The Art of PERUVIAN CUISINE

Juli 2004

Als Erinnerung an unsere gemeinsame Zeit in Südamerika und Inspiration fürs Kochen + 30....

Herzlichst y un abrazo fuerte,
Moritz + Isabel x

Fourth printing 2003

Author: *Tony Custer*

Book and Jacket Design: *Tony Custer & Ursula San Miguel*

Edition and Printing by: *Quebecor World Perú S.A.*

Hecho el depósito legal: *1501032000-0646*
ISBN Number: *9972-9203-0-5*

For further information regarding this book,
please contact: *Felipe Antonio Custer*
e-mail: *facuster@corpcuster.com.pe*
fax: *(511) 461-0030*

CONTENTS

Contents	5	
Preface	9	
Acknowledgements	10	
Introduction	11	
History	15	
Ingredients	23	
Recipes	41	
Aguaymanto sour	42	*Cape gooseberry cocktail*
Algarrobina	44	*Peruvian carob bean syrup cocktail*
Chicha morada	46	*Purple corn and fruit drink*
Pisco sour	48	*Pisco sour*
Hors d'oeuvres & Appetizers	51	
Anticuchos en general & Anticucho de pescado	52	*About Peruvian-style brochettes in general & Sea bass brochette*
Anticuchos de: corazón; pollo; hígado de pollo	54	*Brochettes: Beef heart; Chicken; Chicken liver*
Bolita & Palito de yuca	56	*Mini yuca croquettes & Crisp fried yuca sticks*
Butifarra & Sandwich triple	58	*Peruvian pork sandwich & Triple-decker sandwich*
Chicharrón en general & Chicharrón Novoandino	60	*About* **chicharrón** *in general & Andean "nouvelle cuisine"* **chicharrón**
Chicharrón Otani	62	**Chicharrón** *of crisply fried seafood as prepared by Otani*
Chicharrón de pollo	64	**Chicharrón** *of crisp chicken*
Chicharrón de pulpo	66	**Chicharrón** *of crisp fried octopus*
Choclo estilo José Antonio	68	*Highland Andean corn in warm butter sauce*
Choros a la chalaca	70	*Mussels as prepared in Callao*
Conchitas a la parmesana	72	*Scallops grated with parmesan*
Tamal verde & Humita	74	*Chick-pea tamale & Fresh corn tamale*
Tamal criollo	76	*Dried corn Creole tamale*
Tamal negro	78	*Black tamale stuffed with crayfish*
Tequeños de pulpa de cangrejo & Wantan de mariscos	80	*Crisp crab won-ton rolls & Seafood-filled won-ton*
Yuquita rellena de mariscos	82	*Yuca croquettes with seafood filling*

Soups

Aguadito de pavo	86	*Turkey and rice soup with fresh coriander leaf*
Chupe de camarones	88	*Crayfish chowder*
Concentrado de cangrejo	90	*Stone crab soup*
Cuzqueña de cereales	92	*Cuzco-style soup with Andean grains*
Parihuela	94	*Peruvian Creole bouillabaisse*

First courses

Camarón a la plancha	98	*Fresh crayfish on the griddle*
Carpaccio de pato	100	*Duck carpaccio*
Causas en general & Causa limeña	102	*About spicy mashed cold yellow potato cakes & Sea bass-filled mashed yellow potato cake*
Causa de camarones en salsa tibia	104	*Crayfish-stuffed yellow potato mold with warm coral sauce*
Causa Colonial	106	*Colonial-style mashed yellow potato salad*
Causa de pulpo al olivo & Causa verde rellena de cangrejo	108	*Yellow potato cake filled with octopus in black olive mayonnaise & Crab-filled mashed yellow potato and spinach salad*
Ceviches en general & de Corvina	110	*About **ceviche** in general & Sea bass **ceviche***
Ceviche clásico	112	*Classic sea bass **ceviche***
Ceviche en crema de rocoto	114	*Sea bass **ceviche** in hot **rocoto** cream*
Ceviche mixto	116	*Mixed fish, crayfish and seafood **ceviche***
Ceviche de pato	118	*Duck **ceviche***
Ceviche de camarón a la piedra	120	*Stone-cooked warm crayfish **ceviche***
Ceviche de champiñones y alcachofa	122	*Mushroom and artichoke **ceviche***
Ensalada de pallares	124	*White Lima bean (butter bean) salad*
Ensalada de pulpo con bacon	126	*Octopus and bacon salad*
Escabeche	128	*Cold fish lightly pickled in hot pepper, onions and spices*
Jalea	130	***Chicharrón** mixed platter: crisp fried fish and seafood*
Ocopa & Papa a la huancaína	132	*Spicy Huancayo & Ocopa cheese sauces on potato*
Papa rellena	134	*Meat-stuffed potato croquette*
Pulpo al olivo	136	*Octopus in black olive mayonnaise*
Quinotto	138	*Quinua risotto*
Ravioli de cabrito - "Cabrioli"	140	*Cabrioli - Ravioli with oven roasted kid stuffing in spiced butter sauce*
Solterito arequipeño	142	*Arequipa-style fava bean, corn and cheese salad*
Tiradito en general & de Pescado	144	*About **tiradito** in general & Basic raw marinated fish **tiradito***
Tiradito Alfresco & Tiradito criollo	146	***Tiradito** in Alfresco-style sauce & Creole-style **tiradito***
Tiraditos de Ambrosía	148	*Crayfish, Scallop and Flounder **tiraditos** in 3 kinds of **ají** sauces*
Tiradito dos tiempos	150	*Two tier **tiradito** in lime, sea urchin and vodka sauces*

Main dishes	153	
Adobo de chancho	154	*Annatto spiced marinated pork*
Ají de gallina	156	*Chicken in creamy yellow **ají** sauce*
Ají de langostinos	158	*Shrimps in **ají** cream sauce*
Alpaca en tres cortes	160	*Alpaca in wine*
Arroz chaufa de pescado	162	*Oriental-style stir-fried rice with crisp fish nuggets*
Arroz atamalado	164	*Tamale-style rice with scallops*
Arroz con camarones	166	*Savory rice with crayfish*
Arroz con mariscos	168	*Spicy rice with seafood*
Arroz con pato	170	*Rice with duck and fresh coriander leaf*
Carapulca	172	*Andean dried potato stew*
Cau cau de mariscos	174	*Scallop and octopus stew*
Chicharrón de chancho	176	*Pork confit with home fried sweet potato slices*
Chita refrita	178	*Fried seasoned fish with special creole sauce*
Corvina a la Chorrillana	180	*Grilled sea bass with Chorrillos-style sauce*
Diversión de conejo con ñoquis de yuca	182	*Rabbit "divertimento" with pesto-filled yuca gnocchis in apricot sauce*
Foie gras con tacu tacu de lentejas	184	*Pan-seared foie-gras atop lentil salad, on a bed of re-fried lentils and rice*
Huatia sulcana	186	*Sulco-style pot roast with Andean herbs*
Lechón confitado con especias	188	*Roast suckling pig on a mushroom rösti with hot pepper and honey sauce*
Lechón macerado con frutas al pisco	190	*Slow-roasted suckling pig marinated in Pisco and dried fruit*
Lenguado a lo macho	192	*Grilled flounder in a 'macho'-style spicy seafood sauce*
Locro de camarones	194	*Corn and squash dish with crayfish*
Lomo saltado	196	*Stir-fried tenderloin tips in a sauce of onion, tomato and soy sauce with French fried yellow potatoes*
Olluquito con carne	198	*Savory **olluco** and beef stew*
Pato a la moda de Chepén	200	*Duck in hot pepper, orange and anis sauce*
Pejerrey arrebozado	202	*Crisp fried rainbow smelts*
Pepián de pavo	204	*Turkey with spicy fresh corn sauce*
Picante de camarones	206	*Crayfish in spicy cream sauce*
Pollo al maní	208	*Chicken in peanut sauce*
Risotto de cabrito de leche y culantro	210	*Roast kid with cheese and squash risotto in a cilantro sauce*
Rocoto relleno	212	*Stuffed hot rocoto peppers*
Seco de cordero	214	*Lamb stew with fresh coriander leaf*
Sudado de corvina y conchitas	216	*Braised sea bass in spicy tomato and scallop sauce*
Tacu tacu y sábana de lomo	218	*Re-fried beans and rice, country fried beef tenderloin, egg and banana*
Tacu tacu de mariscos	220	*Re-fried beans and rice stuffed with seafood*
Tacu tacu en salsa de camarones	222	*Crayfish-stuffed re-fried beans and rice with warm coral sauce*

Side Dishes — 225

Arroz a la peruana		Peruvian white rice
Frijol guisado & puré de pallares	226	Canary bean casserole & Large white lima bean (butter bean) purée

Condiments and Sauces — 228

Aderezos: Pasta de ají amarillo; de ají mirasol & ají panca; Salsa madre
— Seasonings: **Ají** pepper paste, Dried **ají mirasol & ají panca** Pastas paste; Mother of sauces

Salsas: Salsa ají y cebolla china; Salsa cruda de rocoto; Jalpahuaica; Huacatay; Mayonesa de rocoto — 230 — Sauces: Hot **ají** pepper and scallion sauce; Fresh **rocoto** pepper salsa; Hot **rocoto** and tomato sauce; **Huacatay** (Peruvian marigold) sauce; Hot **rocoto** mayonnaise

Mayonesa de ají; salsa criolla. — 232 — Hot **ají** pepper mayonnaise; Creole sauce

Aderezos de anticuchos. — Marinades for brochettes

Desserts — 233

Alfajores	234	Delicate cookies filled with **manjar blanco** (caramel cream)
Arroz con leche	236	Peruvian rice pudding
Bienmesabe	238	Caramel fondant candies with nuts and candied orange peel
Encanelados	240	Cinnamon sponge cake
Huevo chimbo	242	Rich sponge cake drenched in Pisco
Mana en frutitas y Bola de Oro	244	Manna fruits & Elegant manna-covered layered sponge cake
Manjar blanco de chocolate, lúcuma y coco	246	**Manjar blanco** and 3 variations: Milk chocolate, **Lúcuma**, Coconut
Mazamorra Limeña y Morada	248	Molasses pudding with dried fruit; Purple corn pudding
Merengue de lúcuma	250	**Lúcuma** meringue
Mousse de chirimoya	252	Custard apple mousse with passion fruit coulis
Picarones	254	Peruvian beignets with fruit-flavored molasses
Ponderaciones	256	Crisp Colonial deep-fried rosette-type wafer
Suspiros de limeña	258	Rich caramel pudding with port wine meringue
Tejas	260	Peruvian fondant-covered **manjar blanco** candies with nuts of fruits
Turrón de chocolate	262	Chilled chocolate and raisin cake
Turrón de Doña Pepa	264	Anise cookie logs bathed in molasses-fruit glaze with sprinkles
Guargueros	266	Peruvian-style cannoli with **manjar blanco**
Volador	266	Oven-puffed egg wafers joined with **manjar blanco** and fruit preserve

Appendix, index

269	Places to purchase Peruvian food supplies in the US and UK
270	Index to some Lima restaurants
271	Bibliography

PREFACE

To '*The Art of Peruvian Cuisine*' by Eric Ripert

My first visit to Peru was of course, enjoyable, but mostly a gastronomic discovery. I was surprised to find an authentic and traditional Peruvian cuisine. It is simple or complex and varied, depending on the region. I found it to be exactly as in France, where we have one cuisine of the 'terrain' and one from the sea. I was delighted with the quality of the products, which were exceptionally fresh, and by the flavors of the fruits and vegetables which remind me of my childhood.

Ceviche, which is one of the most common preparations of Peru, requires perfect quality ingredients, very precise and fast execution, as well as a perfect understanding of the spices and acidity. When a fluke ceviche is prepared, the fluke is transformed into a diamond and the chef, a jeweler. The chef's job is to make the fluke shine and place it in the perfect setting. Through the use of simple and original recipes in this book, the food is transformed into jewels of both land and sea. The reader's imagination is enhanced through the captivating photography.

I congratulate Tony Custer for fostering the idea and bringing this exciting cuisine to the public. I am also excited seeing my friend Jorge passionate about changing Peruvian cuisine. With this book, they are modernizing the cuisine by using lighter ingredients and simplifying and refining the presentation. In fact, revolutionizing their own cuisine, exactly as we do it in the United States and France.

This book is the fruit of the love, passion and work of Tony, Jorge, and Felipe, and their families and friends. It is a great homage to Peruvian cuisine. Enjoy!

New York
March, 2000

ACKNOWLEDGMENTS

First and foremost, my thanks must go to the Ossio/Guiulfo clan: to Marisa for her enormous logistic help and for her contribution of a great many recipes; to Felipe for being the first to believe in this project and lend his unconditional support; and to Coque whose talent as a food stylist and his many chef friends made this book possible.

To Alfredo, Andrea, Apolonia, Cucho, Daniel, Doris, Elena, Flavio, Gastón, Gloria, Isabel, Johnny, Lucho, Luis, Luis Felipe, Rosita and Tito for their wonderful recipes, some traditional and some 'nouvelle', which are the backbone of this book. A very particular thanks to Apolonia, my mother's cook of 40 years, for her wonderful touch with simple dishes and for feeding me most of my life.

Special thanks to Eric Ripert for believing in this project and lending his name to support it. Another great seafood chef, Juan González of the Marisa Guiulfo organization, also deserves endless thanks for the months he has spent cheerfully and patiently preparing and re-preparing these dishes.

Special thanks also to Miguel for his magic touch with light and shutter; his passion for this project is clear in every picture. Thanks, too, to his faithful acolytes Verónica and Ricardo.

To Alison for her dedication to the research, transcription and translation of the recipes which she carried out with a diligence and good humour that went well beyond the call of duty. To Laura and Katia for their unfailing optimism in the face of incomprehensible texts, and to Freda who brought her deep knowledge and love of the Andean peoples, along with her gift for elegant prose, to proofreading all of this.

Big thanks are due to Ursula, my partner in the design of this book, for her dedication and talent as well as her willingness to put up with my deadlines. Thanks also to José Luis without whom she would not have met these deadlines.

My deepest appreciation to Dr. Oswaldo Urbano, Dean of the School of Hotel Management and Tourism at San Martín de Porres University, and to my friend Arturo Rubio, for their kind and generous assistance in the research of this project. Also, where would we be without the multi-talented Gloria Hinostroza who is an invaluable ambulatory encyclopaedia of Peruvian culinary history?

Finally, to Ana, Felipe, Tutu and Malú. Their love of good eating and unconditional support for my adventures has kept me going throughout.

Introduction

The Art of Peruvian Cuisine! Are you surprised? Surprised to find that eating in Peru is one of the world's exceptional gastronomic experiences? You are not alone. In fact, there are so many of you out there who have never heard of our cooking that we have felt compelled to create this book especially to remedy this sad state of affairs. With it we hope to introduce to our country's cooking all those who've never tasted, or even heard of, the glories of Peruvian cuisine.

Around the world, the vast majority of people who have heard of but not visited Cuzco and Machu Picchu, would be astonished to discover that cooking in Peru is of a level that would justify a week's trip here with the single object of visiting Lima's restaurants. I can safely say that all of my acquaintances who have visited Peru from North America and Europe have had a very difficult time dragging themselves away from our bewitching tables. They have pushed along to see our great cultural and archaeological treasures, as well as the headwaters of the Amazon and some of the world's most fascinating flora and fauna, but they've kept a longing eye on our menus.

To complicate matters, few authentic Peruvian dishes have actually made it out of the great curtain of silence that has perennially enshrouded our cuisine. Perhaps **ceviche**, that quintessentially Peruvian dish, is the one that has traveled the most. But how many diners or even cooks around the world know that **ceviche** is Peruvian and that it has been eaten here in one form or another for centuries?

Take the case of **pisco**, our national drink. Until recently Chile to the south of us owned the international rights to the name. Yet the port city of Pisco is on the Peruvian coast 230 kms south of Lima! There are many varieties of this most flavorful, clear and colorless grape brandy but virtually none are known outside Peru anymore. I say 'anymore' because the California Gold Rush forty-niners drank a great deal of **pisco**, shipped from its eponymous port. In 1849 it was infinitely easier to ferry **pisco** up the coast of Peru and Mexico than it was to obtain whiskey from 'back East'. A good Pisco Sour, the most common presentation, is a first rate way to kick off a Peruvian meal. Drinking a 'sipping' **pisco** is a wonderful way to end one.

Goodness knows this book is not meant to be all-inclusive. There are literally thousands of recipes for traditional or nouvelle Peruvian cuisine. We have counted over 250 classic dessert recipes alone. I've attempted only to cover a sampling of dishes that might afford the newcomer a rough glimpse at what Peru has to offer. The signature dishes of countless wonderful restaurants are not in this edition and I must ask those chefs and their fans to forgive me. Peruvians are very serious indeed about their eating.

In the first chapter we will explore how the Quechua and other highlanders of Inca times happily included seafood and shellfish in their diet as a result of their coastal conquests, in the century before Spanish colonization. In its turn, Spanish cooking which had been strongly influenced by 700 years of Moorish domination in southern Spain, fused with the food of the Inca Empire for three centuries, until 1824. Also during this time, the ingredients and cooking methods of the Spaniards' African slaves blended into the Spanish-Quechua fusion.

In the mid 19th century the first Chinese immigrants arrived in Peru. Their influence on Peruvian cooking has been nothing less than fundamental. In the last year of the 19th century the Japanese immigration to Peru got under way. These immigrants and their **nisei** offspring have also had a profound effect on modern Peruvian eating with their wonderfully delicate touch in that very important area of Peruvian cuisine: seafood. As a result, where North America and most of Western Europe have only begun to feel a strong influence of Asian cuisine on their own cooking in the past 30 years, Peruvian cuisine has been integrating the methods and flavors of Japan and China since the 19th century.

In the second chapter, we will give the reader a look at the most important ingredients in our cuisine - what they look like and how they are used. Some will be completely unknown to you and others, though familiar, will be used in unsuspected ways. For example, key limes are rarely used in desserts but are basic to marinating the fish in numerous dishes. And Peruvian yellow potatoes, when mashed, are more often served cold with seafood as appetizers than warm with meat in main dishes. Finally, the third chapter is an overview of recipes which take you from a few key drinks through to dessert.

The talented team of professional and amateur chefs that have helped create this calling card for Peruvian cooking earnestly hope the reader will jump in and not only cook but thoroughly enjoy our food. Even if this book remains on your coffee table, to surprise and amaze your guests, we will feel we have attained our initial objective: to acquaint you, the reader from far away, with the art of Peruvian cuisine.

The making of this book: I had had the idea for this book for some time before my visit to New York City in September of 1999. My wife Ana and I were in Greenwich Village visiting my daughter Isabel, who at the time was beginning her studies at NYU's Tisch School of Film. I made a foray into a bookstore in Union Square. I was disappointed to find that in spite of there being hundreds of cookbooks on Latin American cuisine, there was not one on Peruvian Cuisine. As I left the bookstore I told Ana that upon returning to Lima I'd make a book of my own that would present to the world the true image of Peruvian Cuisine as I see it.

The first person to generously give his time to the project was Felipe Ossio, one of Ana's cousins and General Manager of the Marisa Guiulfo Catering Organization. He helped me pick the dishes and the restaurants. Felipe was also the first person I bounced the idea of a white, plate-less background off of. In the meantime, I had a very sturdy light-table built, purchased several sheets of translucent plastic and began experimenting with different light sources. At this point I selected Miguel Etchepare to join us as team photographer and had him experiment with pictures of food against this lucite background.

Unlike the dishes themselves, I chose to shoot the "Ingredients" against a very large curved sheet of matte white formica. Since Coque Ossio, later the team's chef, had not begun to work with us yet, and Miguel never touched the compositions himself, I had to "wing it" and wash, slice, dice, and set up the ingredients. Miguel then photographed these components. After this harrowing experience, I quickly brought Coque and his culinary/aesthetic talents on board. The two of us spent two weekends filling drawing pads with my sketches, as we struggled to "reinvent" the "look" of Peruvian Cuisine.

I then rented a meeting room at the Club Empresarial in San Isidro, Lima, where Marisa Guiulfo has one of her kitchens. Here all the food was produced as needed. We covered the meeting room windows with black cloth, Miguel set up his camera over my light table and Coque, Miguel and I spent five weeks running this impromptu photo studio while Coque set up the dishes based on our drawings, using his flair as a master chef, and Miguel shot each creation in turn when it was ready.

Beyond this, I designed the layout of the text pages to match what I've always wanted to find in the cookbooks that I buy: a clear presentation of the ingredients and the preparation, as well as a little background on the dish and some helpful hints.

Finally, Ursula and I framed each shot at the end of the picture-taking process. The pictures themselves, however, were created by a joint effort of the three members of the photo team: Coque, Miguel and myself.

HISTORY

FUSION OF FLAVORS

Quisquimite: Moche God of the Sea.

We live in a time when we can buy the ingredients for the cuisine of almost every corner of the world. Our children are used to eating with chopsticks and we pepper our conversation with words like **mesclun** and **dim sum**. Yet our next culinary adventure is right in the Western Hemisphere: the discovery of the rich diversity of dishes and ingredients that make up Peruvian cuisine.

When you sit down to a meal in Peru today, you may not know that you are experiencing the result of a fascinating evolution of foods and cultures. Many Peruvians themselves are only vaguely aware of the unique story of development and adaptation behind the bases of their favorite dishes.

The closest parallel we can draw is the dramatic way that Asian cooking has influenced North American cuisine in the past 30 years. This reinvention of a nation's eating habits has occurred because new ideas and new ingredients have been introduced into the United States. Imagine a similar and continuous revolution, one that stretches back hundreds of years, and you'll begin to get a picture of the evolution of Peruvian cooking.

In fact, the thread begins long before Francisco Pizarro landed in northern Peru with 13 men-at-arms and claimed an empire of 12 million people for the crown of Spain. The basic foods that are represented on the Inca and pre-Inca ceramics in Lima's museums still appear in dishes served at family tables and in restaurants in Peru today.

The Incas - Quechua cuisine

In the 15th century the Inca Empire, building on earlier cultures, already had an ingenious agricultural system using elaborate terracing and irrigation to cultivate food on steep Andean slopes and in coastal river valleys.

Pre-Columbian pottery representing fish.

What they grew mostly was the potato, the basic element in soups, stews and the **pachamanca** -- a mixture of meats and vegetables cooked with hot stones in a covered pit in the ground. Leftover potatoes from the **pachamanca** were put out to dry and, when the bits were re-hydrated and cooked in a stew, they became **carapulca** (p. 172) (from the Quechua **kala**, 'hot stone'; **purka**, 'hole in the ground'), eaten throughout the country to this day.

Pre-Columbian pottery representing maize.

According to the International Potato Center in Lima, the Incas cultivated over 1,000 varieties of potato. While many varieties have disappeared, of the staggering 2,000 varieties of potatoes presently identified, hundreds are still commonly found at market stalls in the Andes and there are still wild potatoes and their relatives growing in rural areas.

Pizarro and his Spanish Conquistadors introduced this modern-day staple to the world when they took it back to Europe in the 16th century. The potato was to become such a common element in the diet of the Western world that in only a hundred years people had forgotten where it came from. Even so, as a linguistic reminder, in Finnish supermarkets today you'll find potatoes under the sign that says **'peruna'**.

Another native food crucial to life in the pre-hispanic Andes was **quinua**. Held sacred by the Incas, they called it the 'mother grain', and at sowing time the soil of the first furrow was ceremonially broken by a golden implement. **Quinua** is once again coming into it's own.

Inca farmers cultivated less frost resistant crops and fruits on the lower mountain slopes and river valleys. The most important of these was maize, the basic ingredient of Andean beer known in urban Peru by the name **chicha**, a Caribbean word brought by the Spanish -- made only by women under the watchful eye of the corn goddess Mamasara. You can still see the **chichera** working her magic today in villages high in the Andes. She continues an ancient tradition of sprouting or macerating the corn, boiling it with water, sometimes adding bits of charcoal to ward off evil spirits and then fermenting the **chicha** in special large, round-bottomed clay jars, set in reed baskets to keep them upright.

The most significant inheritance from the Incas that continues to give contemporary Peruvian food its underlying signature taste, though, is the flavoring from different kinds of **ají** and **rocoto,** or hot peppers, and from herbs such as **huacatay**, which were, and still are, used by Andean peoples to season their boiled and roasted dishes.

The Moors, the Spaniards and their African slaves

During the first 150 years of the Spanish presence in South America, Lima formed the center of one of only two Viceroyalties in the Americas. The Spanish brought the social niceties of court life to Peru and, with great mining and agricultural wealth plus a large native population to provide labor, the leisure class flourished. The biodiversity of Peru's many ecological zones in close juxtaposition is unrivalled in any part of the globe. This newly created leisure class had the time and the wealth to indulge in the fruits of their new land.

Pre-Columbian pottery representing seeds.

Colonial watercolor showing **chicha** preparation.

Trujillo del Peru
Baltazar Jaime Martínez Compañón
Acuarela s.XVIII
1997
Fundación del Banco Continental

Theirs was literally the 'best of both worlds'. The Conquistadors brought with them new species of animals and plants, which rapidly flourished and greatly increased the number of ingredients. Unprecedented integration with the indigenous people gave birth to a colorful new Creole or **criollo** culture and food.

Dishes came to include different types of meat from the goats, chickens, cows and sheep that the Spanish introduced. These were added to the local **llama's** camelid cousin, the **alpaca**, and to guinea pig, wild hare and various types of fowl. Dairy products were added to the original **ají** sauces. Rice, wheat and barley were introduced, along with olives, oils and vinegars, and myriad new vegetables, fruits, notably the grape for winemaking, spices and flavorings. They also brought ovens and introduced new techniques such as pickling and frying.

The new cuisine was an exciting synthesis of ingredients and techniques from the two continents and at all levels of society new dishes began to appear which have evolved into the characteristic motifs of the food that Peruvians love today. For example, **Ocopa**, the signature sauce from the southern city of Arequipa, is a mixture of ground pre-Columbian peanuts and **ají** with the addition of dairy products introduced by the Spaniards.

Iberian peninsular cooking was itself the result of an exotic fusion of Mediterranean influences. As the Conquistadors were natives of Andalusia and Extremadura, the most significant influence for Peruvian cuisine came from the seven hundred years of Moorish occupation of southern Spain. From this culinary inheritance, the Spanish brought with them cumin and coriander, as well as cinnamon and cloves, which went into the famous **criollo** desserts.

The arrival of sugar cane was a delicious surprise to Peruvians and a perfect complement to their herbs and spices. Such a collective sweet tooth evolved that in colonial times the Peruvian Viceroyalty was the largest consumer of sugar in the New World. An angelic touch to desserts and candies came from the many newly established convents in and around Lima. Each convent had it's own delicious specialty. Convents developed most of these confections, which assured the continuity of both the convents and the confections from generation to generation. Still today, almost all Peruvian desserts are Eurocentric with African overtones.

A central ingredient in these new ambrosial mixtures was the vibrant color and style brought to **criollo** dishes by the African slaves who cooked in the kitchens of the Viceroyalty. Peruvians loved and adopted the captivating rhythms of African music and dance, and the aromatic African spices and syrups that they added to the original corn puddings of the Incas resulted in the perfection of a heady mix of blancmanges and custards. African slaves also are credited with the creation of the **anticucho**.

Early Republican engraving of a **picarón** seller.

Lima Antigua
Carlos Prince
1890
César Coloma Porcari

The French

The **criollo** legacy is vigorous and spirited in Peruvian cuisine today, but the 19th century brought new developments, which again added a completely new twist to Peruvian eating habits. The wave of revolution that swept through the world eventually forced Madrid's rulers to concede the loss of Spanish America. On July 28th, 1821, Peru declared its independence and in 1824 the last Spanish soldier left Peruvian soil. The umbilical cord had been cut and a newly independent country was left struggling to forge a national identity.

The flame of the Peruvian revolution was fanned energetically by the **criollos'** fascination with the French Revolution, itself inspired by the American Revolution. It was only natural that, with the Spanish gone, Peruvians looked towards France for inspiration. People felt an emotional link to the new ideals of 'liberty, equality, and fraternity' for which that country had overthrown its monarchy.

Soon after the declaration of independence San Martin issued a decree permitting free entry to foreigners. European immigration took off so effectively that by the year 1857 there were an estimated 20,000 non-Spanish Europeans living in Lima. These included French, Scots, English, Germans, Italians, as well as citizens of most of the Scandinavian countries and the rest of the Mediterranean basin. With the arrival of the French, the cooking and eating habits of France changed forever not only what, but even when **criollos** ate. Mousse is an example of this. For six or seven generations Peruvians have thought of the many mousse desserts at meals and teas as their own. In fact, the mousse's presence in our diet is a direct result of the Libertadores' fascination with all things French, and dates from the early 19th century and independence from Spain.

Mystic Asia - China

Nevertheless, no one could have predicted that the most dramatic impact on Peruvian food in the 19th and 20th centuries was to come from the other side of the earth. A whole new world of flavors and spices was about to burst onto the Peruvian palate with the arrival in 1849 of the first Chinese indentured servants who came to work on the railroad, on coastal sugar and cotton plantations and in the booming **guano** industry.

The Chinese immigrants who survived the grueling and dangerous 120-day trip from Macau often lived and worked under appalling conditions. Life for the 'coolies' didn't improve much after the official abolition of slavery in 1854. But their contracts as indentured servants, though harsh, did include an obligation on the part of the contractor to provide certain foods.

Chinese immigrant with his Peruvian family.

*Los Chifas en el Peru
Historia y Recetas
Mariella Balbi*

A fixed daily quantity of 1.5 pounds of rice was provided as part of their salary and in their specially constructed living quarters, far from their own land, the Chinese workers maintained their culinary traditions along with their cultural identity.

Chinese immigrants imported seeds for vegetables, from snow peas to ginger, that were essential to the Cantonese diet. They introduced soy sauce. Eventually, as they worked off their indentures and settled in the coastal cities, they set up countless small eating establishments. Once again Peruvian cooking blossomed with the discovery of new flavors.

There was initial distrust of these foreigners who 'cooked anything that moved', but Limeños soon began to appreciate the new simple and tasty food appearing in the narrow streets near the downtown central market which today are Lima's bustling Chinatown. To this day, **lomo saltado** is not only a classic Peruvian dish but a typical Sino-Peruvian fusion. The Chinese stir-frying techniques brought over in the last half of the 19th century put Peruvian **ají** into the same pan with ginger and soy sauce for the first time. Modern Peruvians still know most Chinese dishes and ingredients by either their Cantonese name or a hispanicized version of these that has evolved over 150 years.

It is a testament to the impact of Chinese cooking on Peruvian palates that within fifty years of the first immigrant's arrival in the country nearly every one of Lima's wealthy and fashionable families had a Chinese cook. The culture and culinary traditions of Chinatown evolved and adapted and more sophisticated restaurants or **chifas** appeared all over the capital.

Japan - The Rising Sun comes to dinner

In 1899 the first shipload of immigrants arrived from Japan and throughout this century Japanese cooking has left its distinctively 'modern', elegant, and essential mark on culinary trends in the kitchens of Peru. In fact, in the hundred years since the Japanese first arrived, they have been quietly responsible for nothing less than a gastronomic revolution.

Like the Chinese, the first Japanese immigrants initially came to work the coastal plantations. In the beginning they, too, suffered hardship but by the 1920's their families had joined them, their numbers had reached 18,000 and they were economically established.

At this time the first Japanese restaurants gently introduced their own subtle touch to traditional Peruvian dishes. Peruvian cuisine incorporated a delicate hint of **shoyu** and a dash of **miso**.

Japanese immigrants in their restaurant. Early 20" century.

Album Gráfico Informativo del Peru y Bolivia Nippi Shimpo, p.249
1924
Colección del Museo de la Inmigración Peruano Japonesa

At home with their families the Japanese ate something that well-to-do city-dwellers were largely uninterested in - fish! In the first half of the 20th century, eating fish was still seen to be less desirable than meat, but by the end of the 1950's there were a small number of Japanese restaurants that were introducing their clientele to the delights of a whole range of fresh seafood dishes.

Although the Inca ate **ceviche** marinated in **chicha** made from corn and several sour or astringent fruit juices, it was the introduction of limes and onions by the Spaniards and a new approach to fish by the Japanese that gave us the **ceviches** and **tiraditos** that we know and love today.

Conclusion

So here we are in the year 2000. The descendants of the Quechua people number many millions. The Spaniards' descendants have lived in Peru for nearly 500 years, the Chinese and their children for 150 years and the Japanese **nisei** for over 100. During all that time food cultures have been colliding in Peru and succeeding generations have had progressively happier palates as a result. Today, bright young chefs, many of whom have contributed to this book, are once again re-defining Peruvian cuisine. Whether it be through Novoandino creations or progressions on Nikkei food, Coque Ossio and his generation of bright young culinary thinkers will surely continue to elevate Peruvian cuisine to its richly deserved spot among the world's best.

Ingredients

AJI - HOT PEPPERS

Ajíes or hot peppers have been known and used in Peru for seven thousand years. They are an essential element in the flavoring and color of both traditional and modern Peruvian cuisine.

Ají mirasol

This is the dried version of the **ají amarillo**. It has a deep coppery wrinkled orange skin, which should be well washed before using. It has more depth of flavor than in its fresh form and an almost smoky aroma. **Ají mirasol** is dry sautéd or soaked and then ground to make a paste or powder to season and color dishes. Commercially prepared **ají mirasol** paste is also available in specialty food stores.

Ají panca (Capsicum chinense)

Ají panca is another variety of dried hot pepper similar to the **ají mirasol.** Dark reddish purple in color it gives a deeper more 'woodsy' flavor to dishes. Also known in Peru as **ají colorado,** it is marketed in the United States as the Colorado or New Mexico chili. **Ají panca** is dry sautéed or soaked and then ground to make a paste or powder to season and color dishes. Commercially prepared **ají panca** paste is available in specialty food stores.

Ají limo (Capsicum frutescens)

These are multi-colored miniature Peruvian peppers and are extremely hot. They come in a variety of reds, yellows and oranges and are also sometimes purple or white. They are used fresh in **ceviches** and **tiraditos** and also for color and decoration. To reduce spiciness stem, seed and devein them and soak in a little water with vinegar and sugar for 5 minutes. Rinse well and proceed with the recipe.

AJÍ AMARILLO (Capsicum baccatum)

This is the most commonly used hot pepper in Peru. It is also known as **ají verde, ají fresco** and **ají escabeche.** The **ají amarillo** is a long finger shaped chilli pepper, with a bright shiny yellow-orange skin. It has an aromatic fruity flavor and is not very hot. Seeded and sliced, it is added to dishes during cooking and also used raw as an edible garnish. Sometimes a single piece will be put into a dish during cooking to flavor the food and then removed before serving. The **ají amarillo** is also commonly used in paste form. The fresh **ají** is cooked in boiling water to make it soft and then blended to make a paste. When added to dishes during cooking this paste imparts a hot fruity flavor and a pleasant yellow color to the food. The paste can also be mixed with oil and used as a condiment or dipping sauce.

ROCOTO (Capsicum pubescens)

Rocoto is a medium-sized round pepper, which is fiercely hot. Thick fleshed with small black seeds, it can sometimes be yellow or green but is usually red. It can be chopped raw to make a fiery **salsa** and is also ground into a paste to spice dishes. Because of its firmer flesh it is often stuffed as you would a bell pepper. Blanche with vinegar and sugar to reduce spiciness. All chilies should be handled with care as the juice they extract when cut can burn your lips or eyes if you rub them. Oil your hands before handling to prevent stinging. Peruvian chilies give a very distinctive flavor and color to dishes but there are possible substitutes that you can use.
NOTE : Some alternatives are the ancho, jalapeño and serrano chilies.

AGUAYMANTO (Physalis peruviana) Cape gooseberry

This is a native Andean fruit. The berries or hips grow wild on low bushes in the mountains and were once cultivated by the Inca in Cusco's Sacred valley. The berry is green when new, with a green leaf covering, and ripens to a bright orange with dry papery beige leaves. Sweet-tasting with small seeds it can be picked and eaten fresh from the bush. It is also made into commercially produced preserves. **Aguaymanto** is also one of the ingredients featured in the recently popular NovoAndino cuisine where it's marinated in alcohol to make cocktails.

CHIRIMOYA (Annona cherimolia)

Chirimoya is a delicately flavored fruit, native to Peru and Ecuador, but increasingly found all over the world. Its thin dark green skin has an ostrich-leather appearance and the white flesh is sweet with a rich creamy texture. Inside you will find black shiny seeds. Like avocados, **chirimoyas** are picked while still green and left to ripen at room temperature. Once ripe, they will keep in the refrigerator for up to five days. The best **chirimoya** to buy is one which yields lightly to the touch and has no prominent bulges. The skin is peeled with a knife and the flesh broken into pieces. You can use it in whipped cream desserts, mousses and ice creams, or simply eat it fresh.

LIMÓN (Citrus aurantifolia) Key lime

The Peruvian **limón** is called a key lime or tropical lime in the United States. It is similar to a lime, but with more juice. It is small and round with a thin green skin, which turns yellow as it becomes riper. It should be bought when green and still firm to the touch as the more mature the fruit becomes the more bitter the juice will be. A large bowl of **limones** will always be found in any home in Lima. The juice is used to flavor salsas and dipping sauces and also squeezed into soups. Most importantly the acidic juice is used to 'cook' the raw fish in Peru's national dish **ceviche** and its younger sibling the **tiradito**. The juice should always be squeezed immediately before using.

LÚCUMA (Lúcuma obovata) Egg fruit

Lúcuma is a dark green, thin-skinned fruit with yellowish orange flesh and one or more large dark brown shiny stones. The skin of the **lúcuma** will begin to wrinkle when it's ripe. The sweet, aromatic flesh has a cake-like texture. It is used to flavor desserts and pies, and to make ice cream.

Dried corn (Zea mays) MAÍZ MOTE

Maíz mote comes from a variety of dried corn. The dry kernels are soaked overnight and then cooked on low heat for a very long time until they are tender. They must be cooked without salt or they will remain hard. The cooked hominy is then nibbled as a snack and is very popular in the highland villages and towns of Peru. It is also included in **mote soup.**

Large white lima bean (Phaseolus lunatus) PALLAR

The **pallar,** called a butter bean in the United States, is a large white lima bean, usually dried. It can be seasoned as a main dish or included in a cold salad. Peruvians also make it into a delicious purée flavored with butter and cheese. **Pallares** should be soaked overnight, the water in the pot changed, then boiled until the beans are tender. When cooked, the outer skin will loosen and easily slips off, for use in salads.

Wheat (Triticumaestivum l.) TRIGO

Trigo was first brought to Peru and cultivated by the Spanish. It is a nutritious grain with a nutty flavor. In its treated state it is used to give substance to soups and stews. Add during cooking process and it will cook in approximately thirty minutes.

(Chenopodium quinoa) QUINUA

Quinua is a very hardy and extremely nutritious small grain, which looks a little like millet. When cooked, the grains swell and become translucent. It has a slightly nutty flavor and is very versatile. It is good by itself with some butter or oil and seasoning, or as a risotto. It is also used to add flavor and texture to soups, stews and desserts. **Quinua** needs to be picked over for any black grains and then rinsed thoroughly in clean running water to get rid of any of the natural, bitter, detergent-like saponins.

(center) (Solanum tuberosum) CHUÑO

Chuño is the freeze-dried potato, still made today by an Andean technique of preservation 1000 years old. Frozen at night and dehydrated in the day, small and bitter potatoes are converted into a lightweight product high in carbohydrates which literally keeps for decades. **Chuño** is soaked in hot water the night before cooking in soups and stews, or steamed, stuffed with cheese. Found in specialty stores or bottled in brine and labeled **chuño-tunta** (white **chuño**). In urban Peru **chuño** also refers to potato flour used to thicken soups, sauces and desserts.

Frijol (Phaseolus vulgaris) Yellow canary bean

There are many different beans found in Peru but one of the most commonly used is this yellowish brown colored **frijol**. It is soaked overnight and then boiled until tender. It is seasoned to make a savory main dish or accompaniment, and is also used in the dessert **frijol colado** where the beans are puréed and sweetened with sugar and spices.

Papa Seca (Solanum tuberosum) Preserved dried potato

Another ancient method of preserving potatoes produces the **papa seca**. The potatoes are boiled first, then dried in the cold mountain air and sun until they are completely hard. They are then broken up into small pieces. In order to cook them they are reconstituted by first roasting or dry sautéing and then cooking in liquid. **Papa seca** is most commonly found in the stew Carapulca.

Chulpe (Zea mays)

Chulpe are dried kernels of corn toasted or parched with salt to make **cancha** in a rounded clay pot, designed to contain the jumping, toasting kernels. Eaten as a snack, it is also the traditional accompaniment to one of Peru's most popular dishes; tasty deep-fried pork **chicharrónes**.

Kiwicha (Amaranthus caudatus)

Kiwicha is another highly nutritious grain similar to quinua, although the grains are finer. It is sometimes infused to make a refreshing soft drink. It gives texture to soups and stews and the grains are also treated and sold in an air-puffed version similar to puffed rice. This is very popular in Peru with children who eat it as a snack or breakfast cereal. This mini puffed **kiwicha** is also delicious sprinkled on fruit salad or yogurt.

Achiote (Bixa orellana) Annatto

Achiote is a native Peruvian jungle plant. It is used as body paint by jungle peoples and used commercially to color margarine. The irregular terracotta-colored seeds give a distinctive peppery flavor, a little like nutmeg, to stews and cooking sauces, but mostly they impart a bright orange-red color. When buying, the most brightly colored achiote seeds have a fresher flavor. The seeds will keep almost indefinitely in a tightly sealed container if they are stored in a cool, dark place. They can be infused in vegetable oil and the resulting preparation will keep in a tightly sealed container in the fridge for up to a year. **Achiote** is also sold in powdered form.

Camarón (Cryphios caementarius) Peruvian freshwater crayfish

The Peruvian **camarón** is a delicately flavored variety of freshwater crayfish, mainly found in the clear rivers around Peru's second city Arequipa. It has formed part of the local diet for centuries and is also used dried in sauces such as **Ocopa**. It is large and green when raw to pink when cooked and are sold whole or just the tails. All parts of the crayfish are used to give depth of flavor to sauces, chowders or stews. The **coral**, which can be anything from pale grey to deep pink in color, is found just at the base of the head and can be squeezed out and mixed into sauces for added flavor. The heads and shells make a delicious and nutritious stock. The tails themselves are lightly sautéed or boiled and included in soups such as **Chupe de Camarones** or **Parihuela**. They are also delicious cold either as a filling for **causa** or in salads.

Choros (Aulacomya ater) Mussels

The Peruvian mussel has a black and silver shell with sometimes a slightly pinkish tinge. All mussels should be tightly closed when you buy them. Remove the fibrous fringe or 'beard' which attaches mussel to the surface on which it grows and scrub them under cold running water to remove sand and dirt from shells. You may also need to soak them in salted water to purge them of any sand or grit that is inside the shell. Mussels need to be steamed just until they open. (Any that do not open should be discarded.) In Peru they are used in **ceviches** or in soups and seafood sauces. They are also served cold, freshly steamed on their shells with a special piquant topping as in **Choros a la Chalaca**.

Concha Negra (Anadara Tuberculosa) Black scallops

Conchas negras are found in the north of Peru and have a very strong taste. They are found in estuary mud and need to be well cleaned before using. Open and prepare in the same way as you would a normal bay scallop. Reserve the black juice to give more flavor to your dish. They are used mainly in **ceviche.**

Palabrita (Donax Marincovichi) Pipi

Palabritas also have a very strong taste and are mainly used as a flavorful addition to soups and salsas. They are sometimes included in stews or steamed fish dishes. They live in the sand and therefore need to be soaked in cold water before cooking to purge them of any sand or grit that may be inside the shells, and rinsed well in running water.

CAMOTE (Ipomoea batatas) Sweet potato

There are two types of **camote** found in Peru. As the translation suggests they have a sweetish taste. One is pale skinned with bright orange flesh and the other has purple skin with paler flesh and elsewhere is sometimes called a yam. The purple-skinned **camote** is the more starchy and is suited to roasting or baking. The yellow fleshed **camote** has a firmer texture and, when boiled, is one of the traditional accompaniments for **ceviche**. It is sometimes deep fried to make chips and also made into a sweet purée which is included in the recipe for traditional Peruvian beignets, (**picarones**).

OLLUCO (Ullucus tuberosus)

The **olluco** or **papalisa** is a small attractive yellow and red skinned tuber with very moist, juicy flesh. It is eaten in stews and as an accompaniment. In Peru you will often find it in markets sold ready to cook in very thin julienne. It must be sliced before cooking and rinsed in plenty of running water to remove the excess starch.

YUCA (Manihot esculenta) Manioc, Cassava, Yuca

Yuca is another starchy vegetable used extensively in Peruvian cooking. It has a hard bark-like covering with densely textured flesh and a slightly sweet taste. It is prepared in a similar way to potatoes and is excellent fried. It is also often boiled and fried, puréed to make croquettes. Yucas can vary a lot in quality so it's important to buy good ones. Check that the bark is clear of any mold and it should have a slightly bitter taste. The flesh should be clear with no greyish marks, and the juice should be white and starchy.

POTATOES (Solanum tuberosum) Potatoes

There is a staggering variety of potatoes available in Peru today. The International Potato Center in Lima lists over 2,000 known species. Many species were also cultivated thousands of years ago in the Andes and have been lost to us. Peruvian potatoes come in a fascinating array of colors and shapes; from white and bright yellow through to purple and black. Some have variegated coloring. The potato is very rich in nutrients and current research is investigating its medicinal value. Potatoes were a staple of ancient Peruvian cultures as they continue to be today.

Unfortunately it's impossible here to describe the thousands of varieties of Peruvian potatoes and their flavors and uses. The recipes in this book mainly require the yellow-fleshed **papa amarilla.** Some call for white potatoes. If you cannot find yellow potatoes, substitute a dry, floury textured potato such as a good quality Desiree. Likewise King Edwards or Maris Pipers would be good substitutes for the Peruvian varieties of white potato described here. Mix in a small amount of **ají amarillo** paste to get the coloring and flavor.

YELLOW POTATOES Papa amarilla

The **Papa amarilla** is a very dry floury textured potato, perfect for making purées and the Peruvian potato dish **causa**. As it is very starchy it is also good for frying. It is always boiled with its skin on and then peeled when just barely cool enough to handle. Be very careful not to overcook, because the delicate flesh disintegrates easily. **Papa amarilla** is also boiled and served as an accompaniment for many dishes and sauces. Apart from the many dishes made with puréed **papa amarilla**, it is sometimes included in soups and stews.

Huayro

The **huayro** is a fat oval-shaped potato with a rosy red skin and whitish-yellow interior. The flesh of the **huayro** potato is particularly absorbent which makes it a very good accompaniment for dishes with a lot of sauce. It is often included in soups and stews. As the flesh will disintegrate easily, it can be peeled and parboiled before adding to the preparation of the dish so that it finishes cooking with the rest of the ingredients.

Huamantanga

This is a very sought-after Peruvian potato which is only cultivated in the mountains and is therefore available only seasonally. It is long and elliptical in shape with a brown skin. The flesh is white but has the same texture as yellow potatoes. It is good for boiling and also including in stews. The skin is easily peeled after cooking.

White Potatoes Compis, Tomasa

White potatoes such as the Compis, pale skinned with creamy white flesh, and the Tomasa, which has a rosy red skin are not quite so floury as yellow fleshed potatoes and so are more used in the preparation of stews. They withstand cooking well and will maintain their shape and texture.

Perricholi

This potato with pale brown skin and white flesh is the one most used industrially in Peru. The flesh is slightly sweet and has a high moisture content. It is an excellent potato for frying and has an additional advantage in that the flesh does not turn black once peeled.

CHOCLO (Zea mays) Corn

This is a variety of fresh corn with large white kernels. For centuries it has been one of the staple foods of the Peruvian diet. The raw kernels are ground to produce the corn **masa** for making **tamales** and **humitas**. **Choclo** is cooked and eaten as an accompaniment to meat and fish dishes and is used in the preparation of stews, soups and purées. It is the traditional accompaniment to **ceviche** as it complements the lime juice and **ají** perfectly. You can check the freshness of the corn by piercing the kernels with a fingernail to see if they are juicy. Boil corn on the cob in plenty of water with a little sugar and lime juice to ensure that the kernels stay tender and do not become hard. Some people like to boil the ears with the husks and silk intact to add to the flavor.

MAÍZ MORADO (Zea mays) Purple corn.

Maíz morado is a type of corn only found in Peru. It is dark purple in color and cannot be eaten raw or cooked. It is only used for making the fruity drink **chicha morada** and the dessert **mazamorra morada**. The corn is boiled along with fruit and spices to extract the deep purple colored juice used in these preparations.

ACEITUNA DE BOTIJA (Olea europea l.) Alfonso olives

Olives are used extensively in the Peruvian kitchen. Good quality olives are plentiful and inexpensive and are often eaten for breakfast or afternoon tea. They are large fruity-flavored black salted olives similar to Kalamatas to look at but more moist and juicy. They are used to garnish many dishes and are also found whole or in paste form in sandwiches. They are also used to make olive flavored mayonnaise as in the very popular seafood dish **Pulpo al olivo.**

CAIHUA (Cyclanthera pedata) Climbing cucumber

Caihua is a pale green-colored vegetable with a wrinkled surface, sometimes covered with a slight soft down or soft spines. It has a whitish interior with large black seeds. An extremely healthful vegetable, it is very powerful in lowering cholesterol levels in the body. It is used in vegetable and grain soups and also blanched very quickly and eaten almost raw as an accompanying vegetable or dressed as a salad. It should be exposed to only a minimum of cooking time as it will cook very quickly and should remain a little 'al dente'.

CEBOLLA CHINA (Allium fistulum) Scallion

The **cebolla china** is long and slender with a white bulb and dark green leafy top or stalk. It's called **cebolla china** because it was first used in Chinese or **chifa** dishes. It's also used in salads and soups. The white part can be added and cooked during the preparation of the dish and the green part then chopped fine and used as garnish. Both parts of the **cebolla china** also feature as flavoring for dipping sauces in Peruvian cuisine.

CEBOLLA ROJA (Allium cepa) Red onion

The onion most commonly used in Peruvian cooking is the **cebolla roja**. It is medium large in size, with reddish purple skin. It has a relatively mild taste and is used raw in relishes, sauces and salads. It is combined with **ají amarillo,** key lime and oil to make **salsa criolla** which you will find as an accompaniment to many fish and meat dishes. Many of the cooked preparations in this book, as in recipes world-wide, are based on the commonly used mixture of sautéed garlic and onion flavored with herbs and spices. In Peru this is known as an **aderezo** and will almost always also include the addition of **ají.**

HUACATAY (Tagetes elliptica) Marigold

Huacatay is a native Peruvian marigold. It has long, narrow dark green leaves and small white flowers. It is an aromatic herb used to flavor sauces such as the cheese, peanut and **ají** preparation, Ocopa. It's also used in accompanying sauces and salsas for roast and barbecued meats.

ZAPALLO LOCHE (Cucurbita maxima) Winter squash

The **zappallo loche** comes in a variety of shapes, colors and sizes. It has a hard uneven skin and bright orange yellow flesh. The flavor is similar to acorn squash and the flesh is similar in texture to butternut squash. It could be used as a substitute for either of these. The **zapallo loche** is one of the principle ingredients used to make **locro**, an ancient Peruvian stew made in the same way today as it has been for centuries.

ZAPPALLO MACRE (Cucurbita sp.) Pumpkin

Zapallo macre is a large round squash with dark green skin and bright yellow flesh. In Peru these pumpkin can grow to astounding sizes. A favourite soup is **crema de zapallo** served with crispy croutons. The flesh of the **zapallo macre** is also added as a purée to the dough for the Peruvian beignets **picarones**.

QUESO FRESCO Fresh white cheese

The cheese used in Peruvian cuisine is usually this lighlty salted unripened soft cheese. Firm textured, it will keep for up to a week in the refrigerator. It is a very common garnish and accompaniment to all types of dishes and is also an ingredient in sauces such as **Huancaína** and **Ocopa**. It should be kept wrapped in a moist cloth in the refrigerator to maintain maximum freshness and moistness.

Olla de Barro Terraccotta cooking pot

The **olla de barro** is the traditional pot used for cooking in Peru. You will see it everywhere in Andean villages and it is still also very popular in coastal towns and cities. The terracotta imparts a very special flavor to food especially when placed over a wood fire '**a la leña**'. The **olla de barro** can withstand direct heat as well as the indirect heat of oven cooking. A new terracotta pot should always be soaked well before first use. The proper initial curing of an **olla de barro** is quite a hotly debated art/science and every chef has his or her secrets about the best way to go about this. With continual use it will not soak up much moisture from the food

Palitos de Anticucho Bamboo skewers

These traditional Peruvian skewers are sliced straight off the stalks of **carrizo**, which is a plant similar to bamboo or sugar cane. They have a perfect shape for holding **anticuchos** or brochettes on the grill or barbecue. The meat doesn't spin or slide off due to the skewers' shape and fibers. Moreover, it is almost impossible to burn your mouth on one. Finally they have an aroma all their own which complements all of the **anticucho** meats. The most traditional meat for the Peruvian **anticucho** is beef heart which is marinated overnight to retain a succulent taste and texture. Chicken, chicken liver and fish are also very commonly made into **anticuchos.**

PISCO

Aguardiente de Pisco, as is its full name, comes from the grapes grown in the fertile Ica valley, three hundred kilometers to the south of Lima. The 'Piskos' were the native people who inhabited this region centuries ago and when the first vines were brought to be cultivated here by the Spanish, the clear fermented brandy that they started to produce was named for the port of Pisco, from whence the casks were shipped to Lima. Today the production of Pisco continues unchanged in many aspects. The juice from the grape pressing is poured into a **puntaya** or holding vat where it is left for 24 hours. The juice then travels through a series of troughs and channels into the fermentation vats. Fermentation takes about 10 to 12 days and the resulting wine is then transferred to the traditional handmade mud and copper still or **falca**. Here it is carefully heated and distilled until the colorless eau de vie is ready to be transferred again to the special clay **pisqueras** where it will rest for two to three months before being bottled.

There are four types of Pisco :

Pisco Puro is made only from the black Quebranta grape. It is quite dry and is mainly used in mixed drinks and cocktails although the people of Ica will drink it straight.

Pisco Aromático is produced from either Muscat, Italia, Moscatel or Torontel grapes. It has an intense fruity aroma and flavor and is served as an aperitif.

Pisco Acholado is a blended Pisco made from a mixture of two or more varieties of grape. It is excellent drunk straight from shot glasses.

Pisco Mosto Verde is made from grape juice which has not been allowed to ferment completely and therefore still has some sugar content. It has a sophisticated velvety texture and palate and is the most expensive of all the Piscos to produce.

1- Daniel Manrique
2- Doris Otani
3- Alfredo Aramburú
4- Elena Soler de Panizo
5- Humberto Sato
6- Cucho La Rosa
7- Luis Felipe Arizola
8- Andrea Graña
9- Luis Enrique Cordero
10- Carlos Araujo Bado
11- Felipe Ossio G.
12- Gastón Acurio
13- Apolonia Alaya
14- Tony Custer
15- Marisa Guiulfo
16- Jorge Ossio G.
17- Olga Aservi Rosas
18- Rosita Yimura

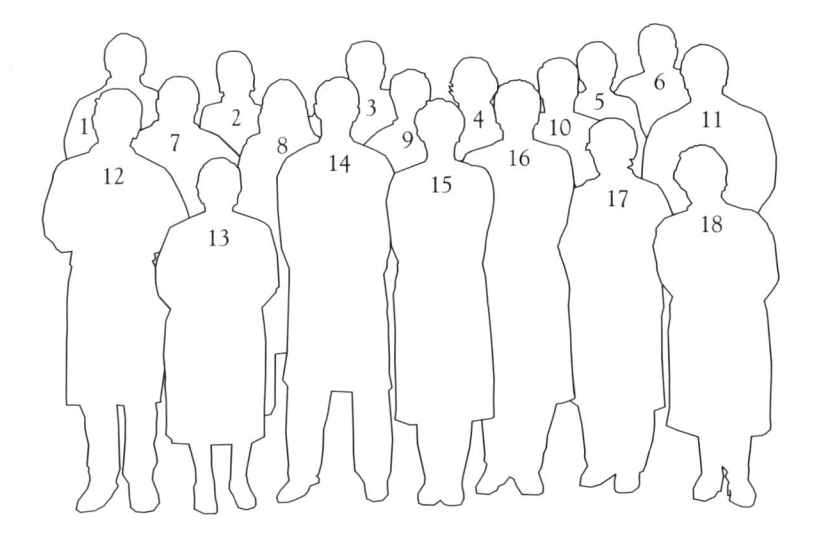

Recipes

Aguaymanto Sour

Aguaymanto is the Andean wild cape gooseberry, orange yellow in color when ripe. In this recipe the berries are marinated in Pisco, to produce a liqueur which makes a refreshing and colorful cocktail. This cocktail was born in the 'Lobby Bar' of the Swissôtel (formerly 'Oro Verde Hotel') in San Isidro, Lima, Peru.

Ingredients:

- 8 tbsp liqueur of **aguaymanto** or cape gooseberries marinated in Pisco
- 2 tbsp key lime juice
- 2 tbsp syrup
- 2 tsp **aguaymanto** or cape gooseberry preserve
- 1 egg white
- 8-10 ice cubes
- Ground cinnamon

Preparation

In blender jar, place first 4 ingredients and blend at high speed for 10 - 15 seconds. Add ice cubes and egg white and blend for a few more seconds.

Serve, well chilled, in a martini glass or flute, topped with a light dusting of ground cinnamon.

Note: To prepare the aguaymanto liqueur, slice 10 **aguaymantos** in half and place in 1 cup of Pisco overnight. If you intend to make more than a half dozen drinks, double these amounts.

Tip: To serve a larger amount simply multiply ingredients by the number of glasses required and serve chilled in a large pitcher.

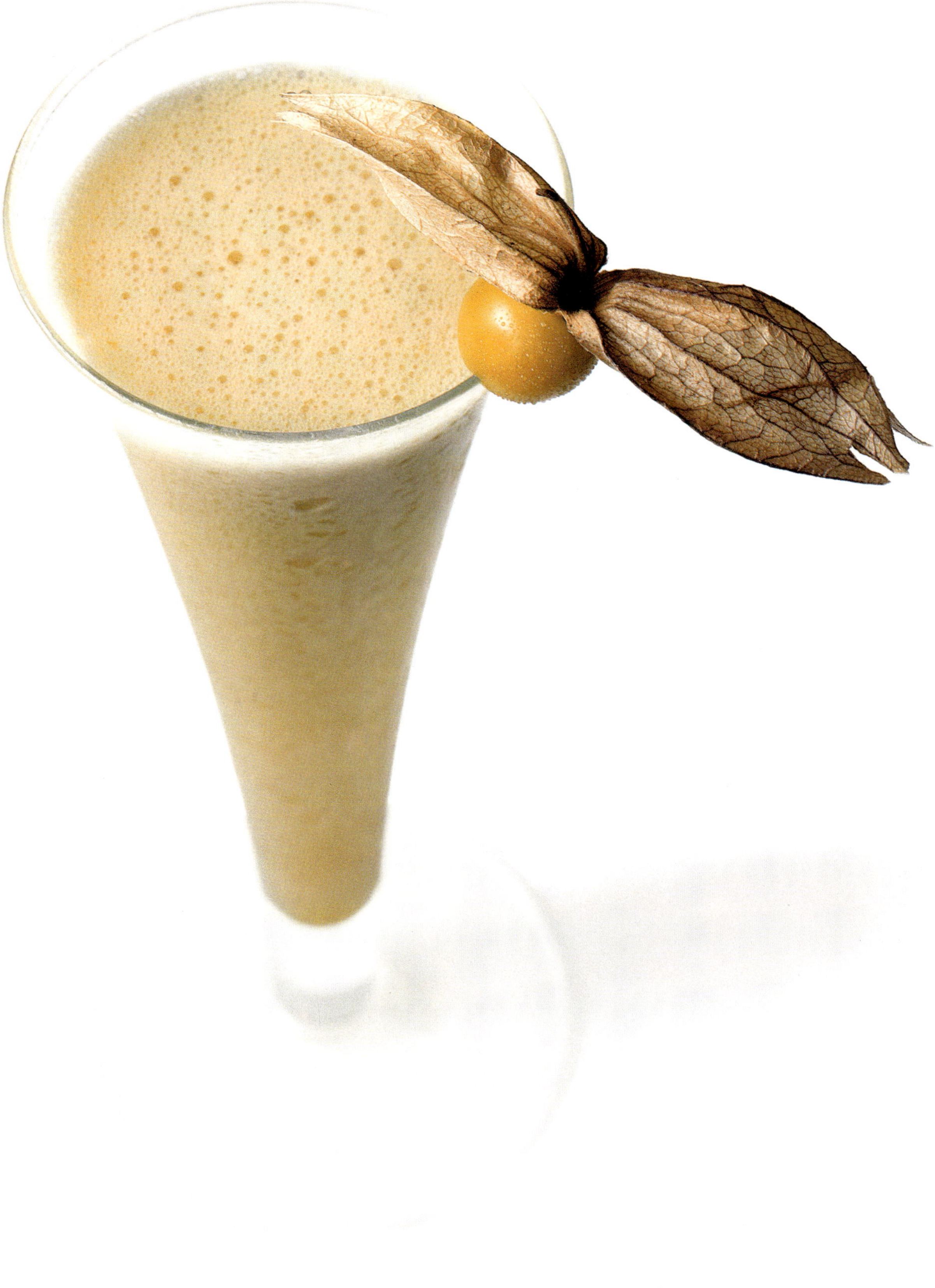

ALGARROBINA

Jarabe de Algarrobina is the sweet syrup made from the fruit of the algarrobo tree, which is a kind of mesquite or carob tree which grows extensively in the northern deserts of Peru. Paired with Pisco, it makes a delicious creamy cocktail.

Ingredients:

- 2 egg yolks
- 4 tsp sugar
- 8 tbsp algarrobina syrup
- 1 cup evaporated milk
- 6 measures Pisco
- 16 ice cubes
- Ground cinnamon

Preparation

Blend all ingredients together on high speed for 1 minute. Serve well chilled, decorated with a light dusting of ground cinnamon.

Tip: To serve a larger amount simply multiply ingredients by the number of glasses required and serve chilled in a large pitcher.

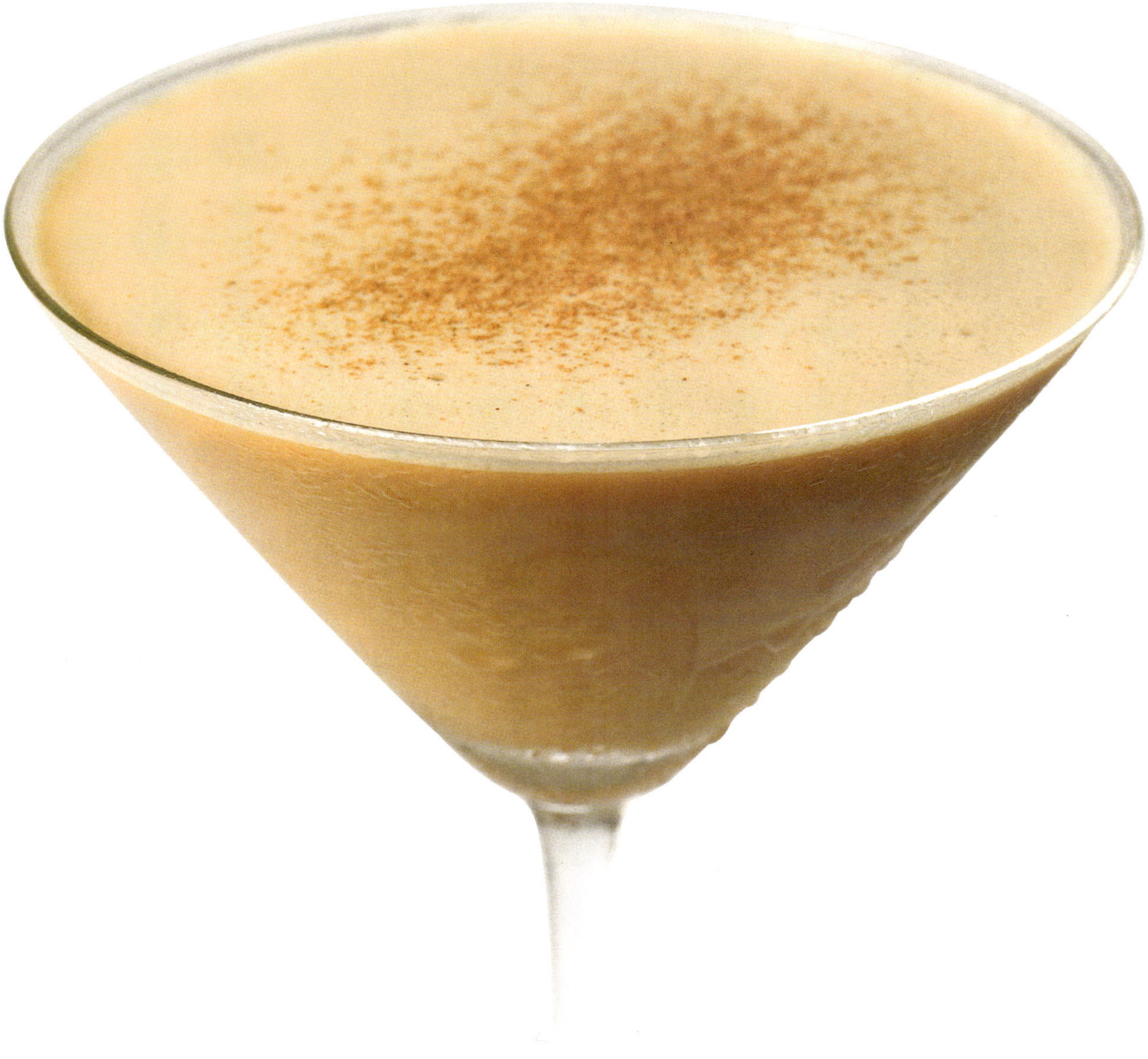

Chicha Morada

This is Cucho la Rosa's recipe. The drinking of **chicha**, *Andean corn beer, was an integral part of ceremonial life in Inca culture. Quechua people would always toss a drop onto the floor as a thanksgiving to the gods before drinking. Purple corn gives a distinctive color to this refreshing nonalcoholic chicha morada. You will always find it on the Peruvian luncheon table in summer.*

Ingredients:

- 3 lbs (1½ kg) fresh ears of corn
- 3 quarts (3 lts) water
- 2 large cinnamon sticks
- ½ lb (250 gr) dried Peruvian sour cherries (**guindas**)
- 1 ½ tbsp cloves
- 2 quinces (quartered)
- 3 cooking apples (quartered)
- Skin of 1 pineapple
- Sugar to taste
- Juice of 4 key limes

To serve:

- ¼ cup finely diced pineapple
- ¼ cup finely diced apple
- ¼ cup finely diced quince
- ½ tbsp ground cinnamon

Preparation

Remove the kernels from the corn and wash well. Bring 3 liters of water to a boil with the corn kernels, the stripped cobs, cinnamon, cloves, cherries, quinces, apples and the pineapple skin.

Boil all the above ingredients just until the corn kernels begin to burst, about 45 minutes to 1 hour. Remove from the heat, strain and leave to cool.

To serve:

Add white or brown sugar to taste, and the juice of approximately ½ key lime per glass of chicha. Finally, add the chopped fresh fruit and ground cinnamon. Stir to combine all ingredients thoroughly and dissolve the sugar. Serve well chilled.

Tip: Some people like to drink their chicha fresh the day it's made. Others leave it to mature for a few days, either in or out of the refrigerator, until it takes on a slightly 'fermented' taste.

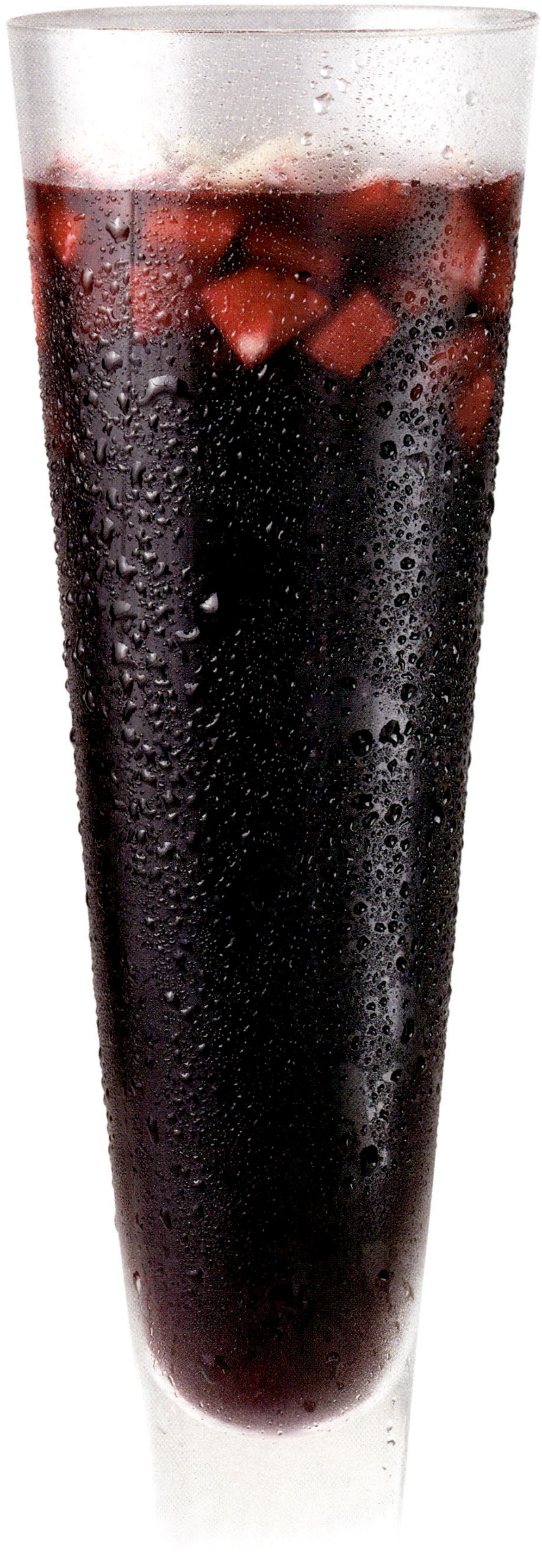

Pisco Sour

Ingredients:

To make the sugar syrup:

- ½ cup sugar
- 3 tbsp water

For the drink:

- 7 ½ oz (225 ml) Pisco
- 2 ½ oz (75 ml) key lime juice
- 1 egg white
- Ice

To serve:

- Angostura Bitters

Pisco *is a clear distilled grape brandy made from the* **quebranta** *grape grown in the Ica valley, and around the Pisco and Ica rivers. Located three hundred kilometers to the south of Lima, the favorable soil and mild climate of the Ica valley made an ideal home for the wineries which were established by Peru's Spanish and Italian immigrant families.*

This is my own recipe which is really quite standard. The only difference is that commercially bottled **jarabe de goma** *(sugar syrup) is more commonly used. I prefer the home-brewed variety.*

Preparation

To prepare the sugar syrup:
Put ½ cup of sugar in a small saucepan with 3 tablespoons of water, just enough to moisten the sugar. Bring the mixture to a slow boil and while stirring, cook until all the sugar has dissolved. Remove from heat and set aside to cool for a few minutes.

To make the sour:
Pour the key lime juice and the Pisco into the warm sugar syrup and stir thoroughly to blend the ingredients completely. Pour the mix into a blender jar and add just enough ice to double the volume of liquid in the glass. Blend on high for an additional 30 seconds to crush the ice. Add one egg white and blend on high for one minute. Transfer to a pitcher and serve immediately in either old-fashioned or white wine glasses. Traditionally, a drop of Angostura Bitters is placed in the middle of the foam in each glass.

The essential mix is 3 parts Pisco to 1 part key lime juice and 1 part sugar syrup: you can use this proportion to increase the recipe to produce any number of drinks.

Tip: A fourth measure of **pisco** may be added for a stronger drink. If you like, the "edge" can be taken off this stronger version by adding a touch more sugar syrup.

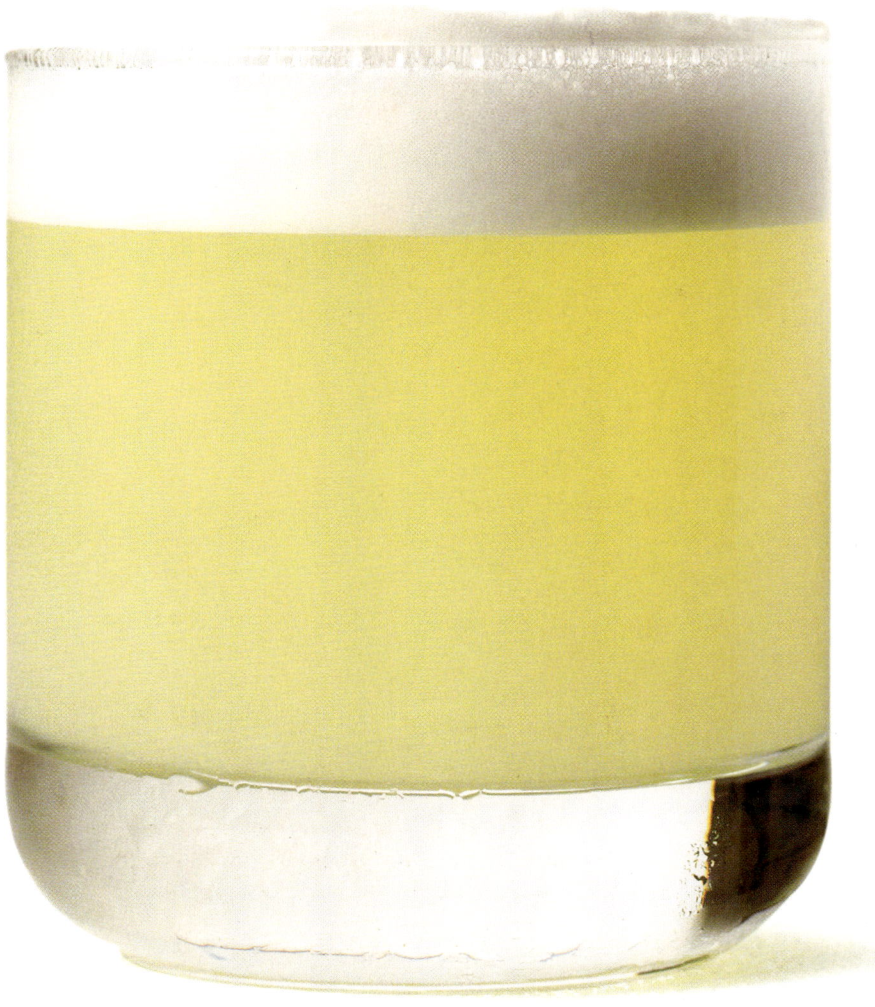

Hors d'oeuvres & Appetizers

ANTICUCHO

*Peruvians are very fond of their **anticuchos**. Before a big Sunday lunch they are indispensable. Often smaller ones will be passed around at cocktails. When I was in my teens, the best **anticucho** in Lima was reputed to be served at small stalls outside the Estadio Nacional, Lima's main football stadium. They tasted wonderful to me.*

*Generally, **anticuchos** must undergo an overnight process of maceration and this is done using one of the basic **aderezos** found in the sauces section of this book.*

Anticucho de Pescado

*Although this is just as much an **anticucho** as its land-based cousins, the preparation is as different as the final flavors.*

Ingredients:

- 1 ½ lbs (750 g) firm fleshed white fish, cleaned and filleted
- 6 cloves garlic, minced
- 1 tbsp **ají panca** paste (p.228)
- ½ tsp freshly ground pepper
- ¼ cup red wine vinegar
- 1 tbsp vegetable oil
- Pinch ground cumin
- Juice of ½ key lime

For the sauce:

- 1 tbsp vegetable oil
- 1 tbsp **ají amarillo** paste (p.228)
- 1 tbsp **ají panca** paste (p.228)
- 1 tsp minced garlic
- ½ tsp salt
- 1 cup fish stock
- 2 tsp cornstarch dissolved in a little cold fish stock
- Freshly ground pepper

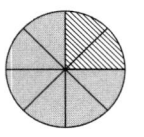

Serves 6-8

Preparation

Choose a firm fleshed fish such as bass, palm ruff or dogfish which won't fall apart on the barbecue.

Cut the fish into 2 in-(5cm-) cubes. Mix together all the other ingredients in a large bowl, add the fish and, once the pieces are covered by the mixture, let stand for no longer than 5 minutes. Thread three pieces of fish onto each bamboo skewer and season with salt just before grilling.

Grill on the barbecue, brushing with oil to prevent from sticking and turning only once, about 5 minutes per side.

For the sauce:
In a small skillet, heat the oil and sauté **ají amarillo** paste, **ají panca** paste, minced garlic, salt and freshly ground pepper, over medium heat for 5 minutes.

Add stock and any leftover marinade. Boil to reduce for 5 minutes. Add cornstarch mixture and bring back to the boil. Cook, stirring for another 2 or 3 minutes until the sauce coats the back of a spoon. Strain and keep warm.

Drizzle sauce over the **anticuchos** when serving.
Serve the anticuchos with **salsa ají y cebolla china** (p.230) as a dipping sauce.

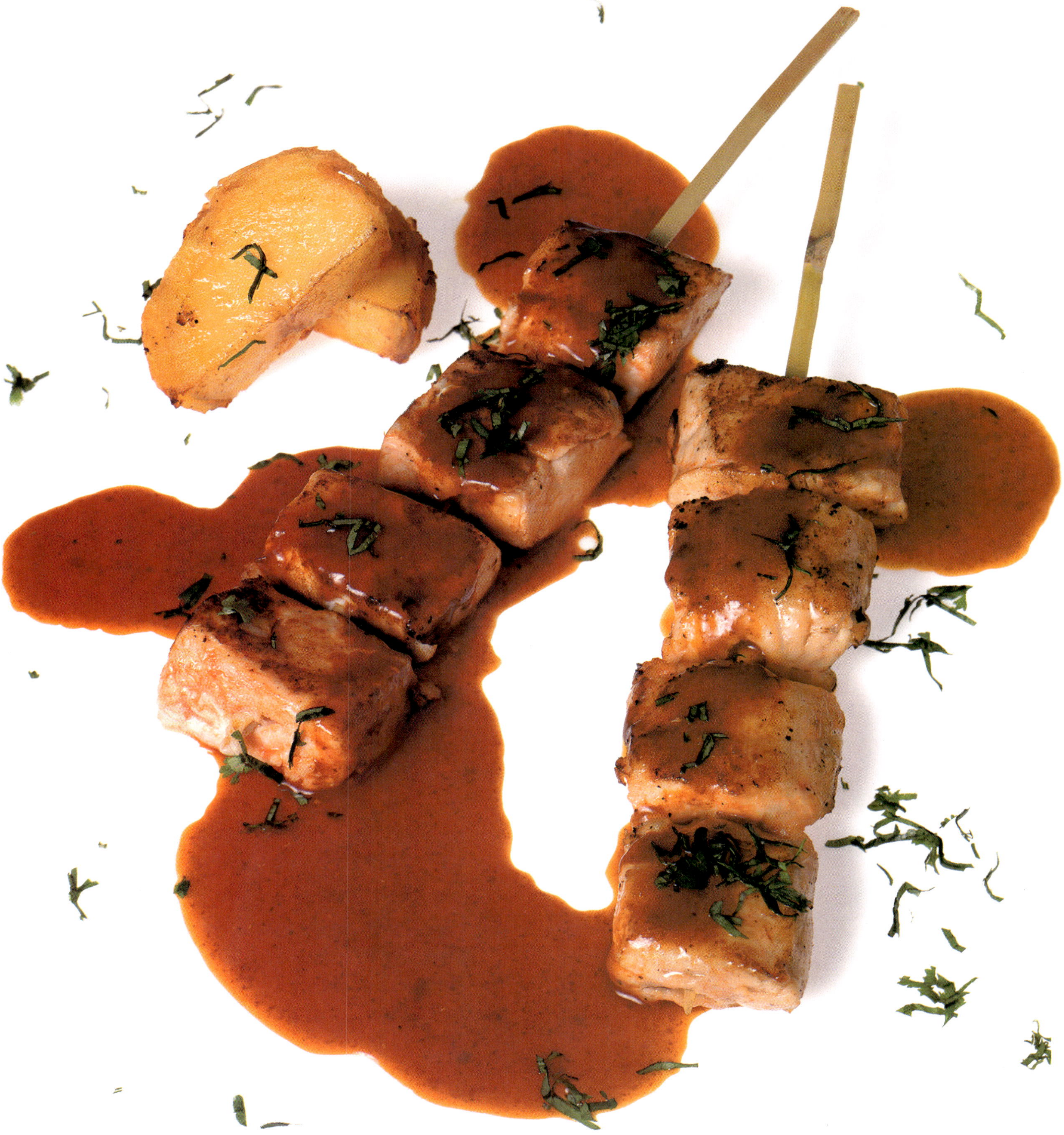

Anticucho de Corazón, Pollo & Higado de Pollo

*Though the raw material, beef heart, may be surprising to some, this rather firm meat is very tasty and, if properly treated, yields a delicious **anticucho** which is considered the most **criollo** and traditional of all. So saying, chicken breast is also a perfect ingredient that if delicately seasoned and lightly marinated, needs a minimum of fuss to prepare succulent brochettes on the grill. Chicken liver anticucho is the Schüler family's recipe from 'La Granja Azul' which has been one of Peru's best loved restaurants for 45 years. During these years it has been known to tourists and locals alike as the place to eat chicken roasted on a spit, and this anticucho.*

Ingredients:

- 1 beef heart, cleaned and trimmed
- Salt
- Oil for basting
- Beef Heart **Anticucho** Marinade (p.232)

Preparation - Heart

Ensure that all skin and sinews are removed from the heart. Cut meat into large bite size pieces. Place the pieces in the marinade overnight. If you like you can thread them onto bamboo skewers, three or four pieces on each skewer, and leave them, assembled, in the marinade.

The next day remove the brochettes from the marinade, sprinkle with salt and barbecue for about 3 minutes per side over very high heat, basting with extra oil and any remaining marinade as necessary. Serve immediately.

Ingredients:

- 6 chicken breast fillets
- Salt
- Freshly ground pepper to taste
- Chicken **Anticucho** Marinade (p.232)

Preparation - Chicken

Cut chicken into bite size pieces and marinate for 20-30 minutes. Remove chicken pieces from marinade, sprinkle with salt and reserve marinade liquid. Thread 3 or 4 chicken pieces onto each bamboo skewer.

Grill brochettes on a hot barbecue for about 8 minutes, brushing with marinade. Serve immediately with **salsa de ají y cebolla china,** (p. 230).

Ingredients:

- 2-2½ lbs (900 - 1135 gr) small chicken livers
- Chicken Liver **Anticucho** Marinade (p.232)
- Salt

Preparation - Chicken Liver

Trim and clean chicken livers and marinate for 15 - 30 minutes. Remove livers from marinade, sprinkle with salt and reserve marinade. Thread 3 or 4 livers onto each bamboo skewer.

Grill brochettes on a hot barbecue for about 6 minutes, brushing with marinade. Serve immediately with **salsa de ají y cebolla china,** (p. 230).

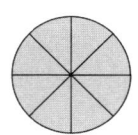

Makes 16 brochettes

Note: A delicious **anticucho de lomo** can be prepared by placing tenderloin bits in beef marinade (p.232) for 2 hours prior to barbecuing.

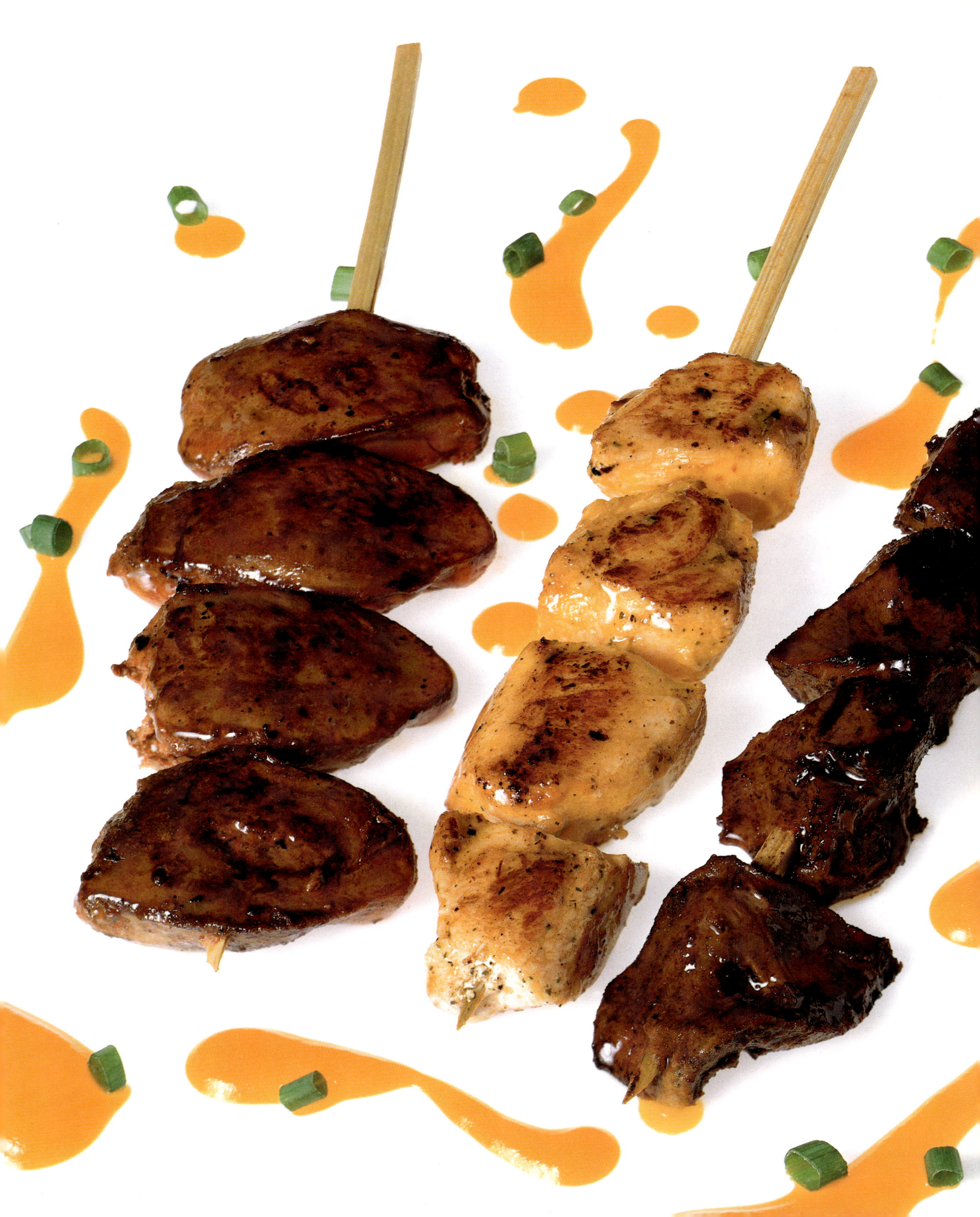

Bolitas de Yuca & Palitos de Yuca Frita

The recipe for **Palitos de Yuca Frita** *comes from my family's cook, Apolonia, who has worked in our kitchen for more than 40 years.* **Bolitas de Yuca** *are a classic* **bocadito** *at traditional Peruvian restaurants such as 'José Antonio', and is one of my favorite nibbles. I find the combination flavors of the yuca and the* **salsa huancaina** *very close indeed to heaven.*

Ingredients:

- 2 lbs (1 kg) yuca
- Salt to taste
- Sifted all purpose flour
- Vegetable oil for deep frying

Makes about 40 cocktail size Yuca balls

Preparation - Bolitas de Yuca

Wash the yuca well and peel. Cut into pieces, place in a large pot of cold salted water, bring to the boil and cook until the flesh is tender, about 25 minutes depending on the yuca. Check individual pieces for doneness. Drain yuca well and take out any grey fibrous core. Mash finely by pressing through a sieve or using a ricer. Add salt to taste. Flour your hands and work surface. Take about a tablespoon of the mixture at a time and form into small balls. Heat the oil in a deep fat fryer or deep frying pan to 365ºF / 185ºC. Deep fry the balls one by one until they are crisp and golden. Drain on paper towel and serve hot with **salsa huancaina** (p. 132)

Note: As a variation on this recipe, add a small cube of **mozarella** or hard cheese to the center of each ball for delicious cheese-stuffed **bolitas de yuca**.

Ingredients:

- 1 large yuca
- Salt to taste
- Vegetable oil for frying

Makes about 18 sticks

Preparation - Palitos de Yuca

Wash and peel the yuca, cut in half lengthwise and then cut each half again lengthwise into three parts. Place in a large pan of salted water and bring to the boil. Cook until the flesh of the yuca is tender when pierced with a fork but not too soft (about 20 - 25 minutes, depending on the size of the yuca). Strain all the water from the yuca and leave to cool in a colander. When cool, remove any fibrous core the yuca may have and cut into small sticks, ½ x 2½ in (1.5cm x 6cm). Deep fry until golden, drain on paper towel. Sprinkle with salt and serve hot with **salsa huancaina** (p.132).

Tip: Once you have made the yuca sticks you can freeze them and then fry them without thawing when you are ready to use them.

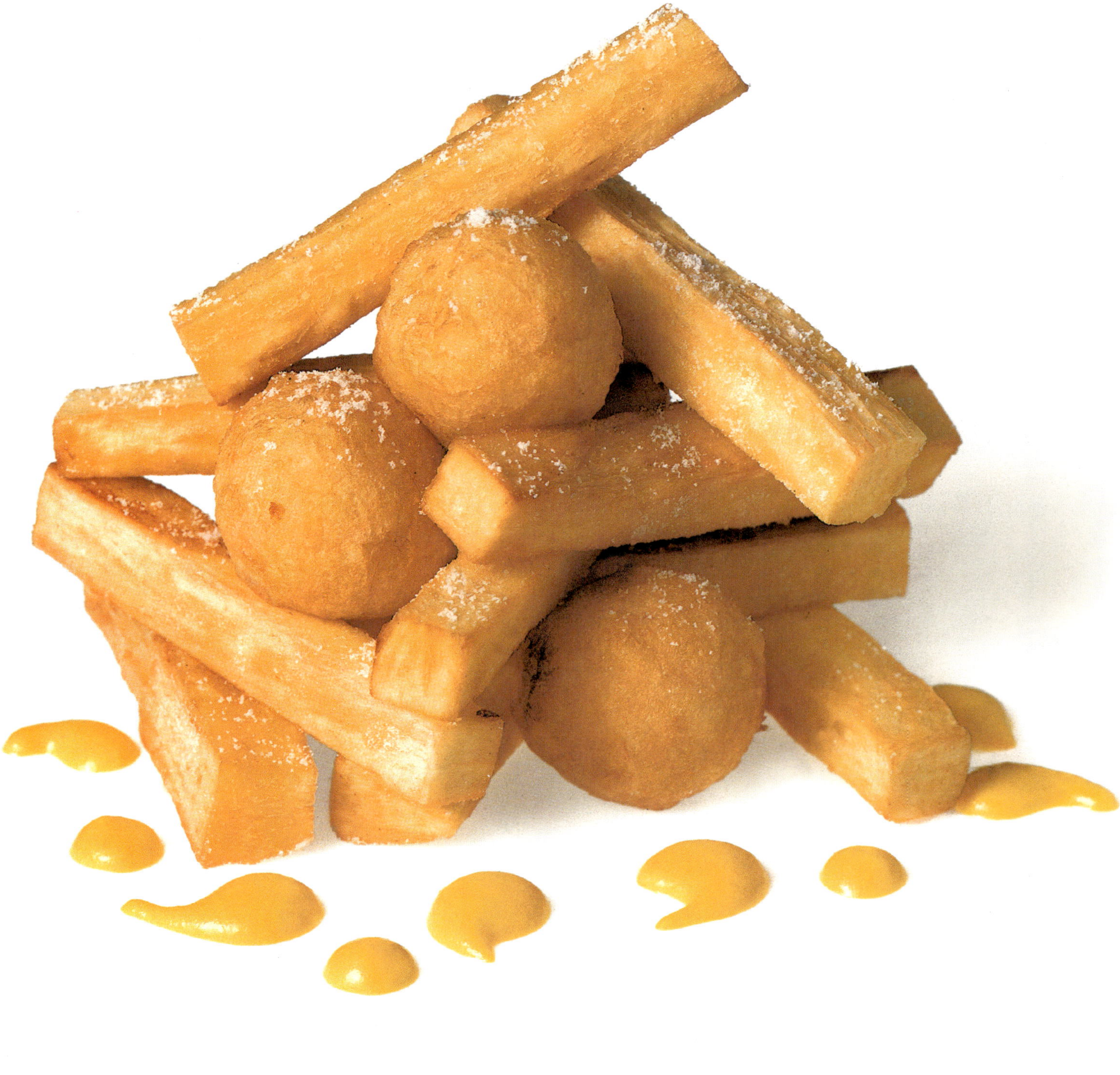

Butifarra & Triple

*The Butifarra, that ubiquitous sandwich with the untranslatable name, is the most classic of all Peruvian sandwiches and can be compared in its popularity to the hamburger in the United States. The sandwich preparation is very simple. What makes it so special is the **jamon del país** (savory pork leg) filling, the secret to which follows in this recipe. The whole pork leg makes a great buffet dish. Butifarras come in a variety of sizes to suit all occasions, from dainty hors d'oeuvres and tea sandwiches to large rolls that are good for lunch on the run. You might try these in individual-size sourdough rolls. The accompanying brightly colored triple decker sandwiches are invariably found on the table at 'lonche', the Peruvian late afternoon tea.*

Ingredients:

- 5-6 lb (2 ½-3 kg) de-boned leg of pork
- 3 tbsp minced garlic
- 3 tbsp **ají panca** paste (p.228)
- 1 level tsp cumin
- 1 tsp turmeric
- 1 medium red onion, grated
- 8 cups salted chicken stock
- 4 bay leaves
- Salt and pepper

Makes 40 large sandwiches

Ingredients:

- 1 large loaf of thinly sliced white bread (3 slices for each sandwich)
- 5 tbsp mayonnaise
- 2 plum tomatoes, peeled and finely sliced
- 1 large Haas avocado
- 4 hard boiled eggs, sliced
- Salt and pepper to taste

Makes about 20 finger sandwiches

Preparation - Butifarra

Combine the garlic, **ají panca** paste, turmeric, cumin, onion, salt and pepper in a bowl. Mix well. Smear the surface of the pork leg with this mixture. Roll the ham tightly and tie securely with kitchen twine. Place the ham roll in a large rondeau or a wide pot. Mix the stock with any remaining seasoning mixture and pour into the rondeau enough to cover a third of the pork. Add the bay leaves.

Simmer the leg of pork, covered, for about 1 ½ to 2 hours, checking liquid level from time to time. To see if the pork is cooked, pierce with a metal skewer and if the juices run clear the meat is ready. Let cool.

To make the butifarra:
Slice the pork leg into very thin slices and place in a roll with lettuce. Sprinkle with salt and add **salsa criolla** (p.232).

Preparation - Triple

Spread one slice of bread with a thin layer of mayonnaise. Cover with a layer of tomato slices. Add another layer of bread spread with mayonnaise on both sides. Layer with avocado slices lightly sprinkled with salt and pepper to taste and a little lemon juice so that they do not become discolored. Spread with another light coating of mayonnaise and add a layer of sliced hard boiled egg. Top with the final slice of bread spread thinly with mayonnaise. Press down firmly and, with a very sharp knife, remove crusts from sandwich. Slice sandwiches into finger or other shaped sandwiches.

Tip: For an extra moist **butifarra**, some people like to add mayonnaise. Peruvians always make their own mayonnaise; if you don't have time make sure you find a good commercial brand.

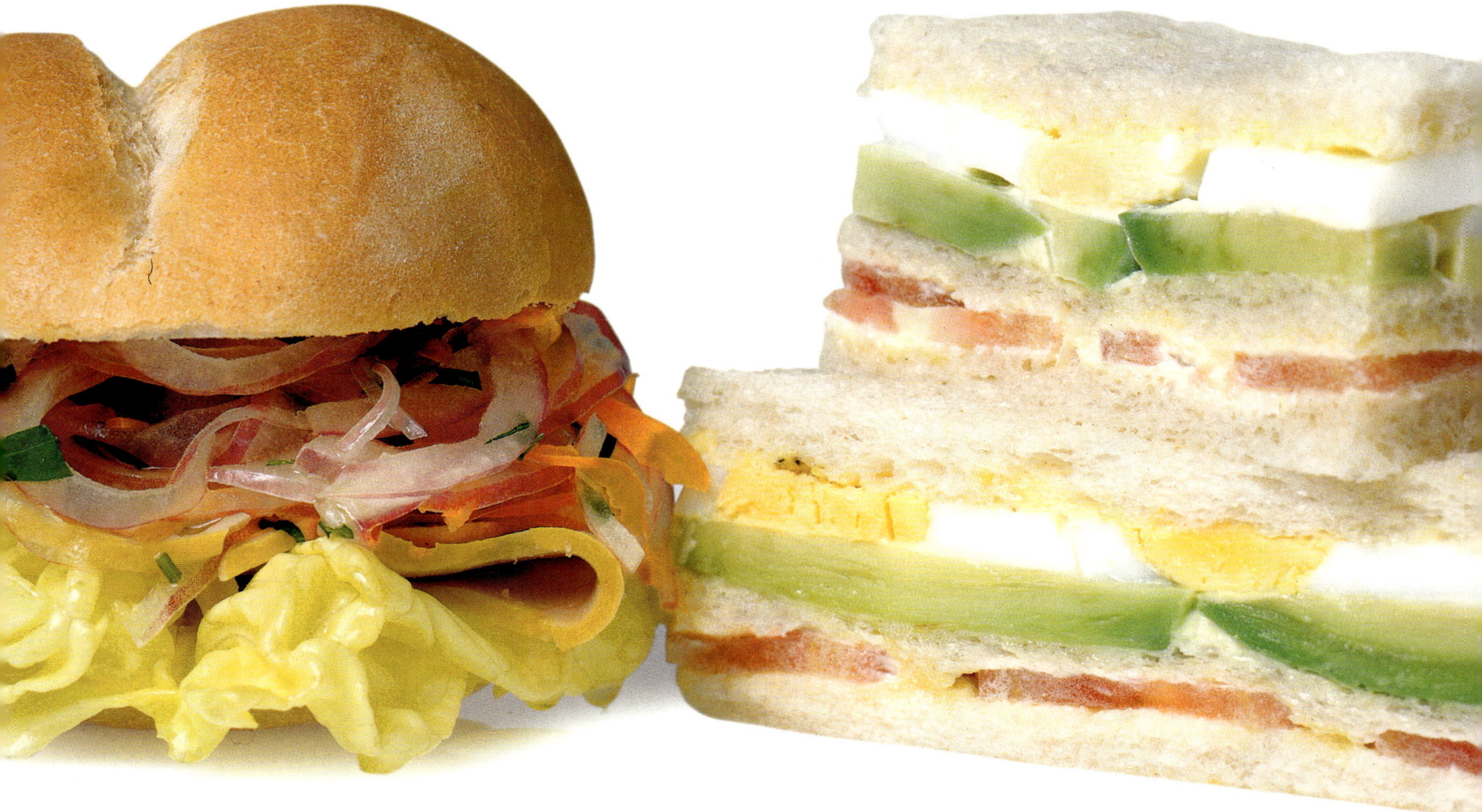

CHICHARRON

Ingredients:

- 3 cups **quinua**
- 1½ lbs (¾ kg) chicken breast fillets
- 1 tbsp oregano
- 1 tbsp curry powder
- 2 tbsp **ají amarillo** paste (p.228)
- 1 cup plain flour, sifted
- 3 eggs, beaten
- Salt and pepper
- Avocado slices

To make the salsa:

- 4 tomatoes, peeled, seeded and finely diced
- ½ **rocoto** pepper, stemmed, seeded, deveined and finely diced.
- Fresh mint leaves
- Salt and pepper to taste
- A little vegetable oil
- A few drops of key lime juice (optional)

To serve:

- Avocado slices
- Fried plantains

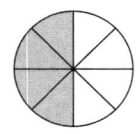

Serves 4

*Traditionally, **chicharrones** are pieces of pork, chicken or fish seasoned, deep fried and served immediately. Peruvians love to eat them either as finger food (**piqueo**) with dipping sauces or as part of a larger meal. The most popular **chicharrones** are probably the crispy fried pork pieces, cooked in their own rendered fat in huge pots over wood fires such as those of the **chicharronerías** in the seaside suburbs to the north and south of Lima. Ingredients should be freshly cut and need a minimum of seasoning. The idea is to keep things light and simple. If the **chicharrón** is of fish, the pieces are normally quickly passed through a coating of cornstarch or flour before frying. Chicken pieces can be fried directly or coated as you wish. Preparation of chicharrones varies according to different family recipes but the one thing that Peruvians will insist upon is that the oil be completely fresh.*

Chicharrón Novoandino

*Cucho la Rosa is the chef of one of Lima's most exceptional avant-garde restaurants, 'Pantagruel', and the pre-eminent figure in what has come to be known as **Novoandino** (New Andean) cuisine. His preparations give a starring role to **quinua** and **kiwicha**, various **chichas**, **alpaca** meat and many other Andean ingredients. Markedly different from coastal **chicharrón**, this dish features a strong **quinua** element.*

Preparation

Wash **quinua** thoroughly in several changes of water. Then boil for 10 minutes. Drain the quinua well, spread out on a baking sheet and leave to dry. Meanwhile cut the chicken breast fillets into strips, 1 ½ x ½ in (3cm by 1cm). Season with the oregano, curry powder and **ají amarillo** paste, and leave to marinate for ½ hour.

When ready, sprinkle the chicken pieces with salt and pepper and coat with the sifted flour and then the beaten egg. Finally, thoroughly coat the pieces with **quinua**. Deep fry in plenty of very hot oil until the **quinua** coating is golden and crisp, about 3 minutes. Drain on paper towel and serve immediately, accompanied by **rocoto** and tomato salsa and fried plantains. Garnish with avocado slice (optional).

To make the salsa:
Combine the diced tomato and **rocoto** in a bowl. Add the fresh mint, salt, pepper, a little oil and, if desired, a few drops of key lime juice.

Tip: The same procedure can be used substituting fresh fish or shrimp for a variation in flavor and texture.

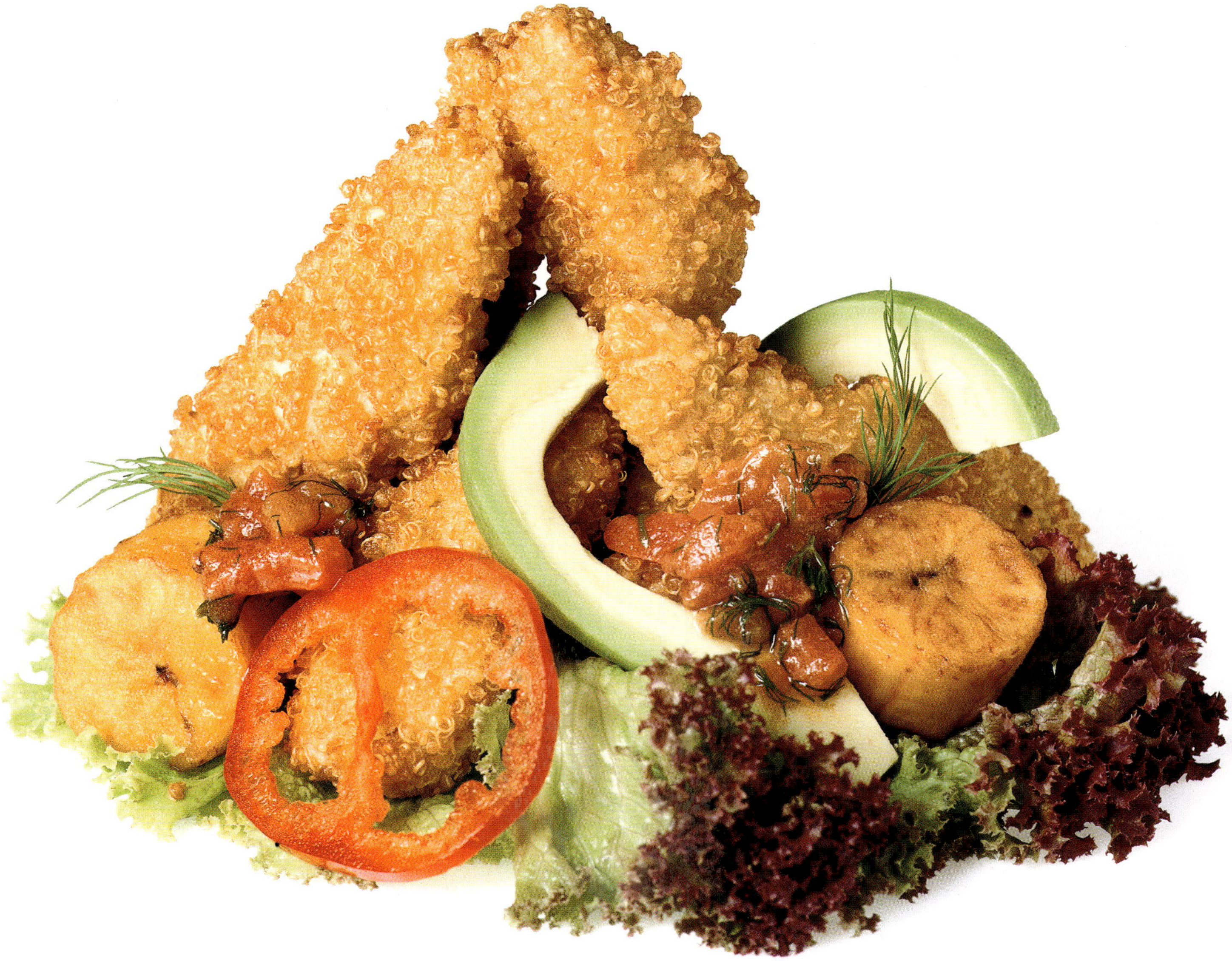

Chicharrón Otani

Ingredients:

- 16 scallops
- 8 fresh crayfish
- 4 medium size squid
- 1 lb (½ kg) shrimp
- ½ tsp minced garlic
- 3 ½ oz (100g) **chuño** or cornstarch
- Salt
- Oil for frying

*Takashi Otani, born in Peru of Japanese parents, was a **nikkei** chef who stamped his own personality on Peruvian cuisine. His daughter Doris now proudly continues her father's tradition at the family restaurant 'El Encuentro de Otani'. These delicate fried seafood morsels, seasoned with just a hint of salt and garlic are simplicity itself - the hallmark of today's **nikkei** cuisine.*

Preparation

Clean scallops and peel shrimp.

Clean and peel crayfish tails, leaving heads intact. Clean and cut squid into rings.

Season with salt and garlic and coat lightly with potato starch (**chuño**) or cornstarch.

Deep fry in enough hot oil to cover completely until lightly golden, about 5 minutes.

Drain on paper towel and serve immediately accompanied by **salsa criolla** (p.232) or tartar sauce.

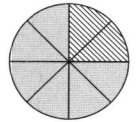

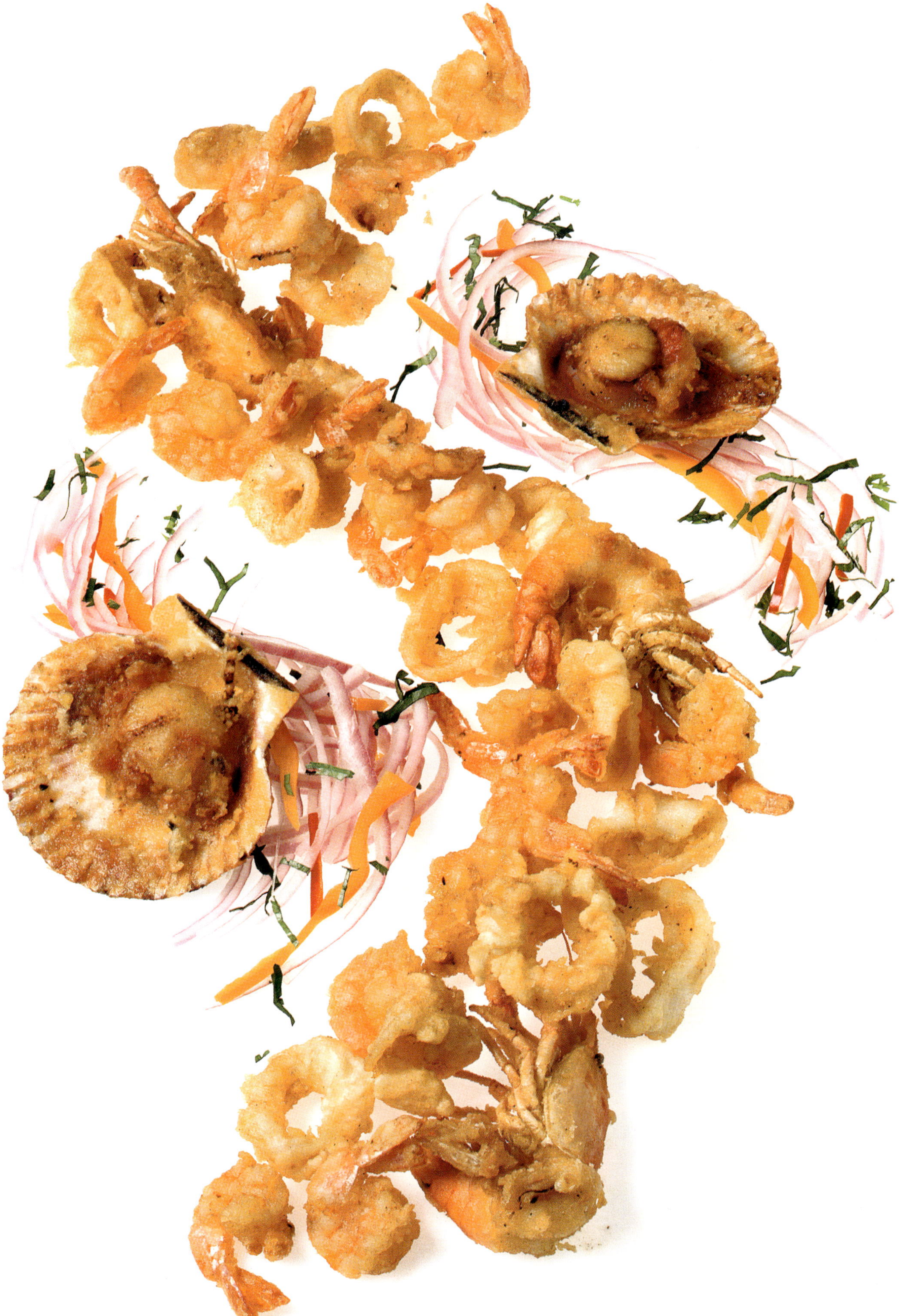

Chicharrón de Pollo

Ingredients:

- 4 chicken thighs
- 4 chicken drumsticks
- 1 tsp Dijon mustard
- 1 tbsp **ají amarillo** paste (p.228)
- 1 tbsp soy sauce
- Juice of 1 key lime
- Salt and freshly ground pepper

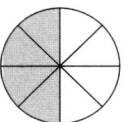

This must be one of the most commonly served hors d'oeuvres in Peru. Tasty deep-fried nuggets of chicken are offered in a stunning variety of presentations of which this is only one. In this recipe the skin is kept on for extra bite and flavor. The fact that soy sauce is included in this popular dish is proof of the influence of Chinese cuisine on Peruvian eating habits.

Preparation

Cut meat from chicken quarters into bite size pieces, being sure to leave on the skin.

Mix the other ingredients together in a bowl and marinate chicken in the mixture for 15 minutes.

Lift chicken pieces from the marinade and deep-fry in very hot oil until golden and crispy, about 10 to 12 minutes. You can test the chicken for doneness by piercing with a skewer. If the juices run clear, the meat is cooked.

Serve immediately accompanied by tartar sauce or **salsa de ají** (p.230).

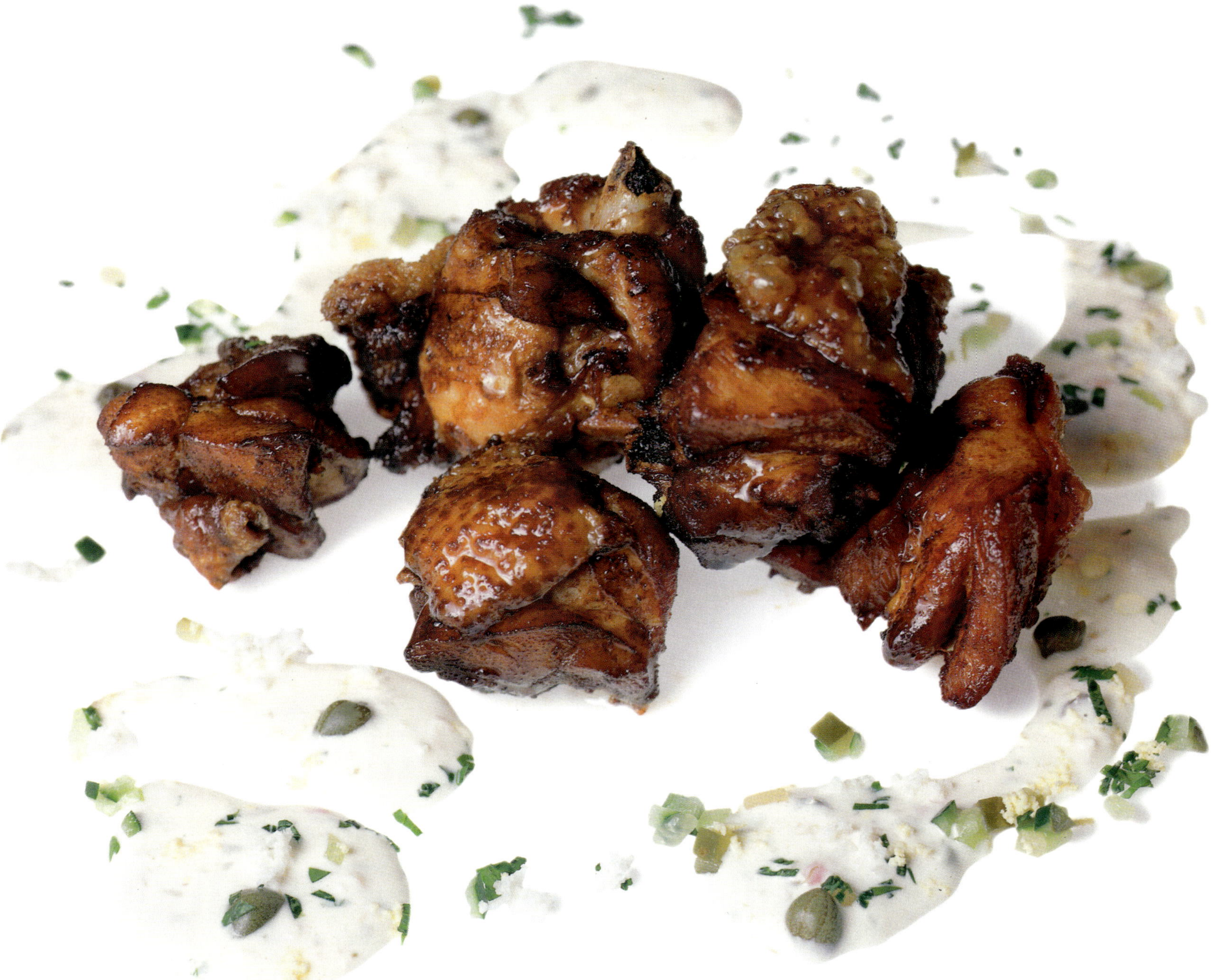

Chicharrón de Pulpo

Ingredients:

- 1 ¼ lb (600g) octopus
- 2 tbsp soy sauce
- 1 tsp mustard
- 4 eggs, lightly beaten
- 2 tbsp milk
- 2 cups all purpose flour, sifted, for coating
- Salt and pepper
- Vegetable oil for frying

Lucho Cordero, chef/owner of 'Kapallaq' in Lima, is a keen diver of renown. His love and respect for the sea, coupled with his great skill in the kitchen bring us several of the recipes in this book. Lucho tends to serve this dish as a mix of octopus and scallops, but we've decided to be purists and serve only the tender and very subtle flavor of octopus.

Preparation

To cook octopus: boil octopus for 40 - 45 minutes until firm but not chewy. Check 'al dente' firmness by piercing with a tooth pick.

Cut the cooked octopus into 2in - (5cm-) long fingers.

In a bowl, combine lightly beaten egg, soy sauce, mustard, milk and salt and pepper. Marinate octopus in the mixture for 10 minutes.

Drain off excess marinade from the octopus pieces in a colander then coat lightly with flour.

Deep fry octopus pieces in very hot oil until deep golden and crispy, about 5 minutes.

Remove from oil, drain well on paper towel and serve immediately, accompanied by ketchup and mayonnaise, tartar, or **ají sauce** (p.230).

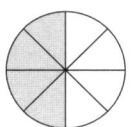

Tip: Be careful not to overcook or the octopus will be tough and chewy.

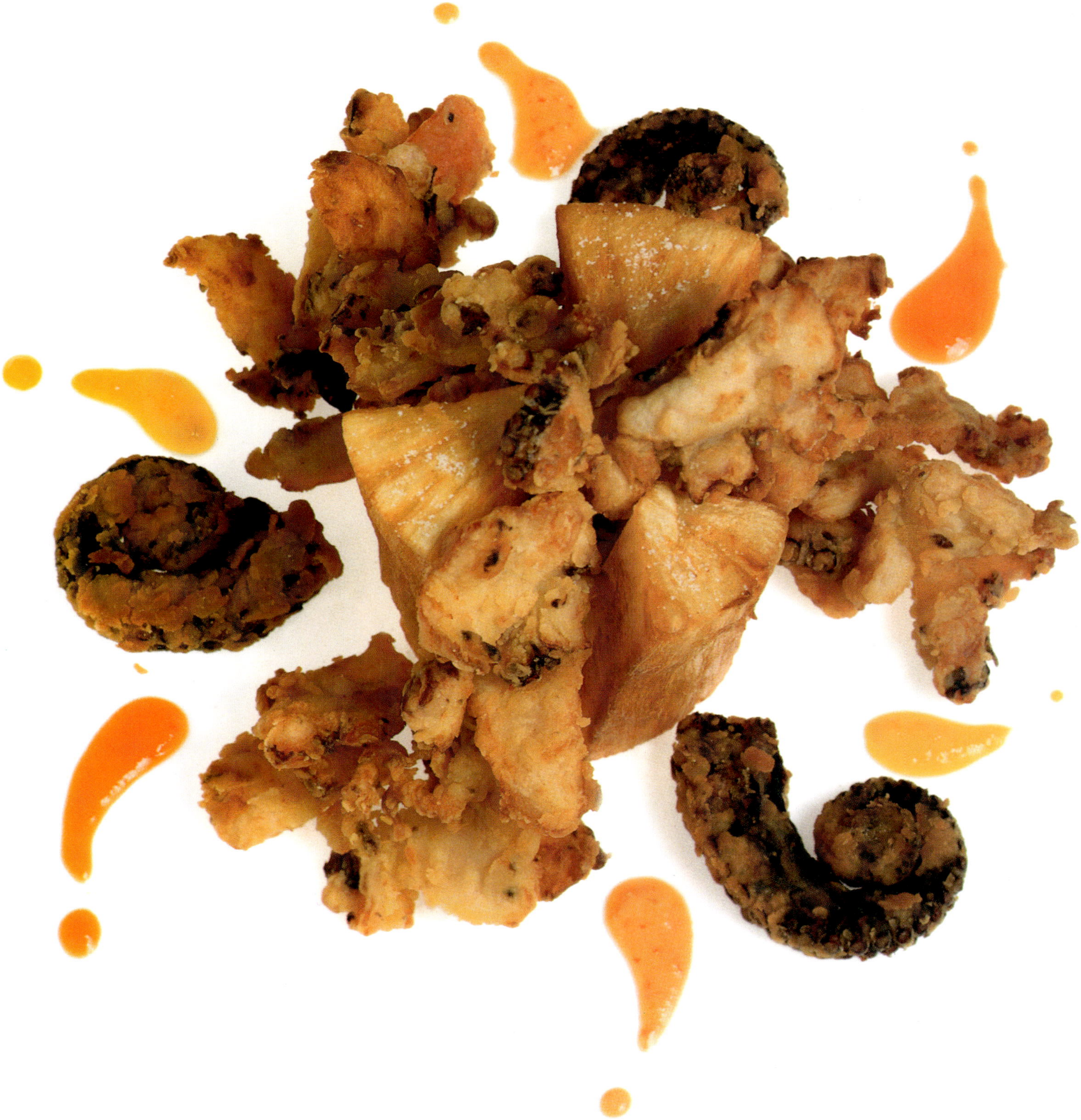

Choclo José Antonio

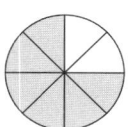

Ingredients:

- 6 ears corn on the cob (unhusked)
- 1 tbsp sugar
- 5 oz (150g) butter
- 1 ½ tsp salt
- 3 level tsp freshly ground pepper
- Juice of 5 key limes

'José Antonio' is one of the most traditional and well-loved restaurants in Lima. This very special treatment of fresh corn is one of the best things about the **piqueo** served there. Corn has always been an essential element of the Andean diet. In Quechua legend, a princess named Saramama pleaded with the sun god to help her avoid her upcoming arranged marriage to an ugly warlock. Obligingly, the sun god transformed her into a maize plant. To this day, in Cusco's Sacred Valley, no man is allowed to touch the corn before it is cooked and served. It is harvested and prepared exclusively by women.

Preparation

Place the ears of corn without removing husks into a large pot of cold water with the sugar and juice of 2 key limes. Bring to a boil and cook until the husk is soft and the kernels are tender, about 10 minutes after the water has come to a rolling boil.

To make the sauce:
In a small heavy pan over low heat melt the butter, taking care that it doesn't burn. Add salt, pepper and remaining lime juice and stir well.

Drain the ears of corn and remove husks and silk.

Serve immediately, bathed in the warm butter sauce.

To serve as an hors d'oeuvre thread 4 - 5 kernels on each toothpick and then bathe in sauce.

Tip: Cooking the corn in the husks will give extra flavor and ensure its tenderness.

Note: You can also eat this with fork or spoon. Shell the kernels from the cob when cooked and mix with the sauce. Turn out into a small bowl and serve immediately.

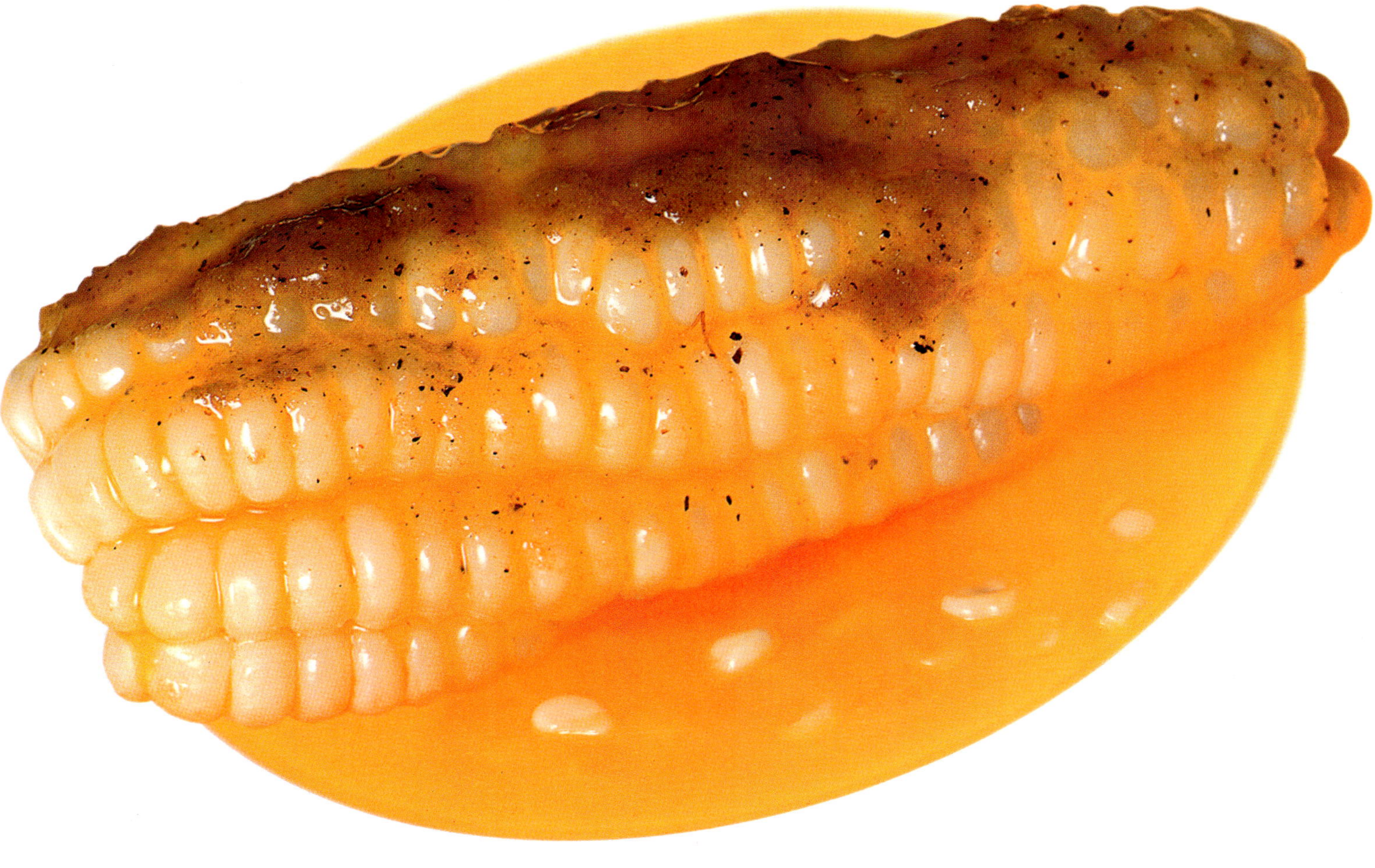

Choros a la Chalaca

This presentation of fresh mussels is a classic of Peruvian seafood cuisine. It is known in slightly different forms along the entire 2,000 kilometer coast of Peru. **Chalaca** *means it comes from Callao, Lima's bustling port area, where this recipe has its roots.*

Ingredients:

- 1 doz mussels
- 1 red onion, chopped as finely as possible
- ¼ cup seeded and finely diced **rocoto**
- 1 tbsp freshly chopped parsley
- ½ cup peeled, seeded and finely diced tomato
- ½ cup fresh corn kernels, cooked
- 1 tbsp **ají amarillo** paste (p.228)
- 1 tbsp vegetable oil
- Juice of 5 key limes
- Salt and pepper

Preparation

Discard any mussels that are not tightly closed. Remove beards (fibrous fringe) with a small sharp knife and rinse mussels very thoroughly under cold running water, scrubbing with a brush to remove any grit or mud. Drain.

Steam mussels gently, removing from steamer as they open to prevent overcooking, discarding any that do not open. Allow to cool.

Place mussels on the half shell on a serving platter.

In a small bowl combine the onion, **rocoto**, tomato, parsley, corn kernels, key lime juice, **ají amarillo** paste and salt and pepper.

Add the oil and mix all ingredients thoroughly. Leave for five minutes to let the flavors develop.

Check and adjust seasonings if necessary and then place 1 tablespoonful on top of each mussel.

Add a few more drops of key lime juice to taste and serve immediately.

Tip: When buying mussels always check that the shells are tightly closed. Shells should be uncracked and unbroken and the mussels should have a pleasant sea smell. Do not store in the refrigerator for any longer than 24 hours. You can also soak the mussels in a solution of salt water for a couple of hours to ensure that all grit and sand is removed.

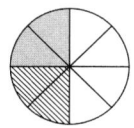

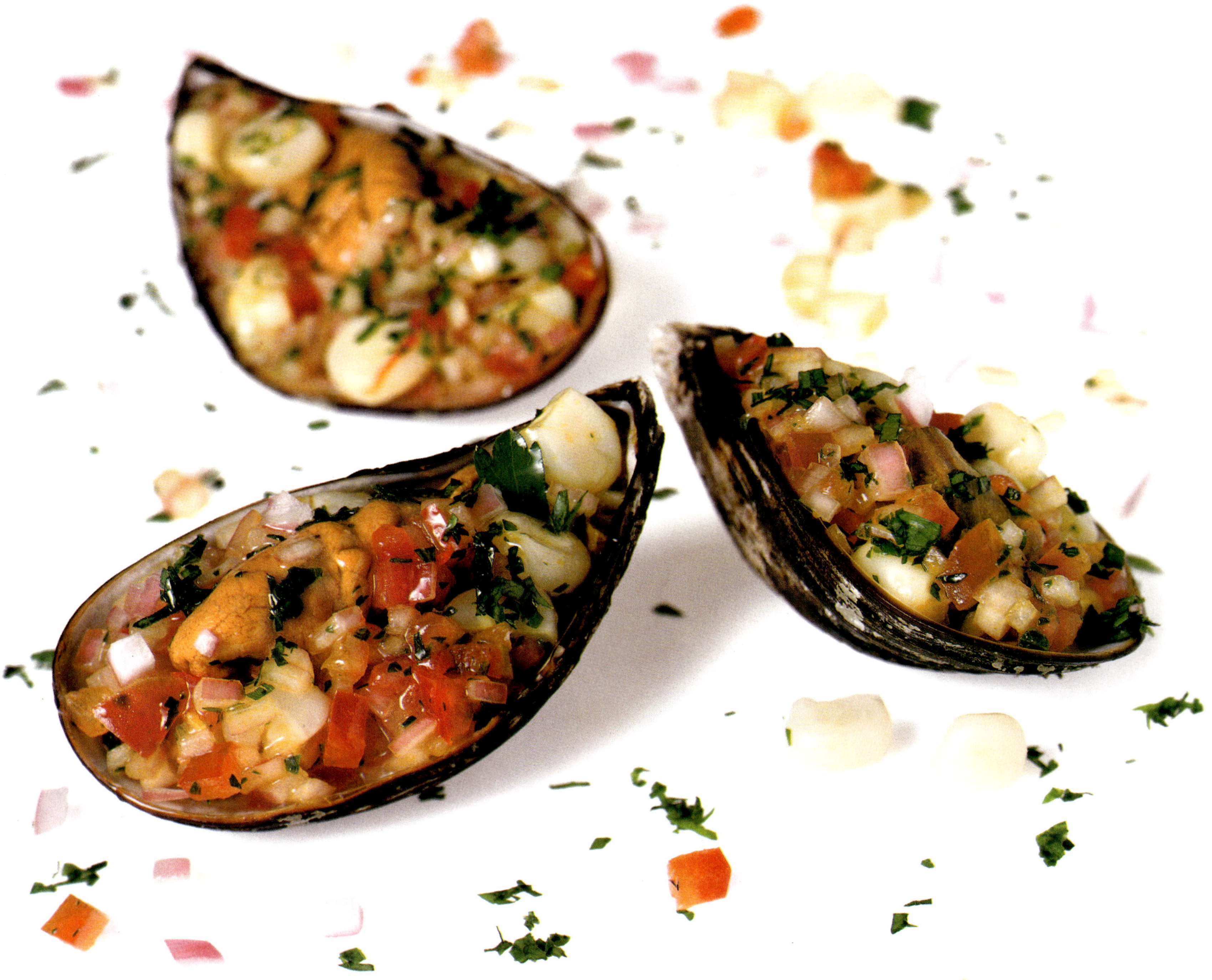

Conchitas a la Parmesana

Ingredients:

- 12 large scallops on the half shell
- 1½ cups grated Parmesan cheese
- 4 tbsp (½ stick) butter
- 1 small glass pisco or whisky
- Olive oil
- Salt and freshly ground black pepper

*Despite its name, no one I know has ever found one of these in Parma, Italy, or for that matter anywhere else in the 'Boot'. In fact I have never seen this preparation of scallops outside of Peru. Personally I like this dish without the red **coral**, but this is the full recipe and includes Humberto Sato's famous 6 drops of pisco on each scallop. Sato, one of the fathers of Peruvian **nikkei** cuisine, says that 6 drops of whisky will do just as well and we each have our own favorite version.*

Preparation

Lightly rinse and dry the scallops, removing the black vein from the round side of the flesh of the scallop if there is one.

Season with freshly ground black pepper.

Cover each scallop generously with grated parmesan cheese and sprinkle lightly with salt. Top with a dollop of butter.

Add a drop of olive oil to each shell and six drops of Pisco or whisky.

Place in the broiler at high temperature for 3 or 4 minutes until the cheese is golden brown.

Serve immediately, garnished with lemon wedges.

Tip: For a delicious variation on this recipe, substitute white wine for the liquor and add a drop of soy sauce to each shell.

Makes 1 dozen

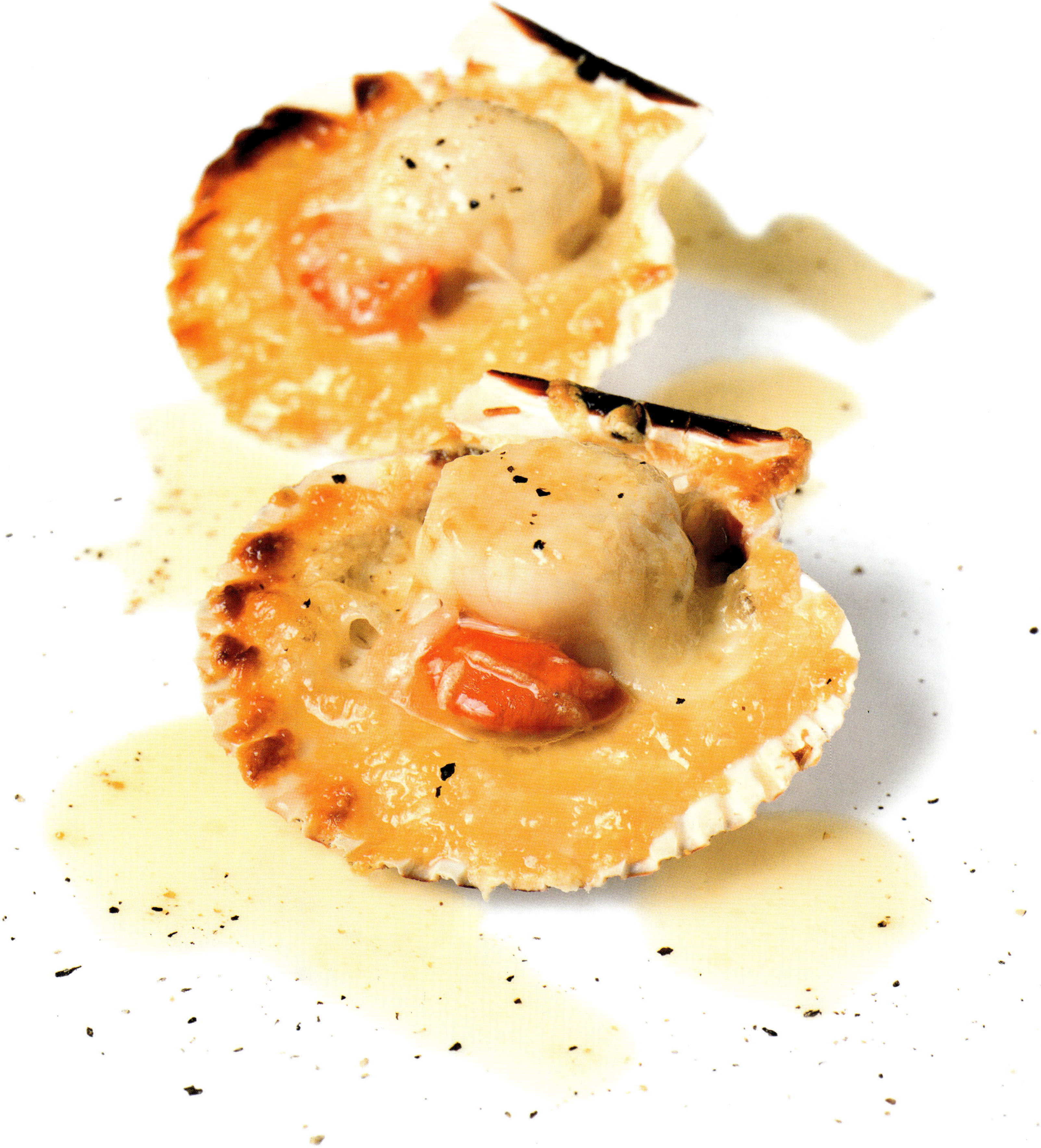

Tamal Verde & Humitas

The recipe for tamal verde comes to us from Andrea Graña who is from one of Lima's most traditional and respected families and a great lover of fine food. The Spanish introduced various savory fillings to the basic Quechua ground corn preparation known as **humintas** *and called them* **tamales**. *The smoky bouquet that fills the kitchen as you unwrap the traditional warm banana leaf covering is central to the experience. Corn husks are a little easier to find and also give their own delicious aroma and taste. The* **humita** *includes* **ají** *and cheese and has a well-balanced sweet and savory flavor.*

Ingredients:

- 1lb (½ kg) chick-peas, soaked overnight
- 1 bunch fresh cilantro leaves, liquified with a little water
- 1 clove garlic, minced
- 2 tbsp lard or vegetable oil
- ½ chicken breast filet, cooked
- 2 hard - boiled eggs
- 1 lb (½ kg) fresh corn husks for wrapping

Ingredients:

- 4 ½ lbs (2 kg) fresh corn on the cob
- 1 cup **ají amarillo** paste (p. 228)
- 4 tsp minced garlic
- 1 tsp ground cumin
- 3 red onions, grated
- 6 oz (170 gr) Philadelphia cream cheese
- 1 **ají amarillo**, seeded, deveined and sliced
- Salt and sugar
- Vegetable oil and lard
- Fresh corn husks

Each recipe serves 6

Preparation - Tamal Verde

Cook the chick-peas in boiling water until they're soft, about 1½ hrs. Strain and reserve some of the cooking liquid. In a food processor, blend the chick-peas with a little of the cooking water and then push the mixture through a fine mesh sieve with the back of a spoon to form a smooth paste. In a large, heavy-based pan, melt 2 tbsp lard, sauté garlic and add the blended cilantro. Season with salt and pepper to taste. Add the chick-pea purée and cook over low heat, stirring continually with a wooden spoon, until you can see the bottom of the pan and the mixture starts to come together in a mass, about 25 -30 minutes. Remove from heat and set aside. Cut chicken into bite-sized pieces. Blanche the corn husks to soften them for easier handling. Assemble (see below). Steam for 10 minutes, serve hot with **salsa criolla** (p.232).

> Tip: For a taste variation, leave out the cilantro and add a black olive to the filling.

Preparation - Humitas

With a very sharp knife remove the kernels from the fresh ears of corn and grind them in a food processor using the pulser until you have a coarse paste. Blanche the corn husks to facilitate handling. In a large skillet, heat the oil and sauté onion for 3 - 4 minutes over medium heat, until translucent. Add garlic and continue sautéing until the onion starts to turn golden, 1 or 2 more minutes. Add **ají amarillo** paste, cumin, salt and sugar to taste and cook for 2 to 3 more minutes. Add onion mixture to the ground corn kernels and combine well. Add a little oil and lard; enough to form a soft dough. Assemble, (see below) and steam gently for approximately 20 minutes. Serve piping hot with **salsa criolla** (p.232).

To assemble the tamales or humitas:

Place two corn husks together lengthwise with the wider ends overlapping. Place a third crosswise in the middle. Place a little of the **masa** or dough in the center of the leaves and then add the filling; for the tamales, fill with one piece of chicken and 1 slice of egg; for humitas, fill each with ½ in (1.25 cm) slice of Philadelphia cream cheese and a 3 x ½ in (8 x 1½ cm) slice of **ají amarillo**. Top with more **masa**. Fold the leaves over to make a neat parcel and tie securely with kitchen twine.

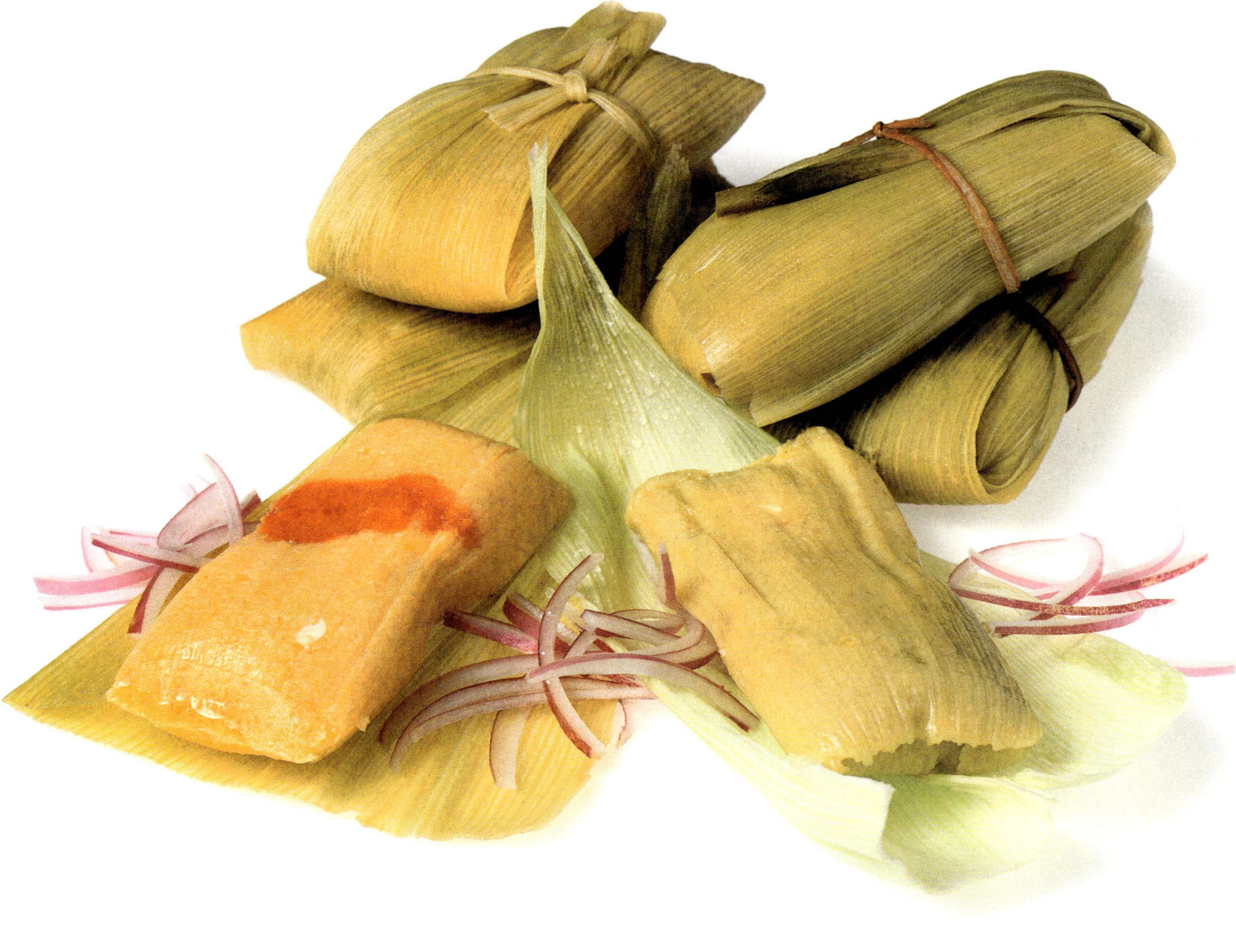

Tamal Criollo

*When travelling in the Andes you are very likely to see people snacking on **maíz mote** or hominy. The dried corn kernels must be soaked and then cooked and hulled before eating. Here the corn kernels are ground into a **masa** or dough for this traditional **creole tamal** recipe.*

Ingredients:

- 4 lb (2 kg) **maíz mote** (large kernels of dried corn)
- 6 tbsp vegetable oil
- 4 tbsp lard
- 3 tbsp **ají mirasol** paste (p.228)
- 1 tbsp **ají panca** paste (p.228)
- 3 tbsp crushed garlic
- 1 tbsp cumin seed
- 6- 8 banana leaves
- Salt and pepper

For the stuffing:

- 6 ½ lb (3 kg) leg or loin of pork
- 1 **ají amarillo**, seeded, deveined and cut into 3 x ½ in- (8x1½cm-) pieces
- 8 olives
- 2 hard boiled eggs
- ¼ cup peanuts, lightly roasted

Preparation

Soak the corn overnight. Bring to the boil in plenty of water, remove from the heat, strain and add more cold water. Repeat procedure. Rinse well and set aside to cool.

When cool enough to handle, slip off hulls and grind in a food processor, adding enough water to form a dough or **masa**. Mix in 4 tablespoons of the oil and the lard. Let the mixture cool thoroughly.

In a small skillet, heat the remaining oil and, over medium heat sauté garlic, **ají** pastes, cumin seed, salt and pepper for 4 minutes.

Add the cooked seasonings to the **masa** and mix thoroughly. Set aside to cool.

Boil the pork in salted water and when it is cooked, (about 25 minutes) let it cool and cut it in slivers.

Place about ½ cup of **masa** in the center of each banana leaf. Top each with a piece of pork, a slice of fresh hot **ají** pepper, one olive, a slice of hard-boiled egg and a roasted peanut.

Fold over the banana leaves to form a rectangular parcel.

Tie up each parcel well with kitchen twine. Bring a large pot of water to a boil and add tamales. Lower the heat and simmer gently for 2½ hours.

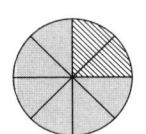

Note: If you cannot find Peruvian **maíz mote**, a mixture of fresh corn (kernels from 2 ears of corn), masa flour (1½ cups) and ½ tsp baking powder will give excellent results also.

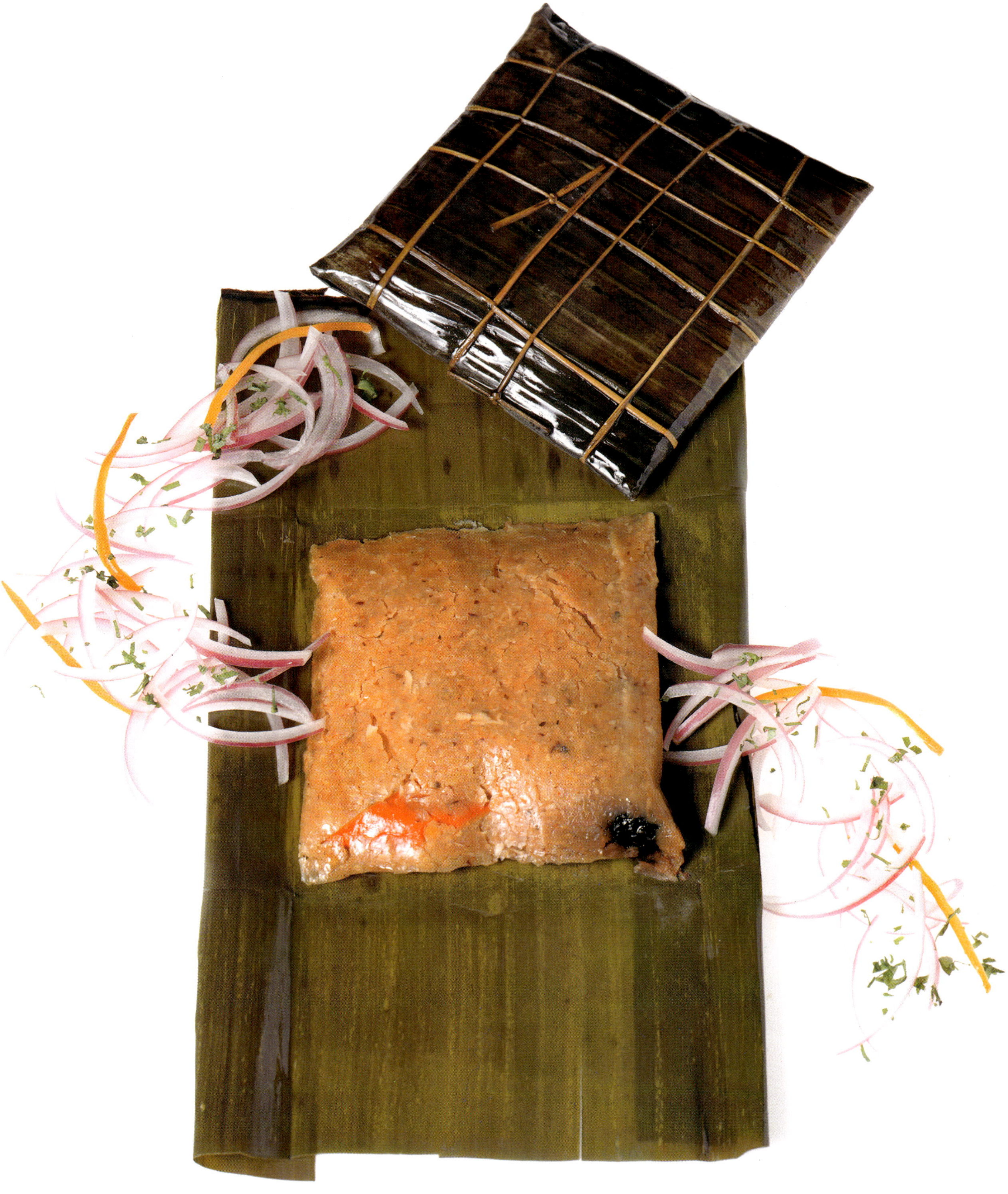

Tamal Negro

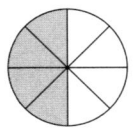

*This is Alfredo Aramburú's delicious seafood tamale. The traditional corn mash **masa** is colored with squid ink and then stuffed with a moist and subtly flavored filling of freshly cooked crayfish tails.*

Ingredients:

- 2 ears of fresh corn
- 8 ½ oz (250g) lard
- 1 tsp minced garlic
- 3 oz (80g) finely chopped red onion
- 1 tsp squid ink
- Salt and freshly ground pepper
- Corn husks

For the filling:

- 1 oz (2 tbsp) vegetable oil
- 1 ¾ oz (50g) white onion, finely chopped
- 1 tbsp paprika
- 3 ½ oz (100g) cooked fresh crayfish tails
- Bechamel sauce
- Salt and freshly ground pepper

To serve:

- 12 fresh crayfish tails
- 1 ½ cups crayfish coral sauce (p. 104)

Preparation

Shell the kernels from the cobs and process kernels in a grinder or food processor to make a coarse paste. (Do not over purée.) Discard cobs.

Heat lard and sauté garlic and onion over medium heat until soft, about 5 minutes.

Add the squid ink, processed corn, and salt and pepper and cook over low heat for about 15 minutes, until the paste comes together to form a light black dough or **masa**. Set aside to cool.

To make the filling:
Heat the oil and sauté the onion over medium heat until just starting to turn golden, about 5 minutes. Add the crayfish tails and paprika. Then add the wine and flambée. Mix in the bechamel sauce and season.

To assemble the tamales:
Lay out the corn husks as for **Tamal Verde** (p.74) place a little of the **masa** in the center. Top with filling and add another layer of **masa**. Wrap and tie securely with kitchen twine, and cook in a minimal amount of water for 30 minutes.

To serve:
Serve warm with crayfish coral sauce, garnished with sautéed fresh crayfish tails.

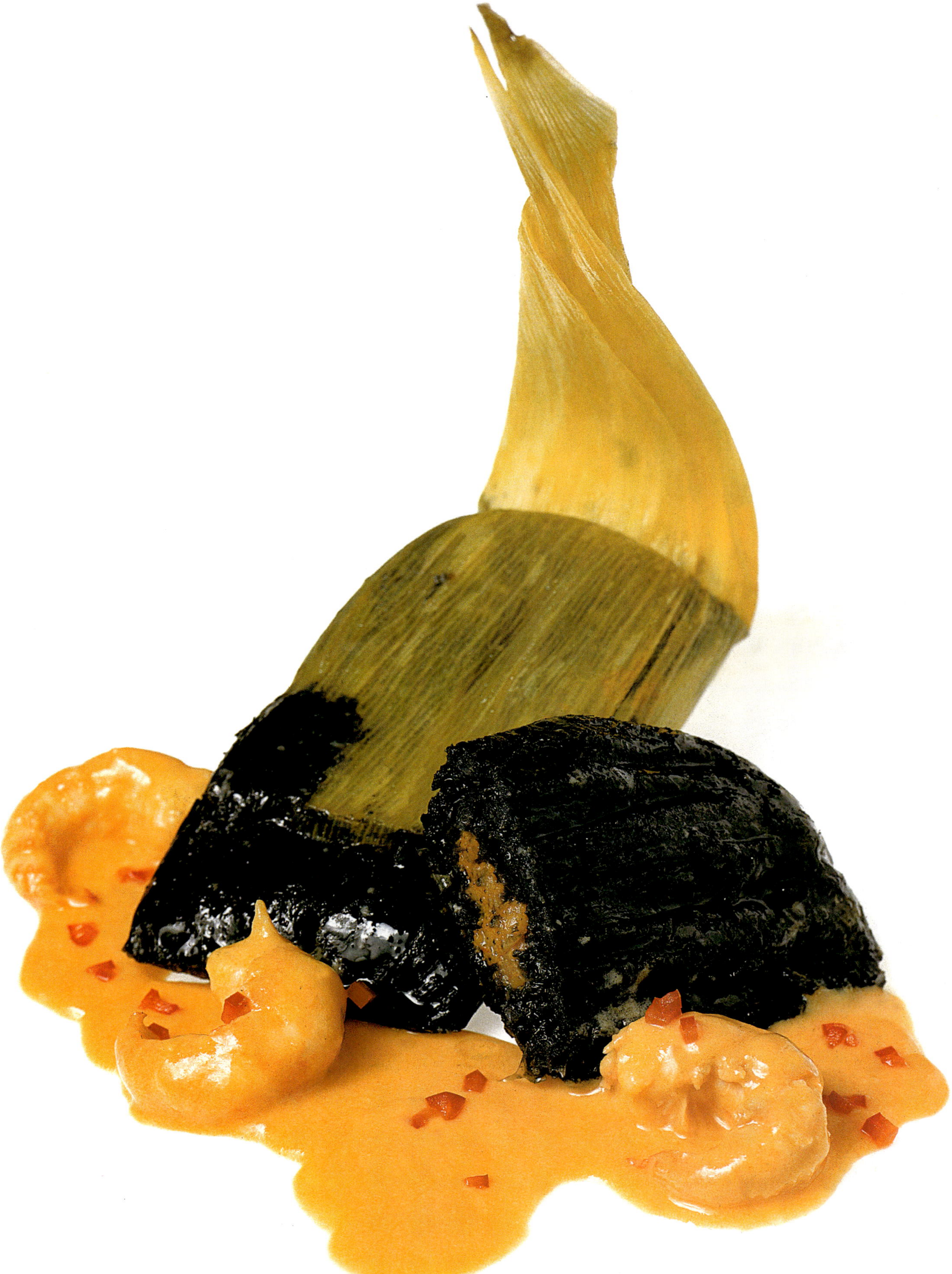

Tequeños Pulpa de Cangrejo & Wantan Mariscos

*Rosita Yimura is a **nisei** lady who has long been a prime force in the creation of **nikkei** food in Peru. Her restaurant is on the ground floor of her home down an intricate set of twisting streets. Finding this house is, as Michelin would say, worth the trip. The sauces and crabmeat filling in Yimura's recipe for crisp rolls combine to produce a very special flavor not found outside of Peru. **Wantan Mariscos** is one of Daniel Manrique's recipes from his restaurant 'Segundo Muelle' and is a classic example of the fusion of Peruvian and Chinese food. In spite of its Chinese heritage, the flavors probably would not be recognized by anyone west of the international date line.*

Ingredients:

- 20 won-ton wrappers
- 8 oz (200g) mozzarella cheese
- ⅔ cup (150g) crabmeat
- ½ tsp dried oregano
- 1 egg yolk, beaten
- 1 cup sifted all purpose flour
- Oil for deep frying
- Salt and white pepper

For the avocado sauce:
- 1 avocado
- 1 tbsp vegetable oil
- 1 tsp key lime juice
- Salt and pepper

Makes 20 rolls

Ingredients:

- 16 won-ton wrappers
- ½ cup (100g) cooked seafood
- 1 ½ tbsp bechamel sauce
- 1 tsp white wine
- 2 tsp finely chopped scallions
- ¼ tsp sesame seed oil
- 1 egg yolk, beaten
- Seven spices (prepared spice)
- Vegetable oil for frying
- Salt

Makes 16 won-tons

Preparation - Tequeños

In a food processor blend the crabmeat and mozzarella until well incorporated. Season with oregano and salt and white pepper to taste. Brush four edges of a won-ton wrapper with beaten egg yolk and place 1 level tbsp of the crabmeat mixture in the center. Spread mixture out a little to form a small roll that covers center of won-ton.

Fold lower section of wrapper over to cover filling and fold top section down. Trim any excess dough from the rolls so that they do not become soggy when cooked. Seal edges firmly by pressing with fingers. Dust rolls lightly in flour. Deep fry in hot oil for 1 - 2 minutes until rolls are crisp and light golden and edges are a slightly darker golden color. Drain well on paper towel and serve immediately, accompanied by the avocado dipping sauce.

To make the sauce:
Combine all ingredients in a blender and process to form a thick, creamy sauce.

Preparation - Won-tons

Mince the seafood; in a bowl combine with the bechamel sauce, sesame seed oil, white wine and scallions. Mix well and season with salt and Chinese allspice. Lay won-ton wrapper on work surface turned as if to forming a diamond. Place 1- 1 ½ tsp of filling at lower end of the diamond and fold up lower point to cover filling, leaving ½ in (1.5 cm) border at the top of the wrapper. Stick with beaten egg yolk.

Take side points of diamond, bring down and around to meet in the center then fold up to form won-ton, sticking with beaten egg yolk. Deep fry in very hot oil until crisp and golden. Drain on kitchen towel and serve with golf or tamarind dipping sauce.

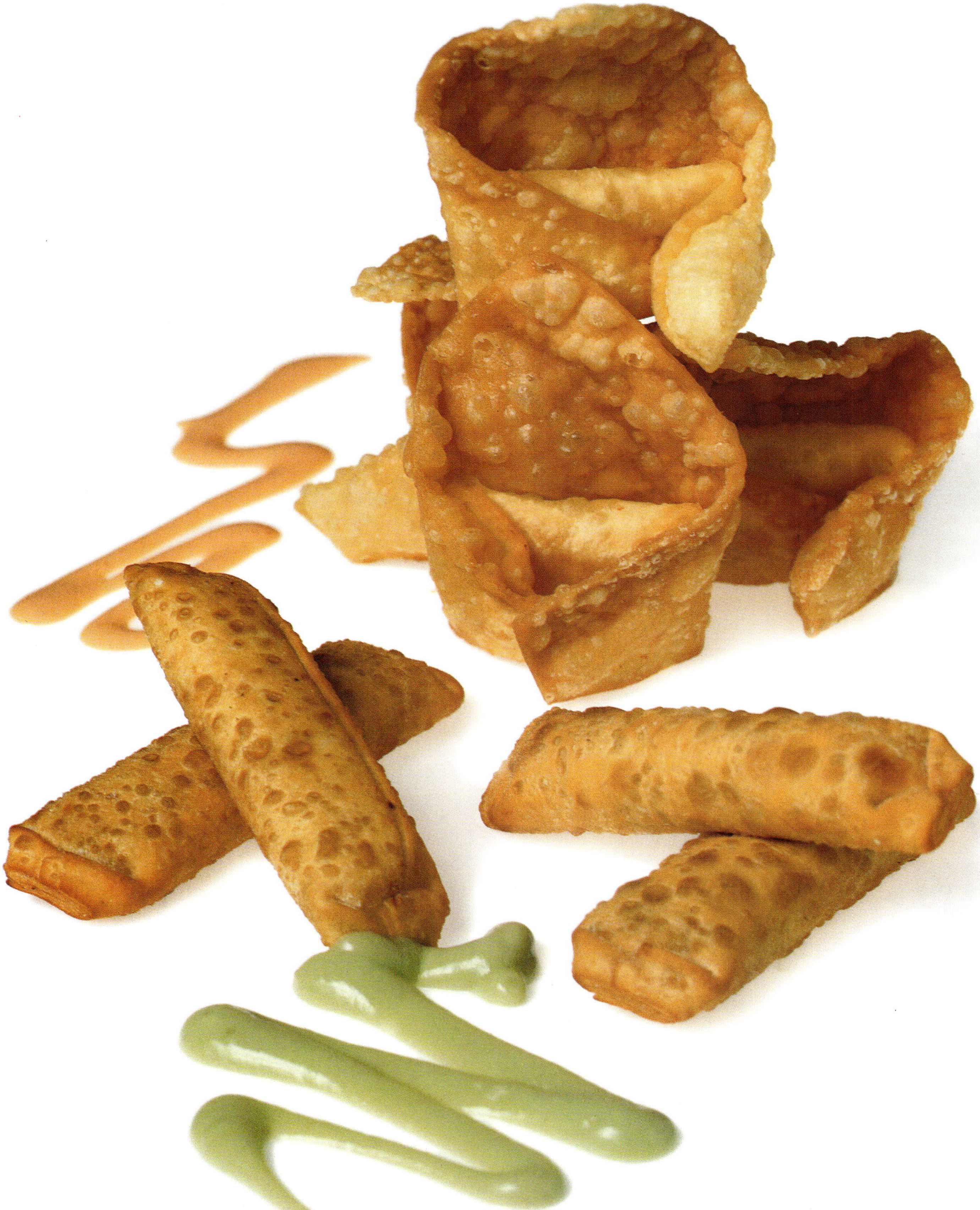

Yuquita Rellena de Mariscos

Ingredients:

- 1 lb (½ kg) yuca
- 1 lb (½ kg) octopus, cooked, chopped fine
- ½ lb (¼ kg) raw shrimp meat
- 1 ½ tbsp (20g) minced garlic
- 1 red onion, grated
- 1 heaped tbsp **ají mirasol** paste (p.228)
- 1 tbsp Worcestershire sauce
- 1 key lime
- 3 tbsp margarine
- 1 egg, beaten
- 1 cup sifted all purpose flour
- Vegetable oil for frying
- Salt and pepper

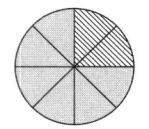

Makes 8 appetizer size servings or 6 first course helpings.

Gloria Hinostroza has collected 3,000 authentic Peruvian recipes from the coast, the Andes and the Amazon jungle. 1,800 of them will soon be published as an atlas of Peruvian cuisine. Gifted with an extraordinary memory for the history of Peruvian cuisine, Gloria has helped us not only with her delicious recipes, but also with many hours of historic narrative. This recipe blends European basics with Peruvian ingredients and flavors

Preparation

Wash and peel the yuca. Cut through in half lengthwise and then again into three parts. Put into a large pot of cold water, bring to the boil, lower the heat and simmer gently for about 25 minutes until the yuca is very tender. Strain and leave to cool slightly in a colander. When cool enough to handle, but still warm, remove any grey fibers in the yuca flesh. Mash finely by pressing through a fine mesh sieve with the back of a spoon or use a ricer.

Season with salt and pepper, and add 1 tbsp of margarine and beaten egg. Mix well until all ingredients are well incorporated. Set aside until ready to use. Cut each shrimp into three or four pieces and season with salt, pepper, Worcestershire sauce and lime juice.

In a small skillet, sauté cooked octopus and shrimp in 1 tablespoon of margarine for 3 or 4 minutes until shrimp turn pink. Remove seafood with a slotted spoon and reserve. In the same skillet, add a little more margarine and sauté onion and garlic until they start to turn golden, about 4 minutes. Add **ají mirasol** paste, cook for 2 or 3 more minutes, remove from the heat and add to the seafood mixture.

To assemble the balls; flour a work surface and your hands. Place about 1 tbsp of the yuca mash into the palm of your hand and squash it down to form a disc. In the center place about 1 level tsp of the seafood filling and then carefully bring the sides round to cover filling and form a croquette.

Lightly coat croquettes in sifted flour. Deep fry croquettes in very hot oil (but not smoking) until golden. Drain on paper towel and serve immediately with **salsa criolla** (p.232) or **mayonesa de rocoto** (p. 230).

Tip: To make a variation on the filling add chopped tomatoes and a little mozzarella.

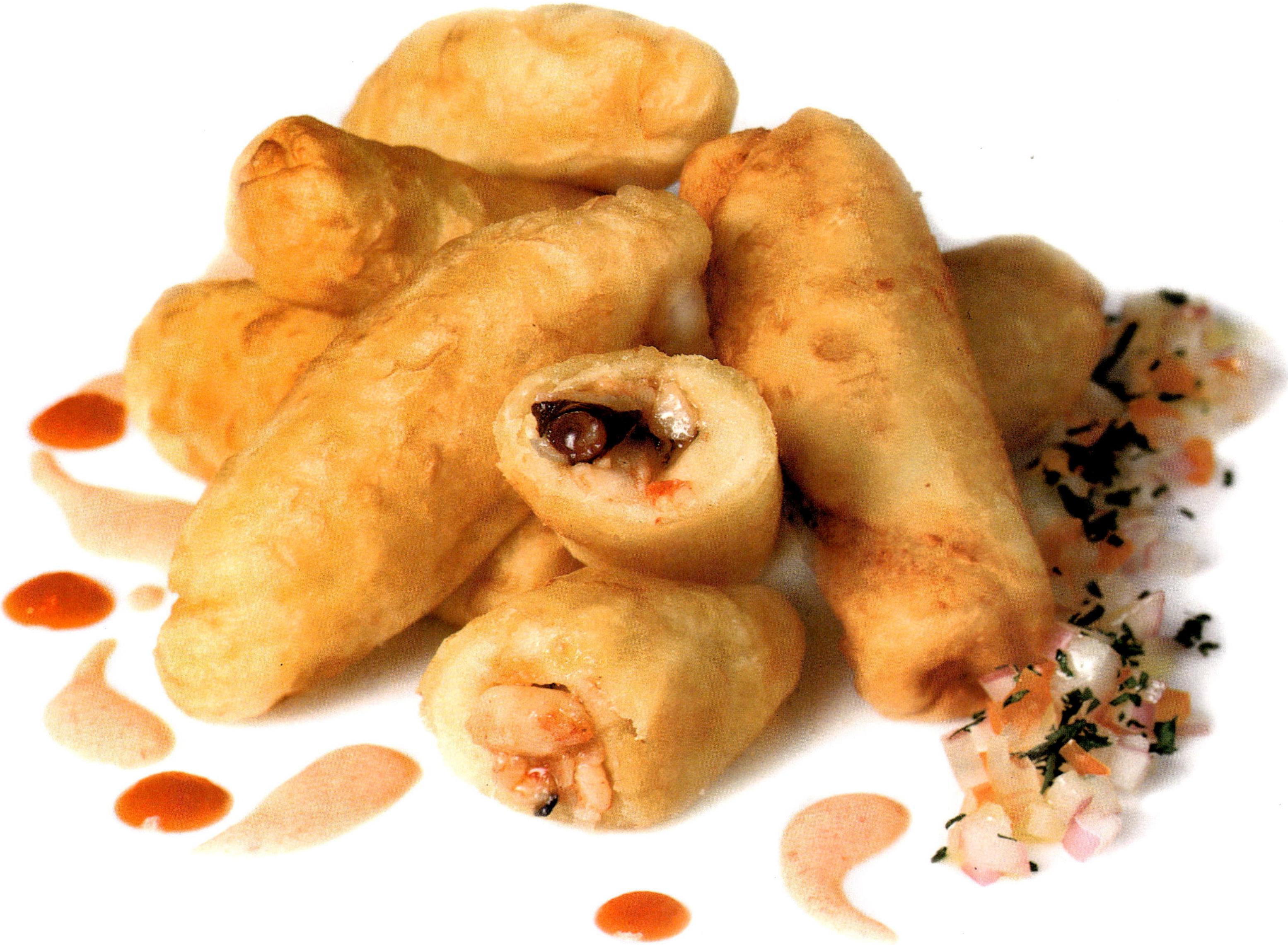

Soups

Aguadito de Pavo

Ingredients:

- 6 turkey pieces
- ¼ cup vegetable oil
- 1 small red onion, chopped
- 2 cloves garlic, crushed
- 1 tbsp **ají amarillo** paste (p.228)
- ½ cup fresh cilantro paste (blend fresh cilantro leaves with a little water)
- 1 cup Pisco or 1 cup beer
- 6 cups chicken stock
- 1 whole **ají amarillo**, cut in half, with seeds and veins intact
- 1 cup rice
- 1 red bell pepper, seeded and chopped
- ½ cup peas
- 1 cup fresh corn kernels
- 3 large yellow potatoes, peeled and diced
- Salt and pepper

*When Peruvians are partying all night, as they often do, the turkey will be discreetly taken from the buffet by the chef, unseen by the guests. At dawn, what's left of it will reappear in this nourishing and reviving soup with vegetables and rice and a 'kick start' of **ají**. A 'levanta muertos', (dish 'to raise the dead') to keep the revelers going well into the next day.*

Preparation

Heat the oil in a large heavy-based pan and sauté the onion over medium heat with the crushed garlic and the **ají amarillo** paste until golden, about 5 minutes.

Cut the turkey into bite-sized pieces, place in the pan and combine thoroughly with the seasonings. Add salt and pepper. Lower heat, cover the pan and cook for 10 minutes.

Add the beer or Pisco, chicken stock, cilantro paste and whole **ají amarillo**.

Bring back to the boil and when liquid is boiling add the rice, red bell pepper, peas and corn kernels.

After ten minutes, add the potatoes and cook for about 5 more minutes or until all the ingredients are tender but not too soft.

Remove the **ají amarillo** before serving.

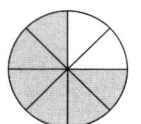

Tip: Peruvian yellow potatoes cook very quickly and will disintegrate if you leave them to boil for too long. If you are using another variety of potato, you will need to add it earlier along with the rice and vegetables.

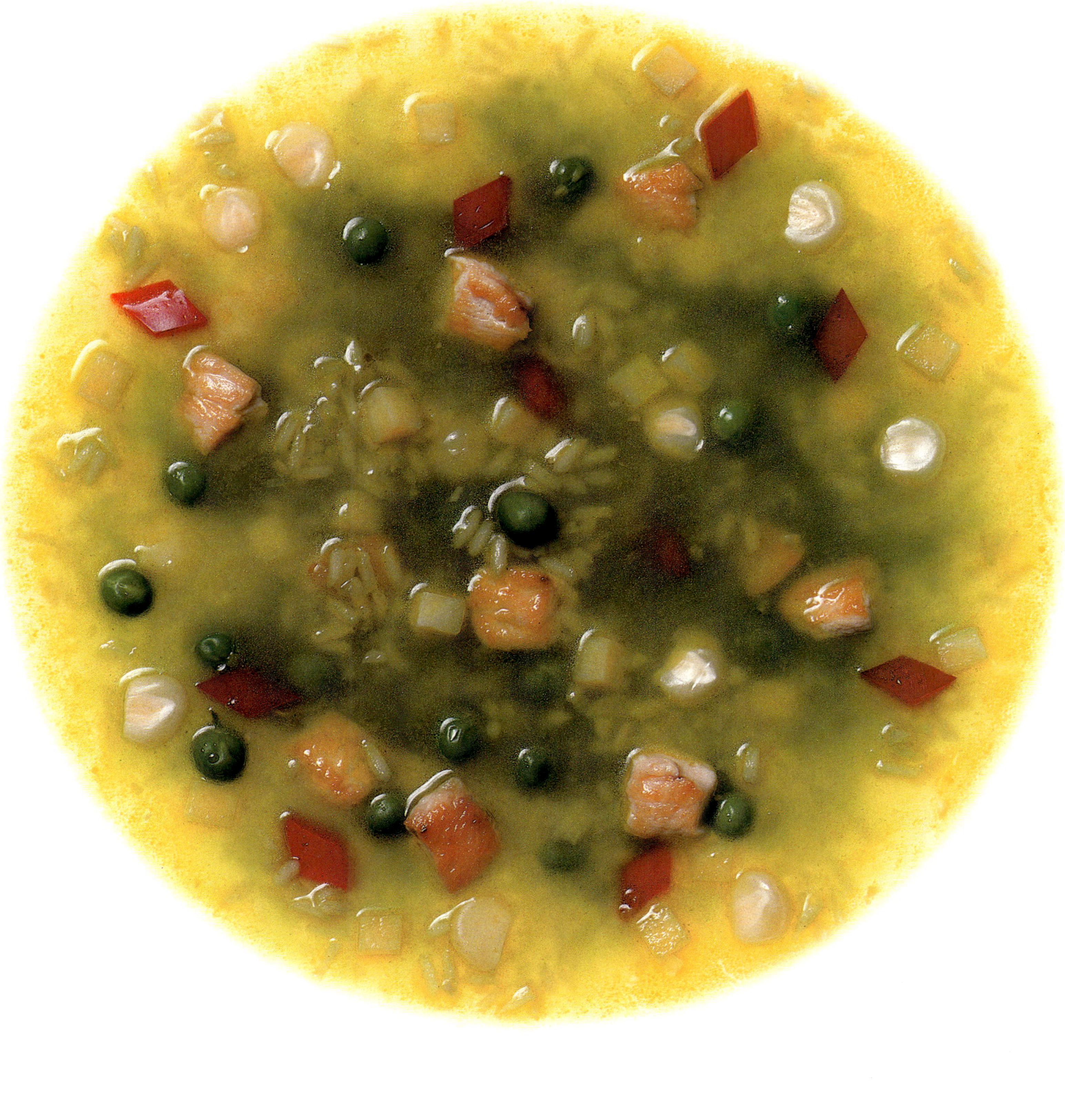

Chupe de Camarones

Ingredients:

- 4lb (2kg) fresh water crayfish
- 1 cup dry white wine
- 8 small sea bass fillets
- 1 cup breadcrumbs
- ¼ cup vegetable oil
- ½ cup (1 stick) butter
- 1 tsp minced garlic
- 2 red onions, finely chopped
- 3 tomatoes, peeled and chopped
- 1 tbsp tomato paste
- 2 ears of corn, cut into rounds
- ½ cup fresh peas
- 4 yellow potatoes, cooked, peeled and cut in half
- ¼ cup rice
- 4 cups concentrated fish stock
- 4 cups crayfish stock
- ¾lb (350g) fresh white cheese
- 1 cup evaporated milk or cream
- 8 dried **ajíes mirasol**, charred
- 8 whole yellow potatoes, boiled and peeled
- 8 poached eggs
- Mirepoix of celery, leek and carrot
- **Ají amarillo** paste (p.228)
- Crayfish corals
- Salt, pepper and oregano
- Chopped cilantro for garnish

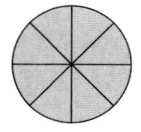

*A hearty and sustaining chowder, **chupe** is one of the many robust soups eaten by country workers and city dwellers alike all over Peru. This recipe is from Arequipa, known as the 'White City', where the Peruvian fresh water crayfish or **camarón** is found in abundance. All parts of the crayfish are used to give a heady intensity of flavor. This **chupe** should be served as a main dish.*

Preparation

Wash the crayfish well and set aside about 20 for serving. Separate the heads from the tails of the remaining crayfish. Peel tails and reserve. Pinch the base of the heads between thumb and forefinger and squeeze gently to extract the coral. Reserve corals and discard the small black sac that is also found inside the head.

To make the crayfish stock:
In a large pan, sauté the crayfish heads in a little butter with the mirepoix for a few minutes. Add the white wine and simmer until almost all the liquid has evaporated.

Add enough water to cover (about 8 cups) and bring back to the boil. Reduce the heat to medium and cook until the liquid has reduced by half, about 10 minutes. Remove from the heat, let cool for a while and then liquefy in a blender, strain and reserve. You need four cups. Season fish fillets lightly with salt and lemon and bread them. Set aside until ready to fry them just before serving.

In a large pan heat the oil and the rest of the butter and, over medium heat, sauté garlic and onion until translucent, about 3 minutes. Do not let them brown. Add the tomato, **ají amarillo** paste to taste, tomato paste and the reserved crayfish corals. Combine well with the onion and garlic and cook, stirring, for 2 or 3 more minutes.

Add the vegetables, rice and the two stocks. Season with oregano, salt and pepper and bring to a boil. Then add the peeled crayfish tails, flame roasted **ajíes**, whole crayfish, cooked potatoes and the heavy cream. Lower the heat so that the mixture does not boil and leave covered. Meanwhile poach the eggs in a little fish stock and milk, and pan fry the fish fillets.

Serve in deep soup bowls. For each portion place in the bowl, first a fish fillet, crayfish tails, corn round, whole crayfish and slice of fresh white cheese. Add the rest of the chupe and top with the poached egg. Garnish with freshly chopped cilantro.

Tip : The dried **ají mirasol** is charred to bring out the flavor. To char the **ají**, hold with a fork over an open flame, or place as close to the heat source in a broiler as you can for a few moments.

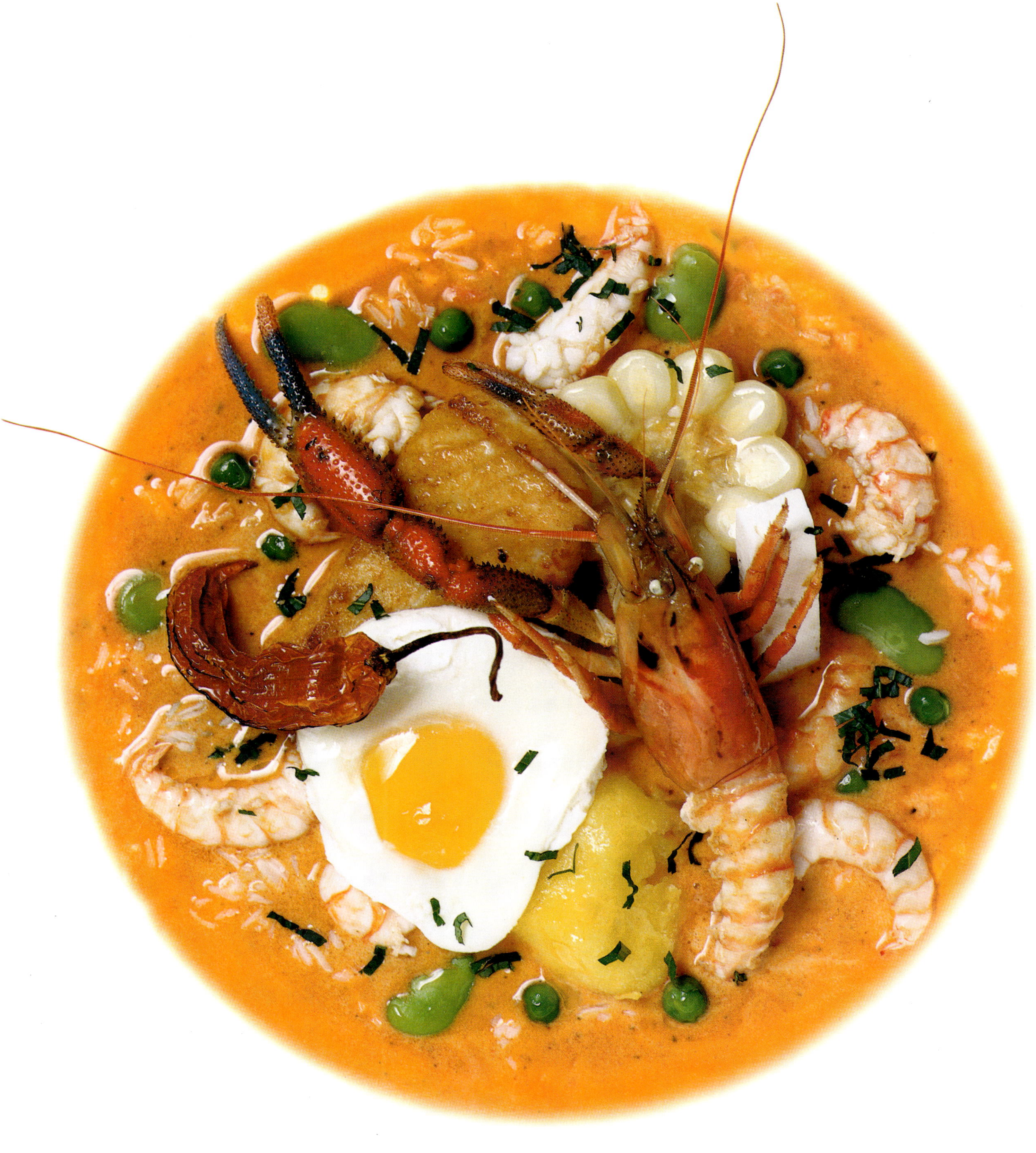

Concentrado de Cangrejo

This is one version of the wonderful crab soup made at the small cevicheria 'Mi Peru'. This tiny restaurant in the coastal suburb of Barranco in Lima is often full of customers asking for this one dish alone. a rustic pleasure for the eyes and the palate - I hope you enjoy this verion.

Ingredients:

- 4 live stone crabs
- 2 tbsp vegetable oil
- 1 cup chopped red onions
- 1 tbsp minced garlic
- 1 tsp tomato paste
- 1 tsp **rocoto** paste (p.230)
- 1 bay leaf
- 4 plum tomatoes, peeled, seeded and chopped
- ½ cup dry white wine
- 4 cups fish or seafood stock
- Pinch old bay seasoning

To serve:

- Freshly chopped cilantro and scallions

Preparation

If you prefer to kill your crabs before cooking, the best method is to place them directly in the freezer for up to an hour before preparing them.

Clean crabs, split in two and smash the claws.

Heat oil in a large pan and over medium heat, sauté onion and garlic until soft, about 3 minutes. Add tomato and **rocoto** pastes, bay leaf, old bay seasoning and tomatoes. Continue cooking for a further 2 minutes.

Add wine and cook until the mixture is reduced by ¾.

Add crabs and when they start to change color (from blue/purple to red) add stock and simmer for another 15 minutes.

Serve immediately, piping hot, sprinkled with freshly chopped cilantro and scallions.

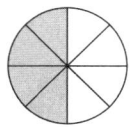

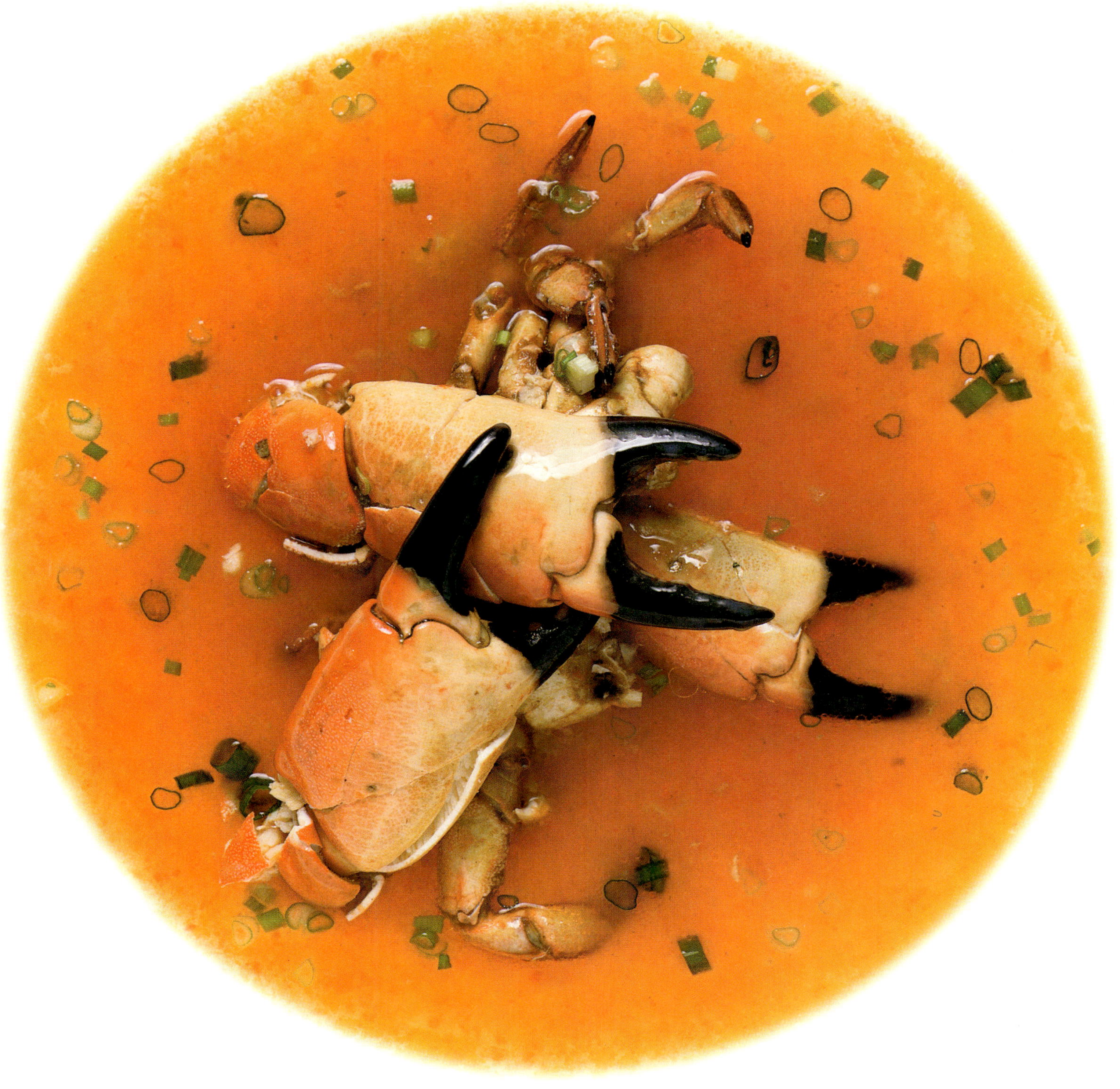

Cusqueña de Cereales

Ingredients:

- 7 cups vegetable stock
- ⅓ cup **quinua**
- 4 tbsp **kiwicha**
- 3 **caihuas**, diced
- ½ cup **ollucos**, finely julienned
- 1 sprig **huacatay**, finely chopped
- Kernels from 1 ear of fresh corn
- Salt and pepper

Another Cucho la Rosa recipe using the ancient grains of Peru. Light, sustaining; modern art in a bowl!

Preparation

Wash the **quinua** and **kiwicha** grains thoroughly under running water until the water runs clear. Leave to drain.

Wash the julienned **olluco** in running water until it once again runs clear, to remove starch. Set aside to drain.

Bring the vegetable stock to a boil in a large pan and add the **quinua, kiwicha** and corn.

Bring to a boil once again and lower the heat. Simmer for 20 minutes.

Add the rest of the ingredients and simmer gently for an additional five minutes. Do not overcook the vegetables, they should be 'al dente'.

Turn off the heat, add the chopped huacatay and serve immediately.

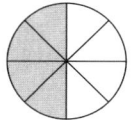

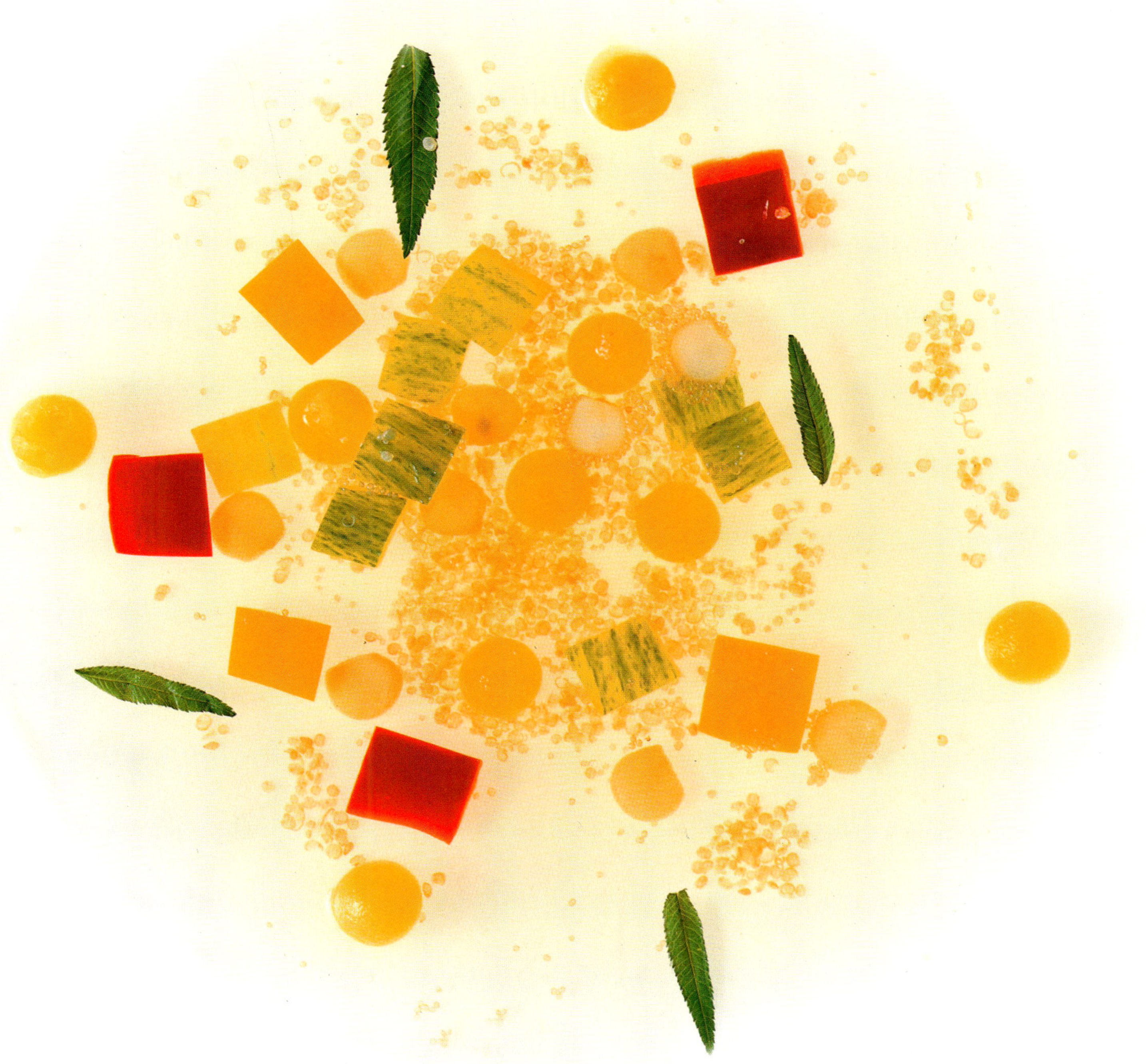

Parihuela

Ingredients:

- ¼ cup vegetable oil
- 1 large red onion, finely chopped
- 3 cloves garlic, crushed
- 2 plum tomatoes, peeled, seeded and finely chopped
- 2 tbsp **ají amarillo** paste (p.228)
- 2 tbsp **ají panca** paste (p.228)
- 1 tsp dried oregano
- 1 bay leaf
- ½ cup dry white wine
- 6 cups fish stock
- 6 small slices of sea bass or any other firm white fleshed fish
- 1 lb (½ kg) peeled and cleaned crayfish tails
- 1 dozen scallops
- 1 dozen mussels, cooked
- 1 cup cleaned squid, cut in rings
- ¼ cup Pisco
- Juice of 1 key lime
- Salt and pepper

*This spicy **criollo** cousin to the Bouillabaisse is a delicious and colorful example of the Mediterranean influences on New World cuisine. With the tempting array of Peruvian seafood available, it's an entertainment in itself.*

Preparation

In a large pan, heat the oil over medium heat and fry the garlic for just a few seconds. Be careful not to let it brown. Add the onion and continue cooking for 4 to 5 minutes or until the onion is completely translucent and just starting to turn golden.

Add the tomato and **ají amarillo** and **ají panca** pastes, bay leaf, oregano and salt and pepper and cook for 2 or 3 more minutes, stirring.

Add the wine. Bring the mixture to a boil, lower the heat and simmer until nearly all the liquid has evaporated.

Then add the stock, bring back to a boil and add first the fish, then the crayfish tails and squid rings and finally the scallops and cooked mussels.

Adjust the seasonings, adding more salt if necessary. Add a few drops of lime juice and the Pisco and serve piping hot.

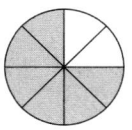

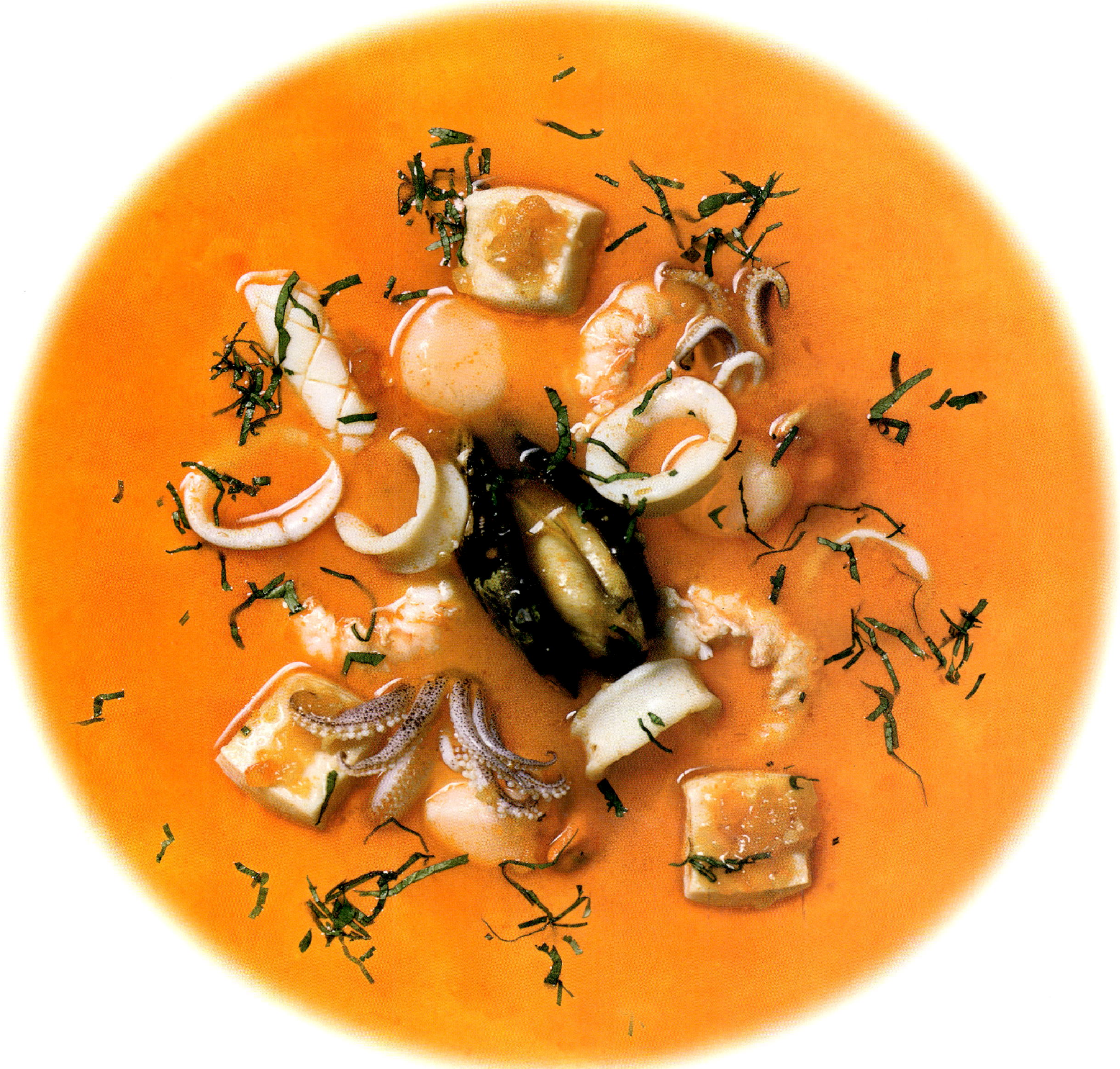

First Courses

Camarón a la Plancha

Ingredients:

- 40 large fresh crayfish
- 1 tbsp vegetable oil
- 2 tbsp butter
- 2 tsp minced garlic
- ½ cup Pisco
- 1 tbsp crayfish corals
- 1 tbsp **rocoto** paste (p.230)
- 2 tsp Worcestershire sauce
- 1 tsp soy sauce
- 2 tbsp chopped cilantro or
- Italian flatleaf parsley

This is a very common coastal dish. It's usually best prepared in the small simple popular restaurants of Lima and the coastal towns. When properly done, the shell should crackle. Marisa Guiulfo is Lima's best known caterer and restaurateur. She is also the head of an incredibly talented culinary family. This is just one of her wonderful collection of recipes.

Preparation

Leave crayfish heads intact, but peel the skin from the tails.

Heat oil and butter together in a large skillet and sauté garlic over medium heat for 1 minute.

Add crayfish and continue cooking 4 to 5 minutes until tails turn a rosy pink.

Add pisco and flambée for another minute or so until the alcohol has evaporated.

Add crayfish coral, **rocoto** paste, Worcestershire and soy sauce and cook for 2 more minutes.

Just before serving, add the chopped cilantro or parsley.

Serve hot with white potatoes.

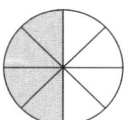

Tip: To extract crayfish coral, pinch base of head between thumb and forefinger and squeeze gently. The coral can be any color from bright orange to dull grey green. Any small black shiny sac or 'gut' you may find should be discarded.

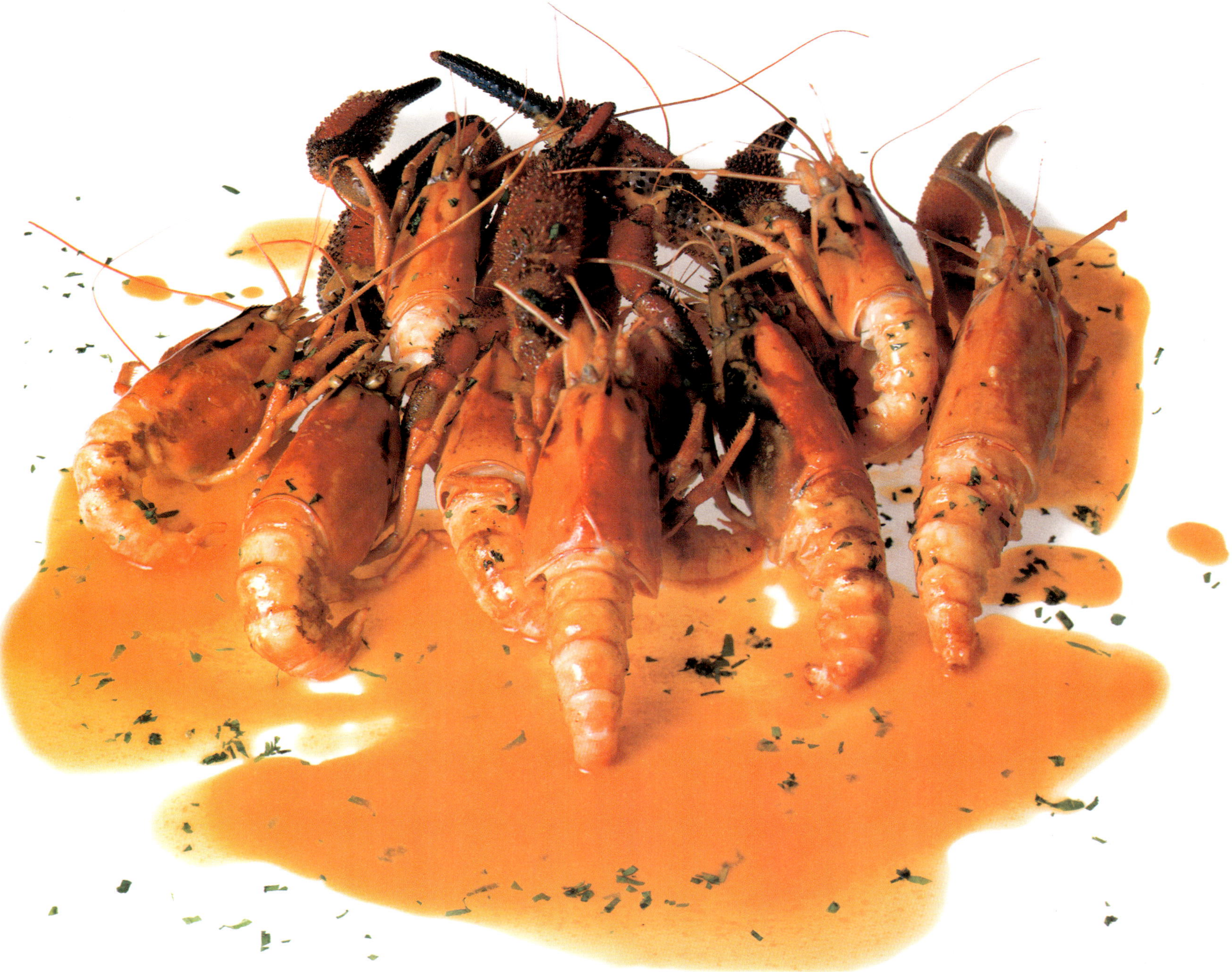

Carpaccio de Pato

This is another of Cucho's extraordinary Novoandino creations. 'Pantagruel's' fascinating menu is divided between classic Peruvian dishes and a series of his mouth-watering modern masterpieces.

Ingredients:

- 2 duck breasts
- Olive oil
- Salt and pepper

For the ají cream:

- ½ cup **ají amarillo** paste (p.228)
- 3 tbsp heavy cream
- 1 tbsp caper vinegar
- 1 tbsp whole grain mustard
- 1 tbsp Chinese hot sauce
- 2 tbsp dry white wine
- 3 tbsp freshly chopped parsley
- 1 tbsp capers
- 5 tbsp concentrated duck stock
- Salt and pepper

To serve:

- Parmesan shavings
- Leaves of lettuce
- Toast

Preparation

Season duck breasts with salt and pepper. Sear on both sides for a couple of minutes over high heat.

To make the ají cream:
Combine all ingredients in a bowl and mix thoroughly to form a smooth cream.

Warm cream sauce in a pan for a few minutes over low heat. Whisk in butter, without letting the sauce come to a boil. Season with salt, remove from heat and set aside to cool.

To serve:
Slice duck breasts as finely as possible and serve cold with the accompanying **ají** cream sauce, lettuce, toast and Parmesan shavings.

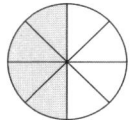

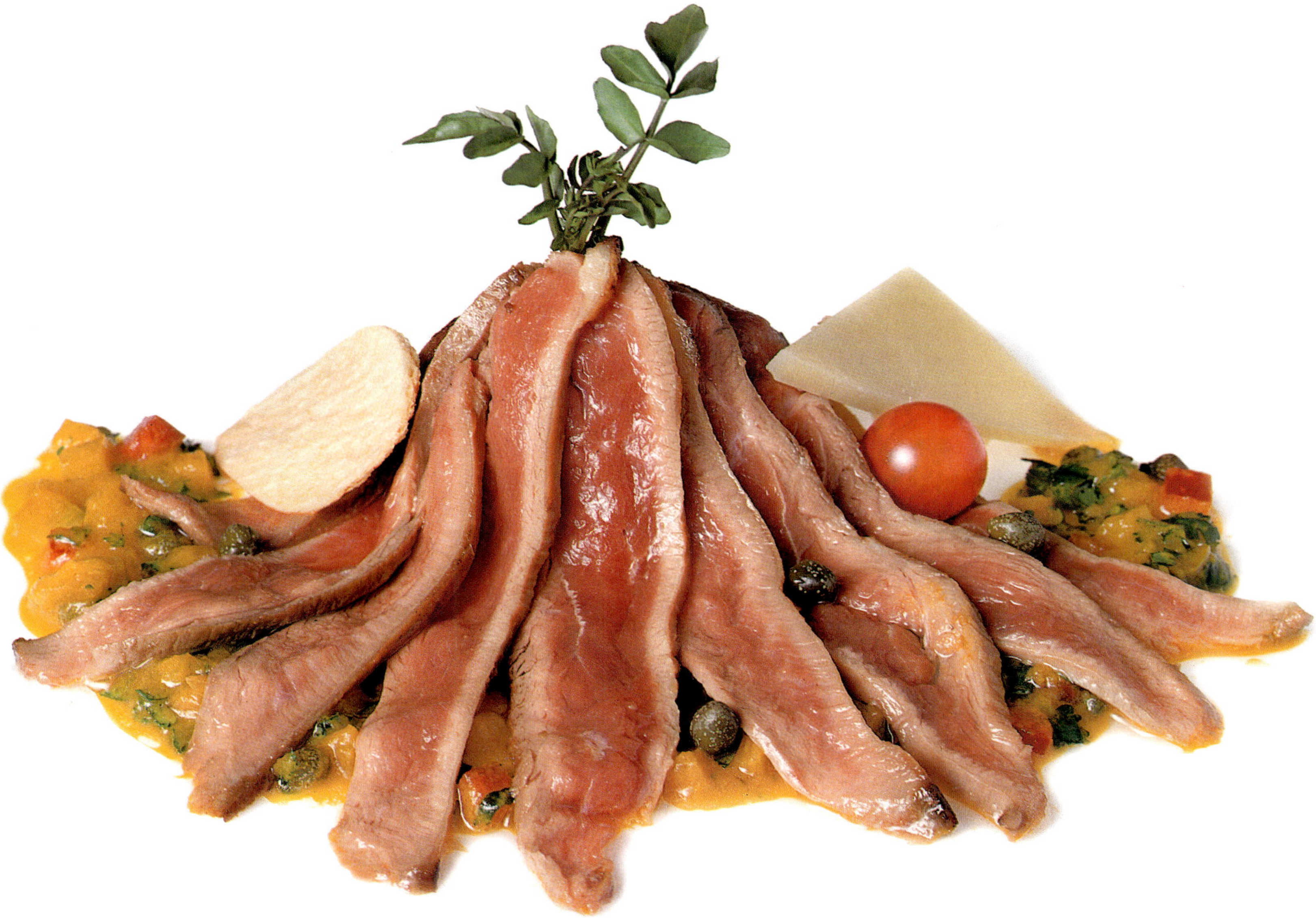

CAUSA

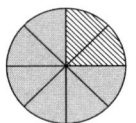

Summer is not summer in Lima without **causa**. *On a hot summer day, no food is more welcome than this cool mashed yellow potato cake stuffed with goodies from the sea. This is one of the most difficult dishes to export in all Peruvian cuisine. It is also one of the most delicious. The sooner yellow potato is exported or grown abroad in large quantities, the happier all our readers shall be.* **Causa** *can be made with a variety of fillings. It can also be made with white or blue potatoes. The important thing is to mash the potato while it is still warm and is easier to handle. Make sure that no lumps remain in the mixture. The filling in a layered causa should be moist so as to balance the texture of the mashed potato.*

Causa Limeña

This very traditional recipe is Apolonia's; she has cooked for my family for over 40 years.

Ingredients:

- 2lb (1 kg) yellow potatoes
- ½ cup vegetable oil
- 2 small fillets sea bass
- 2 red onions, finely chopped
- ¼ cup vinegar
- **Ají amarillo** paste (p.228)
- Juice of 1 key lime
- Juice of 1 orange
- Salt

For the fillings:

- 1 avocado
- 1 cup mayonnaise
- 2 cups cooked corn kernels mixed with mayonnaise
- Juice of 1 key lime

To serve:

- 1 doz cooked crayfish tails
- Lettuce leaves

Preparation

Scrub the potatoes and place them in a large pot with plenty of salted water. Bring to a boil and cook until tender, about 15 - 20 minutes.

Meanwhile, place onion to marinate in a small bowl, with the vinegar and 1 tsp salt until it turns a rosy pink color. Strain the potatoes well and when they are cool enough to handle, peel and mash them finely by pressing them through a fine mesh sieve with the back of a spoon. Alternatively you can use a ricer. Add vegetable oil, key lime juice, **ají amarillo** paste and salt and mix thoroughly until all ingredients are well incorporated.

Poach sea bass fillets and put to one side to cool. Slice the avocado and sprinkle with a little key lime juice and salt. Drain the onion well and combine with the **ají amarillo** paste to taste and with the orange juice. Set aside. Lightly oil and line a 10 in - (25 cm -) rectangular loaf pan or mold with plastic wrap. Line the base of the mold with a layer of the potato mixture, pressing down lightly and leveling with the back of a spoon. Spread a thin layer of mayonnaise on top. Spoon in the corn kernel mixture and add another layer of potato.

Spread another thin layer of mayonnaise on top of the potato layer. Layer the avocado slices on top and cover with another even layer of potato. Cover with the poached fish, spread with a fine layer of mayonnaise and finally top with another layer of potato. Chill in the refrigerator for at least one hour until ready to use.

To serve, invert onto a bed of lettuce leaves, unmold and top with the onion mixture. Garnish with cooked crayfish tails.

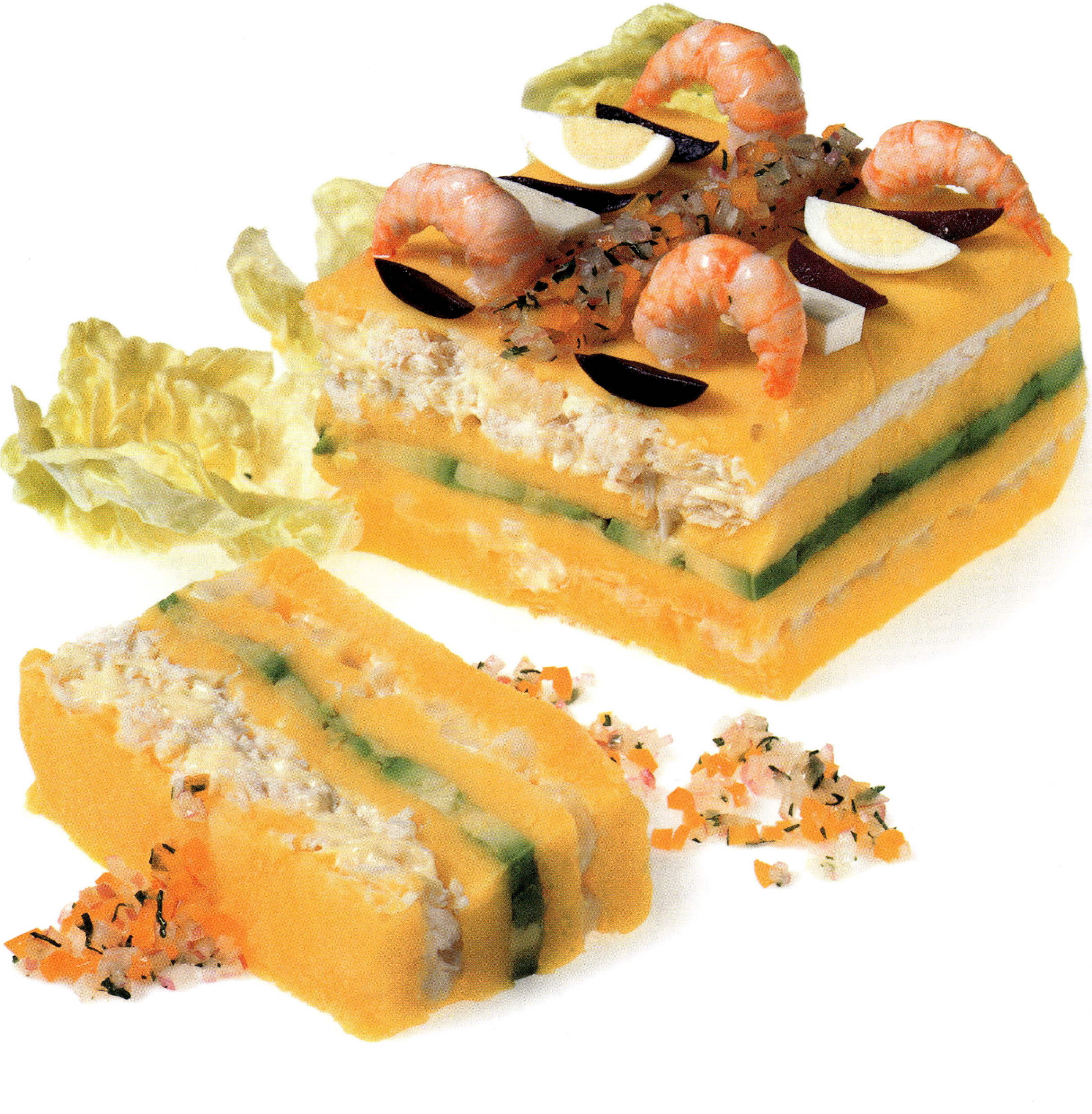

Causa de Camarones en Salsa Tibia

Ingredients:

For the causa:
- 2 yellow potatoes
- 1 tbsp **ají amarillo** paste (p.228)
- 1 tbsp vegetable oil
- Juice of ½ key lime
- Salt and white pepper

For the filling:
- 3 avocado slices
- 4-6 peeled, cooked crayfish tails, mixed with 1 tbsp **salsa golf**

For the crayfish coral sauce:
- 1 tbsp butter
- 1 ½ tbsp crayfish corals
- ¼ cup heavy cream
- 2 ½ tbsp bechamel sauce
- 1 cup crayfish stock (p.88)
- ½ cup white wine

Garnish:
- 1 fresh **ají amarillo**, seeded, deveined and cut into julienne
- 2 black olives, pitted and julienned
- 3 or 4 cooked crayfish tails
- Fresh white farmer cheese
- **Salsa criolla** (optional)

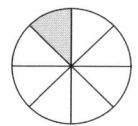

This is a truly spectacular causa from legendary caterer Marisa Guiulfo. The combination of texture and color is matched only by the sensational taste.

Preparation

Scrub the potatoes and place them in a saucepan with plenty of salted water. Bring to the boil and cook until tender, about 10 minutes. Strain and when cool enough to handle (but still warm) peel and mash them by pressing them through a fine mesh sieve with the back of a spoon. Alternatively you can use a ricer.

Add vegetable oil, **ají amarillo** paste, lime juice and salt and white pepper to taste. Mix thoroughly until all ingredients are well incorporated.

Lightly oil and line an individual cup mold with plastic wrap. Line the base of the mold with an even layer of the potato mixture and then spoon in a layer of the crayfish and **salsa golf** mixture. Add another layer of potato and then a layer of sliced avocado sprinkled with a little lime juice and salt.

Finish off with a layer of the potato mixture and chill for at least 1 hour until ready to use.

To make the sauce:
Melt the butter in a small skillet over medium heat and cook the shrimp corals for two to three minutes. Stir in the bechamel sauce and add the crayfish stock and white wine. Bring back to the boil, reduce the heat and simmer until the mixture reduces and thickens to a rich sauce, about 20 minutes. Stir in the cream and adjust seasonings. Keep warm.

To serve:
Invert the **causa** onto an individual serving plate and unmold. Serve with warm crayfish coral sauce and garnish with a julienne of fresh **ají amarillo**, olives, whole crayfish tails and slices of fresh white cheese.

Tip: Do not let the potato cool too much before mashing it. It is much easier to handle while still warm. To make **salsa golf**, mix 1 cup mayonnaise with ½ cup ketchup, 1 tsp Worcestershire sauce and 1 tbsp lemon juice.

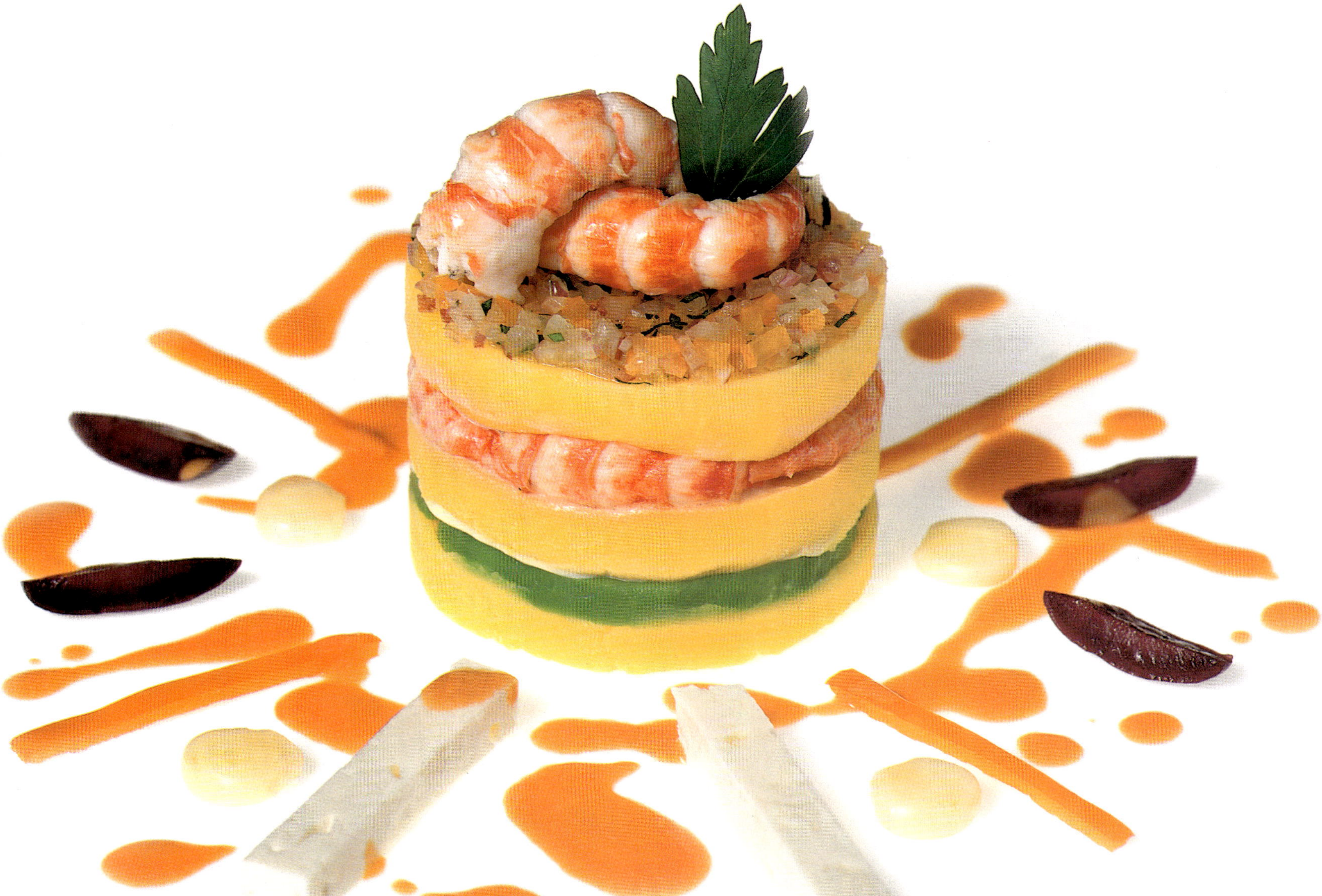

Causa Colonial

Ingredients:

- 48 whole fresh crayfish
- 1 ¾ lb (¾ kg) yellow potatoes
- 4 tbsp **ají amarillo** paste (p.228)
- ¼ cup olive oil
- ¾ cup vegetable oil
- 1 lb (½ kg) small red onions, cut into quarters
- 2 tbsp minced garlic
- 2 **ajíes amarillos**, seeded and sliced
- 3 bay leaves
- 2 tbsp ají panca paste (p.228)
- ½ cup red wine vinegar
- 1 egg
- ½ cup cornstarch
- Vegetable oil for deep frying
- Juice of 2 key limes

To serve:

- 2 hard-boiled eggs
- Black olives
- 4 ounces (100g) fresh white cheese

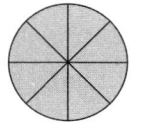

*Another Gloria Hinostroza recipe to surprise and delight the palate. This time a beautifully presented **causa**, which mixes the flavors and textures of 'tempura-ed' crayfish with lightly pickled escabeche.*

Preparation

Separate tails from heads of crayfish. Pinch base of head between thumb and forefinger and squeeze lightly to remove the coral and reserve. (The coral may be any color from bright orange to dull greyish green; any small black shiny sac or gut should be discarded.) Discard heads, clean and peel tails and set aside.

Scrub the potatoes and place in a large pot with plenty of salted water. Bring to the boil and cook until tender, about 20 minutes. Strain well and while they are still warm, peel and mash them by pressing through a fine mesh sieve with the back of a spoon, or with a ricer.

Add olive oil, key lime juice, **ají amarillo** paste and salt and pepper to taste. Mix thoroughly until all ingredients are well incorporated.

In a large skillet, heat vegetable oil and sauté onions over medium heat until they just start to turn translucent, about 3 minutes. Add minced garlic, fresh **ají amarillo**, bay leaf, and **ají panca** paste and cook for a further 2 to 3 minutes.

Add vinegar and let the mixture boil until the liquid has reduced a little, about 5 minutes. Add reserved crayfish corals and cook for 2 more minutes. Remove from heat and let cool to room temperature.

Season crayfish tails with salt, pepper and lime juice.

Beat egg together with 2 tbsp water. Coat crayfish tails in the batter and then in cornstarch before deep frying in hot oil until golden. Remove and drain on paper towel.

To serve, form potato mixture into balls and place on individual serving plates. Top with the **escabeche** sauce and crayfish tails.

Serve garnished with hard-boiled egg, fresh white cheese and black olives.

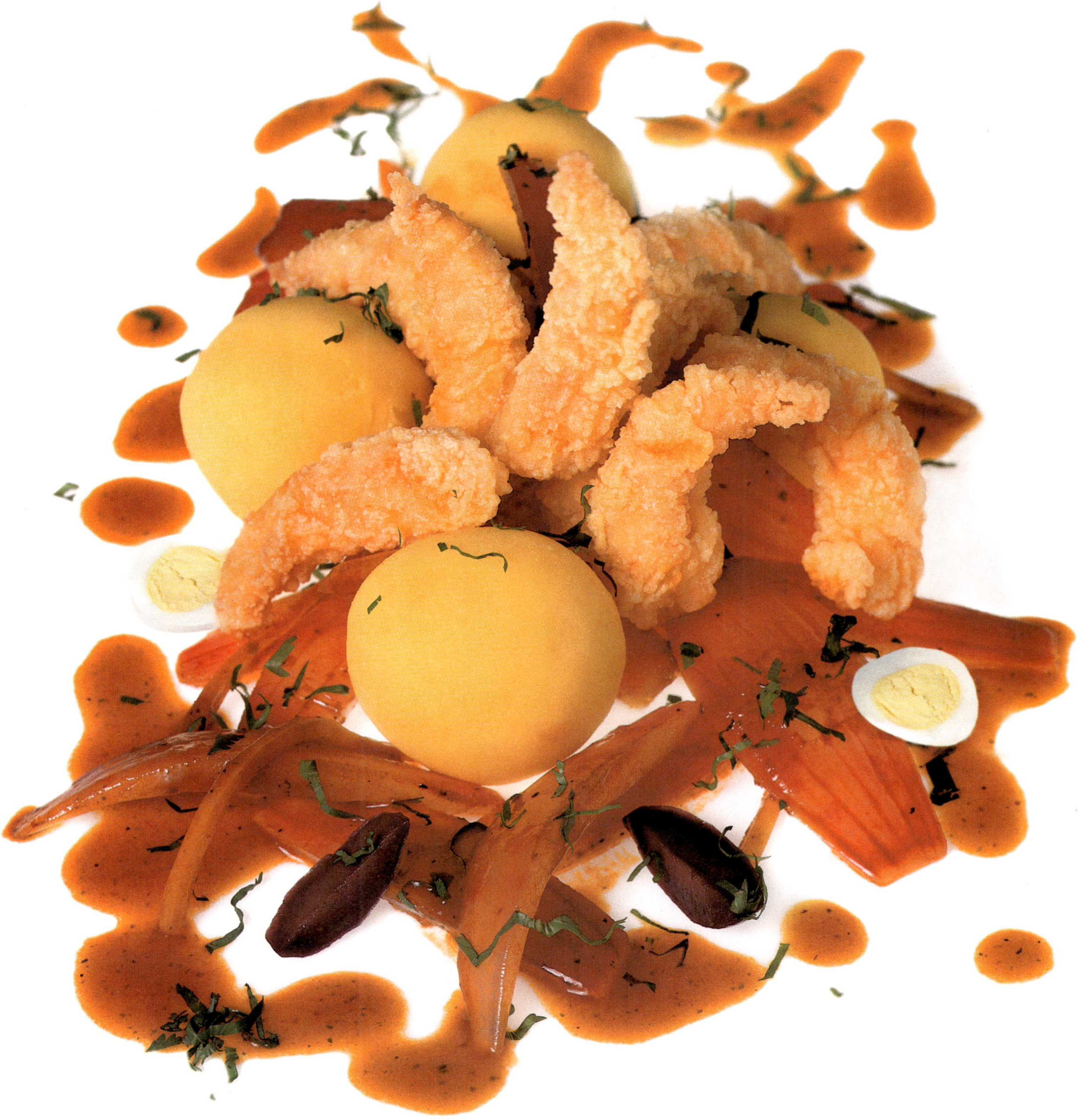

Causas de Pulpo al Olivo & Verde con Cangrejo

*The idea for the colorful **Causa de Pulpo al Olivo** comes from master chef Luis Felipe Arizola at his restaurant 'A Puerta Cerrada'. We gave it a few tweaks. Coque and I threw together the **Causa Verde**, just for fun, to underline the versatility of causa. Once you've got the yellow potatoes mashed, you can let your imagination run wild. Like a good risotto, **causa** lets you put great food on the table with little prior planning.*

Ingredients:

For the filling:
- 2 tbsp octopus in olive mayonnaise (see **Pulpo al Olivo** p.136)
- 3 avocado slices

Garnish:
- 1 tsp capers
- 1 black olive (pitted and diced)

Preparation - Causa de Pulpo al Olivo

Follow the same recipe for the mashed yellow potatoes as for **Causa de Camarones**. For the filling, follow the recipe for **Pulpo al Olivo** except that, instead of cutting the octopus in thin slices, you could cut it into little cubes. Mix with the olive mayonnaise sauce and fill the potato mix with it.

Garnish with capers and black olives.

Ingredients:

For the fillings:
- 2 tbsp cooked crabmeat
- 3 tbsp mayonnaise
- ½ tsp finely chopped **ají limo**
- ½ tsp finely chopped cilantro
- 2 tbsp fresh cooked corn kernels
- Salt and white pepper

To serve:
- Finely diced avocado
- Finely diced tomato

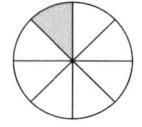

Preparation - Causa Verde con Cangrejo

Follow the same recipe for the mashed yellow potatoes as for **Causa de Camarones**.

Wash the parsley and spinach leaves and blend together with a little water. Place this mixture in a double boiler over low heat and skim off the 'raft' of green solids, which will form after a few minutes.

Add this concentrate to the potato mixture. Mix thoroughly until mixture is evenly green.

To make the fillings:
Mix together crabmeat and 2 tbsp of mayonnaise. Add the **ají limo** and cilantro and mix well. Season with salt and pepper and a few drops of key lime juice. In a separate bowl, combine corn kernels with the remaining mayonnaise and season with salt and pepper to taste.

Assemble the causa with one layer of each filling in between layers of mashed potato. Garnish with diced avocado, tomato and crabmeat.

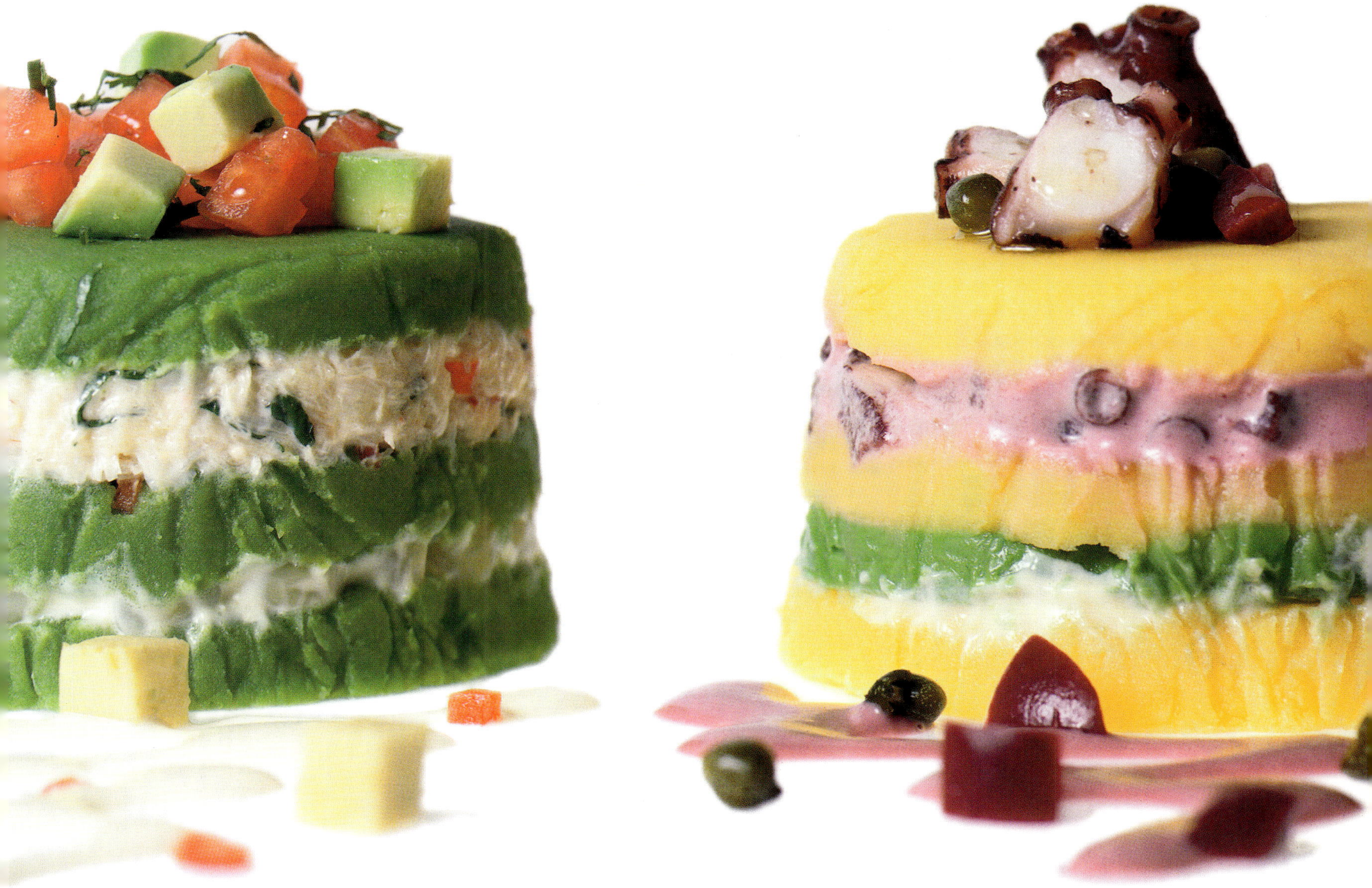

CEVICHE

Ingredients:

- 1 ¾ lb (800g) sea bass or flounder fillets
- 1 red onion, in very fine slices
- ½ red **ají limo**, chopped very fine
- ½ yellow **ají limo**, chopped very fine
- Juice of 16 key limes
- Salt

To serve:

- 1 boiled ear of corn, cut into rounds
- Boiled sweet potato
- Lettuce leaves

Ask Peruvians what their national dish is and the odds are they will proudly tell you **ceviche**. *Like the country and the people themselves, this preparation of spicy marinated fish has a long and varied history. There is a theory that pre-Hispanic peoples 'cooked' fish with a fruit called 'tumbo'. The Inca ate salted fish and a* **chicha**-*marinated fish dish. The Spanish contributed the Mediterranean custom of using lemons and onions. The word itself has been attributed to both Quechua (***sivichi***) and Moorish (***seivech***) influences and even today you'll find it spelled in many different ways.*

It may have a complex lineage, but the basic elements for a good **ceviche** *are freshness and simplicity.*

Use a firm fleshed white fish, which won't disintegrate in the lime juice. Limes should always be squeezed just at the moment of preparation and ingredients kept well chilled. The very special taste of the Peruvian tropical lime is difficult to replace, though closest in flavor is its cousin the key lime. To prevent the **ceviche** *from being too acidic, refresh just before serving by tossing with a couple of ice cubes, but be careful not to let them melt and dilute the taste too much.*

Most importantly, **ceviche** *should be eaten immediately. The lime will 'cook' the fish as you bring it to table and the fish will maintain a sensational taste and texture. Peruvians affectionately call the spicy marination juices of* **ceviche** *'leche de tigre' (tiger's milk), and will drink a small glass to cure a hangover! Eat* **ceviche** *with a fork and provide a spoon for the juices. The traditional accompaniments are corn and sweet potatoes, providing a perfect balance for the complete dish.*

CEVICHE CORVINA

Cucho la Rosa is a true defender of the faith when it comes to **ceviche**. *He only allows 5 ingredients in a* **ceviche**: *fish, lime, salt, onion and* **ají**. *Clean, simple, fresh tastes; here is his recipe.*

Preparation

Cut fish into bite size pieces and mix together with onion in large bowl. Wash onion and fish and drain well. Season with salt and **ají limo**.

Toss fish preparation quickly in lime juice. Refresh by adding a couple of ice cubes, mixing well and removing immediately before they have a chance to melt. Serve **ceviche** immediately in a deep dish, accompanied by boiled sweet potato, fresh cooked corn and leaves of lettuce.

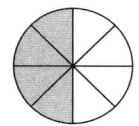

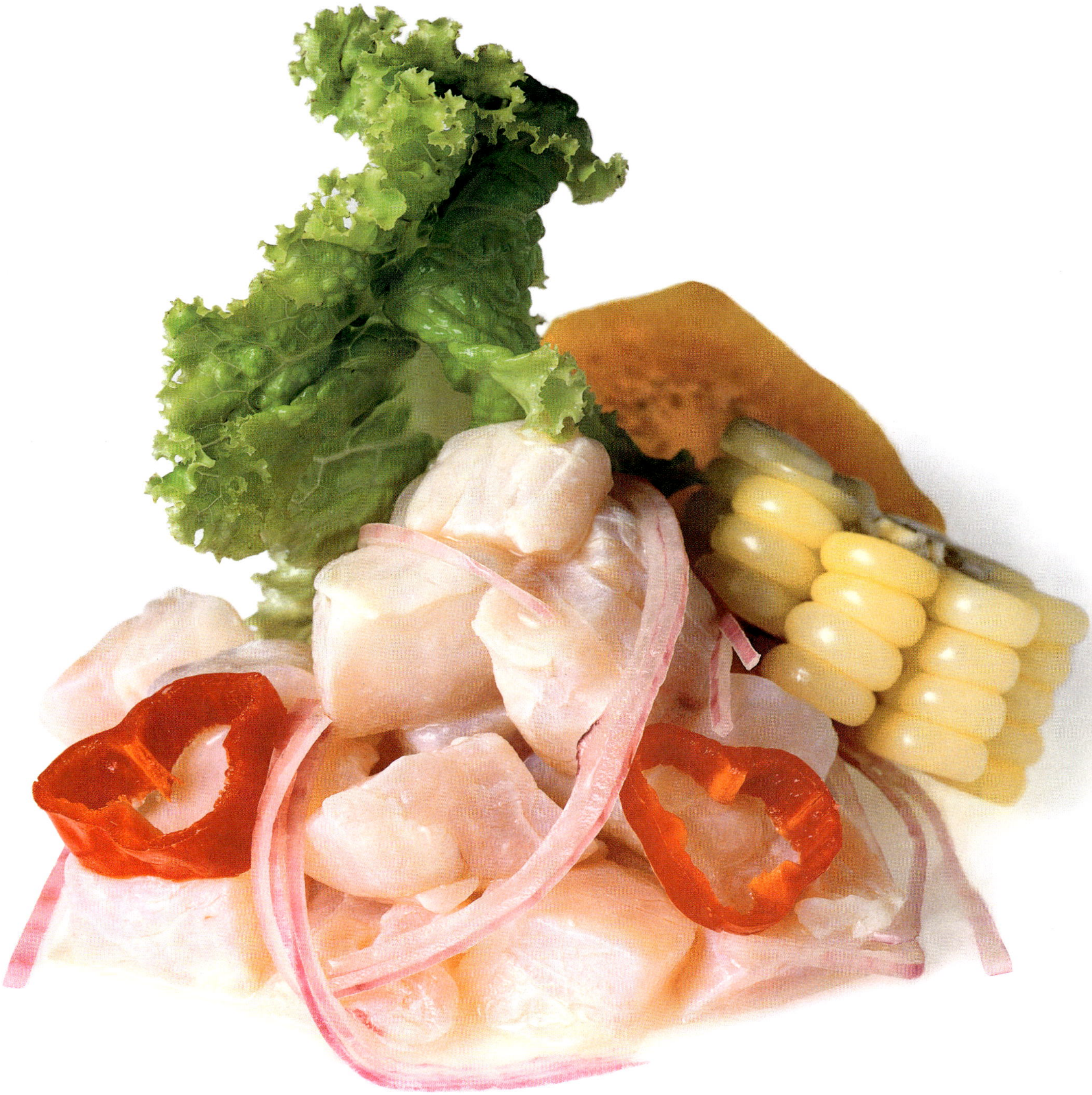

Ceviche Clásico

Lucho Cordero of 'Kapallaq' invented this ceviche and named it for the annual clash of Peru's two top soccer teams: 'El Clásico' between Alianza Lima and Universitario de Deportes. The flavors and colors are strong and vibrant as is the game.

Ingredients:

- 1 cup (150g) cleaned scallops
- 20 black scallops
- 2 tsp minced **ají limo**
- 1 tsp **ají limo** paste
- 1 cup finely minced onion
- 2 tbsp finely minced cilantro leaves
- 2 tbsp fish fumet or stock
- **Cancha salada** (salted toasted "unpopped" Andean corn kernels)
- Salt and freshly ground pepper
- Juice from 8 key limes

Preparation

It's important to prepare the two types of seafood separately for this **ceviche** so that the color from the black scallops does not run into the rest of the dish.

Open the black scallops with an oyster or clam shucker, or the point of a stout sharp knife. Take out all the meat and the juices

In two separate bowls sprinkle the two types of scallops with salt and freshly ground pepper.

Add the key lime juice to both bowls and allow to marinate for about five minutes.

Then add, to each **ceviche**, the **ají limo** paste, minced **ají limo**, onion, cilantro and finally the fish fumet or stock to reduce the acidity of the key lime.

Serve the **ceviches** side by side on the same plate, immediately.

Accompany with salted, toasted 'unpopped' Andean corn kernels (**cancha salada**).

Tips : To make the **ají limo** paste simply blend fresh **ají limo** with a little water in a blender.

If you find this dish is too spicy, serve accompanied with boiled sweet potato; the starch will complement and reduce the hot ceviche flavor.

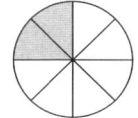

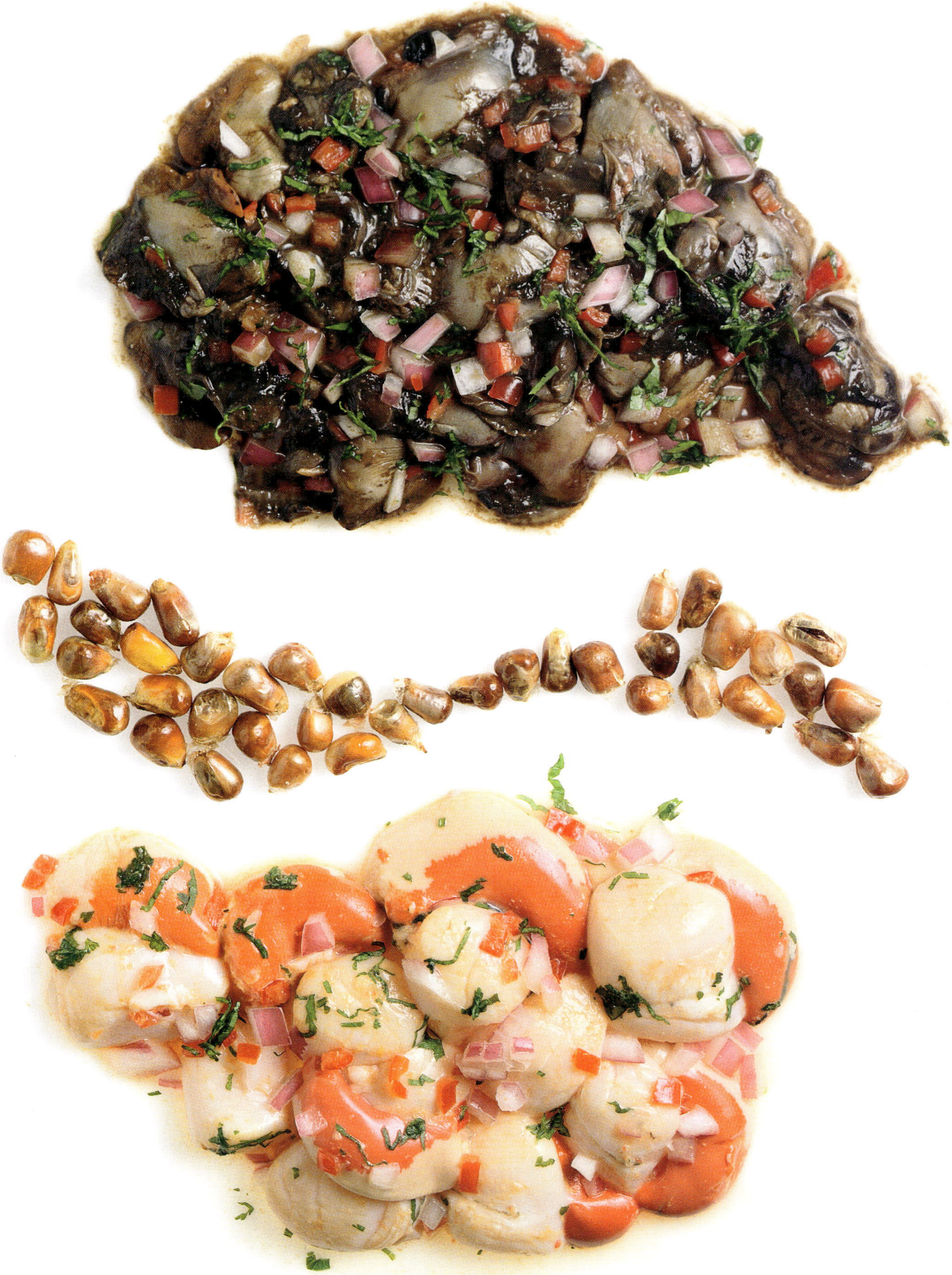

Ceviche en Crema de Rocoto

Ingredients:

- 1 ½ cups (300g) cooked octopus in thin slices (optional)
- 1 ½ kg firm white-fleshed fish
- ¼ leek, white part only, roughly chopped
- ½ stalk celery, roughly chopped
- 2 scallops, corals removed
- 1 tbsp fish stock
- ½ cup vegetable oil
- 3 tsp **rocoto** paste (p.230)
- Half the heart of a medium white onion, roughly chopped
- Juice of 15 key limes
- Salt

To serve:

- 1 red onion, finely julienned
- 1 cup cooked fresh corn kernels

*This exceptional **ceviche** is a signature dish of Daniel Manrique's at his 'Segundo Muelle' restaurant in San Isidro. It blends a white onion, leek and scallop cream with our red **rocoto** pepper, one of the most flavorful peppers in Peruvian cuisine.*

Preparation

Blanche the celery, leek and onion. For a spicy dish, blanche quickly in boiling water. For a milder flavor, blanche dry in a pan over high heat for a minute or two. When cool, blend to make a paste. Set aside and keep chilled.

Combine the scallops and fish stock in the jar of a blender or food processor fitted with a steel blade. Blend for ½ minute at low speed. Then, with the motor running, add the vegetable oil in a slow, steady stream, as you would to make a mayonnaise. The mixture should take on the consistency of a light, chunky mayonnaise. Set aside and keep chilled.

Cube the fish and sprinkle with salt. Combine with sliced octopus (optional).

Mix the white vegetable paste with the fish mayonnaise and finally toss the fish and octopus in the key lime juice. Mix the **rocoto** paste with the fish mayonnaise mixture and pour over the fish and octopus.

Serve immediately, chilled, on a fine julienne of red onions, with boiled sweet potatoes and fresh corn kernels.

Tips : To make the **ají limo** paste simply blend fresh **ají limo** with a little water in a blender.

If you find this dish is too spicy, serve accompanied by toasted corn kernels and boiled sweet potato; the starch will complement and reduce the 'heat' of the ceviche.

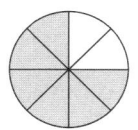

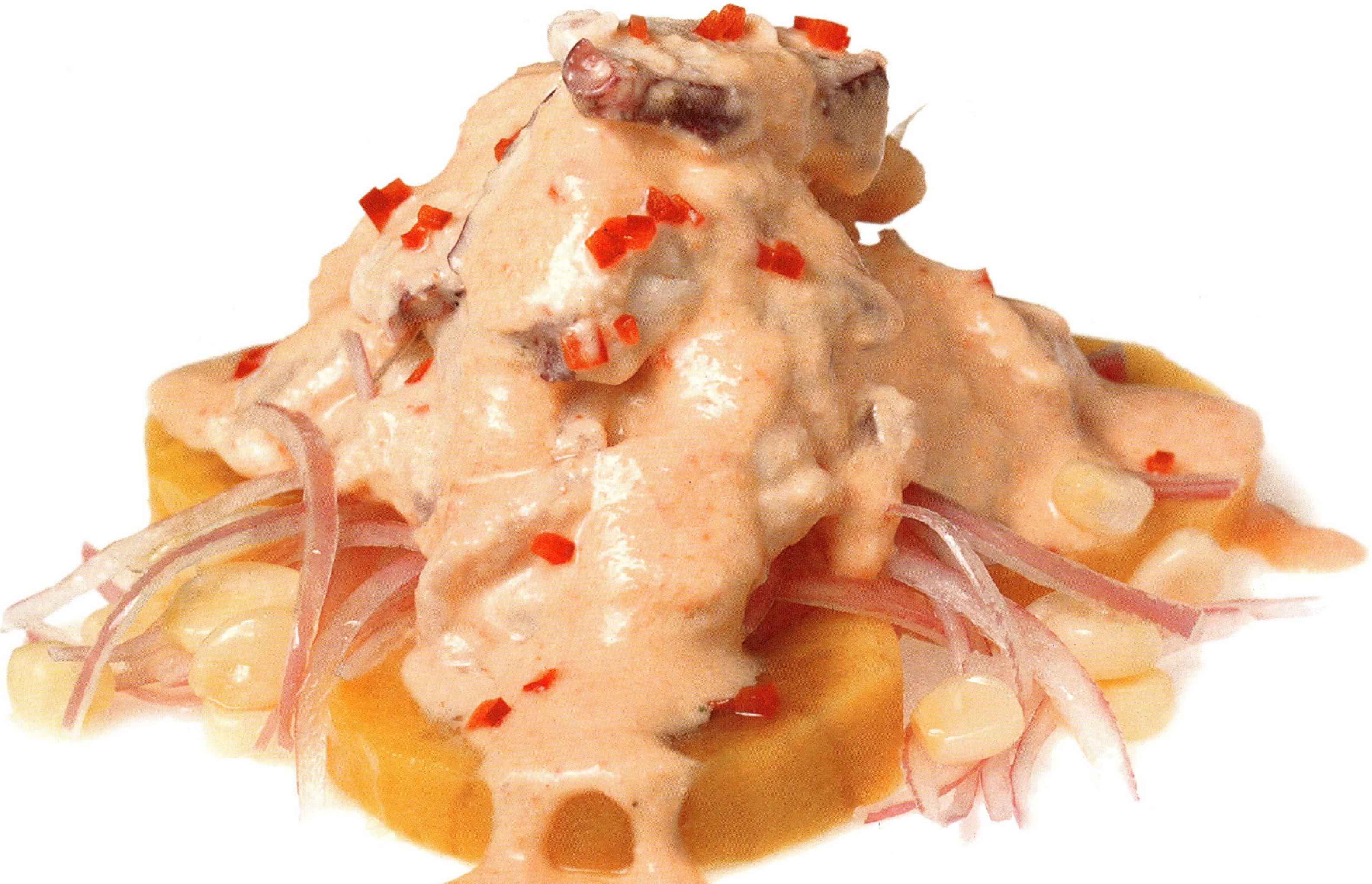

Ceviche Mixto

*This is another variation on Cucho la Rosa's recipe for **ceviche**. The **cevicherías** in Peru serve up a fabulous array of different **ceviches** in all shapes and sizes. The cold Humboldt Current ensures that Peru's Pacific seaboard has a bountiful supply of an enormous variety of fish and shellfish. Let your imagination go wild. There should be a good number of different types of seafood in a 'mixto' to give plenty of contrast in color and texture as well as flavor.*

Ingredients:

- 7 oz (200g) cooked octopus
- 7 oz (200g) blanched squid
- 7 oz (200g) blanched shrimp tails
- 7 oz (200g) scallops
- 1 red onion, sliced very fine
- ½ red **ají limo**, minced
- ½ yellow **ají limo**, minced
- Juice of 16 key limes
- Salt

To serve:

- 2 sweet potatoes, boiled
- 1 large fresh ear of corn on the cob, cooked and cut into rounds

Preparation

Cut octopus into bite-size pieces, or if using baby octopus, leave whole. Cut squid into small rings.

Mix seafood together with onion in a large bowl. Wash and drain thoroughly. Season with salt and **ají limo**.

Toss seafood preparation quickly in lime juice. Refresh by adding a couple of ice cubes, mixing well and removing immediately before they have a chance to melt.

To serve:
Serve on a bed of lettuce with sweet potato and boiled corn rounds.

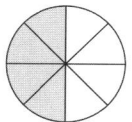

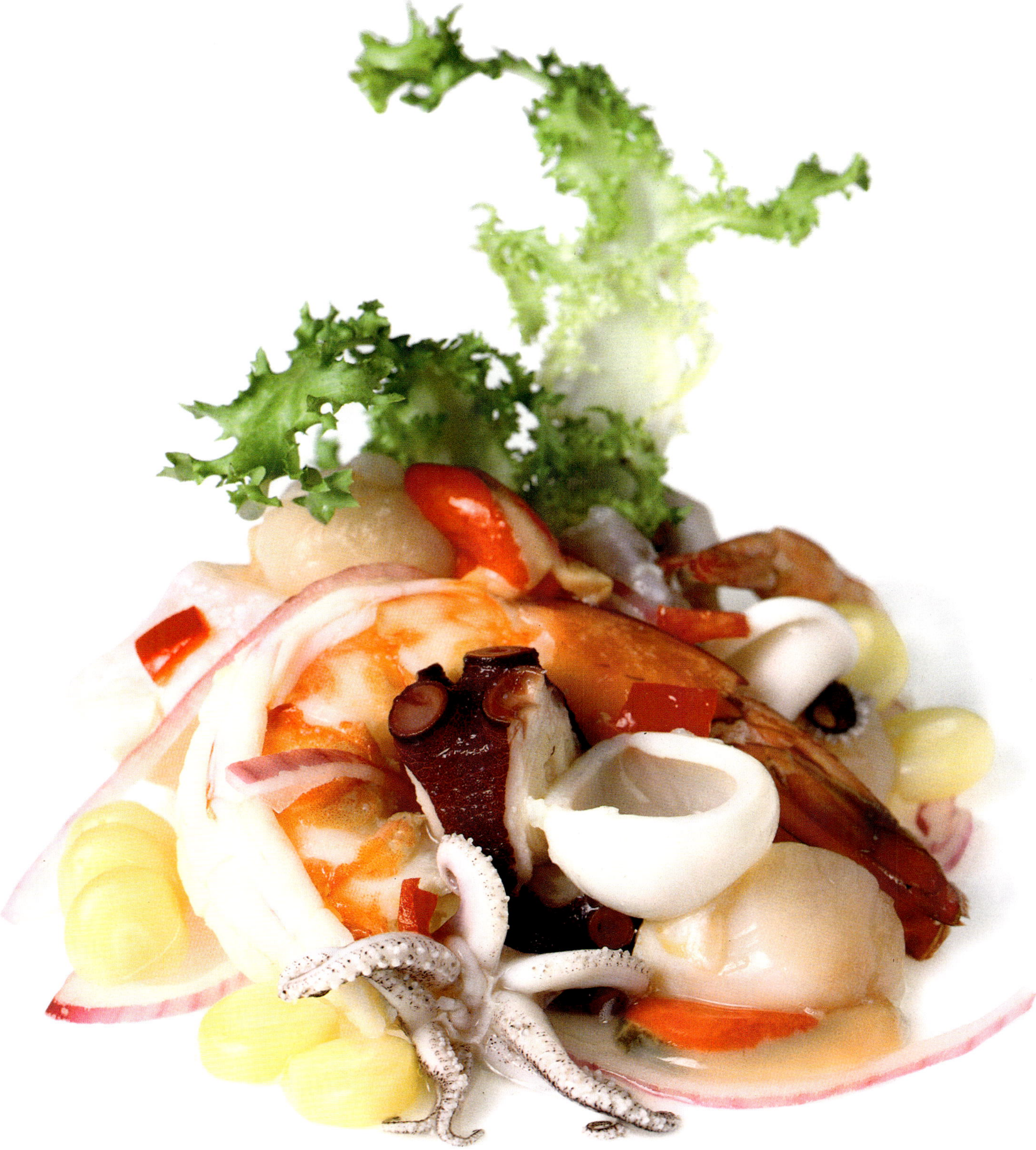

Ceviche de Pato

This unusual ceviche variation comes from the ancient coastal town of Huacho just north of Lima. It's a good solution for the landlocked as well as a change from seafood.

Ingredients:

- 1 duck (about 5 ½ lbs / 2 ½ kg)
- ½ cup water
- 2 tbsp **ají mirasol** paste (p.228)
- ½ cup key lime juice
- 1 tsp salt
- 1 large clove garlic, crushed
- 1 ¾ cups fresh orange juice
- 2 red onions, peeled and sliced fine
- 1 heaping tsp minced garlic
- 1 tsp ground cumin
- ¼ tsp ground white pepper
- 2 sprigs freshly chopped cilantro
- 2 sprigs freshly chopped parsley

To serve:

- 1 lb (½ kg) boiled yuca, cut into slices

Preparation

Cut the duck into 8 generous pieces, including legs, thighs and breast fillets. Remove and discard the skin.

In a small bowl, mix the **ají mirasol** paste with the key lime juice, salt and crushed garlic. Pour this marinade over the duck pieces. Add the orange juice and onions, mix well and allow to marinate for 2 hours.

Lift the duck pieces from the marinade and set aside. Strain the onion and reserve both the onion and the marinating liquid.

In a large skillet, over medium heat, sear the duck pieces without browning, about 5 minutes.

Remove the duck pieces from the skillet. In the same skillet add a little oil, the minced garlic, half the strained, marinated onion, the cumin and white pepper. Sauté for about 2 minutes, until the onion is just becoming translucent.

Add all the marinating liquids, stir and bring to a boil. Lower the heat and add the cilantro and parsley. Cover and cook until the duck is fork tender, about 30 minutes. Add the remaining onion, stir and cook for an additional minute.

Remove from the heat and let cool. Transfer to a platter and serve at room temperature with boiled yuca.

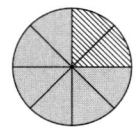

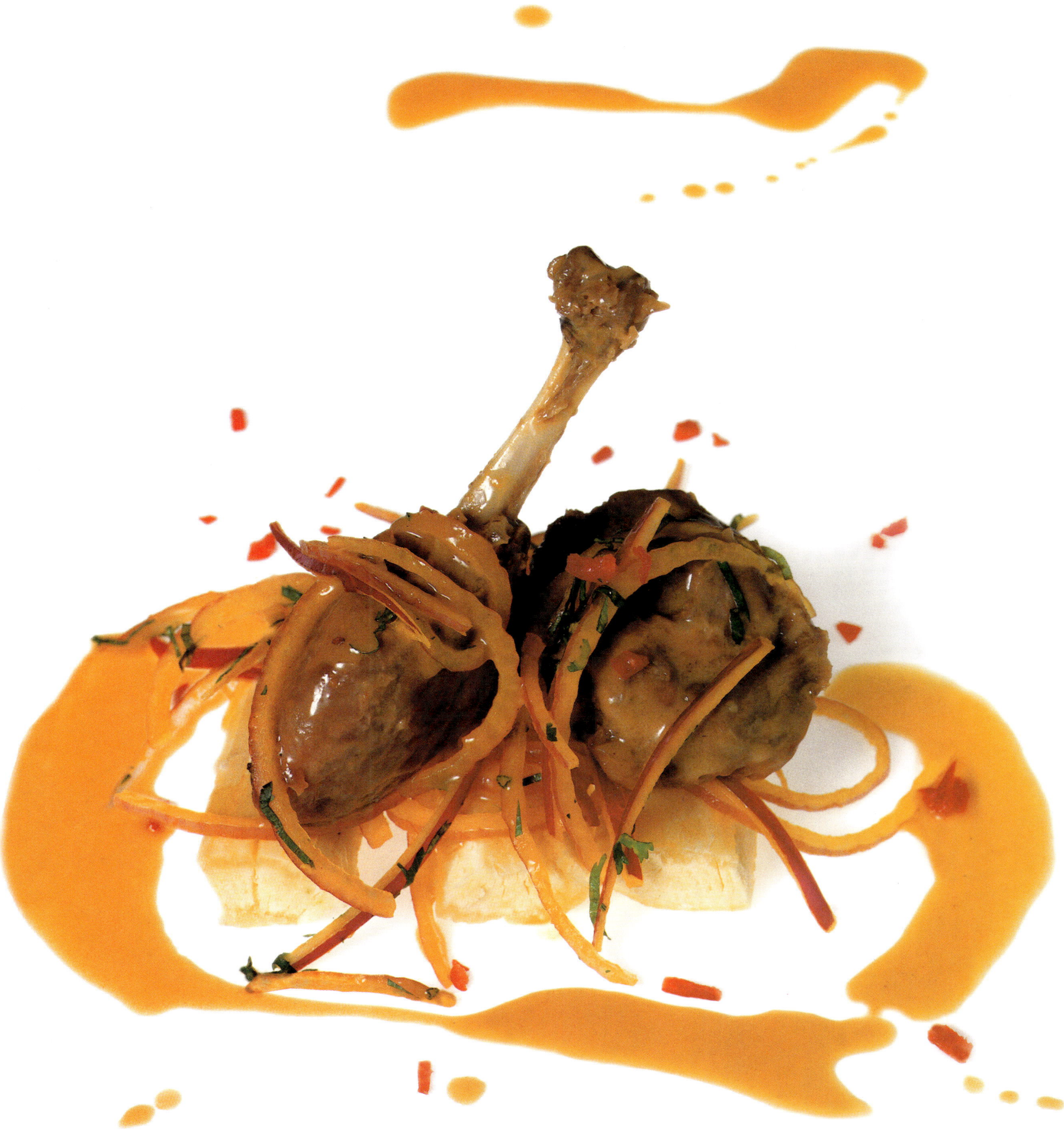

Ceviche de Camarón a la Piedra

Ingredients:

- 2 lb (1kg) fresh crayfish tails, peeled and cleaned
- 2 tbsp vegetable oil
- 2 tbsp minced garlic
- 2 tbsp **salsa madre** (p.228)
- 1 tsp salt
- 2 red onions, sliced finely
- 2 tbsp **ají amarillo** paste (p.228)
- 2 **ají limo**, chopped fine
- 2 tsp fresh cilantro, chopped fine
- Juice of 8 key limes

To serve:

- 1 lb (½ kg) boiled yuca or potato, cut into thick slices

This is another dish from Rosita Yimura. Hot **ceviche** was once cooked using hot stones, hence its name 'ceviche on a stone'.

Preparation

In a large skillet heat the oil and sauté the garlic until golden. Add the **salsa madre** and cook for a further 2 or 3 minutes.

Add the crayfish tails and the salt and sauté for a few minutes until crayfish have just turned a pinkish red color.

Add the onion, **ají amarillo** paste, chopped **ají limo**, chopped cilantro and key lime juice. Cover and simmer gently for 10 minutes.

Adjust seasoning, adding more salt if necessary and serve immediately, warm.

Serve with boiled potatoes or yuca.

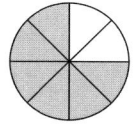

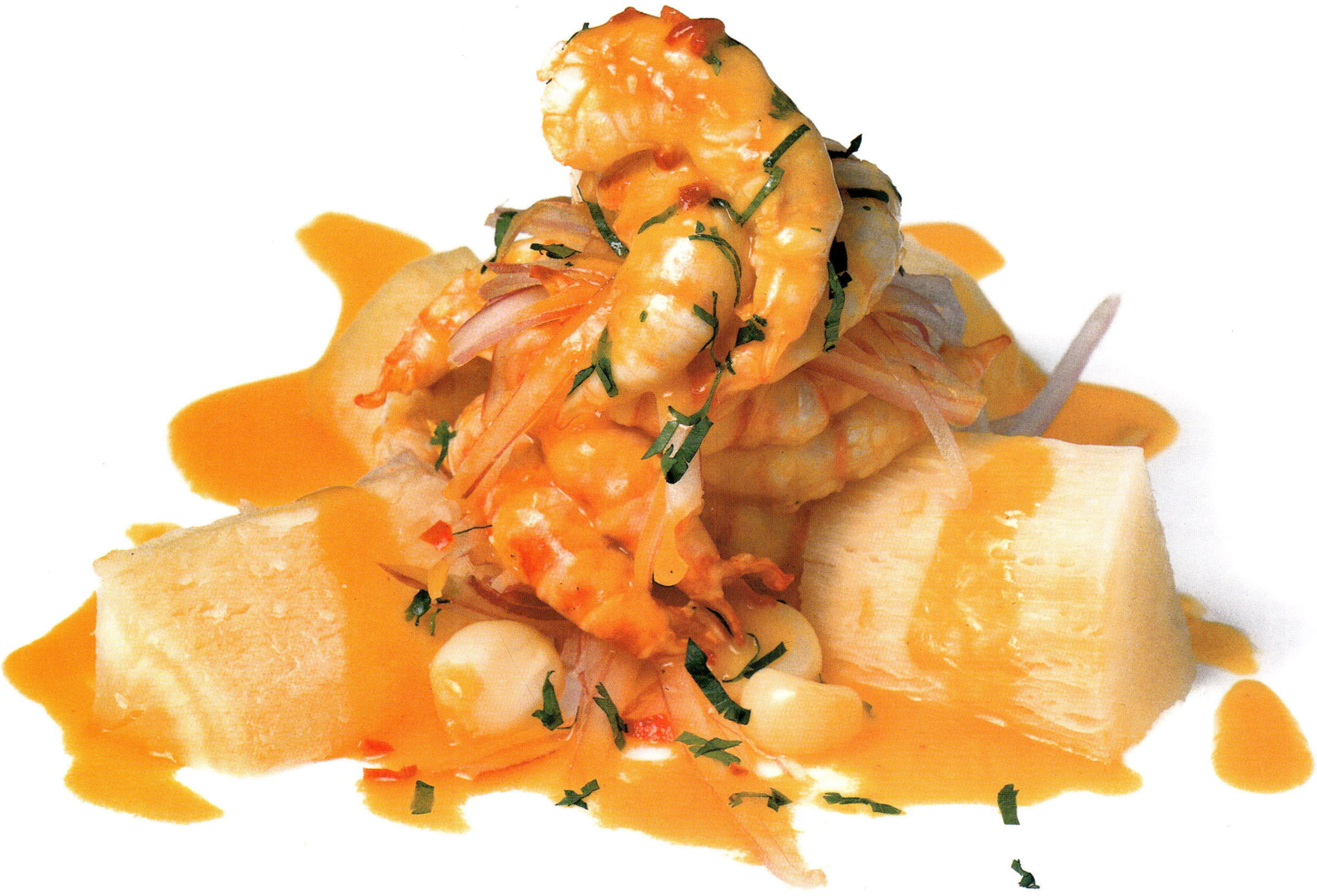

Ceviche de Champiñones & Alcachofa

Ingredients:

- 1¼ lbs (600g) mushrooms
- 6 large artichoke hearts
- ½ tsp freshly ground pepper
- 4 **ajíes limo**, chopped very fine
- 4 cloves garlic, minced
- 1 tbsp freshly chopped parsley
- 1 tbsp freshly chopped cilantro
- 2 tbsp olive oil
- 1 red onion, julienned
- Juice of 8 key limes

*The Mantaro valley, high in the Andes, is the site of Peru's first capital city Jauja, (pronounced 'How-ha'). Here, artichoke fields stretch as far as the eye can see. Understandably the people of this region eat them with everything. This unusual and extremely healthful **ceviche** is light, colorful and delicious.*

Preparation

Clean and trim the artichoke hearts. Bring a large pot of salted water with a little lemon juice to the boil and cook hearts until tender, about 30 minutes. Drain well, let cool and slice.

Wipe mushrooms with a damp paper towel and trim stem ends. Slice fine and place in a large bowl, along with the artichoke slices.

Season mushroom and artichokes with salt, pepper, garlic, **ají limo**, parsley and cilantro. Mix well.

Add the key lime juice, olive oil and onion. Toss well and serve on a bed of endives.

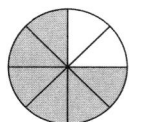

Note: This **ceviche** is particularly fine when made with wild mushrooms. Porcini or cêpes are great. Choose your favorite.

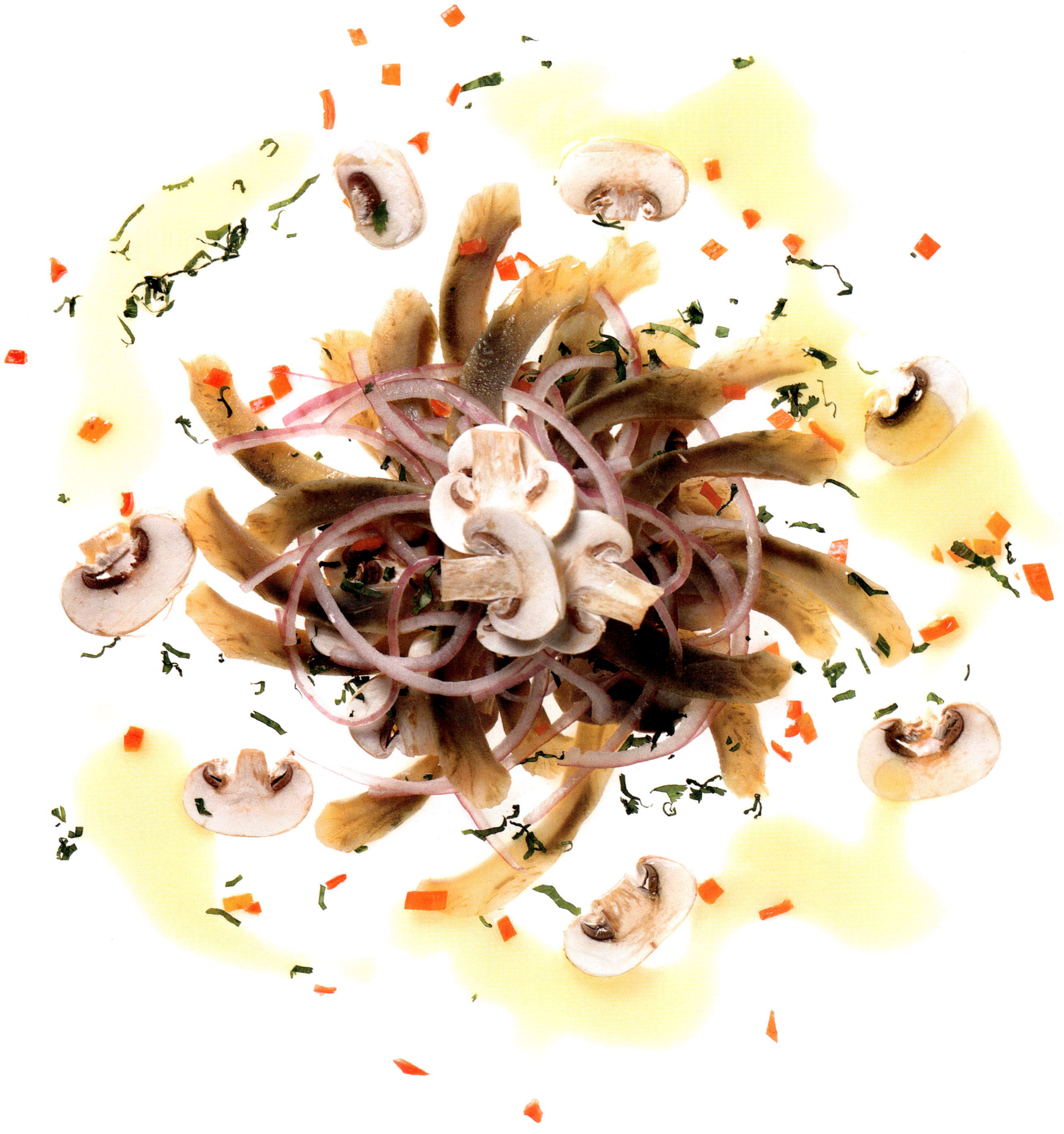

Ensalada de Pallares

This large white lima or butter bean salad is simple and easy to make. It's better made with fresh white lima or butter beans, if you can find them, popped from their skins. If you use dried beans they will need soaking overnight and cooking for a longer time.

Ingredients:

- 1 lb (½ kg) fresh large white lima (butter) beans
- 1 large onion, sliced fine
- ¼ white cabbage
- 1 **ají amarillo**, seeded, deveined and sliced fine
- 8 radishes, diced fine
- 1 tsp oregano
- 2 tbsp olive oil
- 1 tbsp red wine vinegar
- Juice of 3 key limes
- Salt and freshly ground pepper.

To serve:

- 2 tomatoes, sliced

Preparation

Rinse beans and place in a large pot with plenty of water. Bring to the boil and simmer, over medium heat, for about 25 minutes, checking the water level from time to time. The beans should be tender but not too soft. Drain and put aside to cool. Peel if desired.

In a small bowl, combine onion slices with **ají amarillo**, lime juice, olive oil, salt and pepper. Set aside. In a separate bowl combine radish with vinegar, oregano and salt and set aside.

Slice the cabbage, place in a colander and pour boiling water over it. Rinse with cold water and season with salt, white pepper and a little lime juice and vegetable oil.

To serve combine all ingredients on a platter and garnish with sliced tomato. Let stand for 10 to 15 minutes to let the flavors intensify.

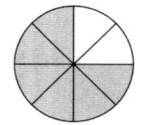

Tip: Dried lima beans can be used in this recipe. Soak them overnight, then rinse thoroughly and boil for about 1 hour until tender.

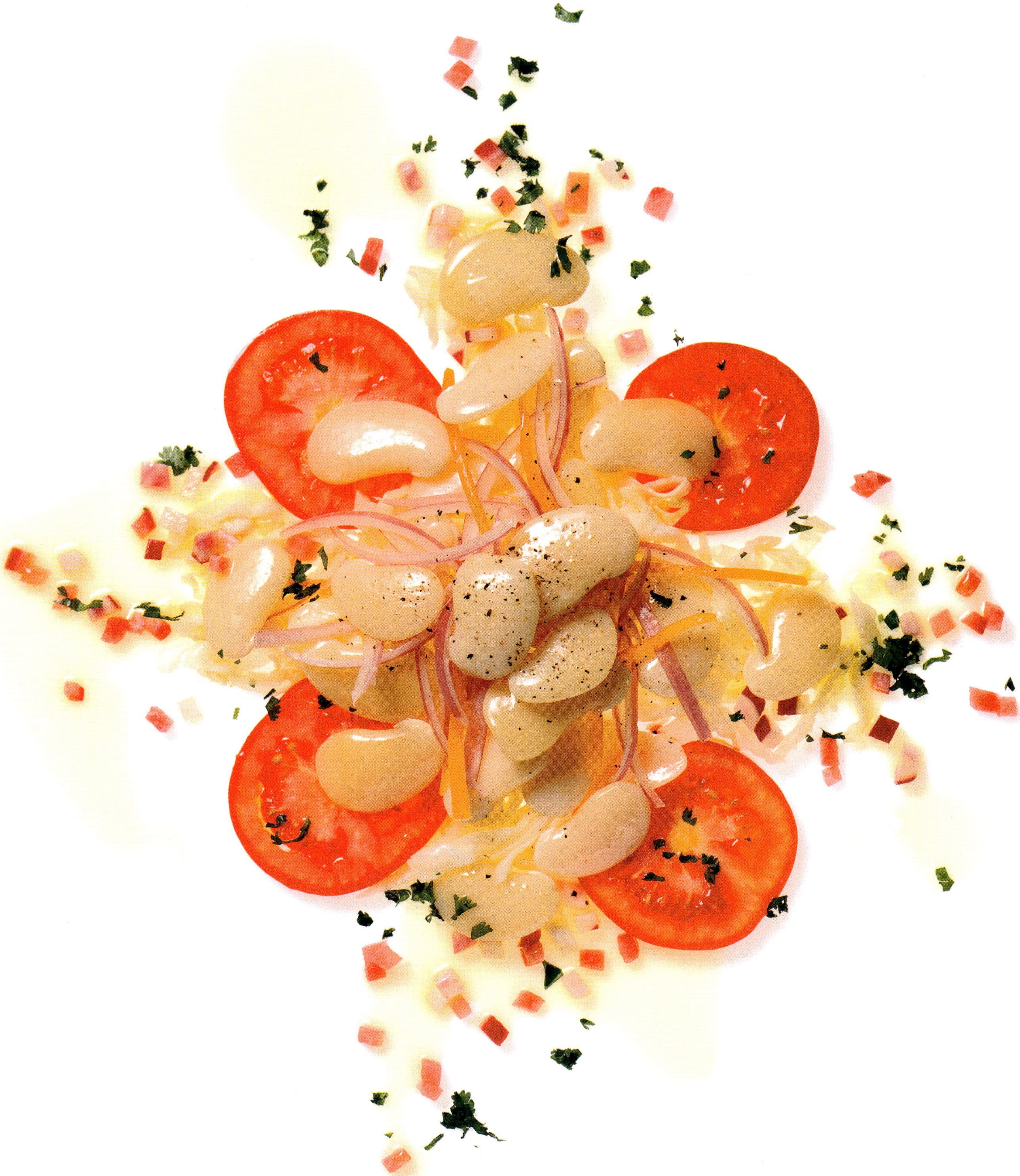

Ensalada de Pulpo con Bacon

Ingredients :

- 1-1¼ lb (480 - 600g) cooked octopus
- 1 red onion, sliced fine
- 1 tbsp vinegar
- ¼ tsp minced garlic
- 2 tbsp mayonnaise
- 2 tbsp bacon bits
- Key lime juice
- Parsley, freshly chopped
- Salt

*This light and zesty salad carries Rosita Yimura's unmistakable stamp. This is a classic example of the best of **nikkei** cuisine: the subtle flavors of a light touch with the octopus married to onions and bacon. Good news! 'Bac-o's' work just as well as home fried bacon.*

Preparation

Wash and cut the octopus into fine slices. Combine in a bowl with the onion slices, key lime juice, vinegar, garlic and salt to taste. Mix well and adjust seasoning as necessary.

Drain all the liquid from the salad and transfer to a serving bowl. Add the mayonnaise and the bacon bits and toss well.

Serve garnished with freshly chopped parsley.

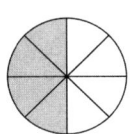

Tip: Rosita Yimura's tip for perfect octopus is to wash and cook it for 40 minutes the day before. Leave to cool and then chill. Once chilled, remove the tentacles and freeze them. Slice the octopus tentacles whilst still frozen, as this makes it easier to handle. Then defrost and rinse well before proceeding.

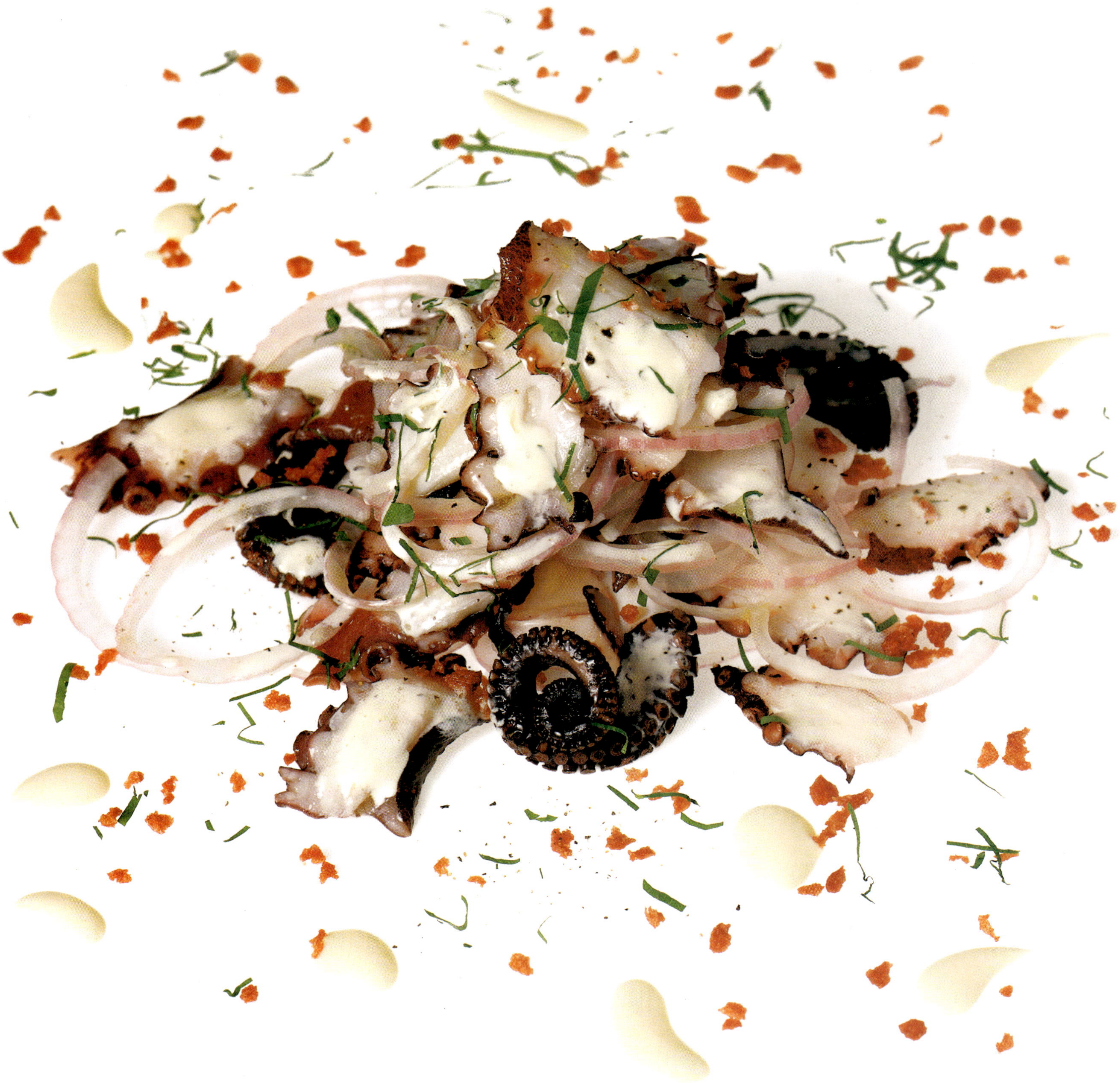

Escabeche

Ingredients :

- 2 lbs (1 kg) white fish
- 1½ cloves garlic, crushed
- 1 tbsp **ají panca** paste (p.228)
- ½ cup vegetable oil
- 1 **ají amarillo**, seeded, deveined and finely sliced.
- 1 ½ lb (750g) red onions, cut into thick slices
- ¼ cup red wine vinegar
- ¼ tsp oregano
- ¼ tsp cumin
- Flour
- Salt and pepper

To serve:

- 4 black olives
- 1 hard-boiled egg
- 1 boiled sweet potato
- Lettuce leaves

Escabeche was a process of pickling and preserving food with sugar and vinegar originally used by the Arabs and brought to Peru by the Spanish. It's now a very common fish dish but can also be prepared with chicken.

Preparation

Clean the fish well and cut into small fillets. Wash and dry the fish pieces, season them lightly with salt and pepper and coat with flour.

Heat the oil in a skillet and pan fry the fish until lightly golden. Remove from the pan and keep to one side.

In the same skillet, sauté the crushed garlic, cumin, oregano, onions, **ají panca** paste, **ají amarillo**, salt and pepper until the onion is translucent.

Adjust the seasonings and add the vinegar. Allow to stand for a few more minutes to let the flavor intensify. Then add more vinegar if desired. Remove from the heat and let cool.

Serve the fish pieces at room temperature, or cooler if desired, on a bed of lettuce leaves arranged decoratively on a platter. Top with the onion mixture.

To serve:
Garnish with slices of hard boiled egg and black olives and serve with sliced boiled sweet potato.

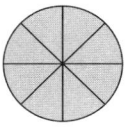

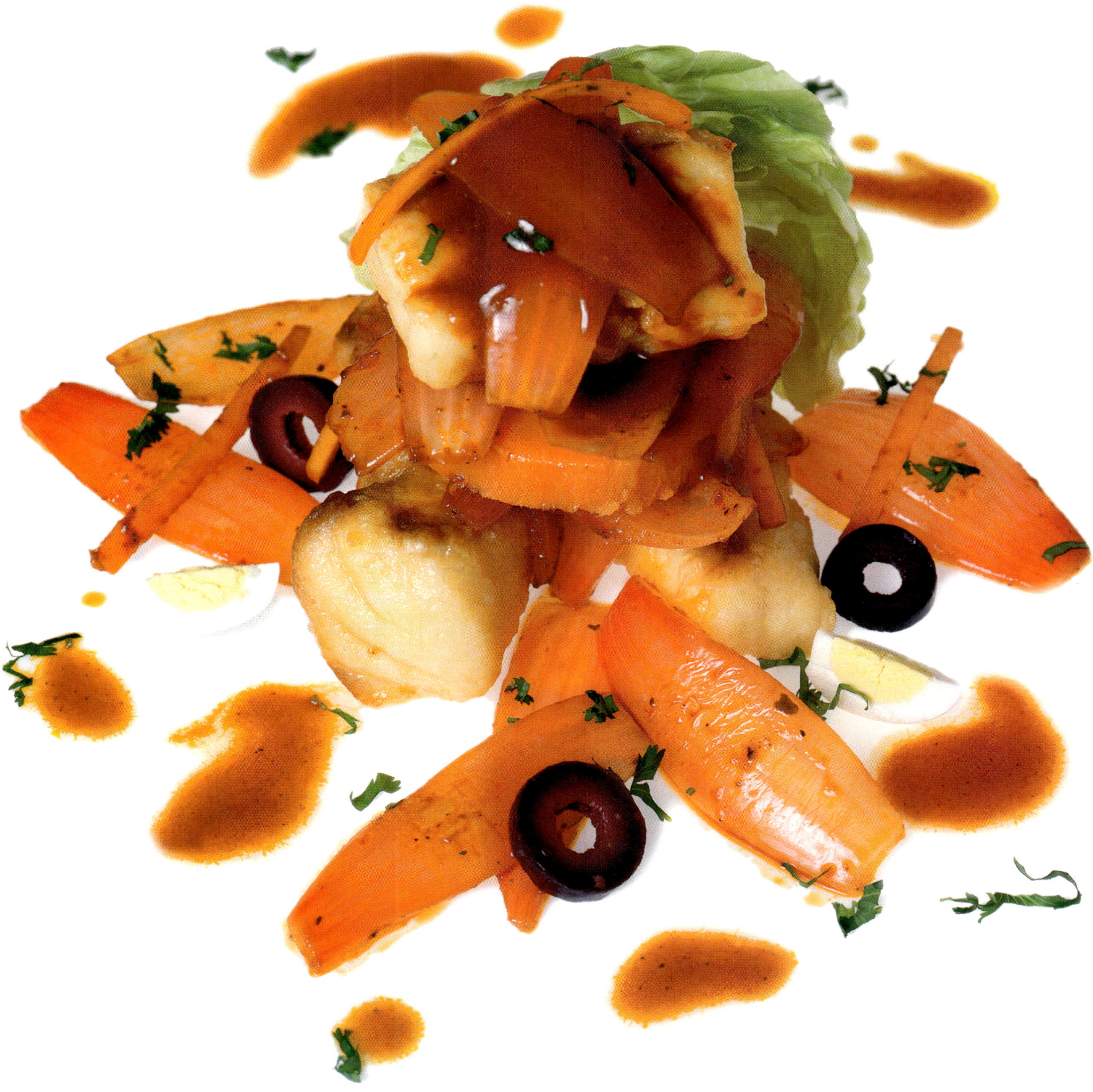

JALEA

Ingredients:

- 4 small white fish fillets
- 2 cups **salsa criolla** (p.232)
- 1 cup cornstarch (for coating)
- 3 cups (600g) raw mixed seafood (octopus, squid, scallops, etc)
- Vegetable oil for deep frying
- Salt, freshly ground pepper and key lime juice

This combination of **chicharrón** *and yuca is a ubiquitous main dish in local seafood restaurants. My favorite version has a strong, thick, dark sauce with coral in it. This recipe is served with a lighter* **salsa criolla**.

Preparation

Use any firm-fleshed white fish, such as sea bass, palm ruff or grouper, and cut the fillets into strips approximately 1 in wide and 3 in long (2.5 x 7.5 cm).

Season fish strips and seafood pieces (use your favorite fish or one in season) with salt, pepper and lime juice, and coat in cornstarch.

Deep fry, first the fish strips, then the seafood in hot oil until golden. Remove and drain on kitchen towel.

To assemble the **jalea**; place the fish strips on a serving platter, spoon **salsa criolla** over the top and add the seafood. Drizzle a few drops of lime juice over everything and serve immediately.

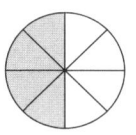

Tip: You can serve it with fish anticucho sauce.

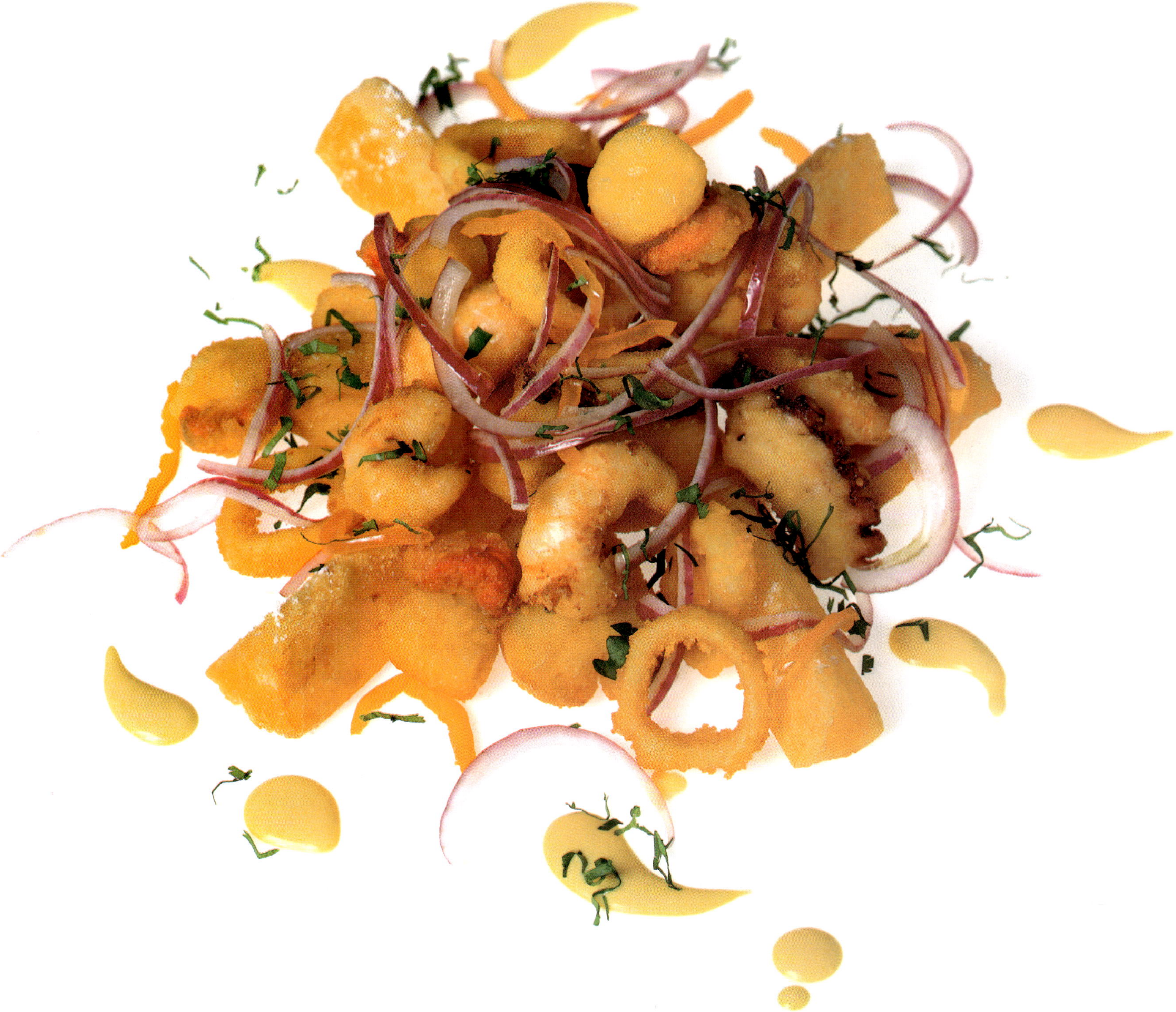

Ocopa & Papas a la Huancaína

*The Inca's 'chasqui' or messengers took **ocopa**, a cloth bag filled with ground peanuts, **ají** and herbs, on their travels. Today, this is considered the city of Arequipa's own signature dish along with their famous fresh crayfish. My grandfather came to Peru in 1918 with his new Parisian bride, to work in Huancayo. In 1919 my father was born in that regional capital of the mineral rich central highlands. This delicately spiced creamy sauce, Huancayo's signature dish, is also great as a dip with your favorite crudité.*

Ingredients:

- 4 small red onions, sliced
- 4 cloves of garlic, crushed
- ¼ cup vegetable oil
- 2 sprigs of **huacatay**, chopped
- 5 **ajíes amarillos**
- 4 vanilla cookies, broken in pieces
- 4 oz (100g) toasted peanuts
- 8 oz (200g) fresh white cheese, roughly crumbled
- Evaporated milk (as needed)
- 6 boiled white potatoes (cold)

Ingredients:

- ½ cup chopped red onion
- 1 tsp minced garlic
- 2 tbsp vegetable oil
- 5 **ajíes amarillos**
- 3 - 4 saltine crackers
- ½ lb (¼ kg) fresh white cheese
- 1 cup evaporated milk
- Juice of ½ key lime
- Oil
- 6 boiled white potatoes (cold)

To serve:

- Lettuce leaves, cooked corn kernels, hard-boiled egg slices, black olives

Serves 6

Preparation - Ocopa

Seed, devein and chop **ají amarillo**. Heat the oil in a skillet and sauté onion, garlic, **huacatay**, **ají amarillo**, salt and pepper, over medium heat, until they are well browned, about 7 minutes. Remove from heat and let cool.

Mix the cooled mixture with the peanuts, cheese and vanilla cookies in a blender. With the motor still running, add enough evaporated milk in a steady stream (as for mayonnaise) for the sauce to form a slightly thick, even, pouring consistency. Adjust seasonings to taste.

Serve at room temperature over the cooked potatoes and decorate with slices of hard-boiled egg and lettuce leaves.

Preparation - Papa a la Huancaina

Seed, devein and chop **ají amarillo**. In a small skillet, heat the 2 tablespoons of vegetable oil and, over medium heat, sauté the onion, garlic and ají amarillo until the onion is translucent, about 3 minutes. Remove onion mixture from the heat and, in a blender or a food processor fitted with a steel blade, blend together with the crackers, white cheese, evaporated milk and salt, adding just enough vegetable oil to give the mixture a smooth creamy consistency.

Add the juice of ½ key lime and blend for a few seconds more. Adjust seasoning to taste, adding more salt if necessary. Let sauce cool to room temperature or chill in the fridge. To serve, pour the sauce over sliced cold boiled potatoes and garnish with boiled egg slices, olives, cooked corn kernels and lettuce leaves.

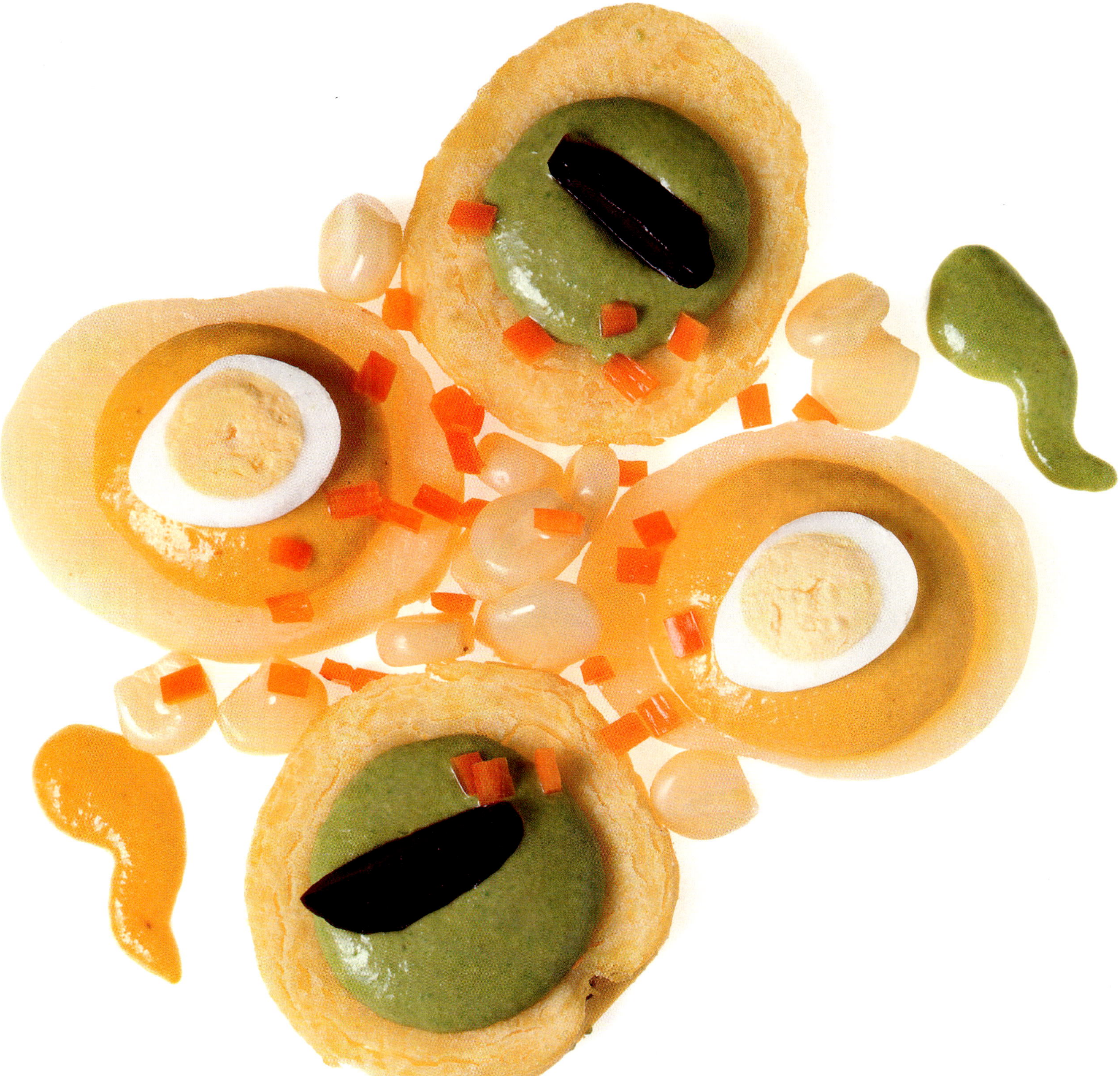

Papa Rellena

Ingredients:

- 2 lb (1 kg) white potatoes
- 1 ¾ lb (750g) meat, half beef, half pork, cut into fine dice or minced
- 3 medium onions, chopped fine
- ½ lb (250g) tomatoes, peeled, seeded and diced fine
- 1 tsp paprika
- 3 ½ oz (100g) pitted black olives
- 3 hard-boiled eggs, chopped
- 1 egg, beaten
- Flour for coating
- Vegetable oil for frying
- Salt and pepper

*This is another of Andrea Graña's delicious recipes. These traditional potato croquettes are served at almost every **criollo** meal. They are delicious served at room temperature in summer or hot in cooler weather.*

Preparation

Place the potatoes in a large pot with plenty of salted water and boil until tender, about 20 minutes.

To prepare the filling:
Heat enough oil to cover the base of a large skillet and brown the meat, seasoning with salt and pepper to taste. Remove the meat from the skillet with a slotted spoon and put to one side.

In the same skillet sauté the finely chopped onion and tomato and the paprika. Cook on low heat for a couple of minutes and then return the meat to the skillet. Simmer all the ingredients together for 5 minutes. Remove from the heat and mix in the hard-boiled egg and the olives.

Strain the potatoes well and when they are cool, peel them and finely mash them by pressing them through a sieve with the back of a spoon. Alternatively, you can use a ricer. Adjust seasoning, adding more salt if necessary, and allow to cool for 10 minutes.

Work the mashed potato with your hands until it resembles a soft, smooth dough. Flour a work surface and your hands. Place about ½ cup of the potato mixture in the palm of your hand and carefully form a thin disc-shaped layer. In the center place about 1 tbsp of the filling. If you like, you can make larger ones after a bit of practice.

Carefully bring sides of the potato layer together to cover filling and form large croquettes. Dip each croquette in beaten egg and then coat with sifted flour. Heat ¼ cup of vegetable oil in a skillet and pan fry the croquettes until golden. Serve immediately with **salsa criolla** (p.232).

Tip: If you are not going to fry the croquettes immediately, do not dip in beaten egg but rather dust with a fine coating of flour to keep them from becoming sticky.

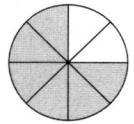

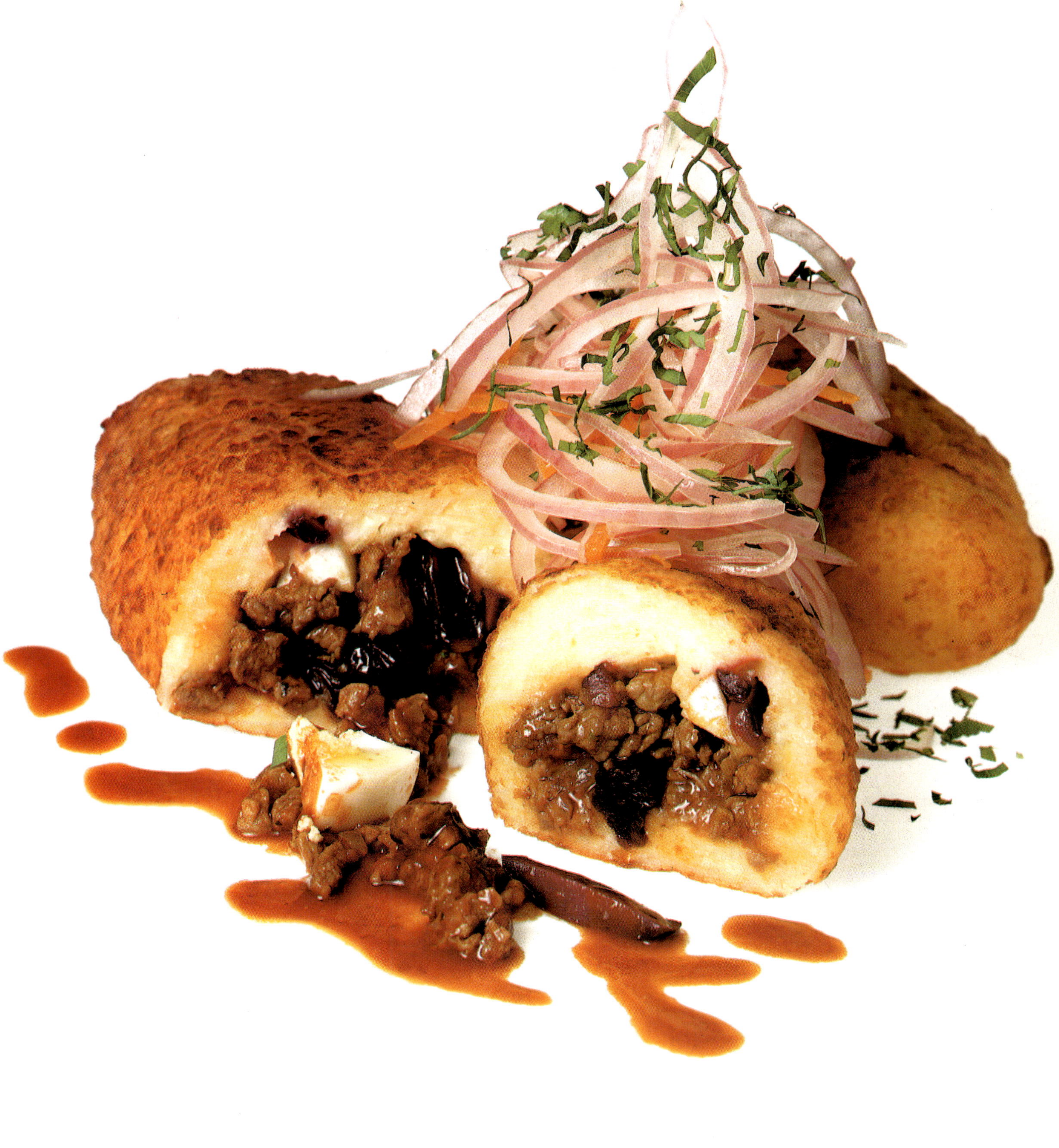

Pulpo al Olivo

This is Rosita Yimura's most famous dish. The contrasting colors of the octopus matched with the glossy purple of the olive mayonnaise make it a particularly attractive opener to any meal.

Ingredients:

- 1 egg
- 1 tsp salt
- 1 cup olive oil
- 2 tsp key lime juice
- 10 large black olives, pitted
- 2lbs (1kg) cooked octopus, sliced fine

Preparation

Combine the egg, salt and key lime juice in the jar of a blender or food processor fitted with a steel blade. Blend for 1 minute at low speed.

With the motor running add the olive oil in a slow steady stream, to form a thick mayonnaise.

When all the oil is incorporated, shut off the motor and scrape down sides of jug with a spatula.

Empty the mayonnaise into a bowl, leaving just enough in the bottom of the blender to cover the blades.

Add the pitted olives and blend for a few more minutes to form a smooth purée. Add the olive purée to the reserved mayonnaise and mix thoroughly until the mixture is a uniform color and consistency. Press through a fine mesh sieve to remove any pieces of olive skin.

Arrange the octopus slices in a single layer on a platter and cover with the olive mayonnaise.

Serve garnished with freshly chopped parsley.

Tip: The key to perfectly formed octopus slices is to cook the octopus the day before (for 40 - 45 minutes) until it is firm but not chewy and then freeze it. Slicing the octopus whilst still half frozen makes it much easier to handle (see **Ensalada de Pulpo con Bacon** p.126).

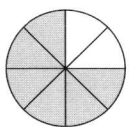

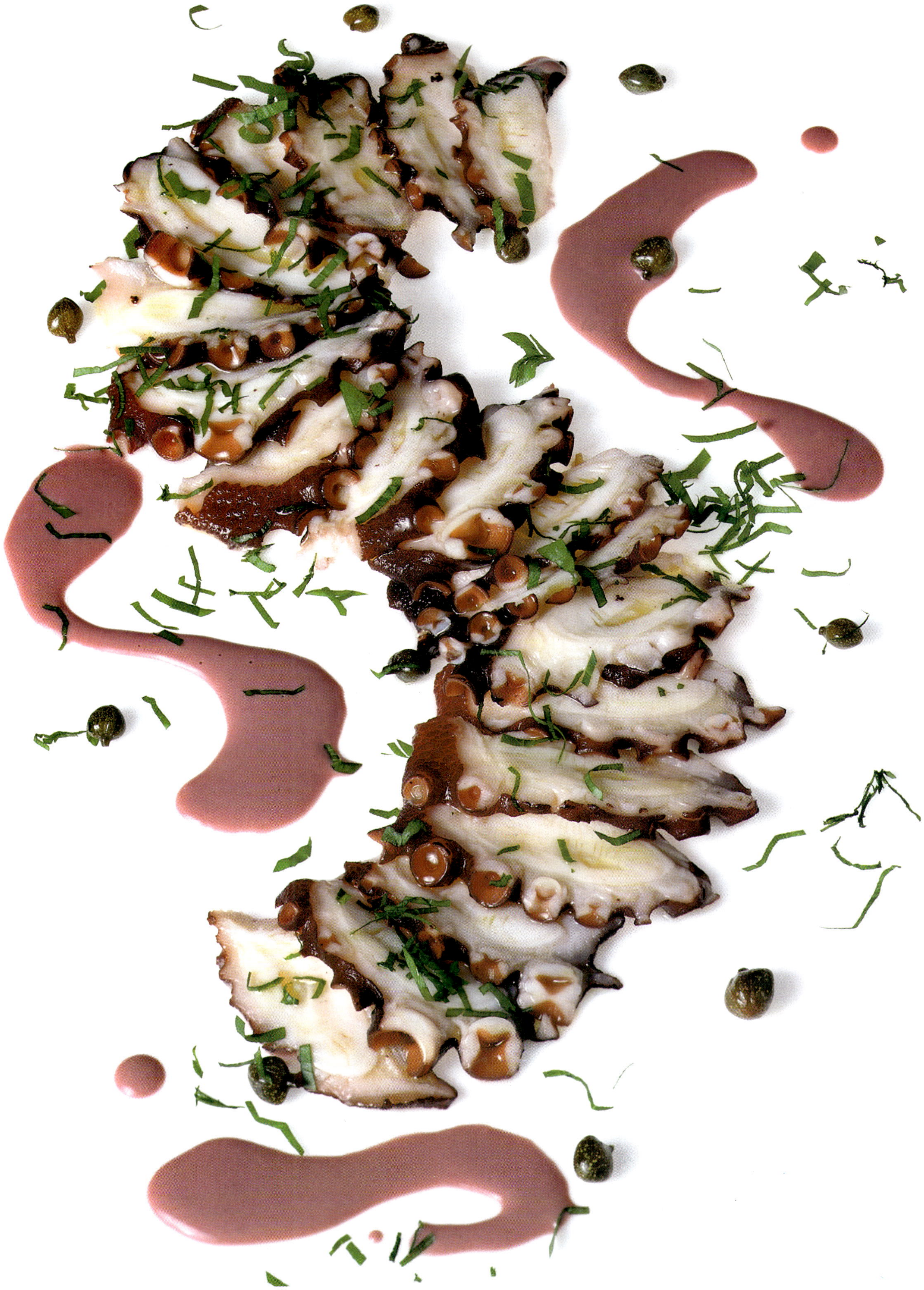

QUINOTTO

*This is another of Cucho's extraordinary 'Novoandino' creations using **quinua**. There's been a modern day resurgence of interest in this ancient 'mother grain' of the Incas. A cereal packed with protein and vitamins it's versatile enough to go from the breakfast table to the most elegant of dinner parties.*

Ingredients:

- ¾ lb (350g) **quinua**
- 5 tbsp **achiote** oil (p.154)
- 1 large red onion, minced
- 2 cloves garlic, minced
- ¼ lb (100 g) bacon
- ¾ cup white wine
- ½ cup crayfish stock (p.88)
- 4 tbsp heavy cream
- ½lb (250g) mushrooms, sliced paper thin
- Parmesan cheese, grated
- Salt

For the sauce:

- 2 doz fresh crayfish tails
- ¾ cup crayfish corals
- 1½ cups heavy cream
- Butter
- Salt

Preparation

Wash the **quinua** in several changes of running water until the water runs clear. Then boil for 7-10 minutes. Be careful not to overcook, the grains should be 'al dente'.

Drain the **quinua** well. Spread out on a baking sheet and leave to dry.

In a large skillet, heat the **achiote** oil and sauté onion and garlic over medium heat until soft, about 3 minutes. Add bacon and mushrooms and cook for another 2 or 3 minutes.

Add cooked **quinua** grains to the skillet with wine, stock and cream. Stir and cook for 5 more minutes.

Just before serving, stir in Parmesan cheese and season with salt.

To serve:

Heat crayfish coral and cream together in a small pan to make a sauce. In a separate skillet sauté crayfish tails in a little butter and then add to the sauce. Season and spoon over risotto.

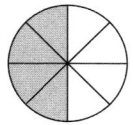

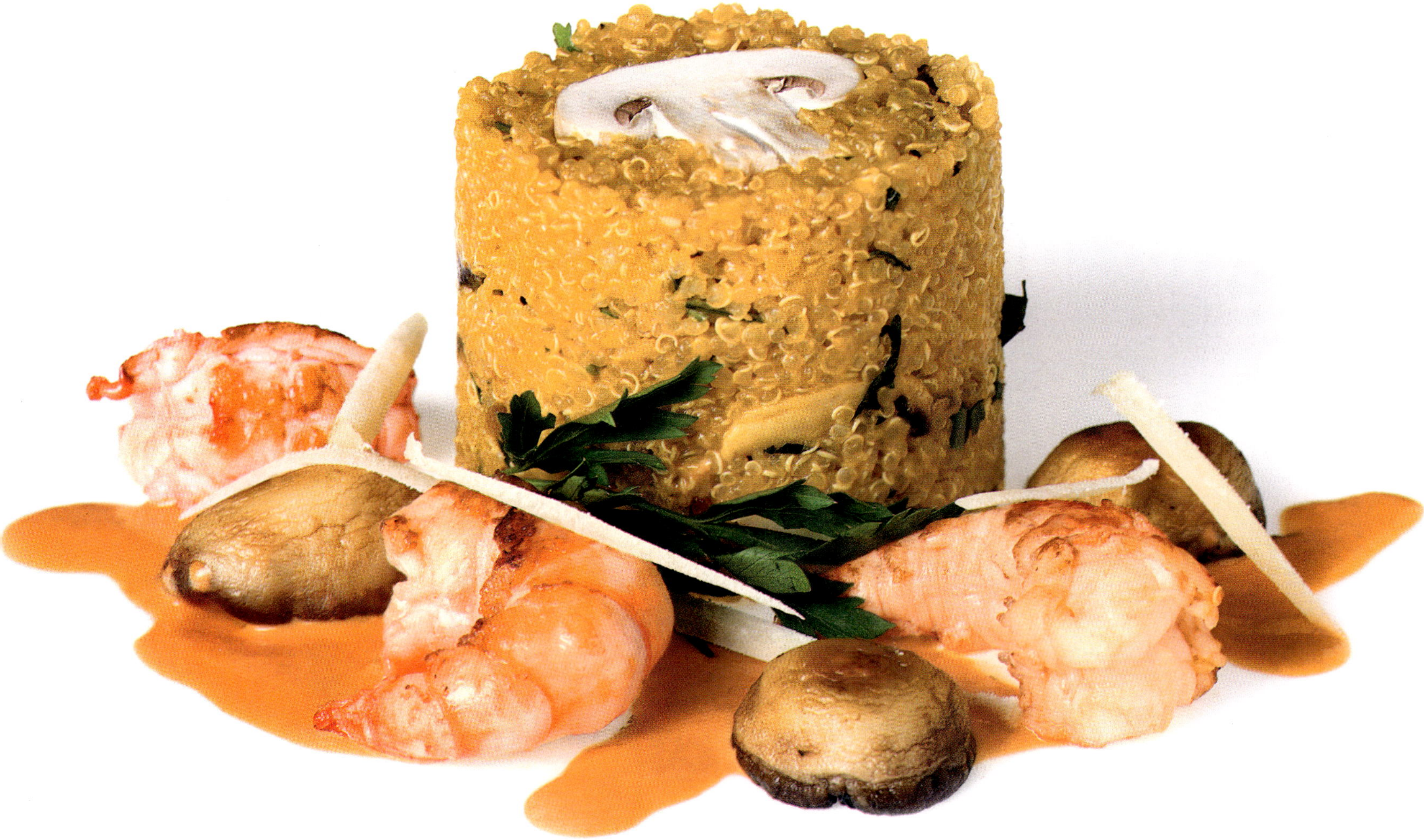

Ravioli de Cabrito - 'Cabrioli'

*This is a recipe that I have thrown together to help illustrate the strong bond between Italy and Peru. In the 19th and early 20th centuries many thousands of Italian immigrants made Peru their home. They thrived here and became great producers of pasta. In 1878, Lima already counted 12 pasta factories. All of them belonged to Italian immigrants. Thus have Peruvians become some of the leading per capita pasta consumers in the Western Hemisphere. This recipe brings the very traditional flavors of **cabrito** (kid goat) and **ají** to both the stuffing as well as the butter sauce.*

Ingredients:

- 2 goat (kid) shanks
- 2 tbsp vegetable oil
- 1 cup chopped red onion
- 3 cloves garlic, crushed
- ½ cup peeled and diced tomato
- 1 tbsp **ají amarillo** paste (p.228)
- 1 cup white wine
- 1 ½ ltrs meat stock
- ½ lb (250g) fresh pasta sheets
- 5 oz (150g) butter
- Juice of 3 key limes
- Salt and freshly ground black pepper

Garnish:

- Parmesan shavings
- Freshly chopped parsley

Makes 24 ravioli

Preparation

To make the goat meat filling:

In a large pan, heat oil and sauté garlic and onion over medium heat until soft, about 3 minutes. Add goat pieces and tomato and cook for a further 2 minutes. Turn goat pieces to ensure that they are well coated in the cooking sauce.

Add **ají amarillo** paste and cook for 1 or 2 more minutes. Add white wine, bring to a boil and reduce for about 3 minutes. Add stock and bring back to a boil. Reduce heat and simmer for about 30 minutes until meat is fork tender. Remove from heat.

Lift meat from pan and, when cool enough to handle, pull from the bone and shred. Empty sauce into a bowl and add meat. Mix well and adjust seasoning. Squeeze out excess cooking liquid from the meat mixture through a fine mesh strainer and reserve.

To make the raviolis:

Lay out fresh pasta sheets on a floured surface. Place 1 rounded tsp filling at 3 in- (7½ cm-) intervals on half the pasta sheets. Brush round the borders of the filling with a little cold water or egg white. Top with the remaining pasta sheets being careful to expel all the air from inside ravioli. Using a round cookie cutter, 3 in- (7½ cm-) in diameter, cut out the ravioli.

Transfer to a floured tray and cover with a cloth towel, until ready to cook. Bring a large pot of salted water to a rolling boil and drop in the ravioli. Cook for about 3 minutes; when they float to the top of the pot they are done.

Meanwhile melt butter and mix in reserved sauce juices. Season with salt, pepper and key lime juice. Remove ravioli from pan with a slotted spoon and drain well.

Arrange on individual serving plates, spoon over warm sauce and top with Parmesan shavings and freshly chopped parsley.

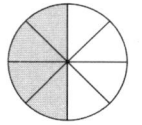

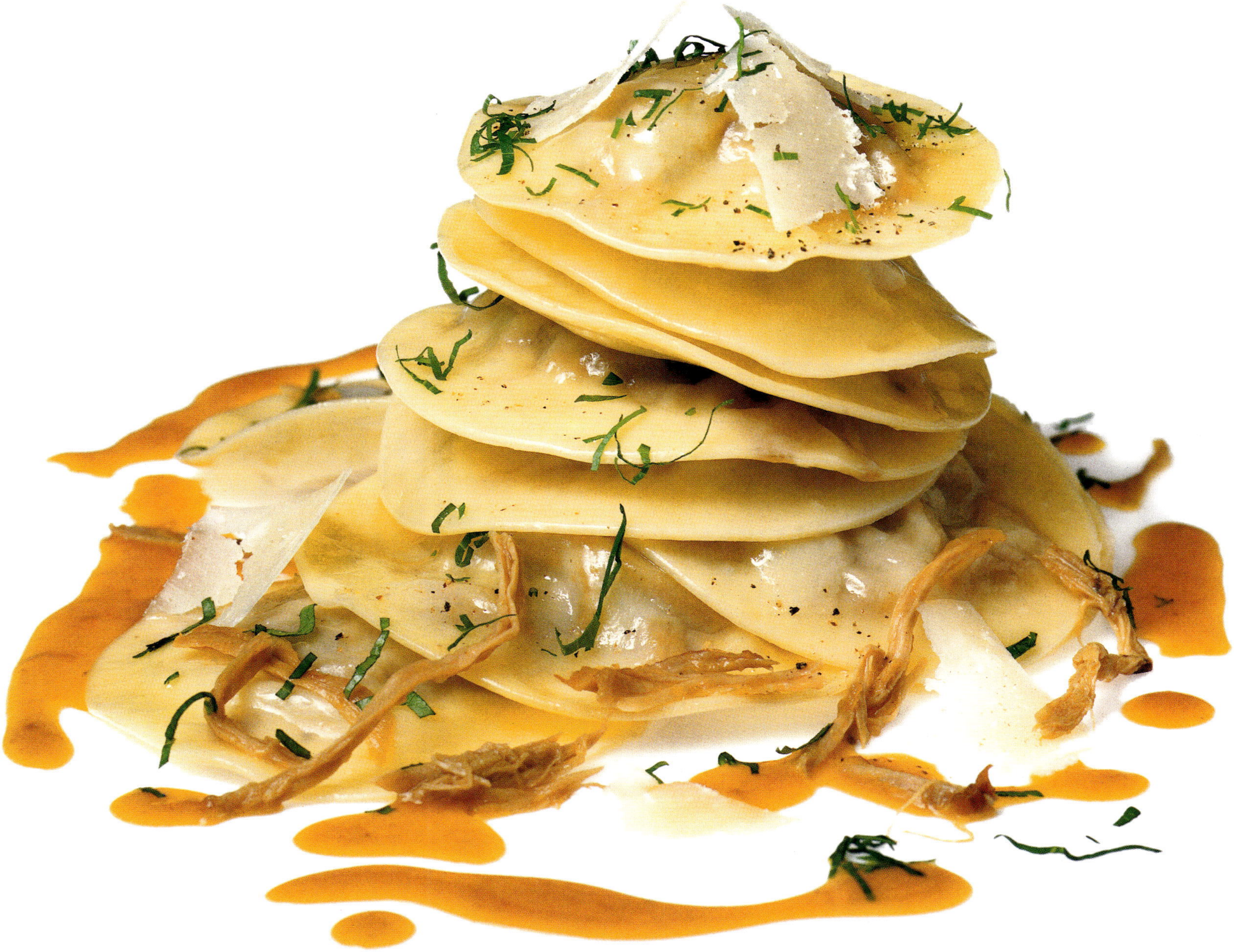

Solterito Arequipeño

Ingredients :

- 1 lb (½ kg) fresh fava or broad beans
- 3 ears of fresh corn
- 6 **ajíes amarillos**, seeded and chopped
- 1 **rocoto**, seeded and diced fine
- 2 large red onions, diced
- 1 lb (½ kg) fresh white cheese, cubed
- 2 tbsp white wine vinegar
- 2 tbsp olive oil
- 12 black olives, pitted and sliced fine
- Juice of 3 key limes
- Salt and white pepper

This is Peru's own version of bean salad and comes to us from the beautiful southern highland city of Arequipa. The color and flavor of fresh fava or broad beans is teamed with fresh corn kernels and juicy olives. Velvety fresh white cheese completes the dish and makes it an ideal candidate for a light luncheon or a first course at supper.

Preparation

Finely chop the **ajíes amarillos** and set aside. In a small bowl marinate for 10 minutes the chopped onion in the lime juice and salt and then drain.

Drop the fava beans into a pot of salted boiling water and boil for 4 minutes. Remove from heat and strain.

Place the corn on the cob in a large pot of cold salted water with the juice of 1 key lime and ½ tbsp sugar. Bring to the boil and cook until the kernels are tender when pierced with a fork, about 10 minutes. Remove from heat and strain.

Pop the beans from their skins and strip the kernels from the corn cobs.

In a large bowl combine the chopped onion with the fresh cheese, **rocoto**, fava beans and chopped **ají amarillo**.

Whisk together the oil and vinegar and pour over the salad. Add salt and white pepper and leave to stand for a few minutes to let the flavors intensify.

Serve decorated with sliced olives.

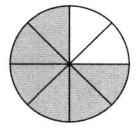

Tip: It's important to add the olives at the end so that they do not discolor the rest of the salad.

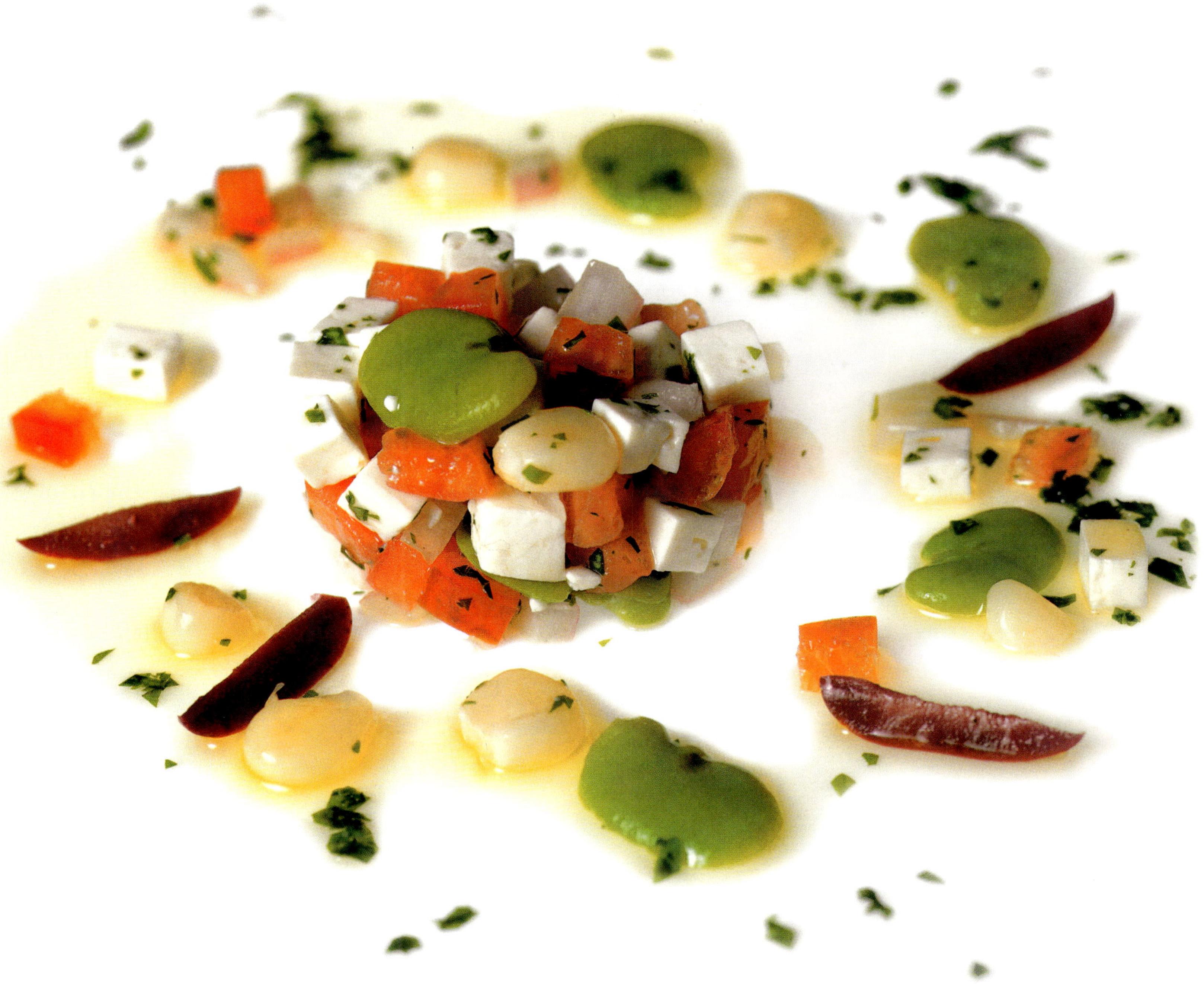

TIRADITO

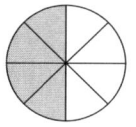

*The simplicity of the ancient coastal people's preparation of raw fish using salt and condiments is echoed in Peru's most modern fish dish: **tiradito**. This is the youngest member of the **ceviche** family and the one growing most in variety of preparation. Unlike **ceviche**, **tiradito** does not include onions, but the main difference is in the cut of the fish, which is sliced fine and then flattened. This way of cutting fish is similar to Peru's northern fishermen's habit of slicing fish with their long knives, but **tiradito** has most markedly been influenced by **nikkei** cooks' treatment of fish. Fresh ingredients are a must and they must be kept well chilled.*

Tiradito de Pescado

*This is Marisa Guiulfo's recipe for **Tiradito**. Crushed celery and ginger give just a hint of added depth to the fresh taste of the lime juice. Simple, elegant and delicious.*

Ingredients:

- 4 halibut fillets (about 5 ½ oz / 150g each)
- 1 piece fresh ginger root (about 1 in / 2.5 cm), minced
- 1 stalk celery, chopped and then crushed
- 1 **ají limo** seeded and finely diced
- Crushed cilantro
- Kernels of two fresh corn cobs
- Salt and white pepper
- Sugar
- Pinch aniseed
- Juice of 15 key limes

To candy sweet potatoes:

- 4 large sweet potatoes
- 3 cups of sugar
- 1 orange peel
- 1 cinnamon stick
- Water

Garnish:

- Freshly chopped cilantro
- **Ají limo**

Preparation

To candy sweet potatoes:
Peel the sweet potatoes and make into small balls with a melon baller. Put them to boil in water that is already hot. Once it comes to a boil, throw out the water. Repeat the procedure 3 times. Add 3 cups of sugar, the orange peel, cinnamon stick and enough water to cover. Simmer until sweet potatoes are candied and shiny (adding more water if necessary).

To boil the corn:
Put corn in cold water and boil with a few grains of aniseed, a pinch of sugar and a few drops of lime juice so corn won't darken. Boil until tender, about 20 - 25 minutes. Drain and let corn cool. Chop cob into 1 in-(2.5 cm-) thick rounds, or strip kernels from cob.

To make the tiradito:
Slice the fish into very fine strips (no more than 1 in (2.5 cm) wide, 3 in (7.5 cm) long and ½ in (1.2 cm) or less thick) and place in a dish, with the strips overlapping each other.

Mix the lime juice with the ginger, crushed celery, crushed cilantro and 1 tsp of the **ají limo**. Season generously with salt and strain through a fine mesh sieve onto the fish 5 minutes before serving. Make sure that all pieces are covered in lime juice. Garnish with sweet potatoes, corn and, if desired, sprinkle with a few chopped cilantro leaves. Serve decorated with remaining diced **ají limo**.

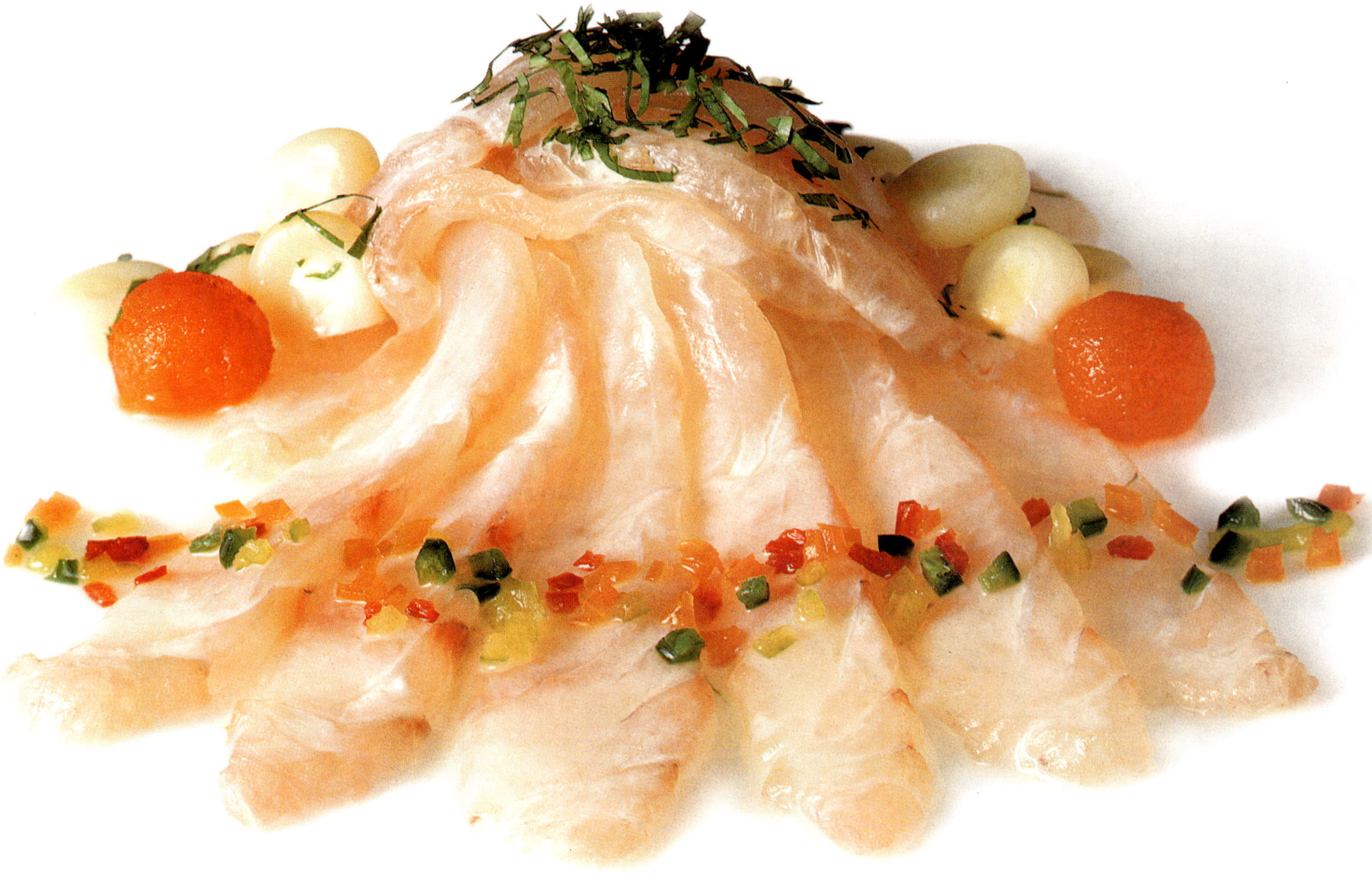

Tiradito Alfresco & Tiradito Criollo

*Alfredo Aramburú is one of Peru's most successful chef/entrepreneurs. His 'Alfredo's' and 'Alfresco' restaurants serve exceptionally flavorful and original dishes with emphasis on fish and seafood. These two recipes are his. The Criollo uses a yellow **ají** based sauce, while the Alfresco signature dish has a bewitching olive oil and garlic blend. Be sure to chill both fish and sauce prior to serving.*

Ingredients:

- 1 ¼ lb (600g) fillet of flounder or sea bass
- 1 ½ cups olive oil
- ¾ cup white wine vinegar
- 1 heaped tsp minced garlic
- 4 tbsp key lime juice
- Salt

Ingredients:

- 1 ¼ lb (600g) flounder fillet
- 4 tbsp key lime juice
- 1 **ají limo**, seeded, deveined and chopped as finely as possible
- 1 tbsp finely chopped cilantro
- 4 tbsp **ají amarillo** paste (p.228)
- ½ tsp minced garlic
- Salt and white pepper

Garnish:
- Cooked kernels from one fresh ear of corn
- Freshly chopped parsley

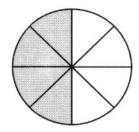

Preparation - Tiradito Alfresco

Mix the vinegar, garlic, key lime juice, salt and olive oil in a blender until they form a well emulsified vinaigrette. Keep well chilled.

Cut the fish fillet into thin slices on the diagonal as for sashimi and flatten with the blade of a large knife.

Pour enough vinaigrette onto the fish to just cover the slices and serve immediately, garnished with cooked corn kernels and freshly chopped parsley.

Preparation - Tiradito Criollo

In a bowl, whisk together the key lime juice, salt, pepper, crushed garlic, **ají limo**, chopped cilantro and **ají amarillo** paste. Keep chilled.

Cut the fish as above.

Spread out on a flat serving platter and sprinkle with salt.

Pour enough **Criollo** cream over the fish slices to just cover them and serve immediately, garnished with the corn kernels.

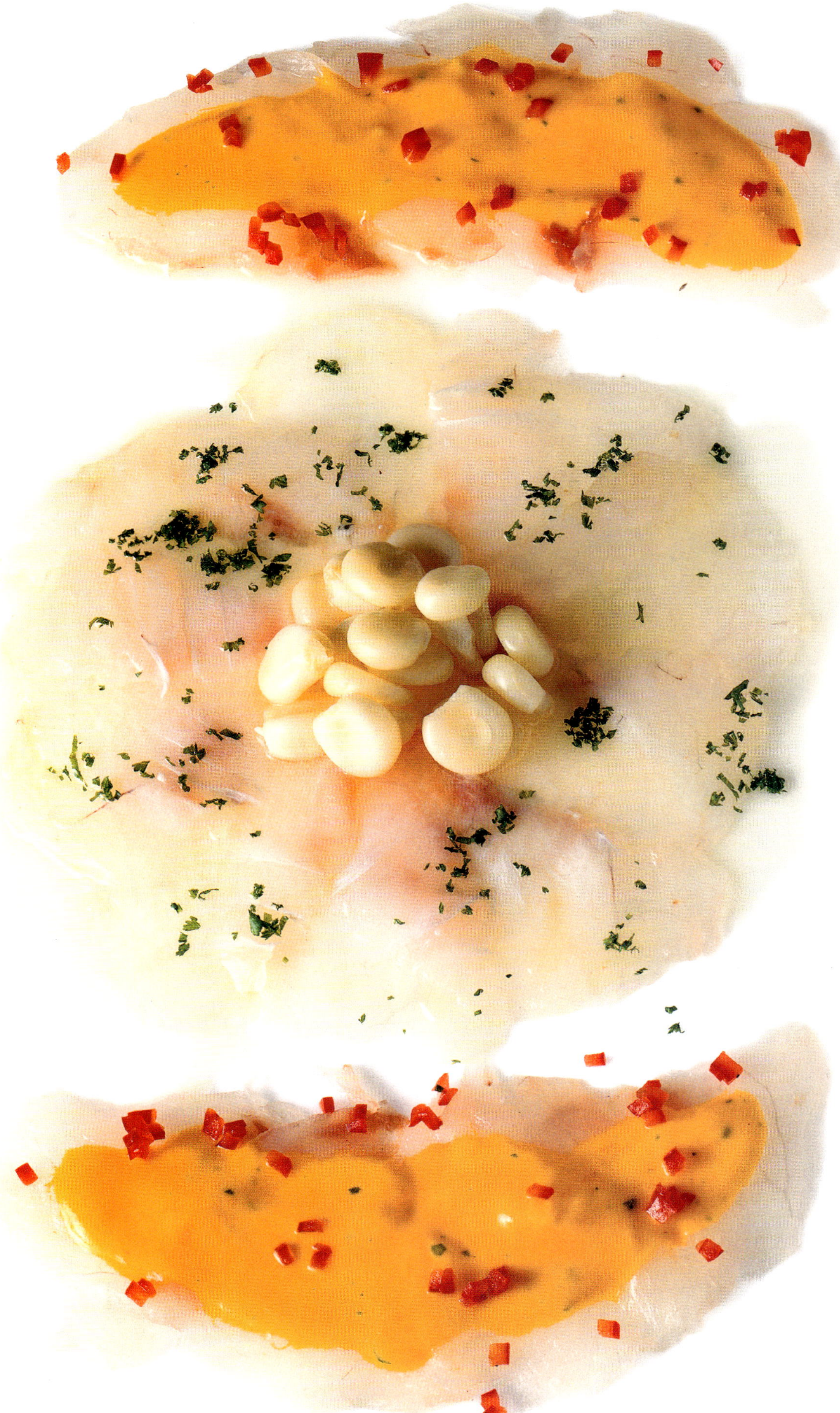

Tiraditos de Ambrosía

Ingredients :

For the flounder:
- 2 oz (60g) fresh flounder fillet
- 2 tbsp **ají amarillo** paste (p.228)
- 1 tbsp key lime juice
- 1 tsp finely chopped cilantro
- Salt and pepper

For the scallops:
- 8 scallops (corals removed)
- 1 tbsp finely chopped shallots
- 1 tbsp finely chopped red bell pepper
- 1 tbsp finely chopped tomato
- 1 tsp finely chopped **ají limo**
- 1 tsp finely chopped mint
- 1 tsp finely chopped cilantro
- 2 tbsp olive oil
- 1 tbsp key lime juice
- Salt and pepper

For the crayfish:
- 8 fresh crayfish tails, peeled and deveined
- 2 tbsp **rocoto** paste (p.230)
- 1 tsp crayfish coral
- 1 tbsp key lime juice
- 1 tsp finely chopped chives
- Salt and pepper

*Ambrosía is one of the top restaurants in Lima. It is run by the food stylist for this book, Culinary Institute of America graduate Jorge Ossio. Jorge, affectionately known as Coque, has put together a stunning trio of **tiraditos** using all three types of Peruvian **ají**. The raw crayfish and **rocoto** pepper are elements from Peru's second city Arequipa.*

Preparation

For the flounder:
Cut the fish fillet into thin strips on the diagonal and flatten with the blade of a large knife. Arrange on one side of an individual serving plate.

Mix **ají amarillo** paste with lime juice, salt and pepper. Pour over fish, just enough to cover. Sprinkle with chopped cilantro.

For the scallops:
Combine all ingredients including scallops. Toss well and place in a small glass container in the center of the plate.

For the crayfish:
Cut each crayfish tail in half lengthwise and flatten with the blade of a large knife. Arrange on plate opposite the flounder.

Mix **rocoto** paste with lime juice, crayfish coral, salt and pepper. Pour over crayfish tails, just enough to cover. Sprinkle with chopped chives.

Cool dish in the freezer for 3 minutes and serve immediately over ice.

Tip: It's essential that **tiradito** be served well chilled to reinforce the sensation of freshness.

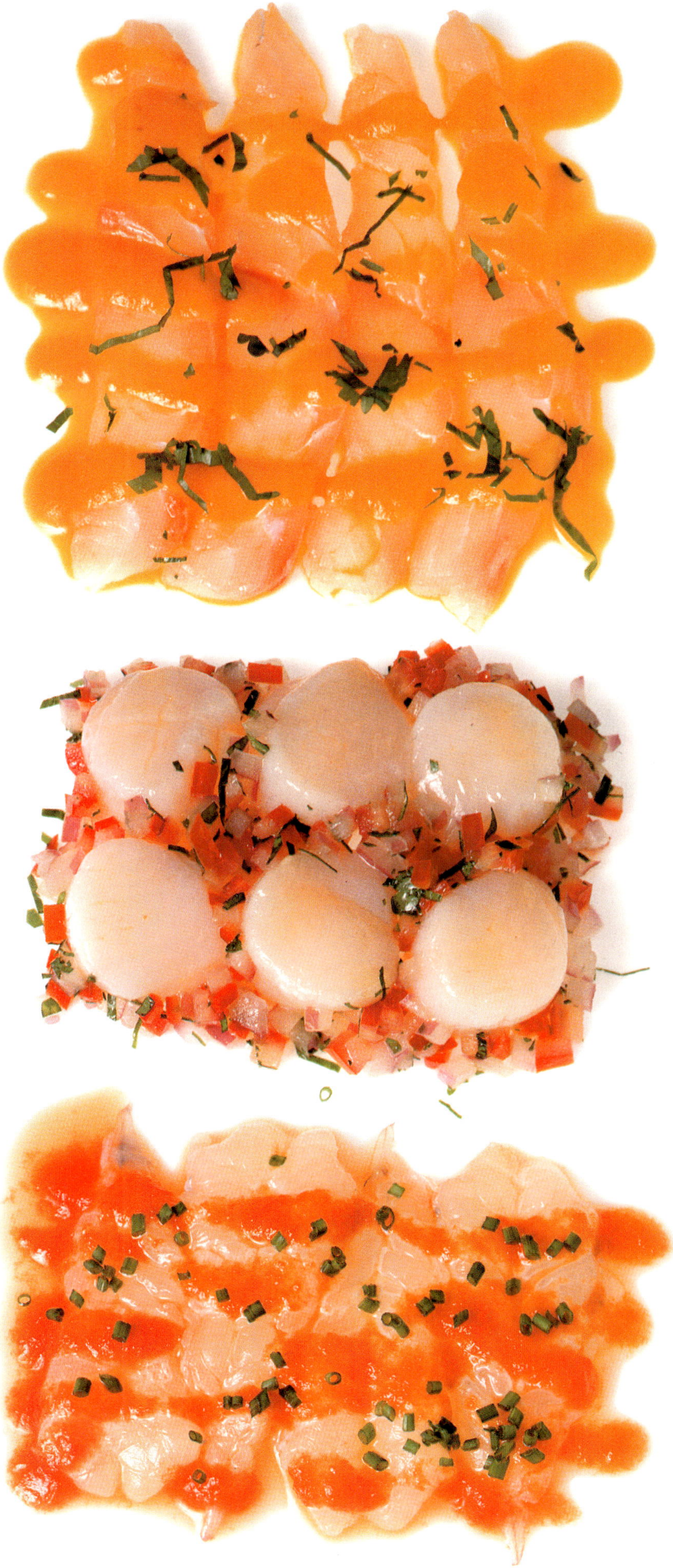

Tiradito Dos Tiempos

Ingredients:

- 4 flounder fillets, approximately 6 ½ oz (180g) each
- 8 fresh, cooked crayfish tails
- 7oz (200g) cooked octopus, sliced
- 7oz (200g) cooked shrimp tails
- 7oz (200g) sea urchin flesh
- 8 scallops
- 1 oz vodka
- 2 **ajíes limo**
- 3 tbsp **ají amarillo** paste (p.228)
- Juice of 2 lb (1kg) key limes

Garnish:

- 4 whole cooked crayfish (optional)
- Lettuce
- Kernels from 2 fresh boiled ears of corn
- Boiled yuca

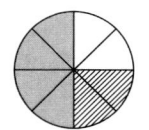

Serves 6 as first course or 4 as main dish

*Olga and Carlos Araujo are a husband and wife team of chefs who have had a dedicated following of fans ever since they opened their first, phenomenally successful, restaurant 'Mamicé' many years ago. Specializing in seafood and Creole cooking, Carlos' imagination and Olga's gifted touch in the kitchen join to create original and inspired recipes such as this striking pair of **tiraditos**. Carlos is the architect of this particular dish and describes **tiradito** as the 'new king' of Peruvian cuisine. He recommends that you experiment with any kind of seafood that you can find.*

Preparation

To make the fish tiradito:
Keeping all ingredients well chilled, with a very sharp knife cut fish fillets into thin strips and then flatten with the blade of a large knife.

Sprinkle with salt and **ají limo** to taste. Set aside.

To make the seafood ceviche:
Blend the key lime juice with the **ají amarillo** paste, vodka and salt to taste. Add the seafood and divide the mixture between four individual martini glasses.

To serve:
Place one martini glass on each serving plate and spread the fish slices around. Pour lime juice onto scallops that you have left in the half shell before serving. Place these two scallops at the base of the martini glass. Pour over just enough lime juice mixture to cover the fish. Garnish with lettuce leaves, freshly cooked corn kernels, boiled yuca and 1 whole crayfish per serving (if using crayfish to decorate). Serve immediately, well chilled.

Tip: Wash the sea urchin flesh thoroughly before using to remove any slimy deposits from the surface.

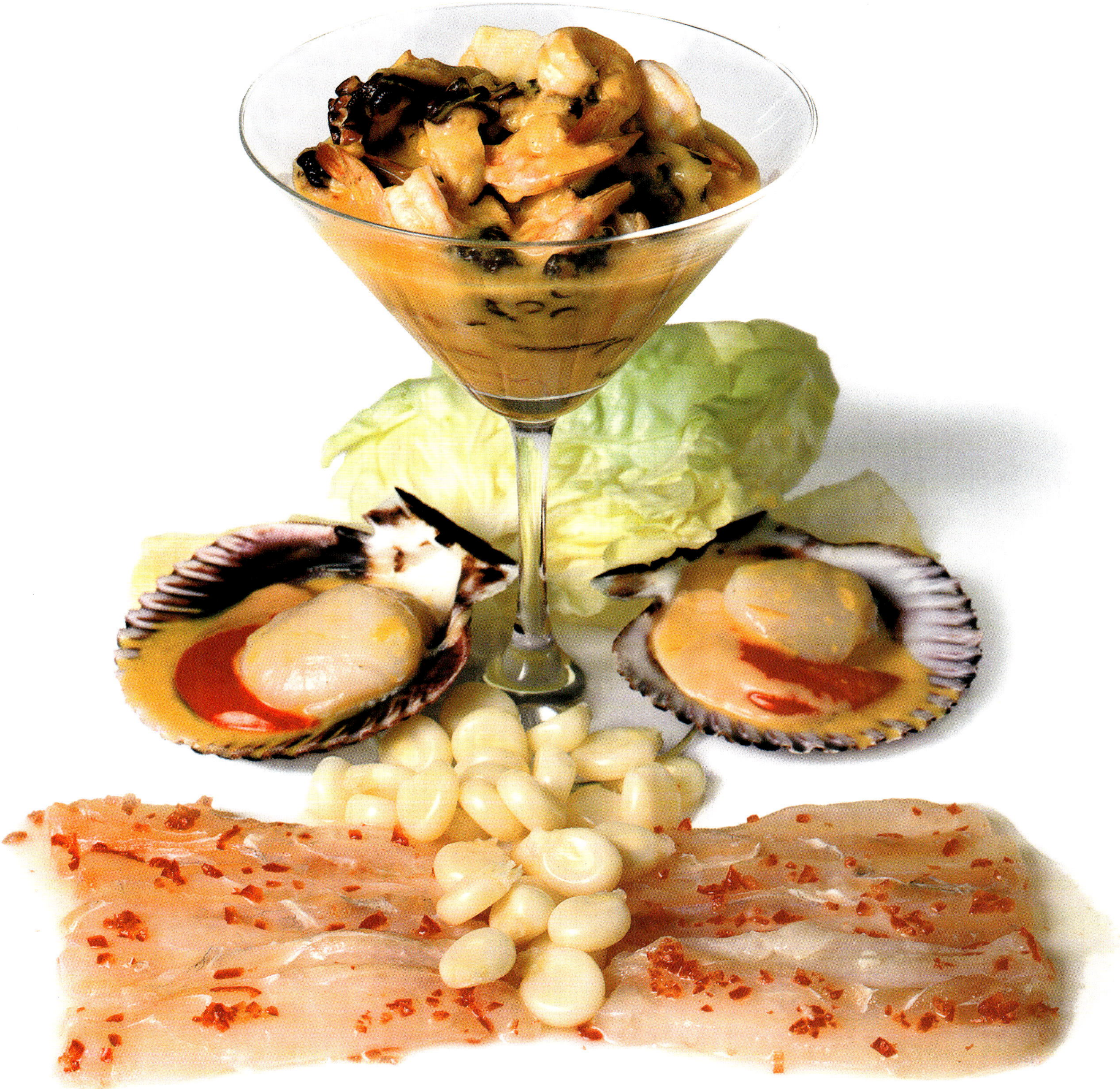

Main Dishes

Adobo de Chancho

Ingredients:

- 2 lb (1 kg) lean leg pork, cut into pieces
- 2 tbsp **achiote** (annatto) seeds
- 2 tbsp vegetable oil
- 6 cloves garlic, crushed
- 1 tsp ground cumin
- ¼ cup **ají panca** paste (p.228)
- 2 red onions, chopped
- 1 cup **chicha de jora** (corn beer) or vinegar
- Salt and freshly ground pepper

***Achiote** or annatto seeds were once used by Amazonian peoples to color their bodies. Today they are used as a commercial colorant for margarine and other food products. In this **adobo** they give a distinctive deep reddish golden color to the pork as well as a pungent spicy aroma.*

Preparation

In a small bowl, combine **achiote** seeds with vegetable oil and let stand, stirring occasionally, for about 30 minutes. Transfer to a small skillet and bring to a boil over low heat, while stirring. Remove from the heat and leave to cool. When cool, strain oil through a fine mesh muslin-lined sieve.

Place the pork pieces in a large glass bowl. Season with salt, pepper, cumin and crushed garlic. Add onion and beer, or vinegar, to cover meat and marinate for 24 hours.

In a large, heavy-based pan heat **achiote** oil and sauté **ají panca** paste over medium heat for 2 minutes. Add the pork and the marinade. Cover and let cook over low heat until meat is fork tender, about 1 hour. Check the liquid level from time to time and add hot water if necessary. The **adobo** should be moist and juicy.

Serve over rice accompanied by sweet potatoes and **puré de pallares** (p.226)

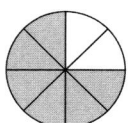

Tip : Achiote seeds can be found in most good markets or specialty food stores. They should be fresh, a bright reddish color, with a peppery aromatic flavor. Avoid any that are brown or burgundy, as they will have lost their flavor. **Achiote** oil can be kept in a sealed container in the refrigerator for up to a year.

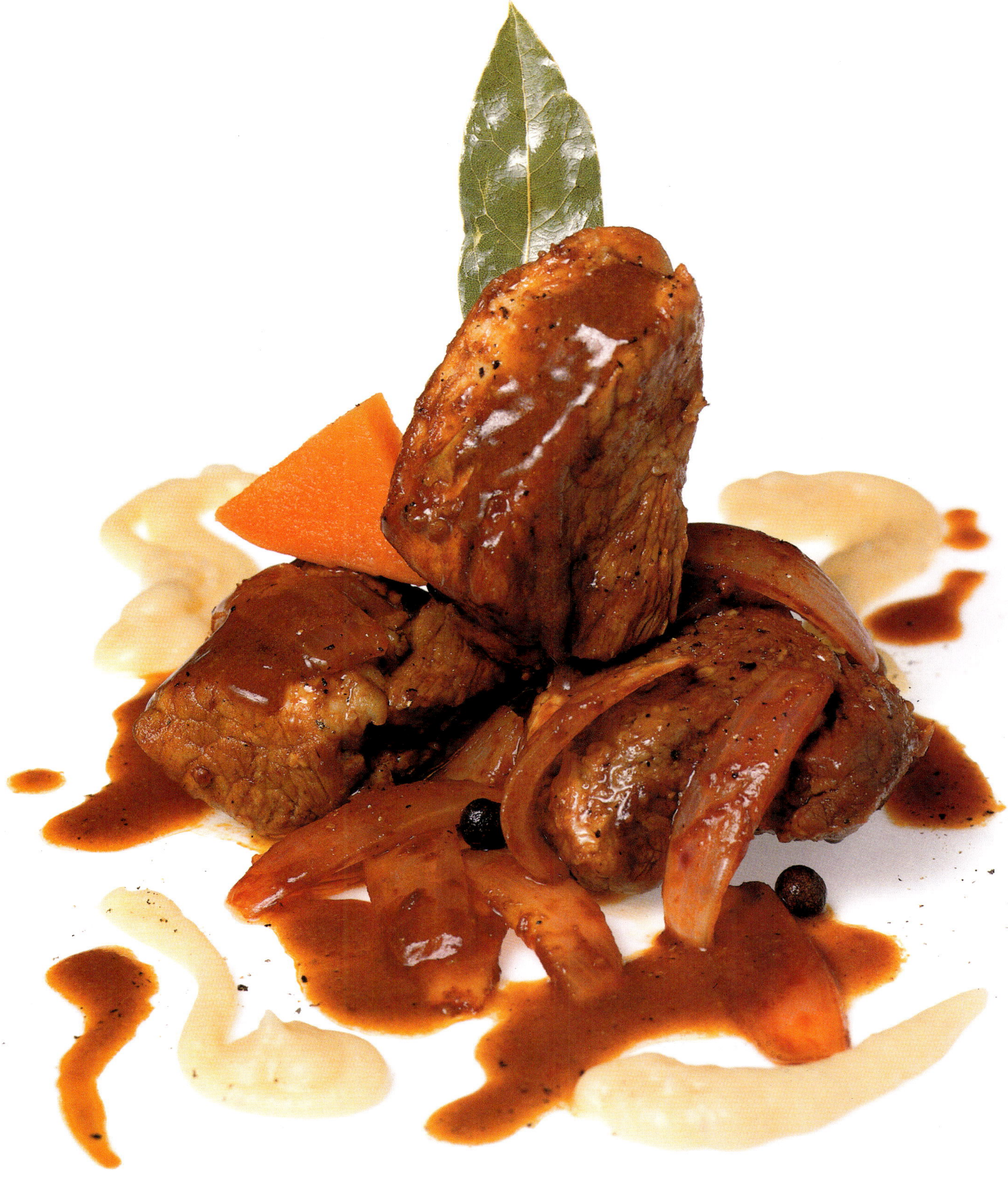

Ají de Gallina

A kind of chicken did exist in Peru in pre-Colombian times. Known as 'hualpa' in Quechua, it was cooked with ají and was important enough to have an Inca named after it. Atahualpa, last of the ruling Incas, was executed by the Spaniards but the dish as it exists today is a perfect example of the fusion of Spanish and Quechua ingredients. The addition of bread, nuts and cheese to the hot spicy chicken gives an added dimension to this very traditional dish.

Ingredients:

- 1 chicken (about 2 kg.) equivalent to 3 complete breasts
- 1 medium chopped white onion
- 1 clove garlic, crushed
- 7 tbsp **ají mirasol paste** (p.228)
- ½ loaf of sliced bread without the crust
- 1 dozen black olives
- 2 cups chicken stock
- 1 ½ cups evaporated milk
- 100 gr. chopped walnuts
- 125 gr. grated parmesan cheese
- ½ cup vegetable oil
- 6-8 yellow potatoes (depending on the size)
- ¼ cup olive oil
- 6 hard-boiled eggs, sliced
- Salt and pepper to taste

Preparation

In a pan of chicken stock parboil the breasts and leave them there to cool. Remove and shred the chicken into bite-size pieces.

Crumble the bread, soak it in the milk and put all this mixture in the blender.

In a large heavy-based pan, heat oil and sauté onion until gold, then add garlic and the **ají mirasol paste** and fry them well.

Add the soaked bread mixture, adjust seasoning. Cook for a further 10 minutes then begin to add ladles of the hot chicken stock, stirring constantly. Add stock each time the sauce thickens. While still stirring constantly, add the olive oil.

Finally, add the shredded chicken, Parmesan cheese and nuts. If too thick add a little more stock while stirring gently in order not to mash the chicken. Simmer until the oil comes to the surface.

Serve hot accompanied by rice (See recipe for "Arroz a la Peruana" p. 225.) and yellow potatoes. Garnish with black olives and hard-boiled egg slices.

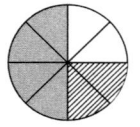

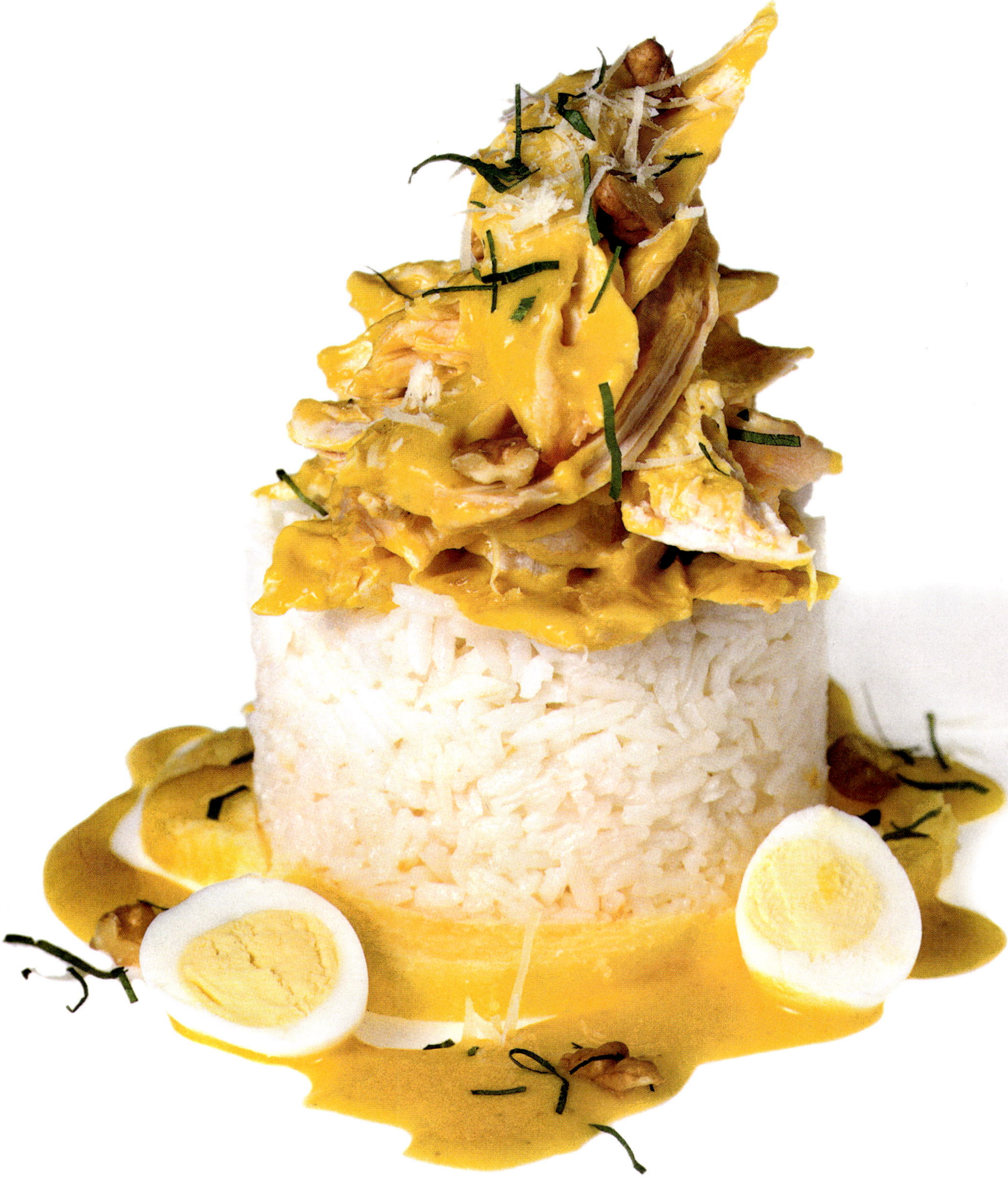

Ají de Langostinos

*This dish from Daniel Manrique is the seafood lover's answer to one of Peru's most traditional dishes: **Ají de Gallina**. Although the preparation is similar, there are some key differences to make allowances for the subtler flavors of the seafood.*

Ingredients:

- 2¾ cups (600 g) shrimp, peeled and deveined (if using octopus it should be previously cooked)
- 2 tbsp vegetable oil
- 3 cloves garlic, crushed
- 4 tbsp **ají mirasol** paste (p.228)
- 1 cup red onion, chopped fine
- 8 slices white bread, crusts removed
- 4 oz (½ cup) evaporated milk
- Chopped pecans, as desired
- Salt and pepper

To serve:

- Hard-boiled egg, sliced

Preparation

Soak bread in evaporated milk and blend to make a thick purée-like mixture.

In a large skillet, heat the oil and sauté onions until translucent, about 4 minutes. Add garlic and continue cooking until just turning golden, another minute. Add **ají mirasol paste** and cook for 2 to 3 more minutes.

Add shrimp, bread mixture and pecans and cook, stirring for a few more minutes until the shrimp turns pink. Season with salt and pepper to taste and add a little more evaporated milk if necessary - the **ají** should be moist and juicy.

Serve hot over rice, garnished with slices of hard-boiled egg.

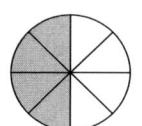

Note: This dish can also be prepared with octopus or a mixture of shrimp and octopus; experiment to find your favorite version.

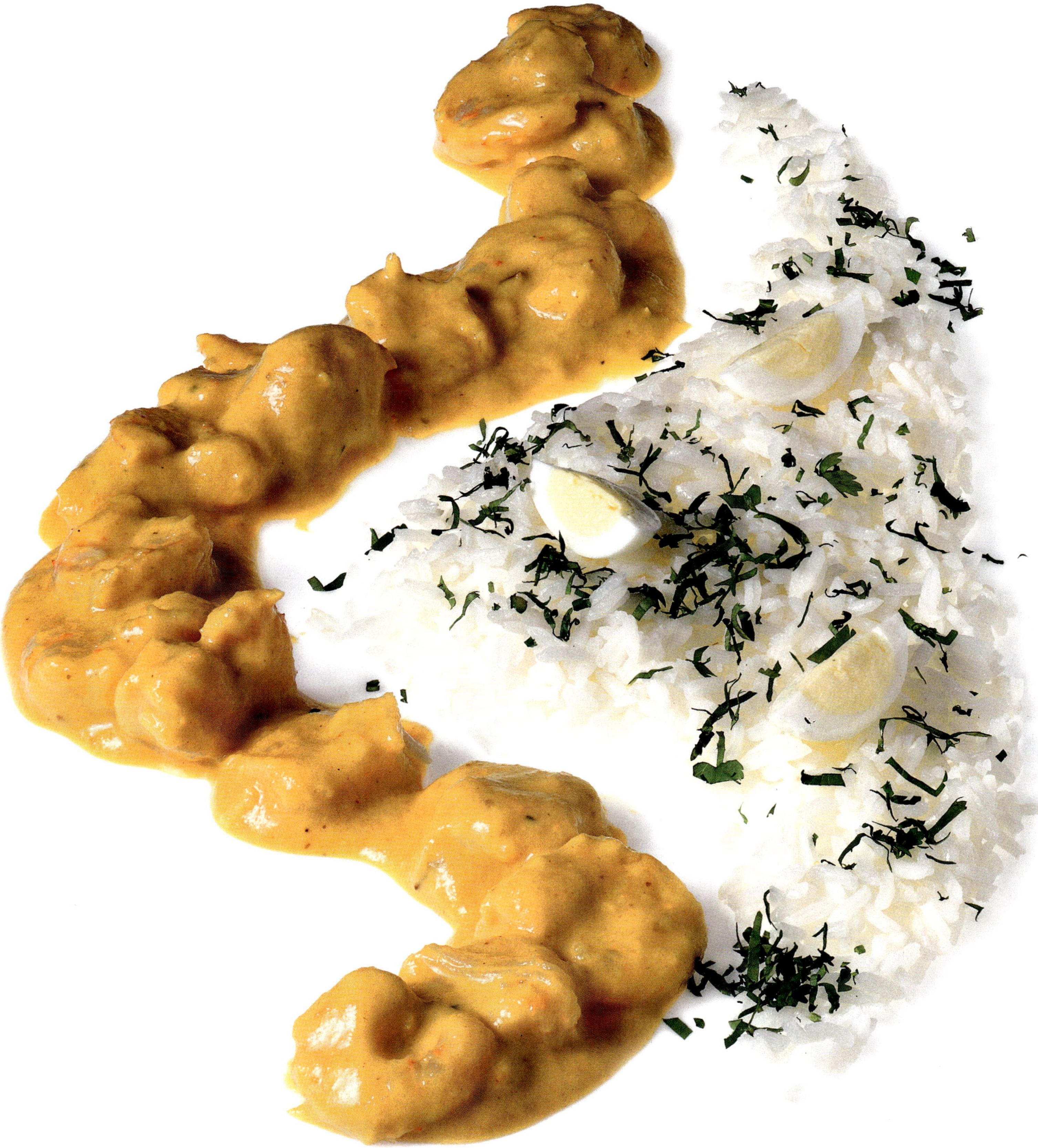

Alpaca en Tres Cortes

Ingredients:

- 6 ½ lb (3 kg) leg of alpaca
- 1 whole small head of garlic, peeled and crushed
- 2 bay leaves
- 6 ½ lb (3 kg) duck fat
- 4 cups (1 ltr) water
- Salt and freshly ground pepper

For the sauce:

- 1 cup red wine
- 1 tbsp sifted all-purpose flour
- 1 tbsp butter
- Alpaca cooking liquid

Another innovation of Cucho la Rosa's fertile imagination, inspired by the dishes served at the royal court of the Inca. The taste of alpaca is somewhat similar to pork or lamb, depending on the cut, with just a touch of game.

Preparation

Mix together the crushed garlic, bay leaves, salt and freshly ground pepper. Rub mixture all over alpaca leg and set aside overnight.

Place the alpaca leg in a large heavy-based pan and add the water and duck fat.

Cook on low heat for about 1 hour or until the alpaca meat is very tender. Add more water if necessary but do not baste.

When the meat is cooked, remove from the pan and set aside (keep warm).

To make the sauce:
Skim fat from the alpaca cooking liquid and discard.

In a small pan, over low heat, reduce the wine by half. Add the skimmed pan juices and cook for a few more minutes. Stir in the sifted flour to thicken sauce and finally whisk in the butter.

To serve:
Slice alpaca and serve hot accompanied by the sauce.

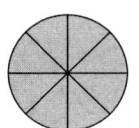

Note: This dish can also be made with other cuts of alpaca meat, such as rib chops or loin.

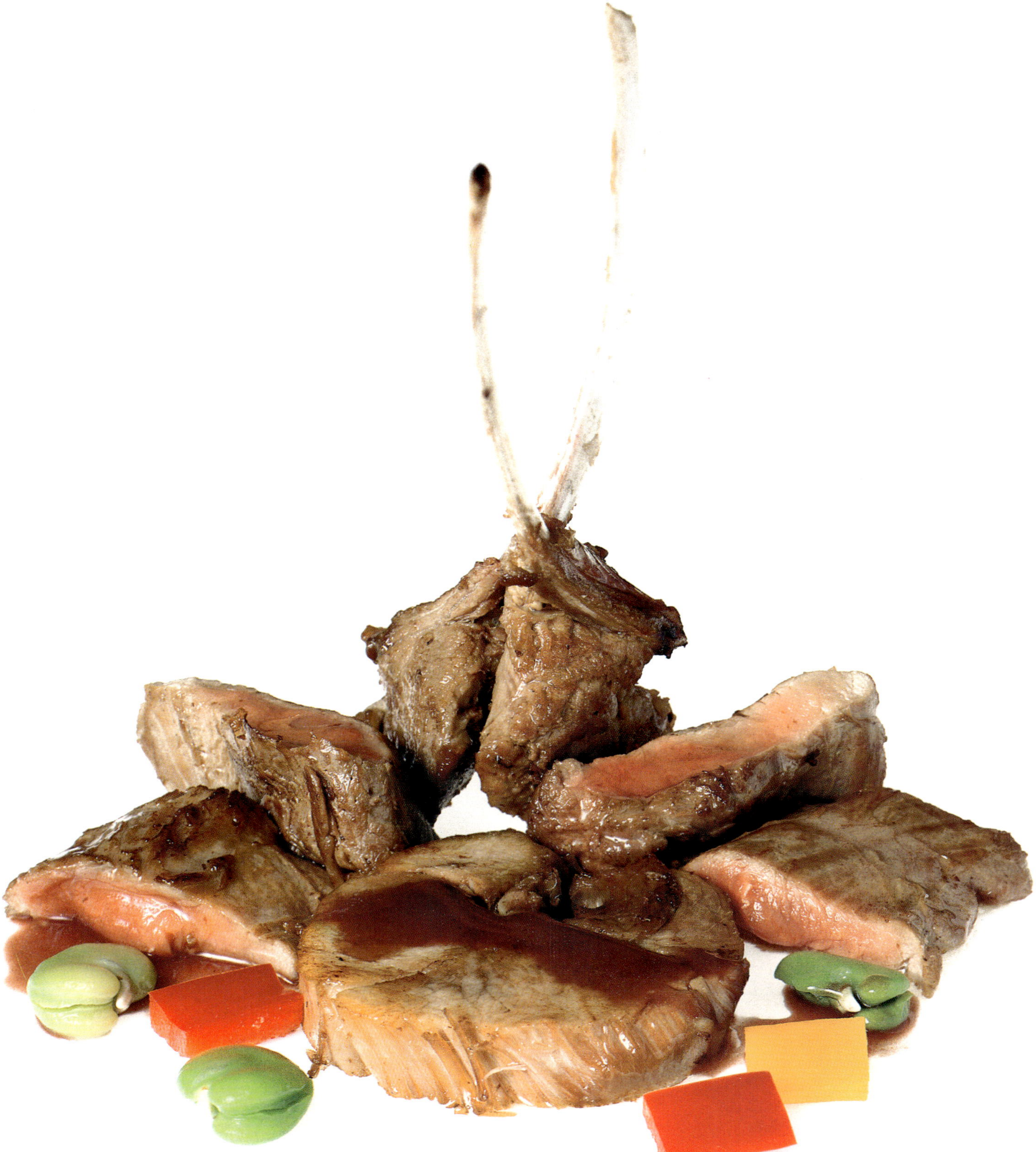

ARROCES

In his 'Historia del Nuevo Mundo', Bernabé Cobo tells us that the first rice seeds were sown in Peru in the same year that Lima was founded, 1535. The Spanish cultivated rice in the favorable climate of the coastal areas. Later on, in the 19th century, the Chinese 'coolies' brought to work in Peru had a clause in their contract stipulating a daily quantity of one and a half pounds of rice as part of their salary. Today rice is one of the mainstays of the Peruvian diet. Visitors to Peru will often coment on the amount of rice we eat. No meal will be served without it and it will often accompany other starchy foods such as potatoes or yuca on the same plate. As well as being served at every meal as a side dish, there are also some delicious dishes with rice incorporated as an ingredient.

Arroz Chaufa de Pescado

Ingredients:

- 2 lbs (1 kg) rice
- 2 lbs (1 kg) firm fleshed white fish fillets
- 2 tbsp minced garlic
- 2 cups cornstarch
- 6 eggs
- 2 tbsp vegetable oil
- 1 bunch scallions, chopped
- 1 red bell pepper, seeded and diced
- 1 tsp sesame seed oil
- Salt and soy sauce
- Oil for deep frying

*This is another of Doris Otani's tasty dishes as served at 'El Encuentro de Otani'. Her menu is varied and multicultural. This is one of the most popular and best loved Chinese-Peruvian fusion dishes. There is a **chifa** or Chinese restaurant on almost every main street in the coastal cities of Peru. The word **chifa** comes from the Chinese for 'to eat rice'. The first tiny cafes and taverns which Chinese immigrants started to open at the end of the 19th century were on the rather seedy Capon Street in downtown Lima. A century later stir fried rice dishes such as this are part of the country's daily diet..*

Preparation

Cook the rice according to **Arroz a la Peruana** recipe (p.225), but do not add the corn kernels.

Cut fish fillets into small strips, approximately 2 x ½ in- (5 x 1¼ cm-) long. Season with minced garlic and salt. Coat with cornstarch and deep fry in hot oil until golden, about 3 minutes. Drain on paper towel and set aside.

Make a thin omelette with the beaten eggs and cut into slender strips. Set aside.

In a large skillet or wok, heat the oil and stir fry red bell pepper and scallions for 1 minute. Continue stir frying adding all the other ingredients including fish and omelette strips. Mix well and cook for a further 3 minutes. Serve immediately.

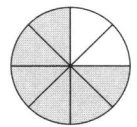

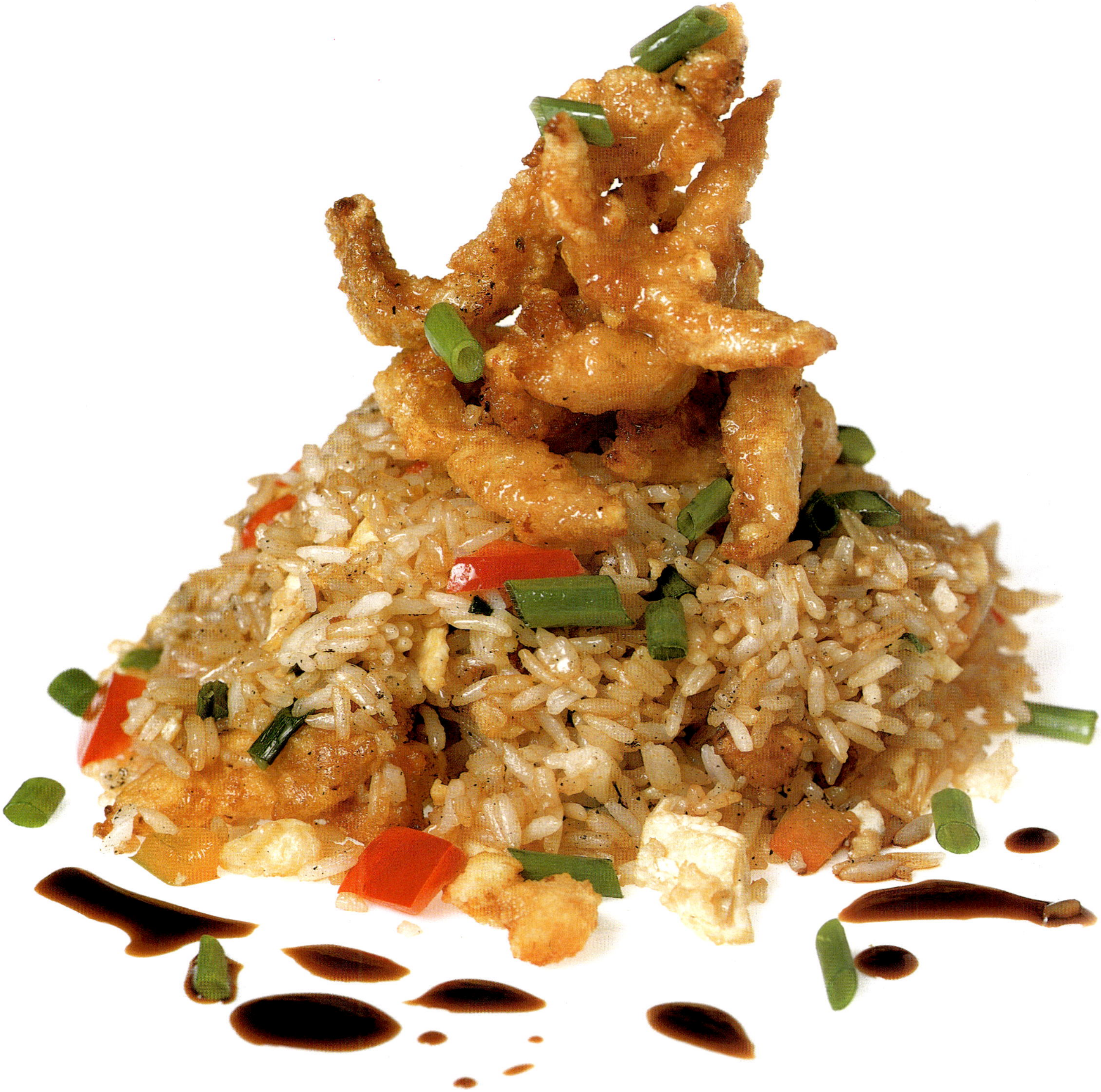

Arroz Atamalado

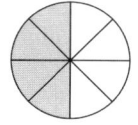

Here, Olga Araujo of the gifted husband and wife duo of chefs Olga and Carlos, presents another original dish. Each member of this talented team has his own particular style with which they have been charming friends and the general public for many years. The fruity flavor of the **chicha de jora** *married to the very special aromatic flavor of the* **zapallo loche** *combine with the scallops to make a delicious rice dish which can be prepared in moments. Beer or wine and acorn or butternut squash will give good results, too. The secret, according to Olga, is to make sure that the rice stays very moist.*

Ingredients:

- 4 doz scallops
- 3 tbsp vegetable oil
- 1 tsp minced garlic
- 1 large onion, diced
- ½ tsp turmeric
- 1 ½ tbsp **ají amarillo** paste (p.228)
- 2 tbsp (50g) acorn or butternut squash
- 4 cups cooked white rice
- 3 cups fish stock
- 1 cup **chicha de jora**, white wine or beer
- 1 tbsp cilantro, chopped very fine
- ½ red bell pepper, cut into julienne
- 1 small **ají amarillo**, cut into julienne
- ¼ cup cooked peas
- 4 yellow potatoes, cooked and halved
- Salt

Garnish:

- Red bell pepper
- **Ají amarillo**
- Freshly chopped cilantro

Preparation

Heat oil in a large skillet and, over medium heat, sauté onion and garlic until golden, about 5 minutes. Grate the squash coarsely, (without peeling it) and add to the skillet along with turmeric and **ají amarillo** paste. Cook for a further 5 minutes.

Add rice, fish stock, **chicha de jora**, cilantro, red bell pepper, **ají amarillo**, cooked peas and salt to taste. Cook stirring continually until the rice grains just start to disintegrate, about 10 minutes. The mixture should have the consistency of a very moist and creamy risotto. Add more liquid as necessary and be careful to keep stirring the mixture so that it doesn't stick.

Add the cooked potatoes and finally the scallops. Cook for about 5 minutes or until the scallops just start to turn opaque.

Serve immediately, removing two scallops per serving and placing them on the side as a garnish. Sprinkle with finely chopped cilantro and garnish with sliced red bell pepper and **ají amarillo**.

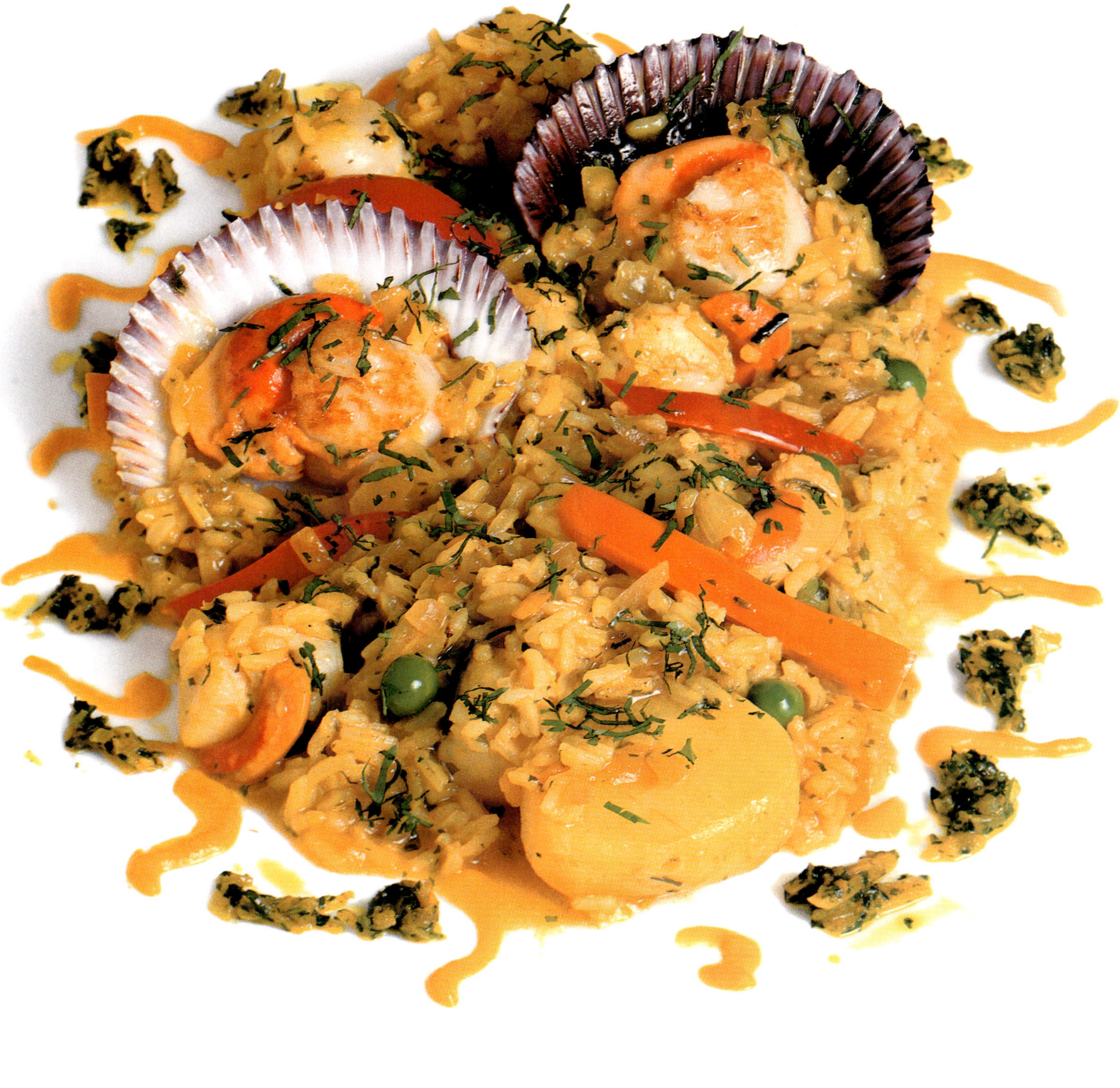

Arroz con Camarones

This is another recipe from master chef/restaurateur Alfredo Aramburú. Here he seasons the crayfish in this traditional rice dish with paprika and a hint of spicy rocoto. The flavor is deliciously enhanced by using the crayfish corals.

Ingredients:

- 2 cups rice
- 3 tbsp vegetable oil
- 1 medium red onion, chopped
- 3 cloves garlic, minced
- 2 tomatoes, peeled and chopped fine
- 1 ½ tbsp paprika
- ½ tsp dried oregano
- 2 bay leaves
- 1 tsp **rocoto** paste (p.230)
- ½ cup white wine
- 2 cups (400 g) peeled crayfish tails
- 1 tbsp crayfish corals
- 2 red bell peppers, peeled and diced fine
- 3 tbsp freshly chopped cilantro
- 1 cup fish stock or fumet
- Salt

Preparation

Cook rice, following recipe for **Arroz a la Peruana**, but without adding the corn kernels.

In a large pan, heat the oil and sauté onion, over medium heat, until translucent, about 3 minutes. Add garlic and continue cooking until ingredients are just turning golden, 1 or 2 more minutes.

Add tomato, paprika, bay leaves and oregano and cook for a further 5 minutes.

Add **rocoto** paste and white wine and cook, stirring, until all the liquid has evaporated. Remove the bay leaves.

Add crayfish tails and corals, stock or fumet and red bell pepper. Once the tails have turned pink, add cooked rice, cilantro and salt to taste. Mix well and serve immediately.

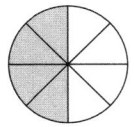

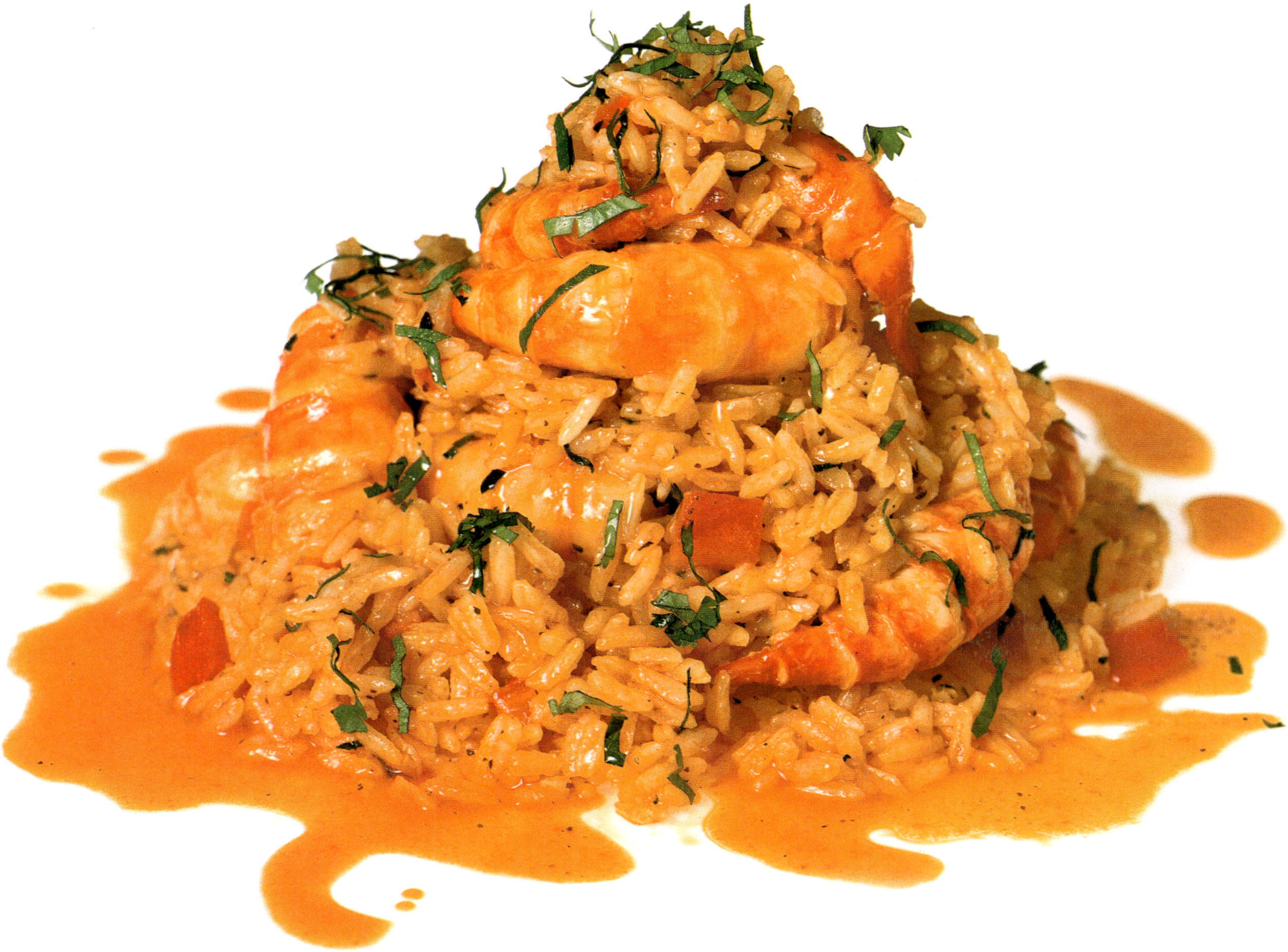

Arroz con Mariscos

Ingredients:

- 2 ¾ cups (600 g) raw mixed seafood (if using octopus it must be cooked previously)
- 2 cups rice
- 3 tbsp vegetable oil
- 1 medium red onion, chopped
- 3 cloves garlic, minced
- 1 tomato, peeled and chopped
- 1 ½ tbsp paprika
- ½ tsp dried oregano
- 2 bay leaves
- ¼ cup **achiote** oil (see recipe for **Adobo de Chancho** p.154)
- ¼ cup white wine
- ¼ cup chicken stock or consommé
- 1 red bell pepper, peeled and chopped
- 1 tbsp freshly chopped cilantro
- Salt and white pepper

The fishing grounds off the Peruvian Pacific coast are blessed with a great diversity of seafood. The meeting of two ocean currents - the southern Humboldt which brings cold water from the seas off the north of Chile, and the El Niño bringing warmer water from the north - provides a rich marine environment where 400 species of shellfish thrive. Alfredo Aramburú puts them to good use in another of his delicious seafood recipes.

Preparation

Cook rice, following recipe for **Arroz a la Peruana**, but without adding the corn kernels.

In a large pan, heat the oil and sauté onion, over medium heat, until translucent, about 3 minutes. Add garlic and continue cooking until ingredients are golden, 1 or 2 more minutes.

Add tomato, paprika, oregano, bay leaves and achiote oil and cook for a further 5 minutes. Add wine and cook, stirring, until all the liquid has evaporated. Remove the bay leaves.

Add the stock or consommé and bring back to a boil. Add the cooked rice, seafood, chopped red bell pepper, cilantro and salt and pepper to taste. Mix all ingredients well and serve immediately.

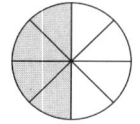

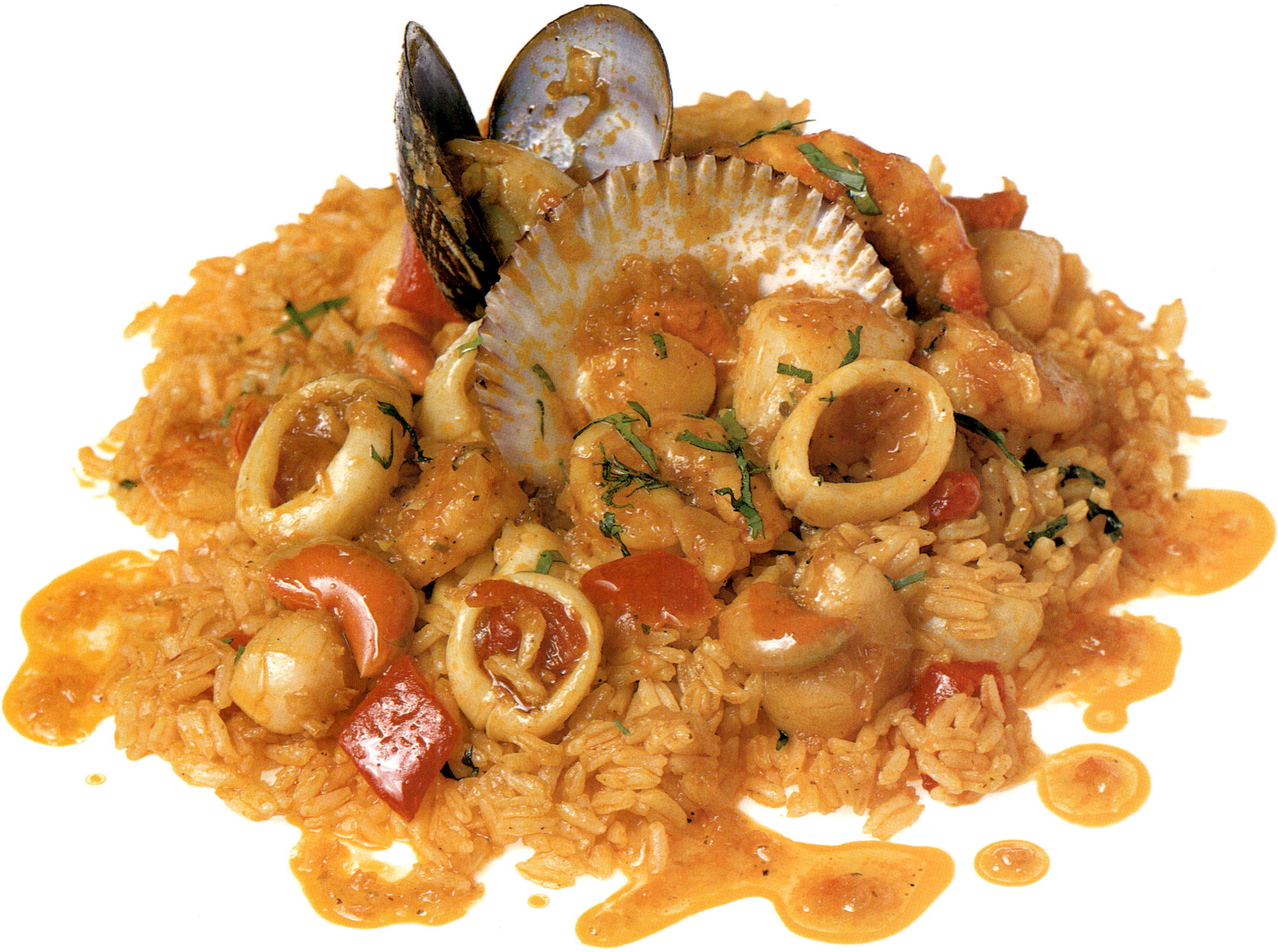

Arroz con Pato

Ingredients:

- 4 duck quarters (thigh and drumstick)
- 2 tbsp olive oil
- 2 tsp freshly ground pepper
- 2 tsp ground cumin
- 2 tsp crushed garlic
- 1 cup mirepoix
- 1 bouquet garni
- 4 cups white wine or dark beer
- 8 cups duck stock or 4 cups beef and 4 cups chicken stock
- Peel and juice of 2 oranges
- Salt

To make the rice:

- ½ cup olive oil
- 4 cups rice
- 2 red onions chopped fine
- 4 tbsp crushed garlic
- 4 heaped tbsp **ají amarillo** paste (p.228)
- 1 large red bell pepper, peeled and diced
- 4 large bunches fresh cilantro leaves
- 1 cup fresh peas and 1 cup fresh corn kernels (optional)
- 2 cups beer
- 8 cups beef or chicken stock

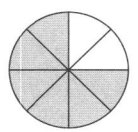

Duck is native to Peru and features in many dishes especially in the northern areas. **Arroz con Pato** *is a recipe that almost every Peruvian cook will know how to prepare. The rice in the dish absorbs the color and flavor of the cilantro. The traditional way to serve this dish is with duck but chicken is frequently substituted.*

Preparation

Season the duck pieces with salt and the freshly ground pepper, cumin, crushed garlic and the peel and juice of the orange. Set aside to stand for 15 minutes.

Heat 1 tbsp of olive oil in a large heavy-based skillet or roasting pan. Seal the duck pieces thoroughly for about eight minutes in all, skimming off as much of the fat as possible. When they are well-browned add the marinade juices plus the mirepoix and the bouquet garni. Add the wine or beer and reduce until about ¼ of the liquid remains.

Add the stock and bring back to a boil. Cover and simmer on low heat until the meat is tender and pulls away from the bone easily (about 2 ½ hours). Add more stock when necessary to ensure that the duck pieces are always covered. When the duck is cooked, remove from the skillet and leave it to cool for a while in order to make it easier to bone. De-fat and strain the cooking liquid and reserve.

Wash the cilantro leaves well, and blend in a mixer with a little water to make about one cup of purée. Reserve a few sprigs for garnishing.

In a large pan heat 2 tablespoons of olive oil and sauté the onion and garlic until they just start to turn golden. Add the **ají amarillo** and cilantro pastes, and season with salt and pepper. Add the rice and cook for a couple of minutes mixing to coat it well with the onion and seasonings. Then add the diced pepper. At this stage you can add corn kernels and peas if desired.

Add the beer and reduce until all the liquid has evaporated. Add, until rice is covered by 2 cm, the stock and some of the reserved strained cooking liquid from the duck for extra flavor. Be sure to leave some of the duck pan juices for serving at the end. Bring to a boil and then lower the heat to minimum and simmer, covered, for about 15 minutes until the rice is cooked. When cooked, separate the grains gently with a fork.

To bone the duck pieces insert a sharp filleting knife behind the drumstick and cut away the meat following the line of the bone. Chop some of the meat into bite size pieces and combine with the rice. Slice the rest and reserve. To serve, place rice on a warmed plate, arrange the sliced duck on top and drizzle with the warm pan juices.

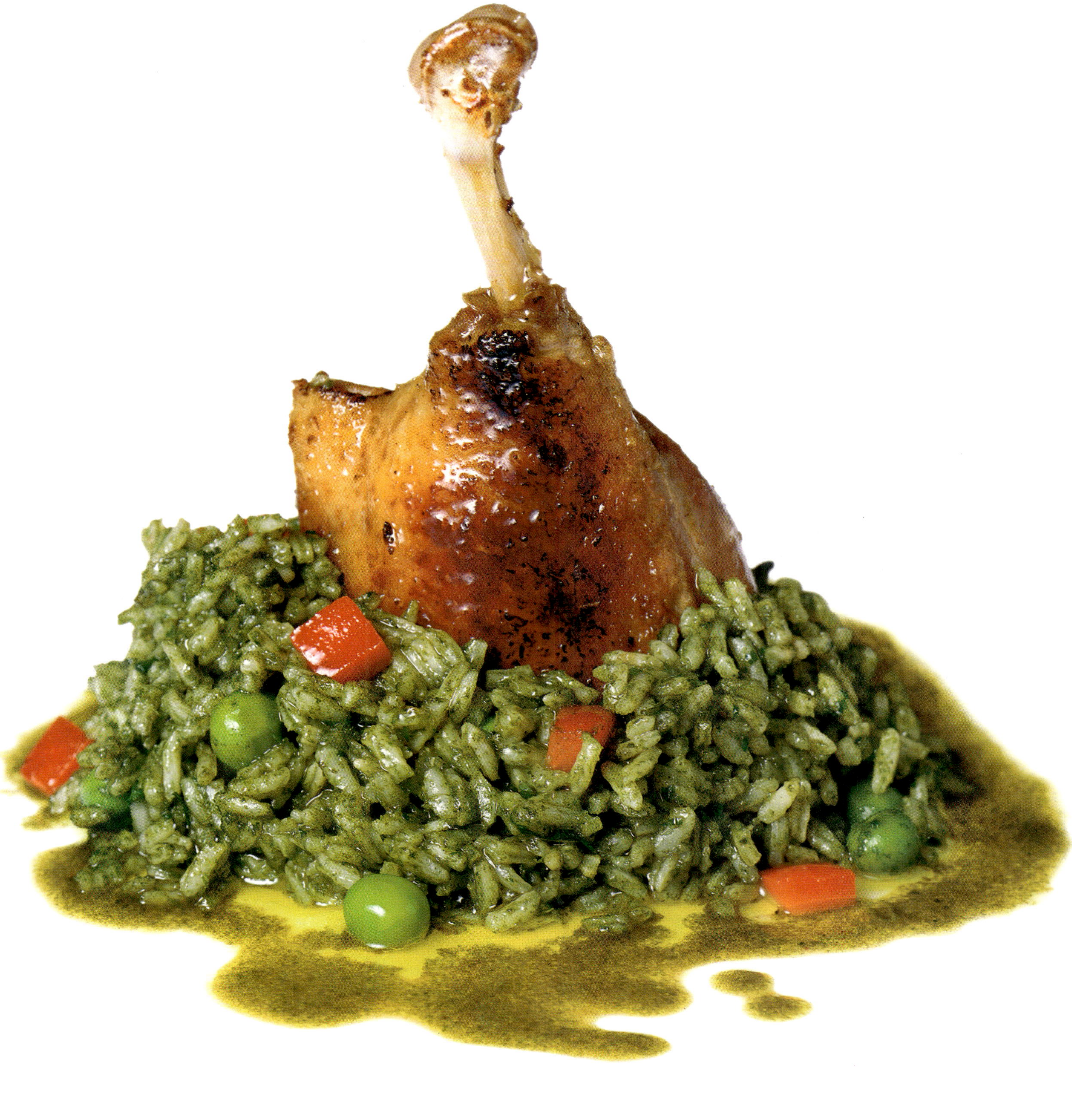

CARAPULCA

Ingredients:

- 2 lb (1 kg) lean pork
- 1 lb (½ kg) dried potato pieces
- 3 tbsp oil or lard
- 2 red onions, chopped
- 1 tbsp crushed garlic
- ¼ tsp cumin
- 3 tbsp **ají panca** paste (p.228)
- 2 sprigs fresh cilantro
- 10 sweet butter cookies, ground
- 2 cloves
- ½ cup port
- 1 square of unsweetened chocolate, grated
- ¼ cup peanuts, roasted and finely chopped
- Salt and pepper

*Kalapurka, as this dish was known to the Quechuas, is one of Peru's most ancient dishes. Named for the hot stones or 'kalas' that were used for cooking, it was originally prepared with dried potato and dried meat (**charqui**). It was also one of the first dishes the Spanish really took to and adapted. Historian Ricardo Palma tells of a huge banquet given in 1608 to celebrate the reconciliation between quarrelling factions within the church, where **Carapulca** was served with rabbit.*

Preparation

Toast the dried potato pieces in a dry skillet over high heat for about five minutes. Shake the skillet from time to time to prevent them from burning and be careful not to let them get too brown. Remove from the skillet and cover with double their volume in hot water. Soak for ½ hour.

Cut the pork into small chunks or short strips. Heat the oil in a large pan over medium heat and brown the pork pieces well on all sides, about 15 minutes. Remove from the pan with a slotted spoon.

In the same pan sauté the onion with the garlic, cumin and **aji panca** paste in the pork fat, until the onion is browned, about 5 minutes. Season with salt and pepper.

Add the browned meat and the dried potato along with its soaking liquid to the pan. Cover and simmer on low heat until the potato is tender, about 40 minutes. If the **carapulca** dries out add some stock or water; keep stirring from time to time to ensure that it doesn't burn.

When the potato is cooked, add the wine, cloves, chopped cilantro, grated chocolate, ground biscuits and chopped peanuts. Cook for a further 15 minutes and adjust seasonings.

Allow to rest for ½ hour before serving. Reheat and serve hot accompanied by white rice.

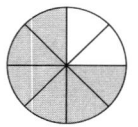

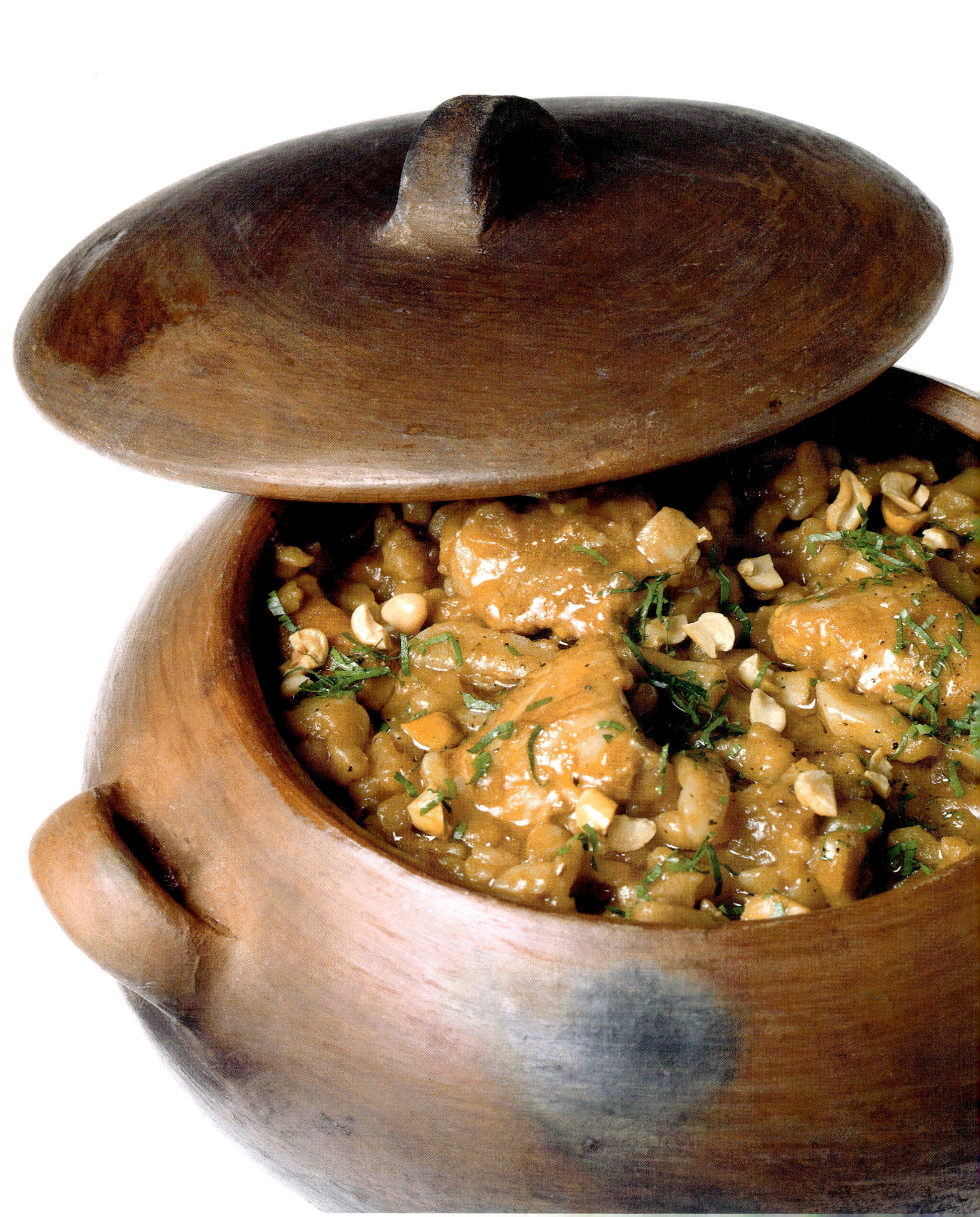

Cau Cau de Mariscos

Ingredients:

- 6 ½ oz (200 g) cooked octopus, sliced
- 6 ½ oz (200 g) raw scallops
- 2 tbsp vegetable oil
- 1 medium red onion, chopped
- 2 tsp minced garlic
- 1 tsp turmeric powder
- 1 ½ cups fish stock
- ½ cup cooked peas
- ¼ cup cooked carrots, diced fine
- 2 medium white potatoes, boiled and diced
- ½ cup cooked corn kernels
- 1 tsp ground fresh **ají limo**
- 3 small sprigs fresh mint, chopped
- 4 cups cooked rice (see **Arroz a la Peruana** p.225)
- Salt and freshly ground pepper

Cau Cau, the original **Rachi Rachi** *tripe and potato stew of the Incas, is eaten in exactly the same form by modern day Peruvians. Here it gets dressed up for dinner and given an elegant twist with the inclusion of octopus and scallops by seafood master chef Luis Enrique Cordero of 'Kapallaq'.*

Preparation

In an earthenware casserole or large heavy skillet, heat oil and sauté onion until translucent, about 3 minutes. Add garlic and continue cooking for another couple of minutes until the mixture starts to color. Add turmeric and cook for a further 2 to 3 minutes.

Add scallops and cooked octopus and cook for 3 minutes.

Add stock, peas, potato, corn kernels, carrots, salt and freshly ground pepper to taste. Bring back to the boil and simmer for 8 minutes. Just before serving add **ají** and mint. Stir through and serve immediately over rice.

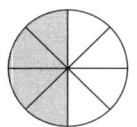

Tip: If a thicker stew is desired add a little cornstarch, dissolved in cold water, along with the stock and vegetables.

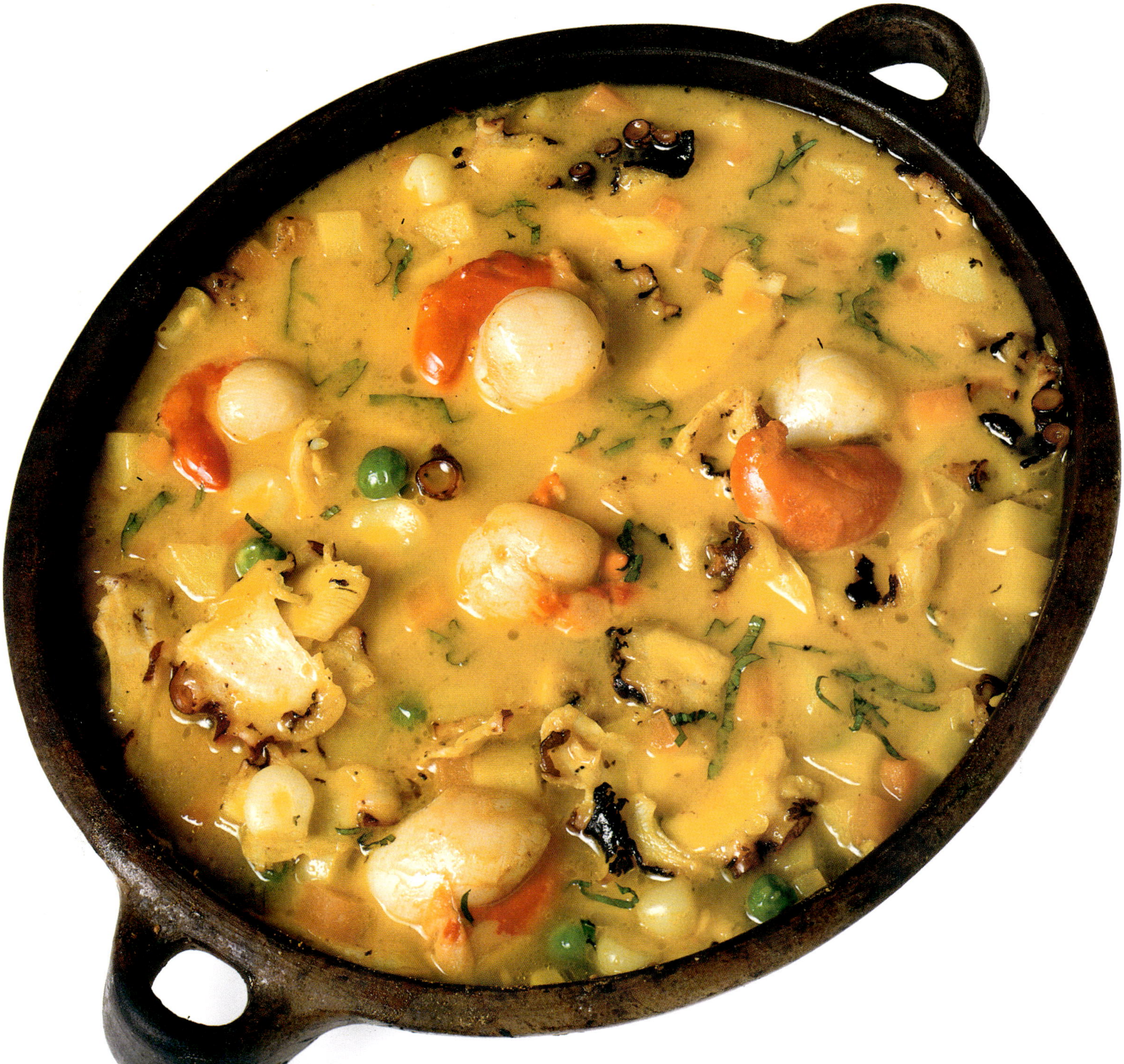

CHICHARRÓN DE CHANCHO

Ingredients:

- 4 ½ lbs (2 kg) pork ribs
- 2 tbsp rock salt
- Water

To serve:

- Fried sliced sweet potato
- **Salsa criolla** (p.232)

Another traditional recipe from Andrea Graña. On Sunday mornings Limeños will head out to the coastal suburbs to eat **chicharrones** *for brunch. These crisp and succulent pork pieces are cooked in large pans over a wood fire in the open air 'chicharronerías' and served with crusty bread, a zesty* **salsa criolla** *and freshly brewed strong coffee. Despite appearances a good* **chicharrón** *is almost all meat.*

Preparation

Chop the pork ribs into 4 in -(10 cm-) long pieces and place in a large, heavy-based pan (teflon finish if possible). Add salt.

Add enough water to cover ribs. Bring to a boil, lower heat to medium and simmer, tightly covered, until all the water has evaporated and the pork begins to render its fat, about 1 hour.

Remove cover and continue cooking ribs in their own fat until they are golden and crispy on the outside and the meat is tender. Turn the ribs to ensure that they brown all over.

Remove ribs from the pan with a slotted spoon, drain on paper towel, cut or break apart into smaller pieces and serve accompanied by fried sweet potato rounds or chips and **salsa criolla**.

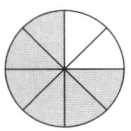

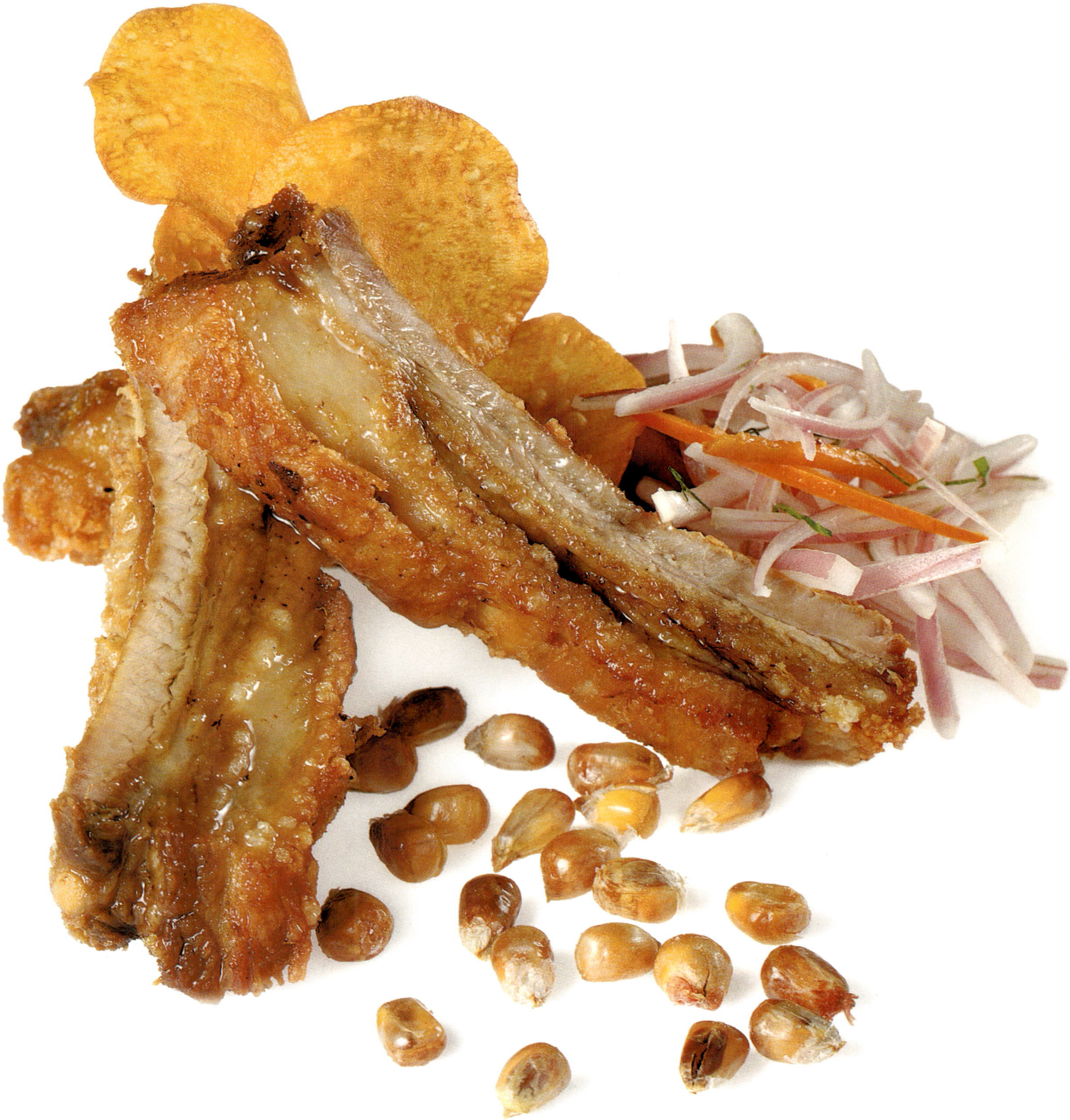

CHITA REFRITA

*When Lucho Cordero chef/owner of 'Kapallaq' talks about the simple rustic dishes such as this fried fish which are traditionally eaten by fishermen in the small coastal towns of Peru, his great love and respect for the sea shines through. His version of **salsa criolla** combines a mixture of fresh vegetables which makes a perfect accompaniment for the fish.*

Ingredients:

- 2 whole chitas (about 2 lb / 1 kg in weight each) cleaned, scaled and gutted
- 2 tsp crushed garlic
- ½ tsp freshly ground pepper
- 4 tsp soy sauce
- Vegetable oil for frying
- Salt

To make the **salsa criolla**:

- 2 small red onions cut into very fine slices
- ½ cup cooked peas
- ½ tomato, peeled seeded and finely diced
- 1 tbsp vinegar
- 1 tsp freshly ground pepper
- ½ cup cooked fresh corn kernels
- **Ají limo** paste (1 tsp - 1 tbsp depending on how hot you want your salsa)
- 4 or 5 sprigs of Italian flat leaf parsley, chopped
- Juice of two key limes
- Salt

Preparation

Mix the crushed garlic with the soy sauce, salt and freshly ground pepper.

Make three diagonal surface cuts on each side of the fish and smear all over with the garlic and soy sauce mixture.

Heat a generous amount of vegetable oil in a large skillet until very hot and fry the fish for about 8 to 10 minutes, turning carefully once, until they are deep golden and crispy. Constantly baste each side with the hot oil by using a spoon to bathe the fish as it cooks.

Drain on kitchen paper and serve immediately, accompanied by the **salsa criolla**.

To make the salsa criolla:

In a bowl combine the onion slices with the vinegar and key-lime juice. Add the **ají limo** paste, salt and pepper, tomato, cooked peas and cooked corn kernels. Allow to stand and, just before serving, add the chopped parsley.

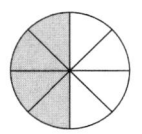

Note: To make the **ají limo** paste, stem, seed and devein fresh **ají limo** and blend with a little water.

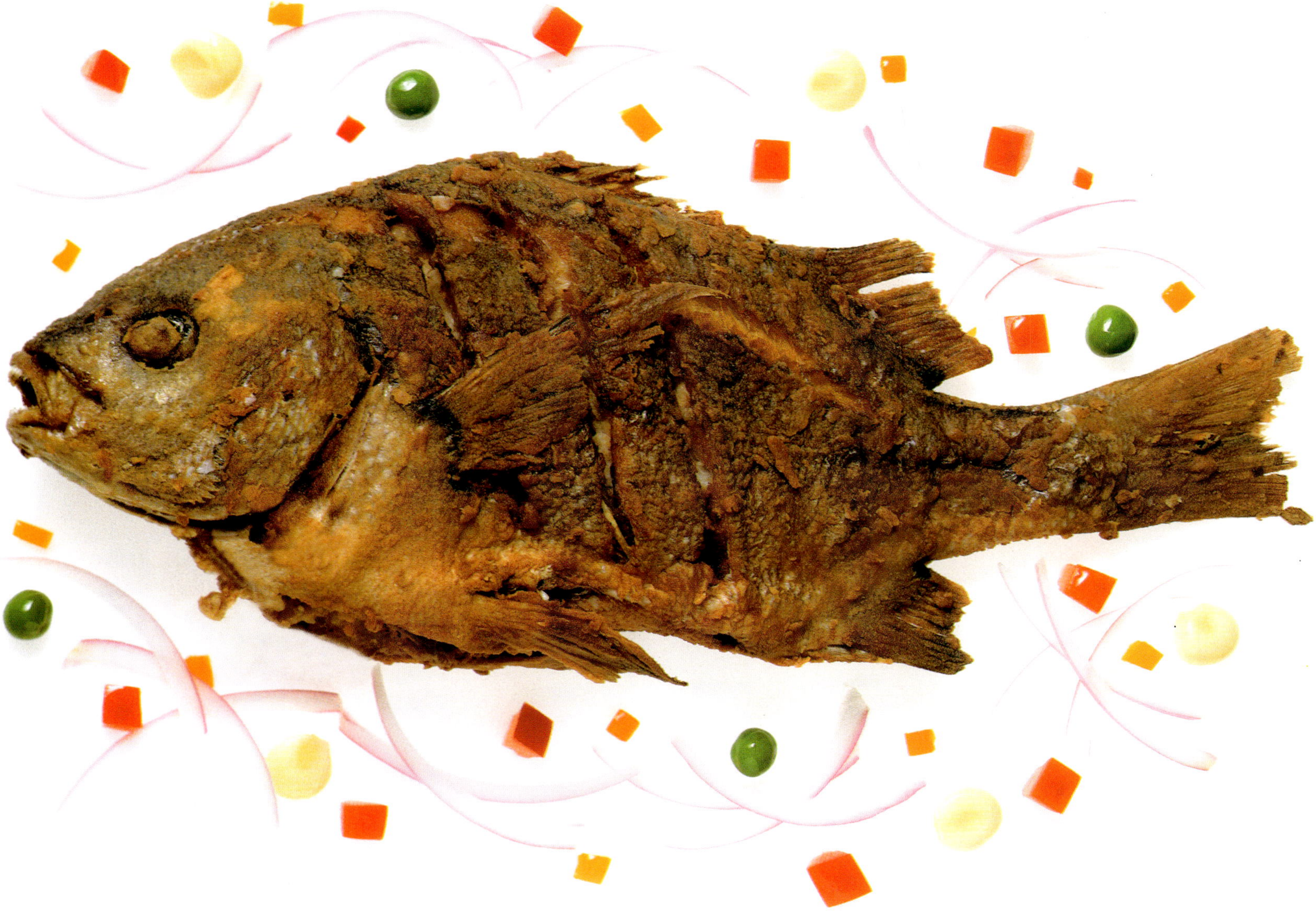

Corvina a la Chorrillana

Cooking fish 'a la Chorillana' originated in the small fishing village of Chorillos, now a suburb south of Lima. Fresh grilled fish is paired with a spicy onion and tomato sauce. This is Alfredo Aramburú's version.

Ingredients:

- 4 sea bass fillets (about ½ lb / 200 g each)
- 2 tbsp vegetable oil
- 1 tbsp butter
- 1 tsp minced garlic
- 2 medium red onions, sliced
- 2 bay leaves
- 1 ½ tbsp paprika
- 2 tbsp all purpose flour
- 2 **ajíes amarillo**, seeded and finely sliced
- 1 red bell pepper, peeled and diced
- 2 tbsp white wine vinegar
- ½ cup dry white wine
- 1 cup fish stock or consommé
- 3 tomatoes, peeled, seeded and quartered
- 1 tbs freshly chopped cilantro
- ¼ cup cooked peas
- ½ tsp dried oregano

Preparation

Heat oil and butter and sauté garlic and onion over medium heat until golden, about 5 minutes. Add paprika and flour and mix well. Add bay leaves, red bell pepper, wine, vinegar, fish stock or consommé and fresh ají amarillo. Continue cooking, stirring occasionally, until the liquid has reduced and the sauce coats the back of a spoon, about 5 minutes.

Add cooked peas, freshly chopped cilantro, tomato and oregano. Cook for a few more minutes until the tomatoes are warmed through. Remove bay leaves.

Cook the fish fillets on a griddle for about 3 minutes each side, brushing with oil to prevent them from sticking. Serve immediately topped with the warm sauce.

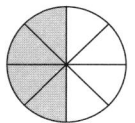

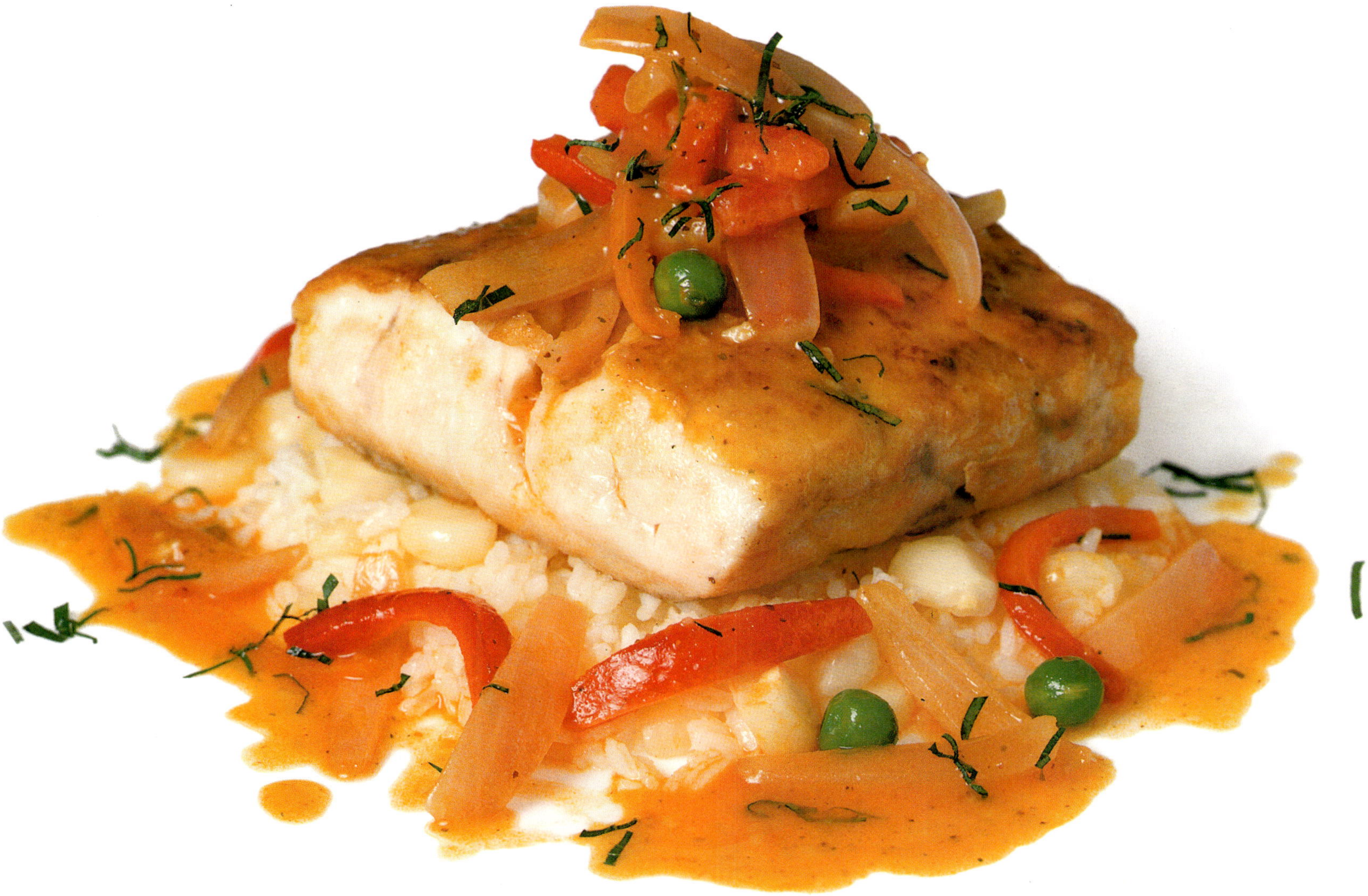

Diversión de Conejo con Ñoquis de Yuca

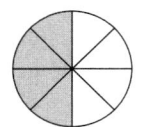

*This trio of rabbit preparations is another spectacular Gastón Acurio recipe. His colorful and delicious **diversión** or 'entertainment' pairs this delicate white meat with the assorted flavors and textures of pine nuts, swiss chard and a fruity apricot sauce. All accompanied by pesto-stuffed gnocchis.*

Ingredients

For the rabbit:
- 1 rabbit, about 3 lbs (1½ kg), cut in pieces
- ¾ lb (300 g) swiss chard (silver beet)
- ¼ cup (100 g) pine (piñon) nuts
- Scant 2 tbsp (50 g) butter
- 1 ¼ cups chicken stock
- Salt and freshly ground pepper

For the gnocchi:
- ¾ cup (300 g) cooked and mashed yuca
- ¾ cup (300 g) cooked and mashed yellow potatoes
- ¼ cup (100 g) sifted, all purpose flour
- 2 eggs, beaten
- ¼ cup (100 g) pesto
- 3 tbsp (85 g) butter
- ½ cup heavy cream
- Parmesan cheese, grated
- Salt

For the sauce:
- 3 ½ tbsp (100 g) apricot preserves
- 2 tbsp chicken stock
- Fresh tarragon
- Scant 2 tbsp (50 g) butter

Preparation

To prepare the rabbit:
Separate the rabbit forelegs, hind legs, loin piece and ribs. Melt butter in a small pan over medium heat and sauté swiss chard together with the pine nuts and salt and pepper to taste. Trim rabbit loin from the bone and lay on a flat surface. Spread with the swiss chard mixture, roll up and tie with kitchen twine at 2in-(5cm-) intervals. Preheat oven to 350ºF / 180ºC. Place stuffed rabbit loin into a baking dish and brush with a little vegetable oil or melted butter. Bake in the preheated oven for about 40 minutes or until juices run clear. Grill rabbit ribs for a few minutes each side, set aside and keep warm.

In a heavy-based pan, over medium heat, melt the butter and the oil and brown remaining rabbit pieces all over. Add chicken stock and bring to a boil. Reduce the heat, cover and simmer gently on very low heat for about 20 minutes until the rabbit is tender. (The timing will depend on the age and size of the rabbit.)

To make the gnocchi:
Mix the mashed potato and yuca together thoroughly and place in a mound on a work surface. Make a well in the center and add a small handful of flour, the beaten egg yolks and salt to taste. Fold mixture together, gently bringing the dry ingredients towards the center, gradually adding just the necessary amount of flour to make a fine soft dough. Too much flour will make the gnocchis tough. Once dough has come together, let the mixture rest for 5 minutes. Dust hands with more flour and place about 1 ½ tsp of the mixture in the palm of your hand, add a little pesto and bring mixture together to surround and form an individual gnocchi. Bring a large pot of salted water to a rolling boil and poach gnocchi until they rise to the surface. Meanwhile place butter in a small pan on high heat until it turns a nut-brown color. Turn off heat. Toss gnocchi in butter, drizzle with a little heavy cream and sprinkle with Parmesan.

To make the sauce:
Heat the apricot preserve with the chicken stock in a heavy-based pan and reduce by ½ over medium heat (about 10 minutes). Finally whisk in the butter and remove from the heat.

To serve:
Arrange sliced stuffed rabbit loin, ribs and a leg on each plate. Serve with the gnocchi, drizzled with a little of the warm apricot sauce.

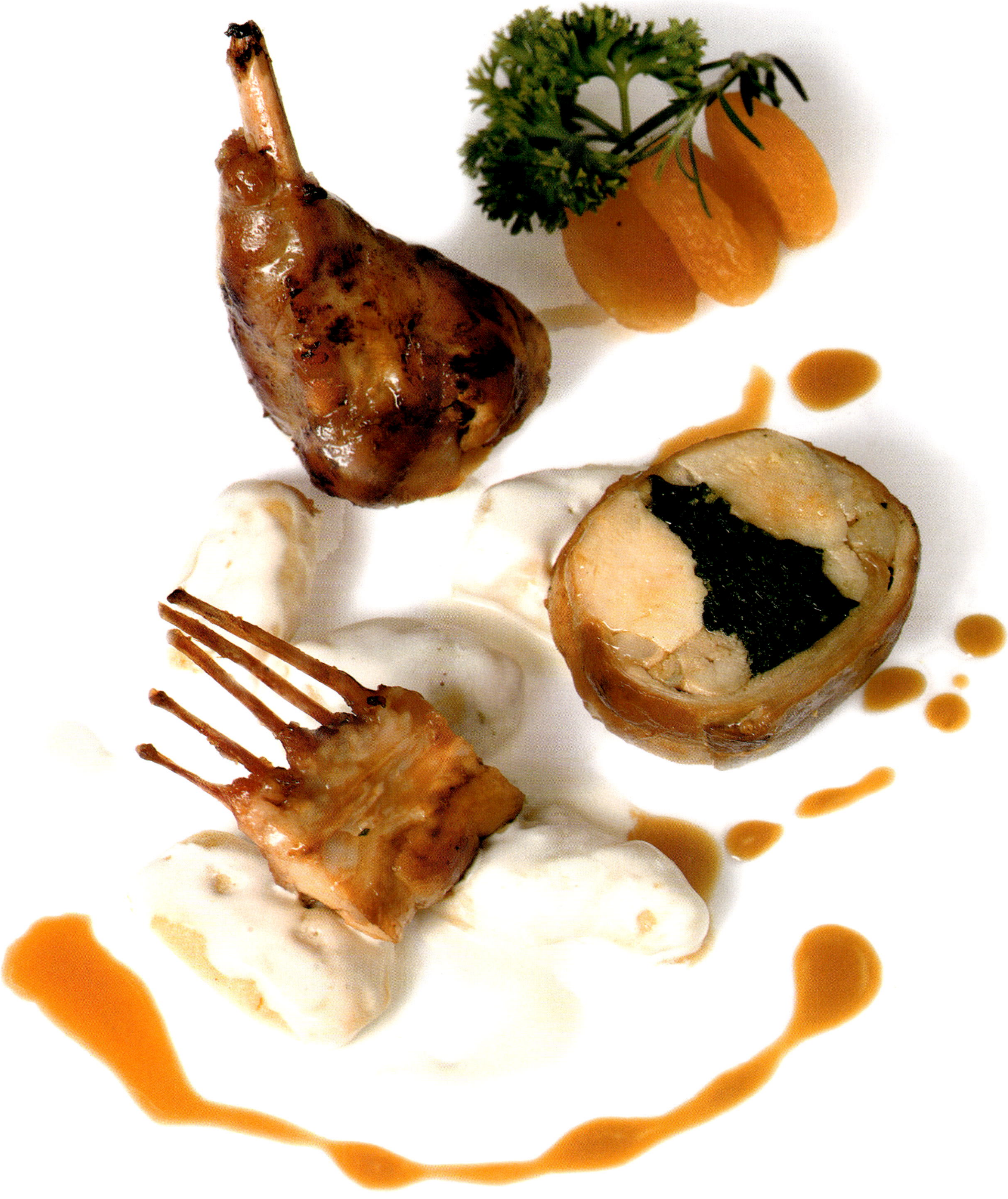

Foie Gras con Tacu Tacu de Lentejas

*This is one of Coque's wonderful 'nouvelle cuisine péruvienne' dishes served at 'Le Bistrot de mes Fils'. The pairing of lentils with foie gras and fruit works particularly well. The result is a spectacularly innovative way to serve traditional Peruvian **tacu tacu**.*

Ingredients:

For the salad:
- ¼ cup (50 g) cooked brown lentils
- 1 tbsp chopped onion
- 1 tbsp freshly chopped cilantro
- 1 tbsp freshly chopped parsley
- ½ tbsp chopped banana
- 1 tbsp peeled and diced red bell pepper
- 1 tbsp balsamic vinegar
- 2 tsp olive oil
- 1 tbsp chopped tomato
- One 2 oz (50 g) piece of foie gras
- Pinch fresh oregano, chopped
- Pinch fresh thyme, chopped
- Salt and pepper

For the tacu tacu:
- ¼ cup (50 g) brown lentils
- ½ cup (100 g) cooked white rice
- 1 tbsp vegetable oil
- 2 tbsp chopped onion
- 1 tbsp minced garlic
- ½ tsp dried oregano
- 1 tsp **ají panca** paste (p.228)
- 2 lady finger bananas

For the sauce:
- 1 glass port, reduced
- 2 tbsp concentrated beef stock
- 1 tsp butter

Serves 1

Preparation

To make the lentil salad:
In a bowl, combine cooked lentils, onion, red bell pepper, parsley, tomato, cilantro and banana. Add herbs, a few drops of sherry vinegar, balsamic vinegar, olive oil and salt and freshly ground pepper. Toss all ingredients well.

For the foie gras:
Clean the liver well and score with a sharp knife. Sear in a pan with a little oil.

For the Oporto sauce:
In a small pan, reduce the port, add the beef stock, reduce and stir in a little butter. Adjust seasonings, adding salt.

For the tacu tacu:
Cook lentils until soft, about 40 minutes. Blend just a couple of spoonfuls of the lentils to make a little purée. Leave remaining lentils intact.

In a large skillet, heat oil and sauté onion and garlic, over medium heat until just starting to turn golden, about 4 minutes. Add the lentils and lentil purée. Add the rice and mix well.

Heat a thin film of olive oil covering the base of a teflon pan. Place the **tacu tacu** mixture 3 - 4 in-(8 - 10 cm-) in diameter in the pan (as if making a small thick tortilla) and cook for a few minutes. Gently lift the edges to see if it is browned. When browned on one side, carefully flip over to cook the other side. Slide on to a plate.

Slice and fry the lady finger bananas and place on top. Then spoon on a layer of lentil salad. Finally, top with the foie gras.

Serve with the port sauce.

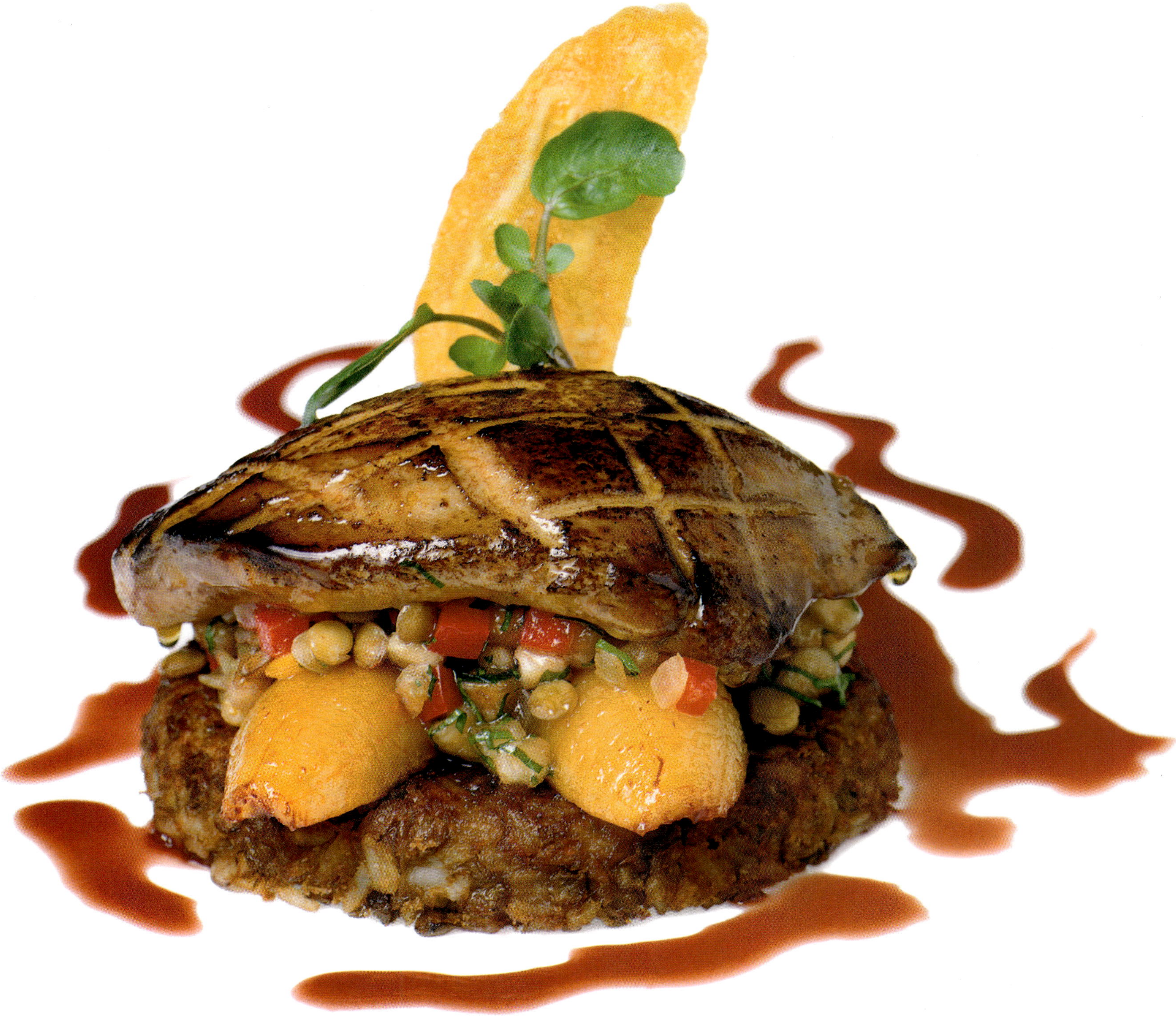

Huátia Sulcana

Ingredients:

- 2 lbs (1 kg) rib eye roast
- ¼ cup vegetable oil
- 1 tbsp minced garlic
- 2 tbsp **ají panca** paste (p.228)
- 2 tsp freshly ground pepper
- ¼ cup red wine vinegar
- 1 lb (½ kg) red onions, sliced
- 1 cup cilantro leaves
- ¼ cup fresh rosemary
- ¼ cup fresh oregano
- ½ cup fresh mint
- 2 ajíes amarillo, seeded and sliced
- Salt

*This is a very special recipe from Isabel Alvarez at her restaurant 'Señorío de Sulco'. In ancient Peru, before the advent of ceramics, stews or **huatias** would be cooked in hollowed out squash or pumpkin called **mates**. Because they couldn't withstand direct heat the food was cooked by placing hot stones or **kalas** inside the **mate** along with the ingredients. Nowadays the container may be different, but the robust and lively flavors of this slow cooked rustic stew make it a winner for both family meals and entertaining.*

Preparation

Heat oil in a deep, heavy, flameproof casserole or stock pot. Sauté garlic and **ají panca** paste over medium heat until garlic is golden, about 5 minutes. Season with salt and pepper.

Remove from heat. Add vinegar, onion, **ají amarillo**, rosemary, cilantro and oregano. Mix well to combine ingredients. Add meat, place mint leaves on top and cover pot tightly.

Cook over low heat for 1½ to 2 hours, making sure that the pot is tightly covered. If, by any chance, the steam should escape during cooking and the stew starts to dry out, add a little stock.

When meat is cooked, remove from pan, slice and serve hot with cooking sauce, accompanied by baked sweet potatoes.

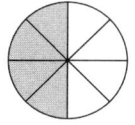

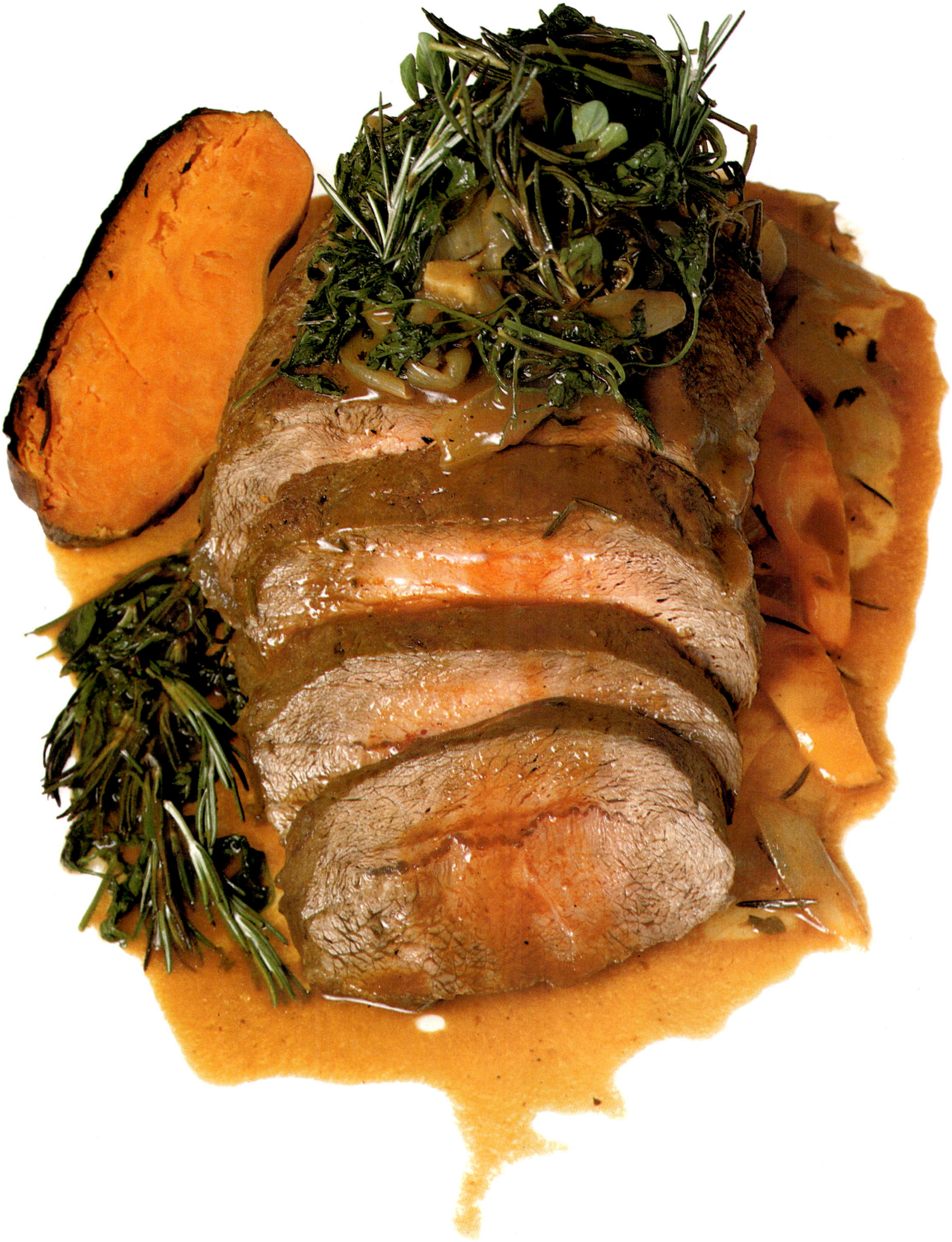

Lechón Confitado con Especias

Ingredients:

- 2 legs of suckling pig of about 1½ lb (700 g) each
- 1 tbsp coriander seeds
- 1 tbsp star anise
- 1 tbsp fennel seeds
- 1 tbsp allspice
- 1 tbsp cumin
- 1 tbsp powdered ginger
- 2 cups (½ ltr) duck fat
- Salt

For the sauce:

- 2 cups (½ ltr) pork pan juices
- 1 **rocoto** seeded, deveined and puréed in blender
- 1 tbsp honey
- 1 tbsp maple syrup
- 2 tbsp white vinegar
- 3 ½ oz (100 g) butter

For the rösti:

- 2 lb (1 kg) **tomasa** (white) potatoes
- 1 red onion, chopped fine
- 3 ½ oz (100 g) bacon, chopped
- 7 oz (200 g) **callampas** or **portobello** mushrooms, sliced fine
- Clarified butter

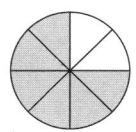

This recipe comes to us from Gáston Acurio, a graduate of the Cordon Bleu School of Cooking in Paris and chef/owner of one of Lima's premier international restaurants, "Astrid y Gastón".

Preparation

Toast the spices lightly and grind in a spice mill or food processor.

Reserve about 1 tbsp of the spice mixture for the sauce and rub remaining spices over pork. Leave overnight.

The next day lift pork from the spices. Preheat oven to 212º F / 100º C. Cook pork in a slow oven with the duck fat for 2 ½ hours. Remove from the oven, set aside and reserve roasting juices.

To make the sauce:
Over medium heat reduce the honey with the vinegar, adding the pan juices from the pork and the **rocoto** purée. At the end whisk in butter and add the reserved spices.

To make the rösti:
Boil the potatoes and, when cool, grate coarsely. Sauté mushrooms, onion and bacon in a skillet until the onions are golden, about 5 minutes. Mix in the grated potatoes and season with salt and freshly ground pepper to taste.

Heat a little clarified butter in a separate teflon frying pan. Add a little of the rösti mixture and brown lightly on both sides giving it the form of a thick round "cake", very crisp and golden on the outside and soft on the inside.

Before serving, put the pork in a very hot oven (approximately 450ºF / 232ºC) for 10 minutes to caramelize the skin. Serve on top of the rösti surrounded by the sauce.

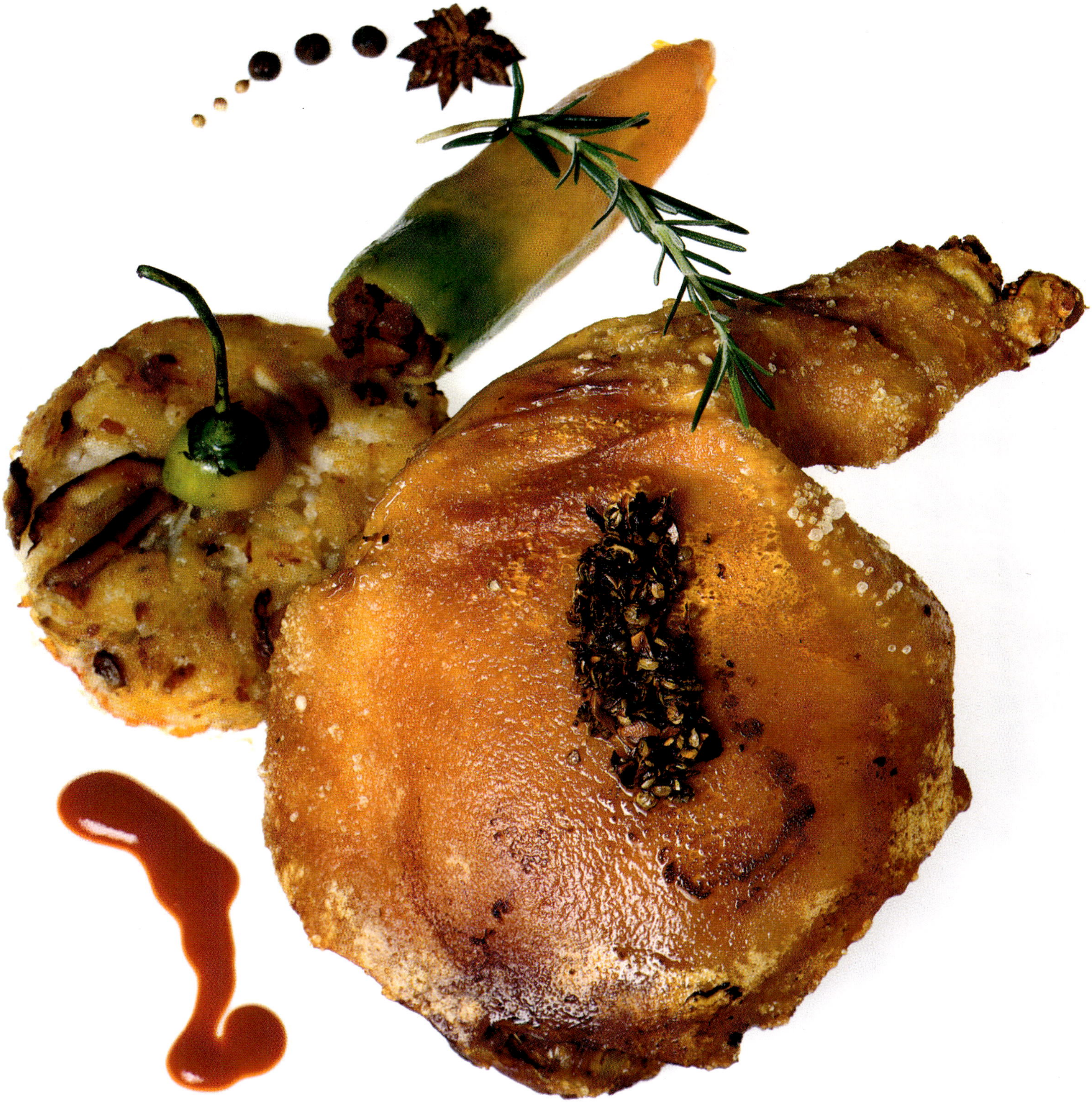

Lechón Macerado con Frutas al Pisco

Ingredients:

- 4 lb (2kg) leg of pork
- ½ tbsp minced garlic
- 1 tbsp freshly ground pepper
- ½ tsp cumin
- 4 tsp **ají amarillo** paste (p.228)
- 1 tbsp soy sauce
- 2 tbsp sugar
- ½ tbsp fresh rosemary
- ½ tbsp fresh oregano
- Juice of 1 key lime
- Salt

For the pisco:

- 2 cups pisco
- ½ cup raisins
- ½ cup dried apricots
- ¼ cup pitted prunes
  (Place all ingredients in a sealed jar and let marinate for two weeks)

This is a very typical celebration dish in Peru. A suckling pig or leg of pork is always preferred for parties and special occasions. At 'Señorío de Sulco', Isabel Alvarez' son, Flavio Solorzano, gives us this recipe, in which the pisco-marinated fruits give the pork a special touch. Note that you'll need to marinate the fruits in pisco two weeks prior to cooking this dish.

Preparation

Rub pork leg all over with key lime juice. Set aside to rest for 3 hours. Pre heat oven to 300ºF / 150ºC. Combine all other ingredients in a bowl (except the pisco mixture) and mix well.

Place sauce in the base of a roasting pan and lay pork leg on top. Roast for approximately two hours or until juices run clear. Add more liquid to the sauce as necessary to keep it moist but do not baste; the pork should be very crispy on top.

Remove from oven and set aside pork leg. Scrape sauce from the roasting pan and blend. Return to a small pan and reheat. Adjust seasoning and add pisco-marinated fruits. Simmer for a few more minutes to heat through and finally add pisco. Remove from heat.

Slice pork and serve with warm sauce.

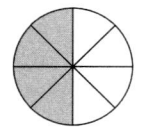

Note: This recipe also gives spectacular results made with a suckling pig. Adjust the quantities and cooking time accordingly.

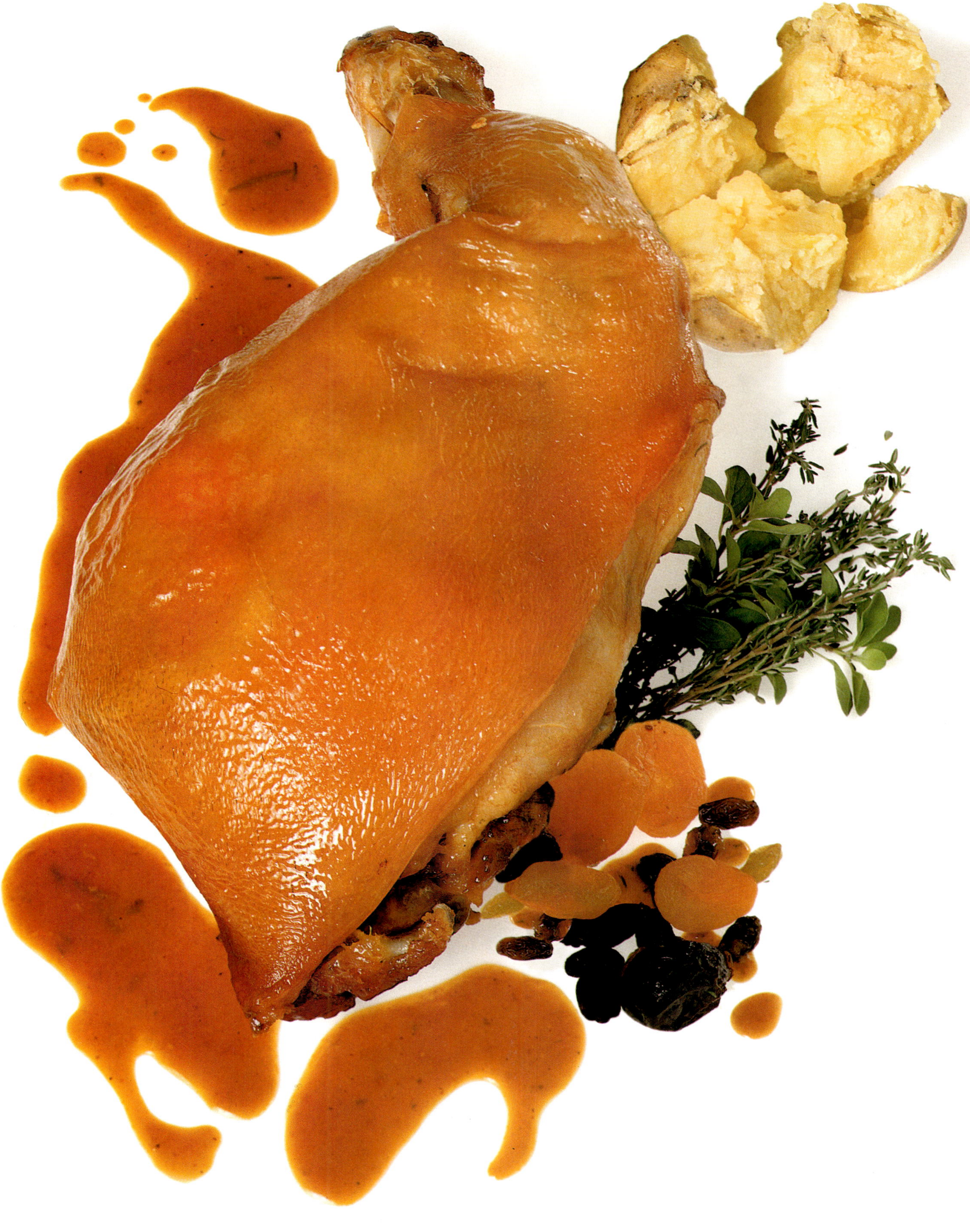

Lenguado a lo Macho

This is another of Alfredo Aramburú's delicious fish dishes. I'm not sure whether the name of the dish refers to how hardy ('macho') you need to be to eat all that seafood or to the possible results of doing so.

Ingredients:

- 4 flounder fillets, approximately ½ lb (200 g) each
- ¾-1 lb (400 g) mixed raw seafood
- 2 tbsp butter
- 2 medium red onions, chopped fine
- 3 cloves garlic, minced
- 2 tsp all purpose flour
- 2 oz (¼ cup) dry white wine
- 1 cup (¼ ltr) chicken consommé
- ½ cup cream
- ½ cup evaporated milk
- 1 ½ tbsp paprika or cayenne pepper
- 1 tbsp finely chopped cilantro
- ½ tsp **rocoto** paste (p.230)
- 1 red bell pepper, peeled and diced
- Pinch dried oregano
- Tomatoes, peeled, seeded and chopped
- Salt and pepper

Preparation

Melt the butter in a medium-sized skillet. Over medium heat sauté the onion, garlic, oregano, and paprika or cayenne pepper for about 4 minutes until the onion is translucent and starting to turn golden.

Add the tomato and flour and cook for an additional 2 or 3 minutes.

Add the wine and simmer until nearly all the liquid has evaporated. Add chicken consommé and bring to a boil. Add the cream, evaporated milk and the seafood and cook until the seafood turns opaque, about 3 minutes. Remove from heat and keep warm.

Cook the fish fillets on a griddle, 3 minutes a side.

Just before serving, return the sauce to the heat. Add salt, pepper, rocoto paste, red bell pepper and cilantro and stir well.

Transfer the fillets to individual plates and serve topped with the seafood sauce.

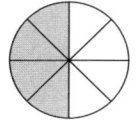

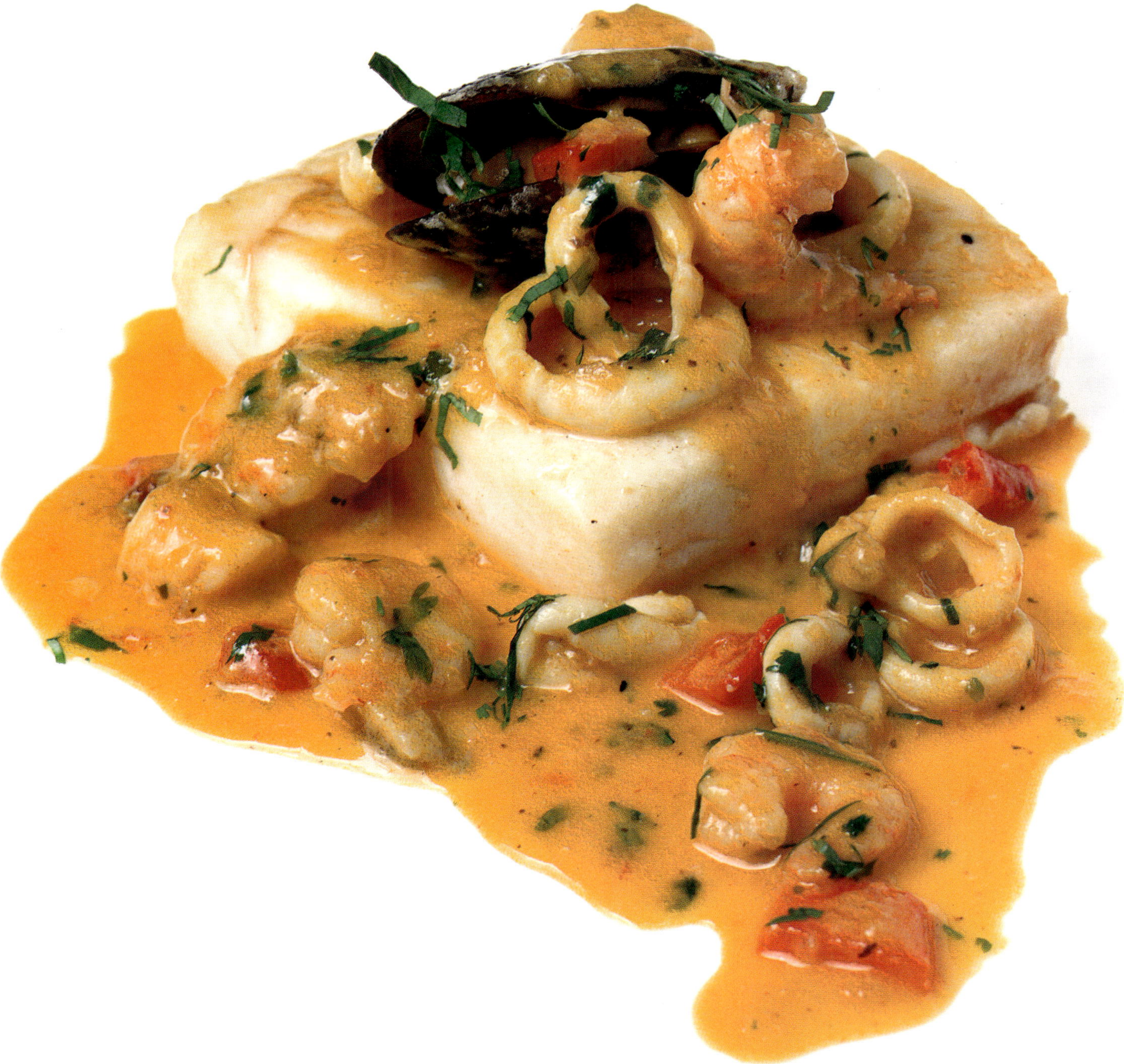

Locro de Camarones

*Locro is a pre-Columbian stew, eaten pretty much in the same form now in Peru as it has been for centuries. It's an evolution from the even more ancient pre-Inca **Rokro** which was traditionally made from potatoes, **ají** and any other single ingredient.*

Ingredients:

- ¼ cup vegetable oil
- 1 small red onion, chopped
- 3 cloves garlic, crushed
- ½ tsp dried oregano
- 3 lbs (1½ kg) pumpkin, peeled and chopped
- 3 white potatoes, peeled and chopped (optional)
- 1½ cups fresh corn kernels
- 1 cup fresh peas
- 4 tbsp butter
- 4 doz crayfish tails, peeled and cleaned
- 2 cups chicken stock
- 3 oz (100 g) fresh white cheese, crumbled
- ½ cup cream
- **Ají amarillo** paste (p.228)
- Salt and pepper

Garnish:

- Cilantro chopped fine
- Fresh white cheese cubes or slices

Preparation

Heat the oil in a large heavy based pan and, over medium heat, sauté the onion with the garlic, **ají amarillo** paste, oregano, and salt and pepper until just turning golden, about 5 minutes.

Add the pumpkin, peas, corn kernels, and the potato if you are using it.

Add chicken stock. Cover and leave to simmer on low heat until all ingredients are well cooked and the pumpkin is beginning to dissolve, adding more liquid as necessary, for about 30 minutes.

Meanwhile, in a separate skillet, sauté the crayfish tails in the butter only until they've just turned pink, season with salt, pepper and a little lemon juice to taste.

When everything is cooked, add the white cheese and milk. Then add the sautéed crayfish tails, reserving some for decoration.

Pile onto a serving dish and garnish with white cheese cubes or slices and the reserved sautéed crayfish tails. Sprinkle with fresh chopped cilantro.

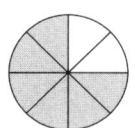

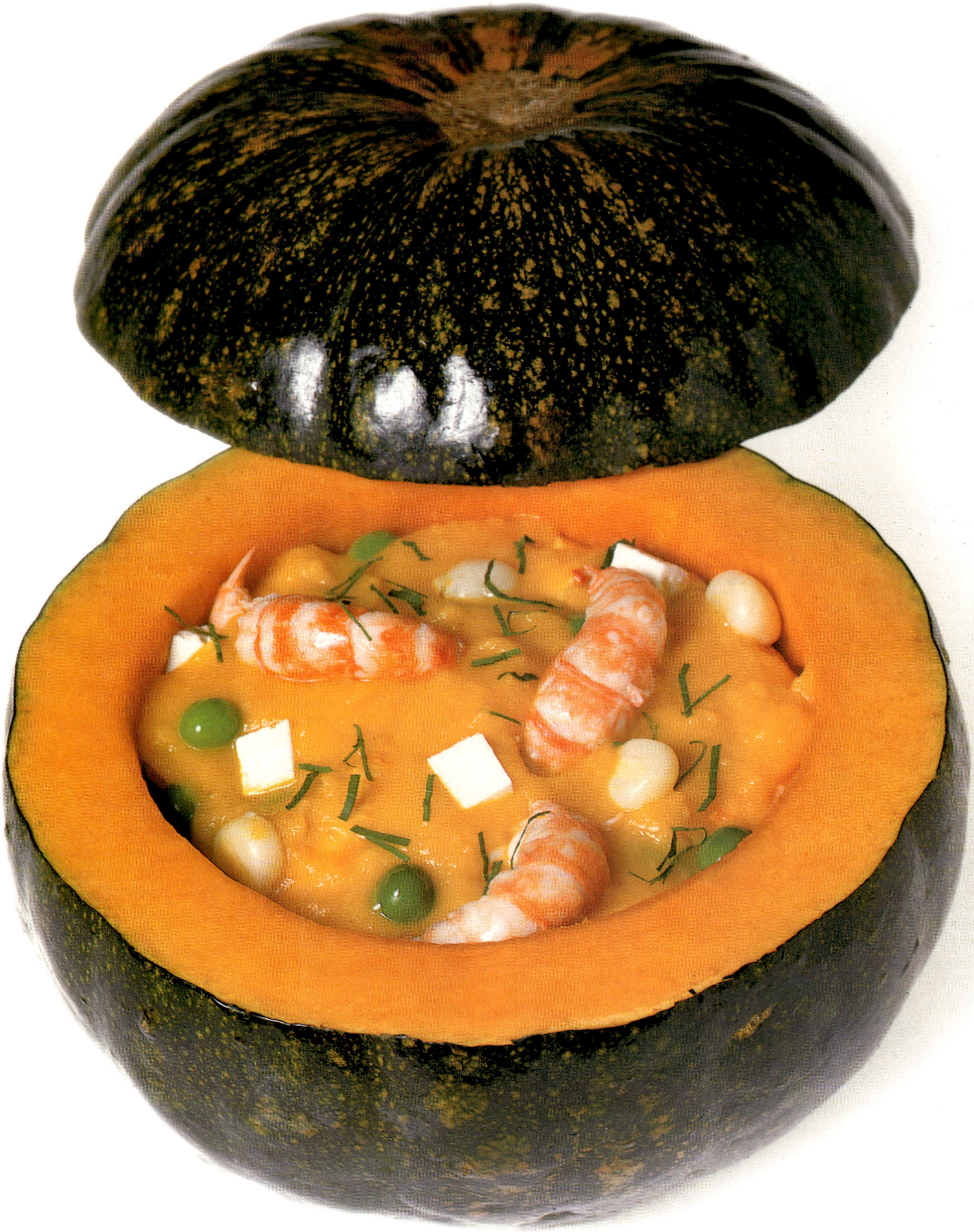

Lomo Saltado

Ingredients:

- 1 tsp minced garlic
- 2 tsp finely chopped **ají limo**
- 2 lbs (1kg) beef steak
- 1 lb (½ kg) red onions, sliced
- 1 lb (½ kg) plum tomatoes, sliced lengthwise into sixths
- 2 lbs (1 kg) large yellow potatoes, peeled and cut into sticks
- **3 ajíes amarillos**, sliced fine
- 6 tbsp soy sauce
- 2 tbsp freshly chopped cilantro
- Pinch ground cumin
- Red wine vinegar
- Salt and freshly ground pepper
- Oil for stir frying and deep frying.

*Here Andrea Graña gives us her recipe for **Lomo Saltado**. The arrival of Chinese indentured servants to work the coastal plantations and the railroads in the mid 19th century had a profound effect on Peruvian eating habits. **Lomo Saltado** is probably the modern day dish that best symbolizes Peruvians' enthusiasm for the stir fry technique. With its traditional ají flavoring, and a soy sauce twist, this meat and potato dish is a family favorite all over Peru.*

Preparation

Cut meat into ½ in- (1¼ cm-) wide strips or into gougeonettes.

Heat enough oil to cover the base of a large pan or wok and, over medium heat, sauté garlic and **ají limo** for 2 minutes. Raise the heat, add meat and brown all over. Season with salt, freshly ground pepper and a pinch of ground cumin.

Remove the meat from the pan along with the juices so as to keep it moist. Set aside.

Add a little more oil to the pan if necessary and stir-fry onion until barely soft, about 1 minute. Season with salt and pepper. Add a few drops of vinegar and continue stir-frying until it has evaporated, about another minute. The onion should still have some bite. Remove onion from the pan, set aside and repeat procedure with tomato.

In a separate skillet, deep fry potato slices until just slightly golden. Remove with a slotted spoon, drain on paper towel and season with salt to taste.

Return meat, onion and tomato to the wok. Add **ají amarillo** and soy sauce and cook for ½ minute. Finally add the large French fries and mix everything together carefully. Garnish with freshly chopped cilantro and serve immediately, accompanied by white rice.

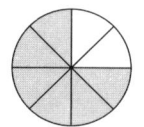

Note: The same recipe can be followed substituting crayfish tails, fish fillets or chicken fingers for the meat.

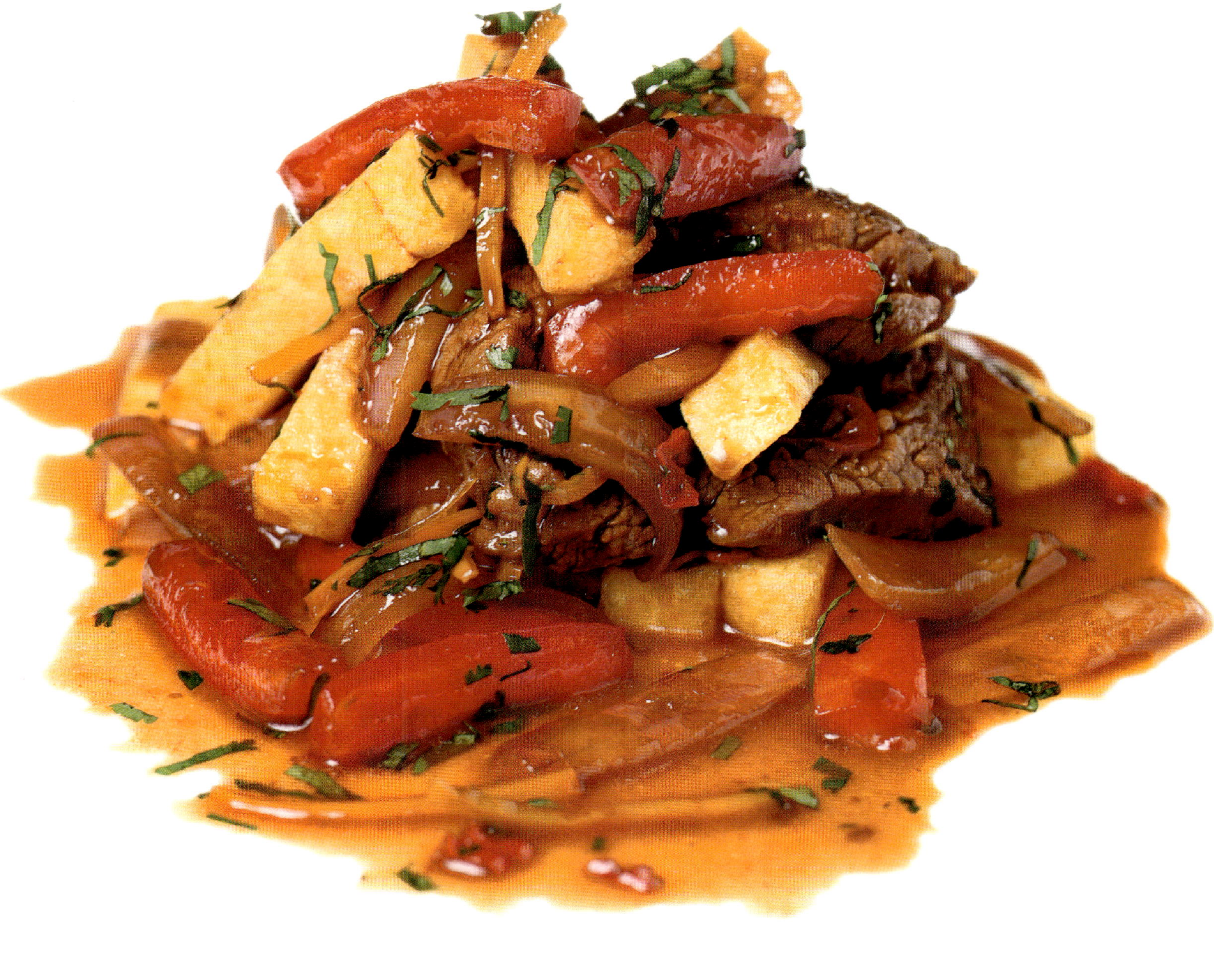

Olluquito con Carne

Ingredients:

- 2 lb (1 kg) olluco
- 2 tbsp vegetable oil
- 2 tsp crushed garlic
- 2 tbsp **salsa madre** (p.228)
- 2 tbsp **ají panca** paste (p.228)
- ¼ tsp dried oregano
- ½ tsp ground cumin
- ½ lb (250 g) ground beef
- 1 **ají amarillo** chopped fine
- 12 mint leaves
- Salt

Olluco is an attractive relative to the potato. Yellow and pink in color, it has very moist flesh and will cook very quickly. Its subtle flavor makes it a perfect companion to meat. This stew from Rosita Yimura is a simple, quick and easy dish, which makes it a great favorite for busy family cooks.

Preparation

Cut the olluco into fine julienne. Wash thoroughly in a colander until the water runs clear and leave to drain.

Heat enough oil to cover the base of a large pan, and sauté the garlic over medium heat until just turning golden, about 5 minutes. Add the **Salsa Madre**, **ají panca** paste, salt, oregano, and cumin and cook for 2 or 3 more minutes.

Add the meat and brown lightly, mixing to coat with the other ingredients and seasonings. Then add the finely chopped ají amarillo and the julienned olluco, and leave to cook for approximately 20 minutes, turning occasionally.

Chop the mint into very fine strips and combine with the meat and olluco mixture.

Garnish with finely chopped parsley and serve with white rice.

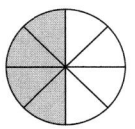

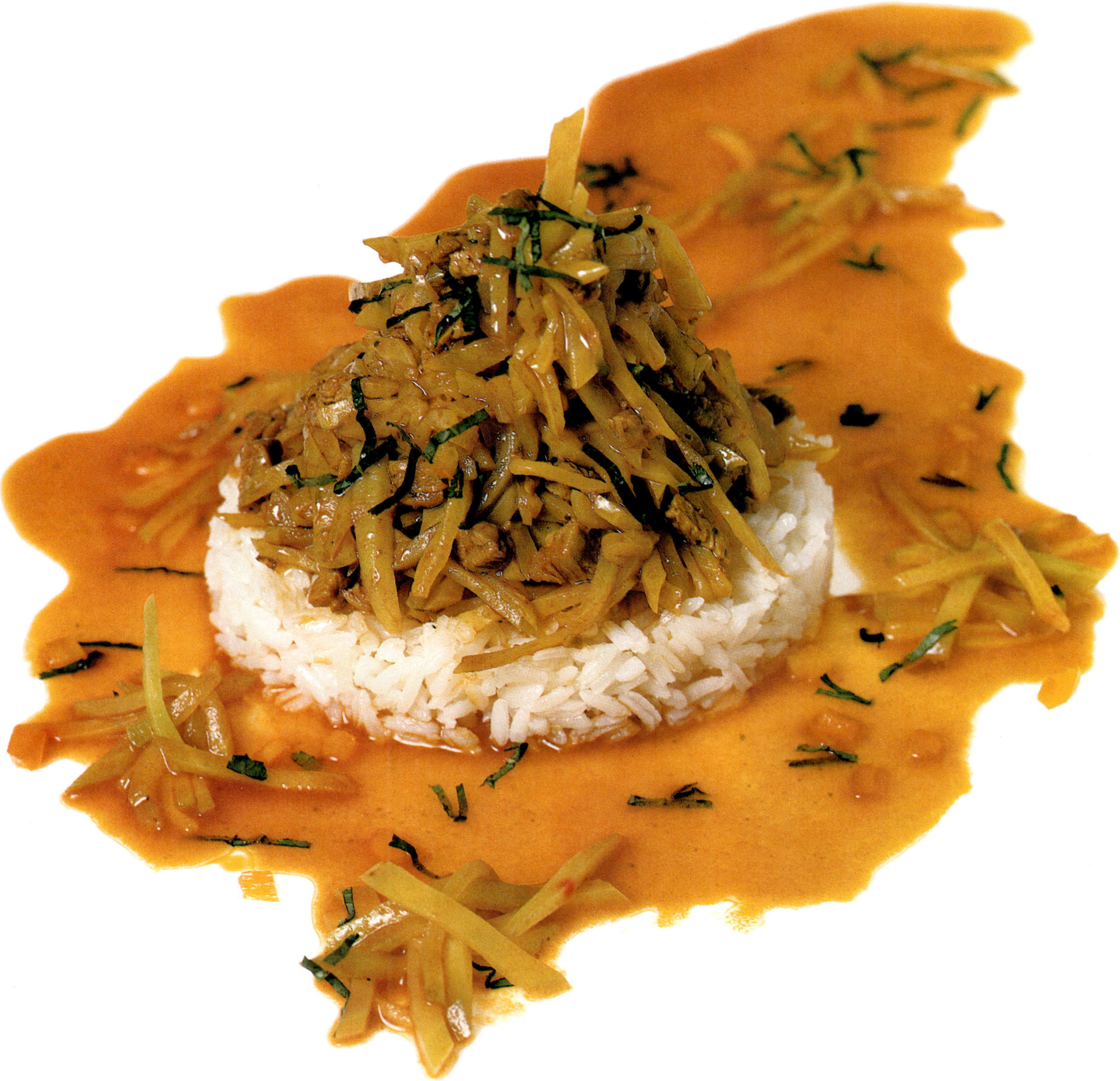

Pato a la Moda Chepén

Ingredients:

- 2 duck breasts (½ breast per portion)
- 4 duck drumsticks
- 2 tsp vegetable oil
- Salt, pepper and cumin

For the Salsa Chepen:

- 2 cups red onion, chopped fine
- 2 cloves garlic
- 2 tbsp **ají mirasol** paste (p.228)
- 3 cups stock
- 2 tsp anise liqueur
- Juice of 1 orange
- Sugar (optional)

Garnish:

- Black olives
- Orange slices
- Candied orange peel

*This is one of Marisa Guiulfo's favorite recipes. Cooked regularly at her grandparents' hacienda, it is still a dish that she likes to make for family occasions. The Peruvian native duck or 'ñuñuma' was domesticated by the Inca and appeared in several pre-Columbian stews and preparations. It was much heftier than its European counterpart. Duck still features importantly on menus in northern parts of Peru. This dish from the ancient northern town of Chepen is flavored with orange, **ají** and a hint of anis.*

Preparation

Heat oil in a large pan and when it's very hot add the duck drumsticks. Sear the drumsticks quickly and then lower heat immediately. Cook turning frequently, until golden brown, about 8 minutes. Remove from pan and set aside.

In a blender or food processor fitted with a steel blade, blend onion, garlic and **ají mirasol** paste. Sauté mixture in the same pan used for sealing duck for 3 minutes on low heat. Replace drumsticks and add enough stock to cover them.

Cover and cook on low heat until meat is fork tender (1 - 1 ½ hrs). After about 1 hour of cooking time, add the orange juice.

When you are almost ready to serve, score the duck breasts on each side and season with salt, pepper and cumin. Sauté breasts in a heavy skillet until medium rare, about 4 minutes each side. The breasts should still be pink in the center. Remove and keep warm.

Just before serving, stir anise liqueur into sauce, adjust seasonings and add a little sugar if sauce is too spicy.

To serve:

Spoon sauce onto warmed individual serving plates and arrange sliced duck breast and 1 drumstick on top of each. Garnish with sliced orange, candied orange peel and black olives.

Serve warm accompanied by cooked fava or broad beans.

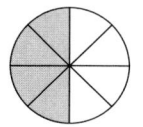

Tip: To make the candied orange peel. Blanche strips of peel of 1 orange in 4 changes of water. Then boil in syrup (½ cup water to ¼ cup sugar) for approximately 8 minutes.

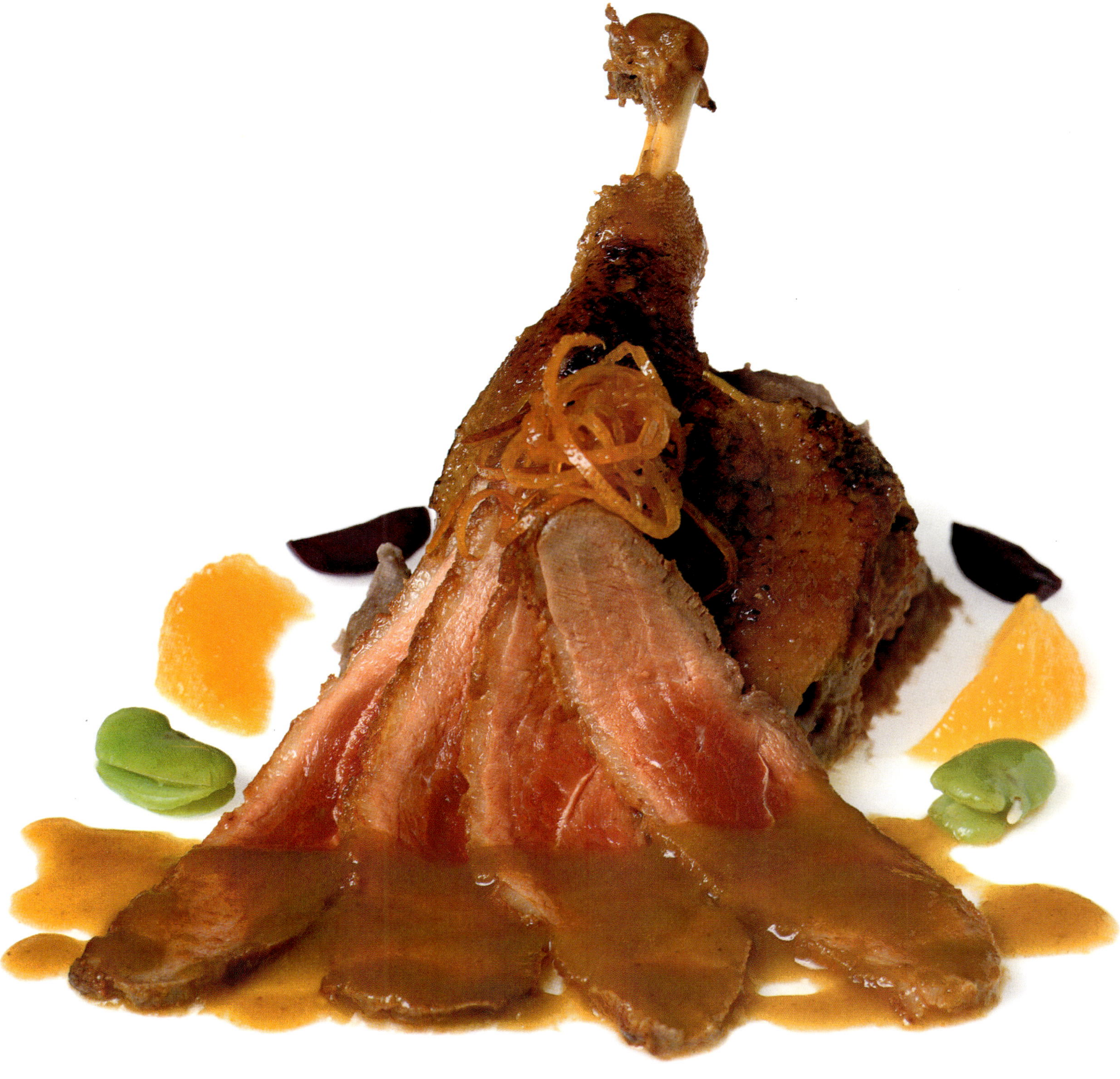

Pejerrey Arrebozado

This is a fondly remembered dish from my childhood, as prepared by our family cook, Apolonia. The Peruvian silverside or rainbow smelt is a small, attractive fish, of a sparkling translucent silver color with a flash of yellow. Careful! These crispy things can become an addiction.

Ingredients:

- 2 doz smelts or Peruvian silversides
- 2 tbsp all purpose flour
- ¼ cup milk
- 5 eggs
- Vegetable oil for frying
- Salt and freshly ground pepper

To serve:

- 3 white potatoes peeled, sliced into wheels and deep fried

Preparation

Get your fishmonger to clean and gut the fish for you removing the backbone but leaving the tail intact. Rinse the fish, drain well and pat dry on kitchen towel.

In a small bowl, combine milk and flour and stir until flour is dissolved.

In a separate bowl, beat the egg whites to form soft peaks. Fold in beaten egg yolks, the milk and flour mixture and salt and pepper.

Dip the smelts in the batter and coat well.

Heat the vegetable oil to 375ºF / 200ºC. Deep fry the smelts, a few at a time, until they are golden brown on all sides, about 1 or 2 minutes each. Serve with golden fried potato wheels and home made mayonnaise.

Note: These fish are also wonderful either breaded or dipped in a beer batter, or simply floured and served with oriental dipping sauce. With this same preparation, they also make an excellent filling for causa.

Tip: If you need to remove the backbone yourself, pinch close to the tail to loosen it then spread fish on a plate and sprinkle with the lime juice (this makes it easier to take out the backbone and will also give the fish additional flavor). Leave to drain in a colander for a few minutes before gently removing the backbone.

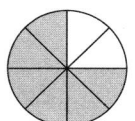

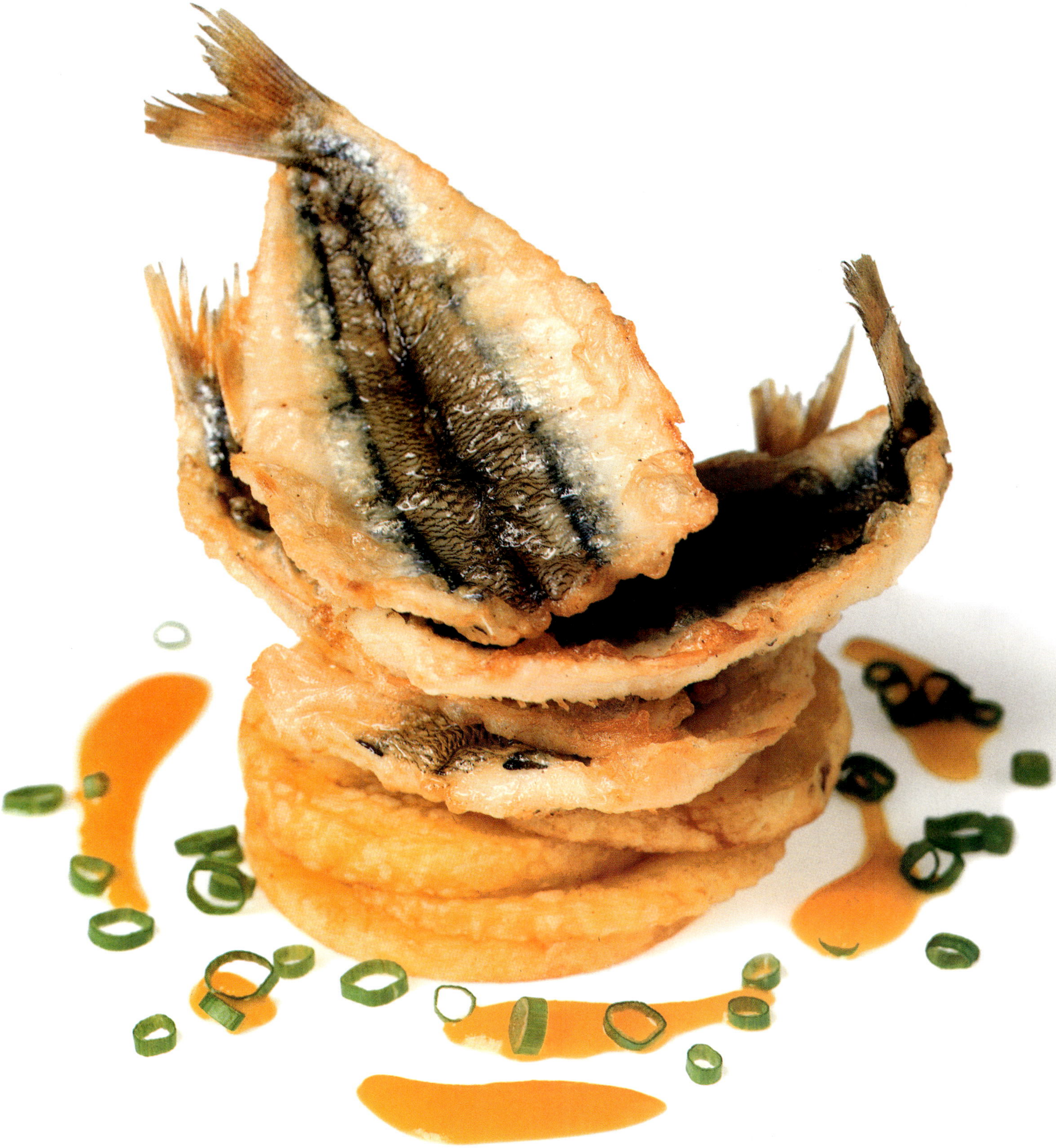

Pepián de Pavo

*Pepián is another ancient Peruvian preparation which is still eaten regularly in its original form. As with many other dishes, each region or town has its favorite way of preparing it. A creamy, more liquid form of the classic **humita** or **tamale**, it can be made with rice or corn and teamed with duck, turkey or any kind of meat that rings your palate's bells.*

Ingredients:

- 1 small turkey breast (about 3 lb / 1.5 k)
- 2 tbsp vegetable oil
- 1 tbsp **ají amarillo** paste (p.228)
- 2 cloves garlic, crushed
- 2 tomatoes, peeled, seeded and diced fine
- 1 large onion, diced fine
- Salt and freshly ground pepper

For the pepián:

- 1 cup ground fresh corn kernels
- ½ cup pea flour
- ¼ cup **ají mirasol** paste (p.228)
- 1 cup chicken stock
- ¼ cup peanuts, toasted and ground

Preparation

Season turkey breast with salt and pepper. Sear on all sides in a large skillet. Transfer to a preheated oven (400ºF / 200ºC) and cook until meat is tender, about 20 - 30 minutes. Set aside and keep warm.

In the same skillet that you used to sear the turkey breast, add a little more oil and sauté onion and garlic over medium heat until soft, about 3 minutes. Add tomato and **ají mirasol** paste and cook for a further 2 or 3 minutes.

Meanwhile, combine all **pepián** ingredients except for the stock in a large bowl and mix thoroughly.

Add **pepián** mixture to skillet. Mix well and add chicken stock. Cook, stirring continually, over medium heat until the mixture thickens to a thin purée, about 5 minutes. Add more stock or water if necessary. Season with salt and freshly ground pepper.

To serve:
Slice turkey breast and assemble layered with the **pepián** on warmed individual serving plates.

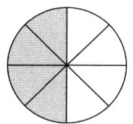

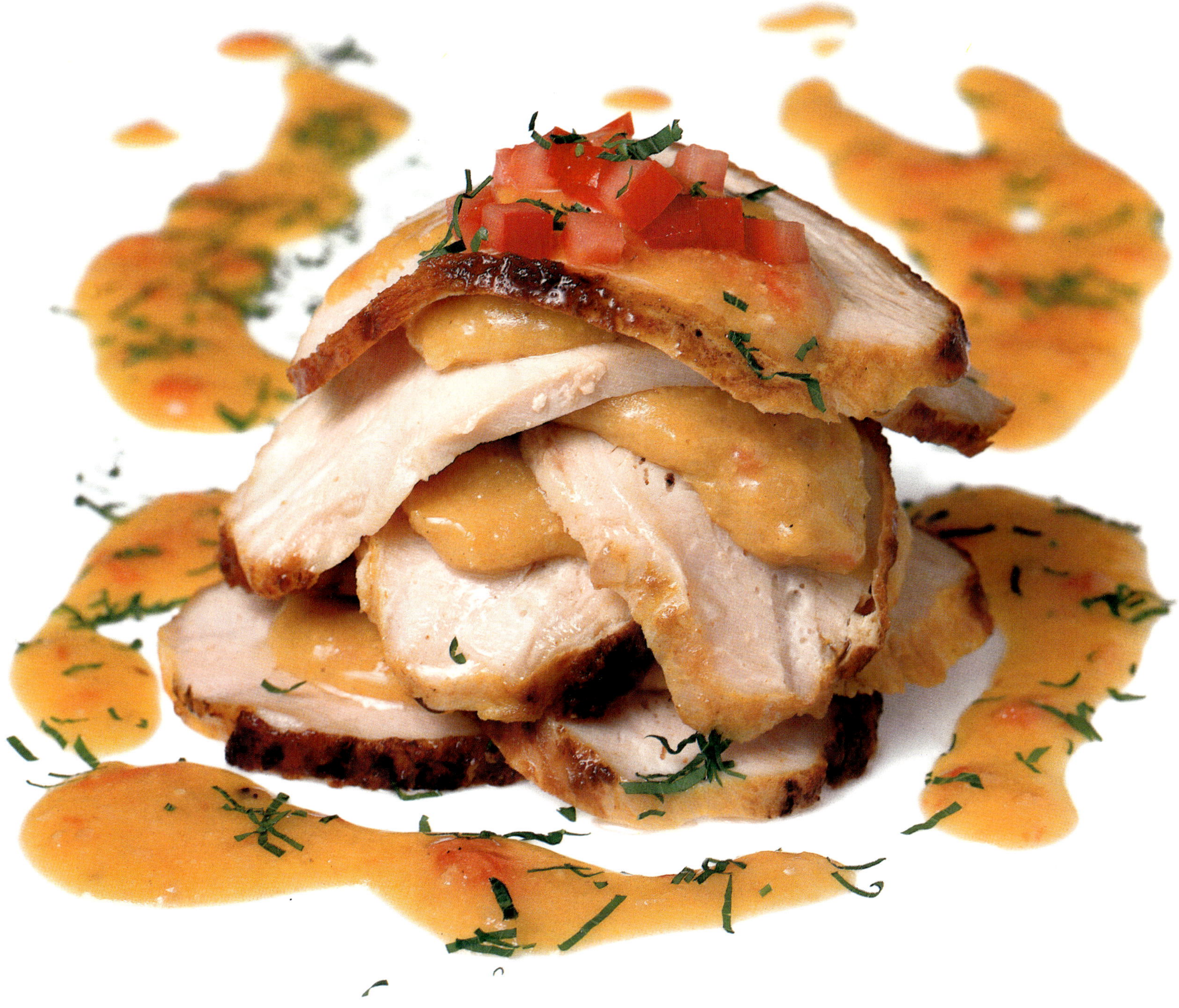

Picante de Camarones

Ingredients:

- 36 fresh crayfish tails
- 3 cups crayfish stock (p.88)
- 3 slices white bread, crusts removed
- 2 tbsp vegetable oil
- 3 cloves garlic, crushed
- 1 large red onion, chopped
- 2-3 tomatoes, peeled, seeded, and finely diced
- 2 tbsp **ají amarillo** paste (p.228)
- 1 cup olive oil
- 2 tbsp chopped walnuts
- Salt

Garnish:

- 4 whole cooked fresh crayfish

*This is another dish Marisa Guiulfo likes to prepare. The traditional use of **migas** or crumbled bread as a thickening and a base for the hot **ají** pepper flavors gives this dish both substance and consistency. It's definitely worth making the crayfish stock yourself from scratch. the amount of **picante** depends on how much **ají** you want to add.*

Preparation

Boil crayfish tails in 3 liters of salted water for 3 minutes. Remove and put on ice to prevent further cooking. When tails are cool, peel and set aside.

Put bread to soak in 1 cup of the crayfish stock.

In a large heavy-based pan, heat oil and sauté garlic and onion, over medium heat until soft, about 3 minutes. Add tomato and cook for a further 2 minutes.

Remove onion mixture from the pan and blend with the soaked bread to form a thick paste. Return to pan. Add **ají amarillo** paste, olive oil and remaining 2 cups crayfish stock. Cook for 10 minutes.

Stir in nuts and reserved crayfish tails and warm through. Season with salt to taste. Serve hot, garnished with cooked crayfish and accompanied by rice or yellow potatoes

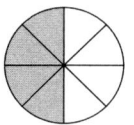

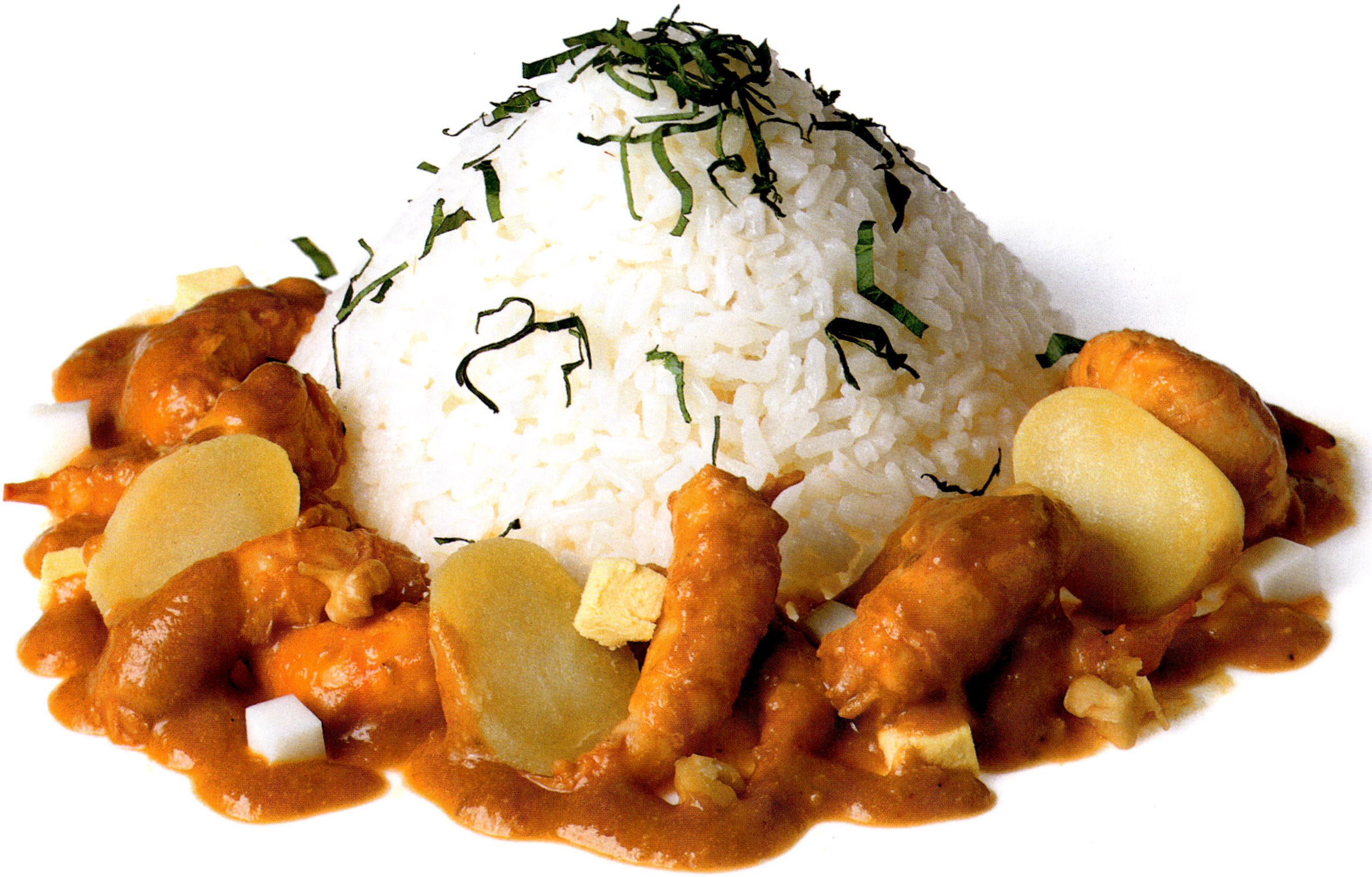

Pollo al Maní

*This is Rosita Yimura's variation on this typical Andean dish. She substitutes chicken for the trational **cuy** (guinea pig) served with this spicy peanut sauce.*

Ingredients:

- 1 chicken, cut into pieces.
- 1 red onion chopped
- 1 ¼ tbsp crushed garlic
- 4 tbsp **ají panca** paste (p.228)
- 1 cup vinegar
- 5 oz (150 g) peanuts, roasted and ground
- 3 cups water or chicken stock
- 2 tbsp vegetable oil
- Salt, pepper and cumin

For serving:

- 6 yellow potatoes, boiled and cut into slices
- 6 cups of **Arroz a la Peruana** without corn kernels (p.225)

Preparation

Place the chicken pieces in a dish and season with salt, 1 tbsp of the crushed garlic, 2 tbsp of the **ají panca** paste, pepper and cumin. Pour the vinegar over the chicken pieces and leave to marinate for 30 minutes.

In a large skillet heat the oil and sauté the onion over medium heat until translucent. Add the remaining ¼ tbsp of garlic and sauté for a further 2 to 3 minutes until the ingredients are just turning golden. Then add the rest of the **ají panca** paste and cook for another 2 to 3 minutes.

Add the water or chicken stock, 1 tbsp of the chicken marinade and salt, pepper and cumin to taste. Bring the sauce back to the boil, reduce the heat and simmer gently.

Meanwhile make sure the chicken pieces are well drained. Lightly coat them with flour and deep-fry them in plenty of hot oil. Drain on paper towels.

Add the ground peanuts and the deep-fried chicken pieces to the sauce and mix thoroughly. Warm through for a few minutes.

Serve immediately over slices of cooked yellow potatoes. Accompany with white rice.

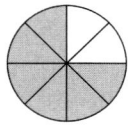

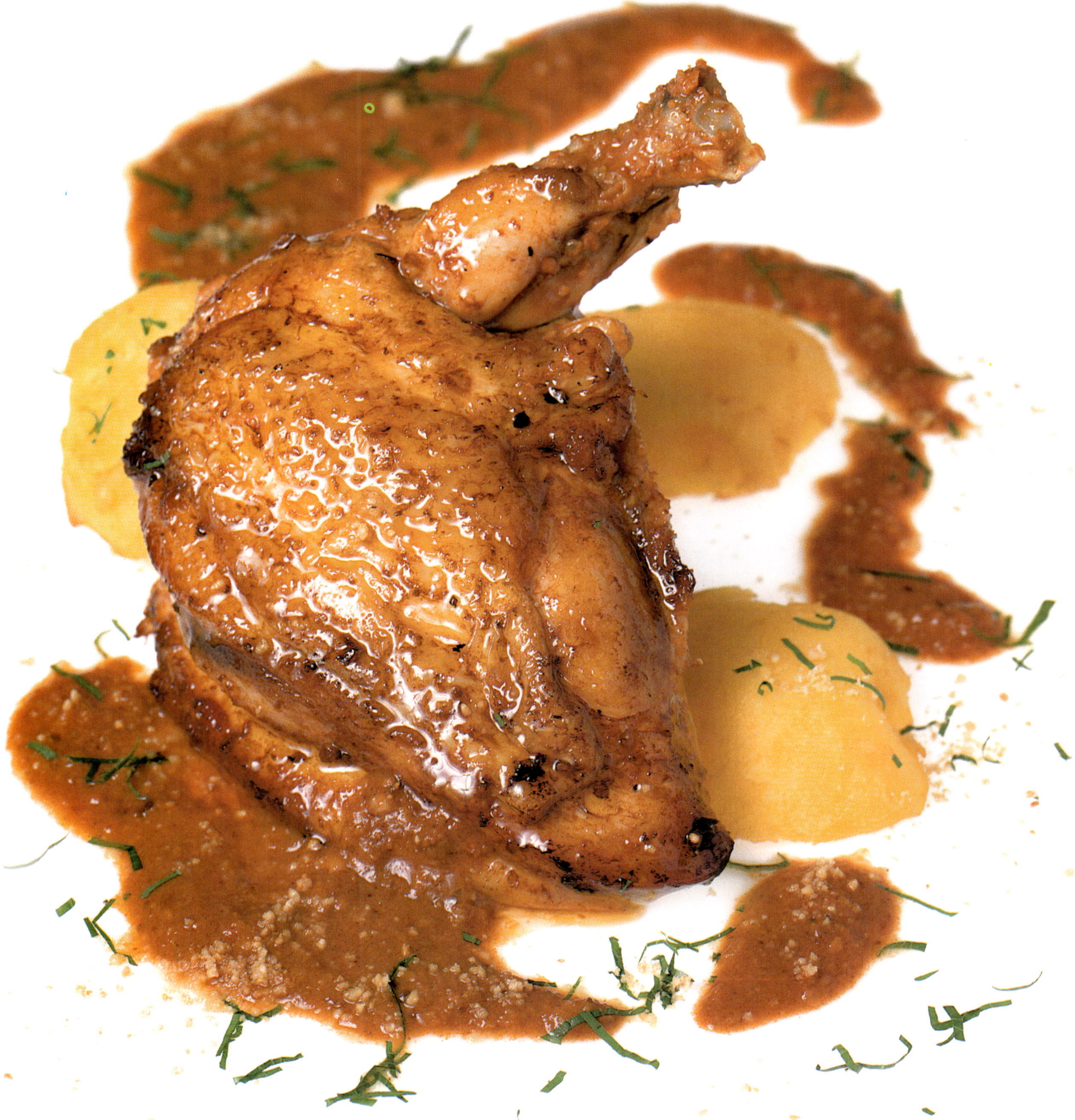

Risotto de Cabrito de Leche & Culantro

This is another recipe from talented chef Gastón Acurio. The European technique of risotto here is put together with what have become the very typically Peruvian flavors of goat and cilantro.

Ingredients:

- 4 baby goat shanks
- 1 tbsp butter
- 1 lb (½ kg) spinach
- 3 ½ oz (100 g) cilantro
- 2 tbsp vegetable oil
- 1 red onion, finely chopped
- 2 cloves garlic, minced
- 2 tomatoes, finely chopped
- 1 cup (¼ lt) goat stock
- ¼ cup Noilly-Prat
- 2 tsp coconut milk
- 2 oz (50 g) butter
- Curry powder to taste

For the risotto:

- 2 tbsp butter
- 1 tbsp olive oil
- 1 cup arborio rice
- ½ red onion
- 1 clove garlic
- ½ glass white wine
- 3 cups chicken stock
- 3 ½ oz (100 g) fresh white cheese
- 7 oz (200 g) peas, cooked
- 2 cups squash, cooked and puréed
- 1 ¾ oz (50 g) butter
- 1 ¾ oz (50 g) Parmesan cheese
- Virgin olive oil to taste
- Cooked kernels from 1 fresh corn cob

Garnish:

- Fresh mint leaves

Serves 4

Preparation

Have your butcher partially de-bone each goat shank, leaving the upper bone intact. Reform and tie with kitchen twine. Wash spinach leaves and cilantro and wilt in a closed pan over low heat with a little butter and salt for 1 minute. Blend to make a purée, strain and reserve.

In a large skillet, heat oil and sauté onion and garlic for 2 minutes. Add shanks and brown for a further 3 minutes. Add curry powder, tomato and Noilly-Prat. Bring to the boil and simmer until liquid has evaporated.

Add goat stock to cover ingredients, adding a little water if necessary. Cook on very low heat until the meat is fork tender, about 30 minutes. Add coconut milk and reserved spinach and cilantro purée. Reduce and add butter.

To make the risotto:

In a large heavy-based skillet over low heat, melt the butter with the oil. Add the onion and sauté until soft, about 5 minutes. Add the garlic and cook for a few minutes longer. Add the rice and stir until well coated with the oil and butter. Sauté for a few more minutes until rice is opaque.

Pour the stock into a separate saucepan and bring to a boil. Reduce heat so stock is barely simmering. Add wine to the risotto and bring mixture back to a simmer. Cook, stirring occasionally, until liquid is absorbed. Add 1 or 2 ladles of hot stock to the risotto and continue to cook, stirring, until the stock is absorbed, about 3 or 4 minutes. Repeat the procedure until all the stock is absorbed and the rice is creamy but the grains are still 'al dente' in the center.

Finally, stir through squash purée, corn kernels, peas and fresh cheese pieces. Add butter, Parmesan and olive oil.

To serve:

Place a little risotto in the center of an individual plate. Top with the semi-boned goat shank and drizzle with a little of the green sauce. Garnish with fresh mint leaves.

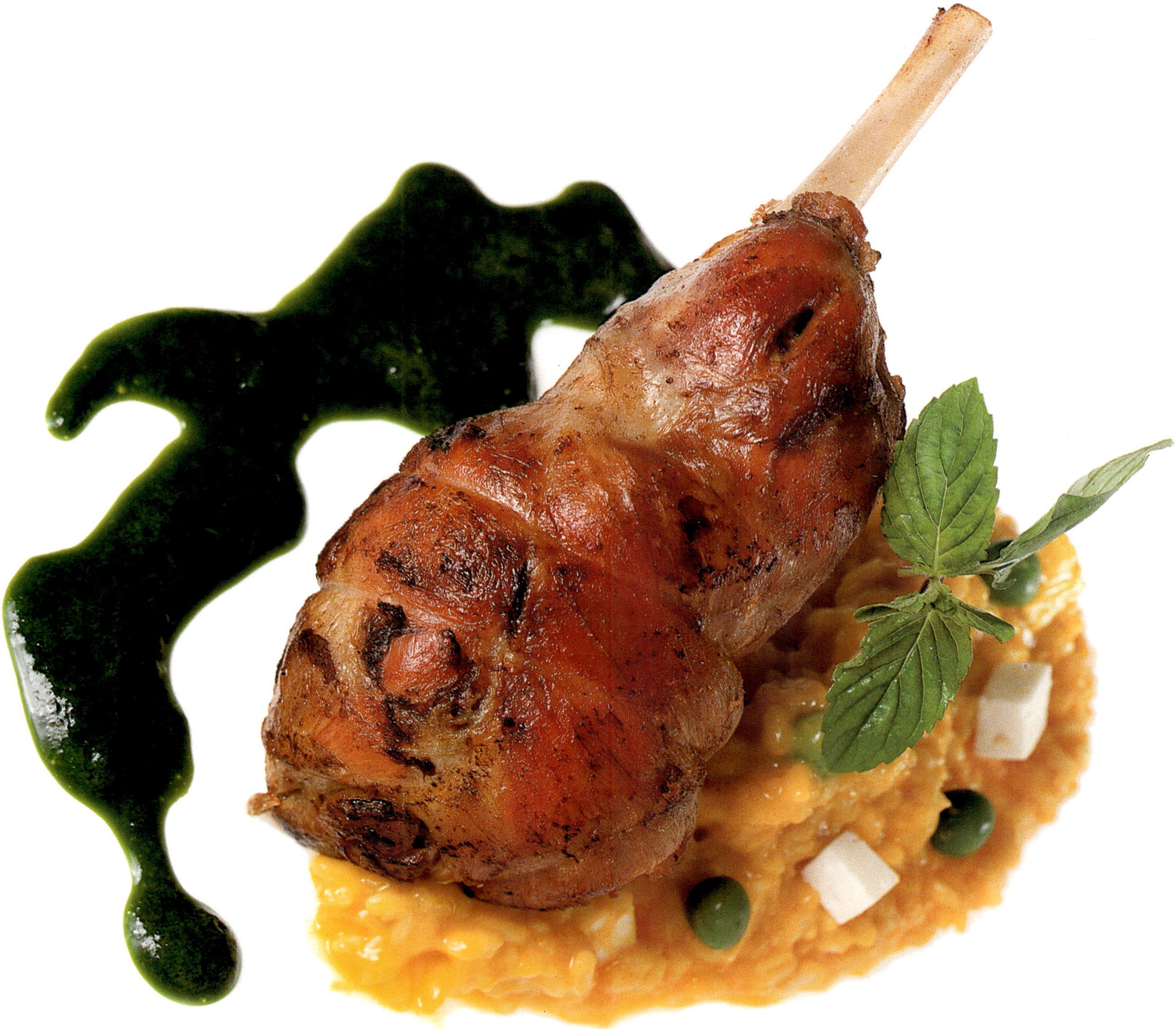

Rocoto Relleno

Ingredients:

- 8 **rocotos**
- 6 tbsp sugar
- 3 tbsp vinegar
- 4 tsp crushed garlic
- 14 oz (400 g) ground chuck
- 14 oz (400 g) ground pork
- 4 cups red onion, finely chopped
- 8 tomatoes, peeled, seeded and chopped fine
- 4 oz (120 g) raisins, soaked
- 4 tbsp **ají panca** paste (p.228)
- 8 tbsp vegetable oil
- 8 black olives, pitted and chopped
- 2 hard-boiled eggs, chopped
- Grated cheese for gratin
- Salt, pepper and cumin

For the crema de rocoto:

- 1 cup heavy cream
- 2 tbsp rocoto paste (p.230)
- ¼ cup white wine

A great traditional favorite. Captivating to the eye, the consecutive boiling of the peppers makes them as deliciously digestible as edible.

Preparation

Heat the oil in a large skillet and sauté the onion and garlic over medium heat until golden, about 5 minutes.

Crumble the ground pork and beef into the skillet and cook over medium heat, stirring often until meats are browned. Spoon off as much excess fat as possible.

Add the **ají panca** paste, tomato, raisins, salt, pepper and cumin and cook for a further 10 minutes.

Remove from heat and add the olives and hard-boiled egg. Cover and keep warm.

Carefully slice the tops off the **rocotos** and scoop out all seeds and veins.

Add 2 tbsp sugar and 1 tbsp vinegar to a large pan of water and bring to the boil. Blanche the **rocotos** and their tops in three separate changes of water, adding 2 tbsp sugar and 1 tbsp vinegar to each change of water. This will reduce their spiciness.

Drain the **rocotos** well and fill with the meat mixture and cover with grated cheese. Replace the tops.

Place under a broiler until cheese is melted and golden. Serve immediately with **crema de rocoto**.

To make the crema de rocoto:
Reduce wine in a small pan over medium heat until almost totally evaporated, about 4 minutes. Add cream and **rocoto** paste. Lower heat and continue cooking until the sauce has reduced to a thick pouring consistency.

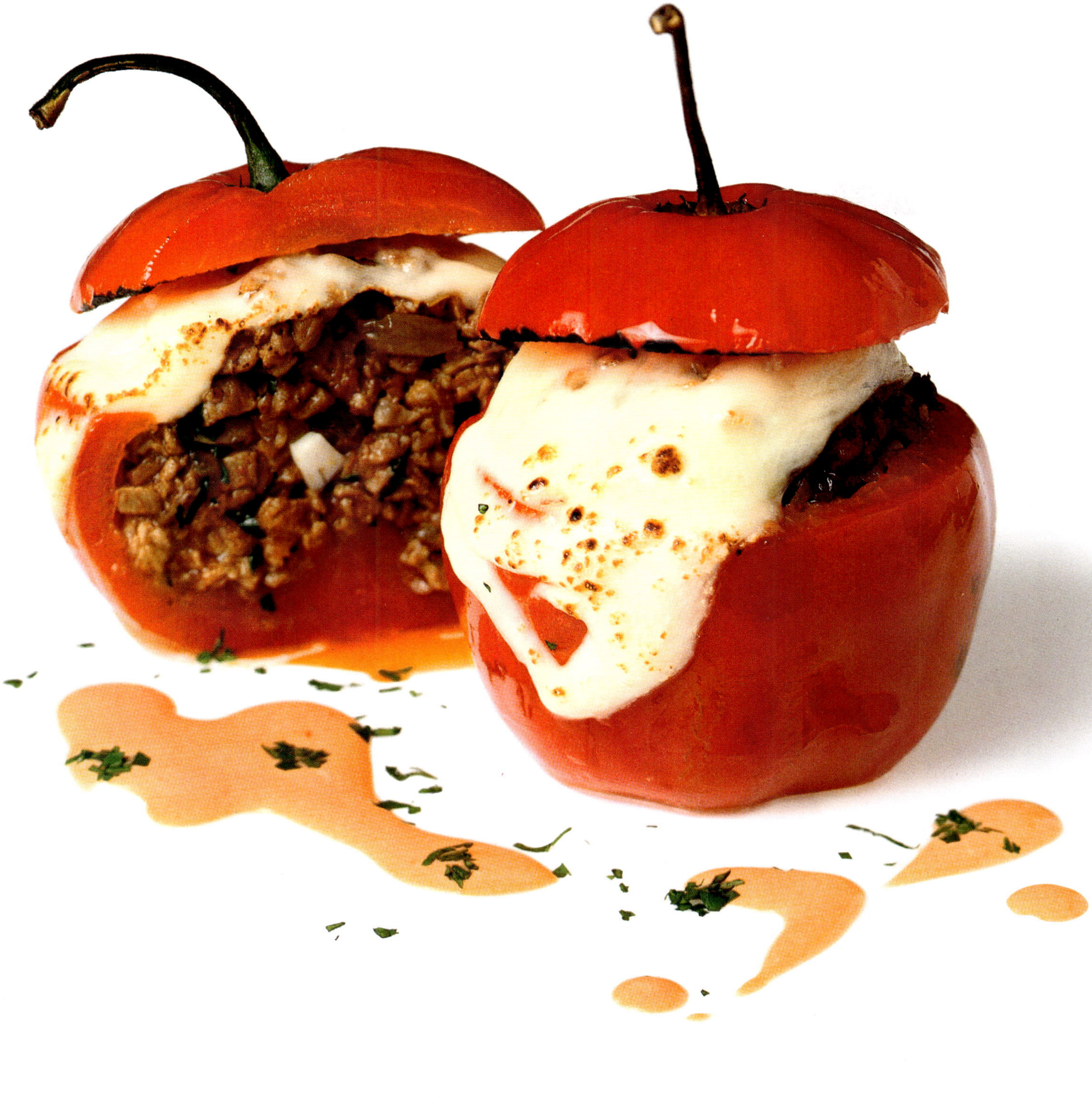

Seco de Cordero

Ingredients:

- 6 lamb shanks, weighing approximately ¾ lb (325 gr) each
- 2 cups (½ lt) **chicha de jora** or corn beer
- 1 tsp paprika
- 3 tbsp **ají amarillo** paste (p.228)
- 1 tsp oregano
- ½ cup vegetable oil
- 1 red onion, chopped finely
- 4 cloves garlic, crushed
- 1 cup cilantro purée
- 2 cups stock
- Salt and pepper

To serve:

- 6 cups cooked rice (see **Arroz a la Peruana**, p.225, without the corn kernels)
- 1 lb (½ kg) yellow potatoes
- 3 cups cooked **Frijoles Guisados** (p.226)

Cilantro is one of the balmy hints of Arabian flavors brought to Peruvian cuisine by the Spanish. The characteristic velvety green sauce essential to a seco is also used to accompany several other meats and fish in Peruvian cuisine.

Preparation

In a large bowl, combine beer, paprika, oregano, **ají amarillo** paste, salt and pepper. Trim lamb shanks and marinate in the beer mixture for at least four hours.

In a large pot, heat a little of the oil and sear lamb shanks until golden brown all over. Remove shanks from the pan and set aside. In the same pan, heat remaining oil and sauté onion, over medium heat, until translucent, about 3 minutes. Add garlic and continue cooking for another couple of minutes until the mixture starts to color. Add ½ cup of the cilantro purée and cook for a further 2 minutes.

Add stock and bring to a boil. Replace lamb shanks, cover and simmer gently, on very low heat, until meat is fork tender, about 2 hrs.

When meat is cooked, stir through the remaining cilantro purée and the peas. Serve immediately with rice, yellow potatoes and **Frijoles Guisados** (p.226).

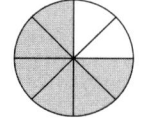

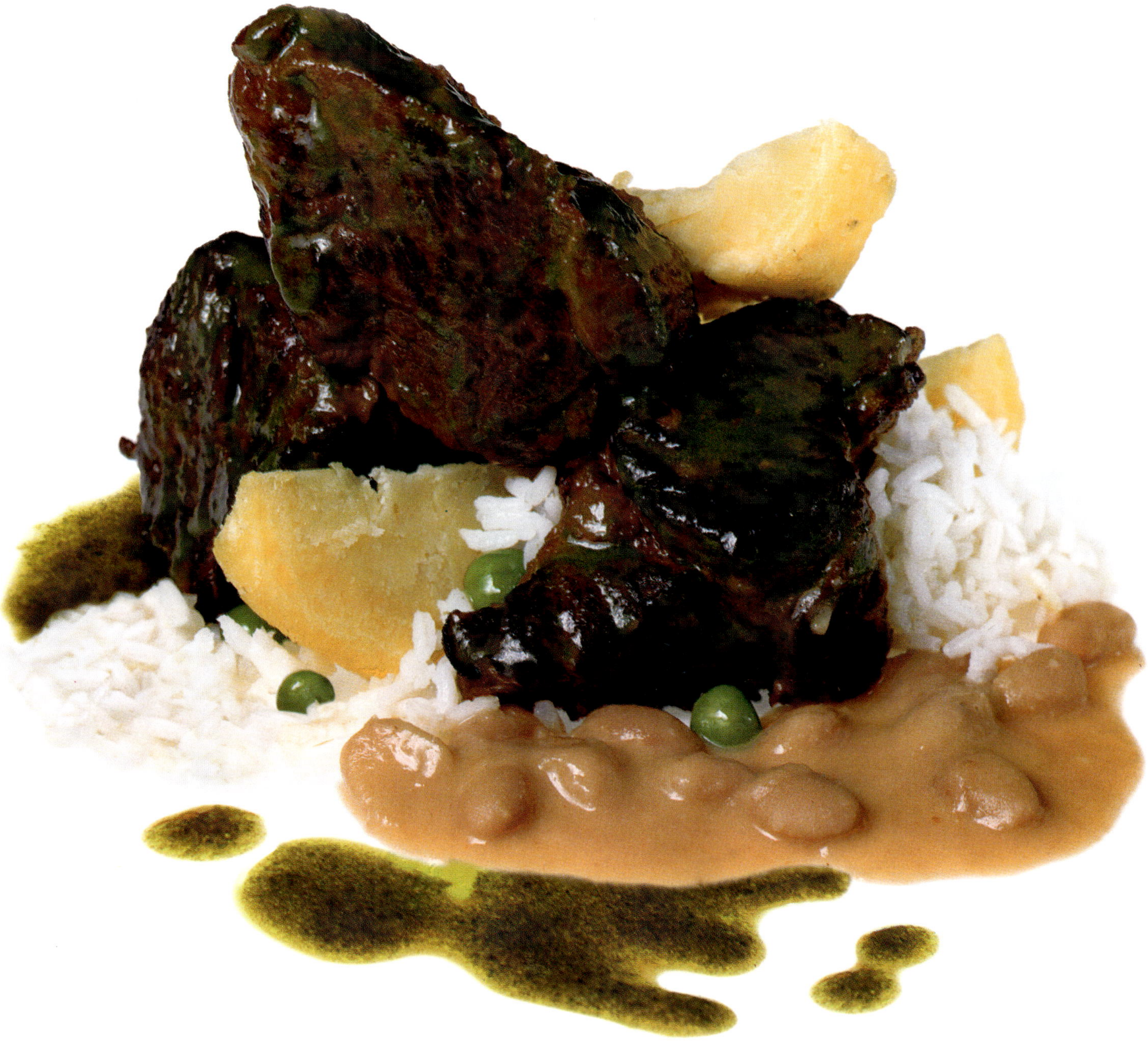

Sudado de Corvina y Conchitas

Ingredients:

- 4 sea bass fillets (about 6 ½ oz /180 g each)
- 20 scallops
- 2 tbsp vegetable oil
- 1 cup finely chopped red onion
- 3 cloves garlic, crushed
- ¼ cup **ají amarillo** paste (p.228)
- 5 cups fish stock
- ½ cup white wine
- 3 tomatoes, peeled, seeded and diced fine
- 1 tbsp finely chopped cilantro
- 1 cup cooked peas
- 1 tbsp butter
- Salt and freshly ground pepper

To serve:

- 2 large white potatoes, cut into oval spheres and steamed

When Marisa Guiulfo has guests at her beautiful beach house in the fishing port of Pucusana, this is what she likes to serve in the evening as the sun sets and the air turns chilly. After a large leisurely lunch the guests are ready for something light and simple. This gently braised fish with a delicate seafood sauce is perfect for the occasion.

Preparation

Season fish fillets with salt and pepper.

Heat oil in a large skillet and sauté onion and garlic over medium heat until soft and transparent, about 3 minutes. Add **ají amarillo** paste and cook for 1 more minute.

Add wine and reduce over medium heat until almost dry. Then add stock and bring to the boil. Add fish fillets and half of the tomato.

Lower the heat, cover and simmer fish for 6 to 8 minutes in the sauce until fish is just turning opaque and is almost ready. Be careful not to overcook.

Add remaining tomato to the skillet with peas, scallops and cilantro. Cook, stirring, for two minutes. Finally whisk in butter and season sauce with salt and pepper.

Serve fish in a deep dish, topped with the scallops and sauce. Accompany with steamed potatoes.

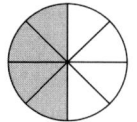

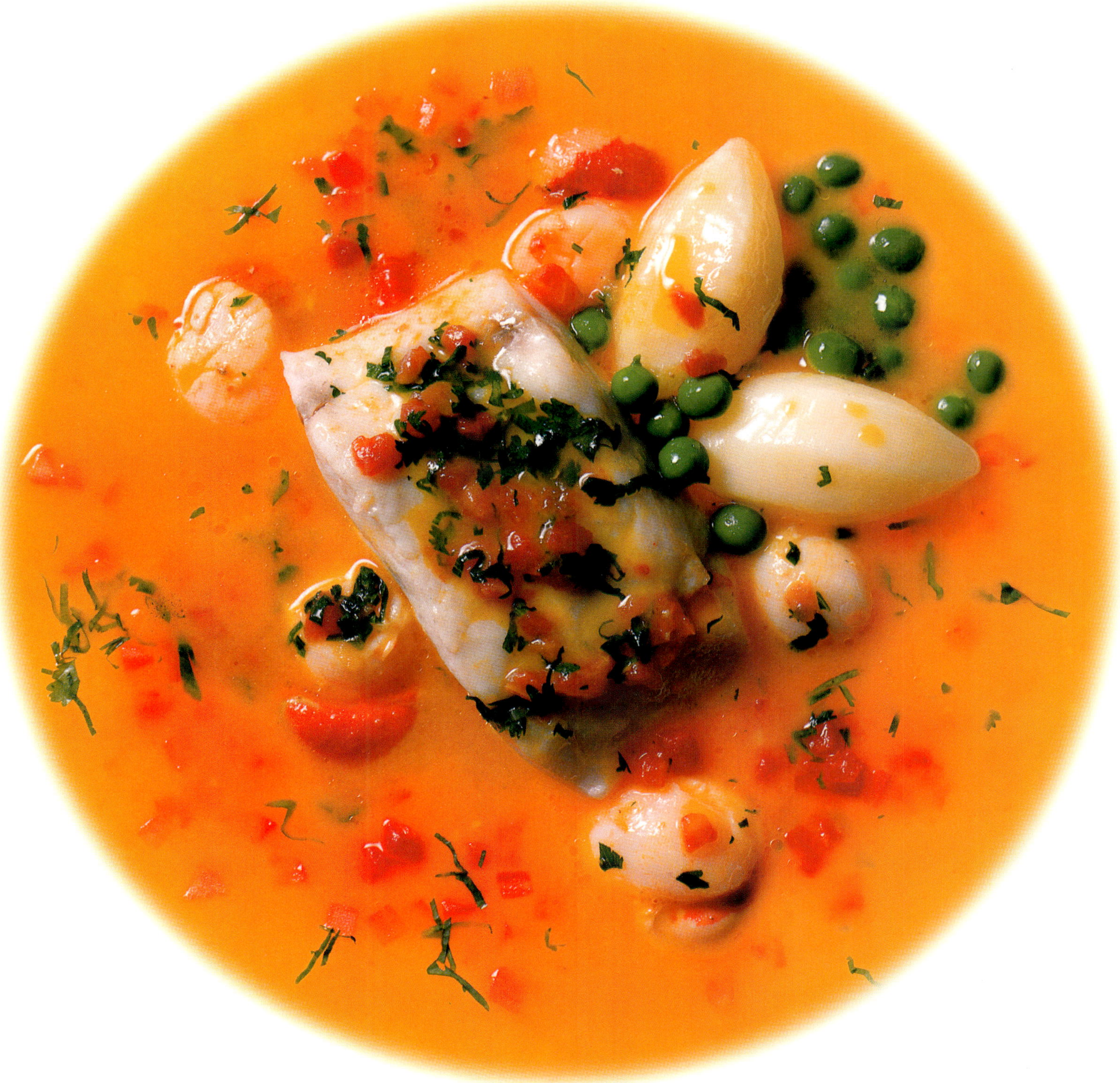

Tacu Tacu

Ingredients:

- 1 lb (½ kg) canary beans, soaked overnight
- 1 lb (½ kg) fat back or salt pork, diced
- ½ lb (¼ kg) cooked rice
- 2 tbsp vegetable oil
- 1 large red onion, chopped fine
- 4 cloves garlic, crushed
- ½ cup **ají amarillo** paste (p.228)
- 1 tbsp dried oregano
- Salt and pepper

*Tacu tacu was a dish invented by the black African slaves who worked the coastal cotton and sugar plantations in colonial Peru. This economical and nutritious dish of seasoned beans and rice is just part of the culinary and cultural heritage of that era. It is a perfect way to use leftovers, but why wait till then? Cook the beans and rice specially to make this hearty meal, served best the day after preparation. This recipe is the one that Luis Felipe Arizola serves at his restaurant, 'A Puerta Cerrada' and is simply the best **Tacu Tacu** I have ever tasted. He usually uses lima (butter) beans but here we've substituted canary beans. You may use either one.*

Preparation

Drain beans. Place in a large pot with plenty of water and cook together with fat back or salt pork until beans are soft, about 1½ hours. Set aside to cool and, when cool, beat with a wooden spoon to form a coarse purée.

In a large skillet, heat the vegetable oil. Sauté crushed garlic and onion over medium heat until golden, about 5 minutes. Add **ají amarillo** paste and oregano and cook for an additional 2 or 3 minutes.

Add the cooked rice and beans and mix to combine thoroughly. Season with salt and pepper to taste. Remove from the heat.

To make the tacu tacu:

Heat another skillet with a little oil. Add ¼ of the bean and rice mixture and, with the help of a spatula, turning it constantly to avoid it sticking and drying out, form mixture into a thick tortilla. Turn out onto a warmed serving plate. Repeat with the remaining mixture.

This dish is traditionally served with fried eggs, fried bananas and a 'blanket' of breaded fried tenderloin.

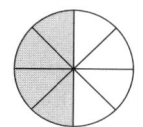

Tip: For a finer textured Tacu Tacu, blend up to ¾ of the bean mixture before adding to the cooked rice and seasonings.

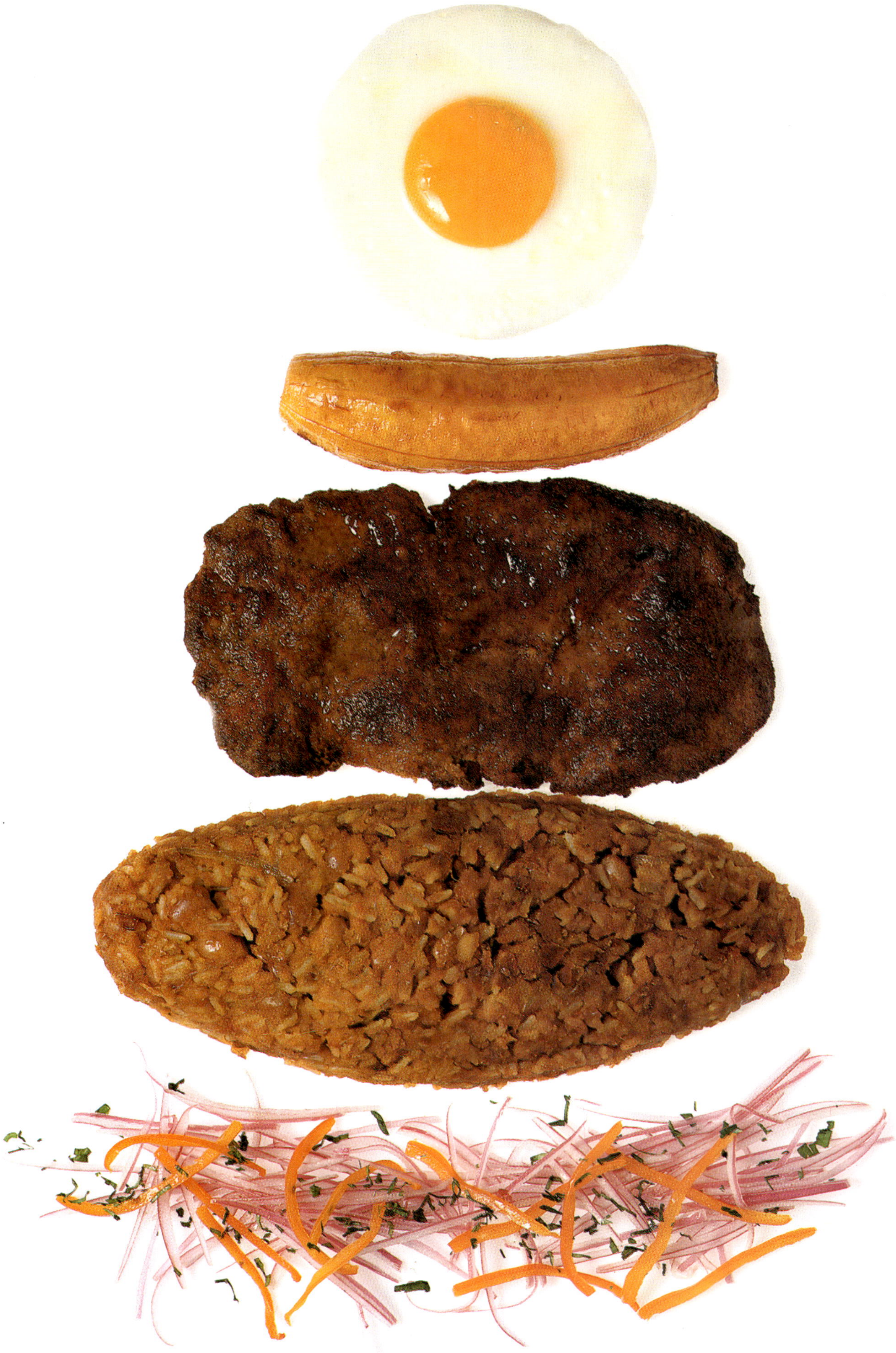

Tacu Tacu de Mariscos

Ingredients:

- 3 cups cooked beans
- 3 cups cooked rice (see **Arroz a la Peruana** (p.225) without the corn kernels)

For the filling:

- 2 cups mixed cooked seafood (shrimp tails, scallops, octopus, squid, mussels…)
- 3 red onions chopped fine
- 2 large tomatoes, peeled and diced
- ½ tsp oregano
- 1 tbsp freshly chopped cilantro
- 2 tbsp soy sauce
- 6 tbsp vegetable oil
- **Ají limo**, seeded, deveined and chopped fine
- Salt

*Otani was reportedly the first person to create a **Tacu Tacu** with seafood filling. His daughter Doris now lists this as one of the most popular dishes in their family restaurant. The wrist action needed to turn the 'tortilla' is a delight to watch in the restaurant kitchen. It might take a while for an amateur to master but the finished dish is so delicious, that you won't worry too much about perfect presentation. Doris Otani recommends using day old beans as they will be softer and make a moister dish.*

Preparation

To make the filling:

First make the filling. In a large skillet, heat 3 tbsp oil and sauté onion, tomato, oregano and salt, over medium heat until onion is translucent, about 3 minutes.

Raise heat and add cilantro, **ají limo** and soy sauce. Cook, stirring for 1 minute, and then add mixed seafood. Cook for 2 more minutes and remove from heat. Set aside until ready to fill the **Tacu Tacu**.

To make the tacu tacu:

If possible use a teflon skillet to avoid the rice sticking. Heat just enough oil to cover the bottom of the skillet. Add a pinch of oregano, about a quarter of the cooked beans and a quarter of the cooked rice.

Continue cooking and mixing all ingredients together, over medium heat, for a few minutes. When rice and beans are well mixed, leave without stirring for a few moments to let the mixture form a thick 'tortilla'.

When the underside of the mixture just starts to turn golden, place about a quarter of the filling along the center of the **Tacu Tacu** and using a large spoon and a gentle flipping movement of the wrist, bring sides of mixture over to cover filling. Check to ensure that all the filling is covered and slide **Tacu Tacu** onto a warmed serving plate.

Repeat with the remaining mixture.

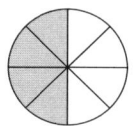

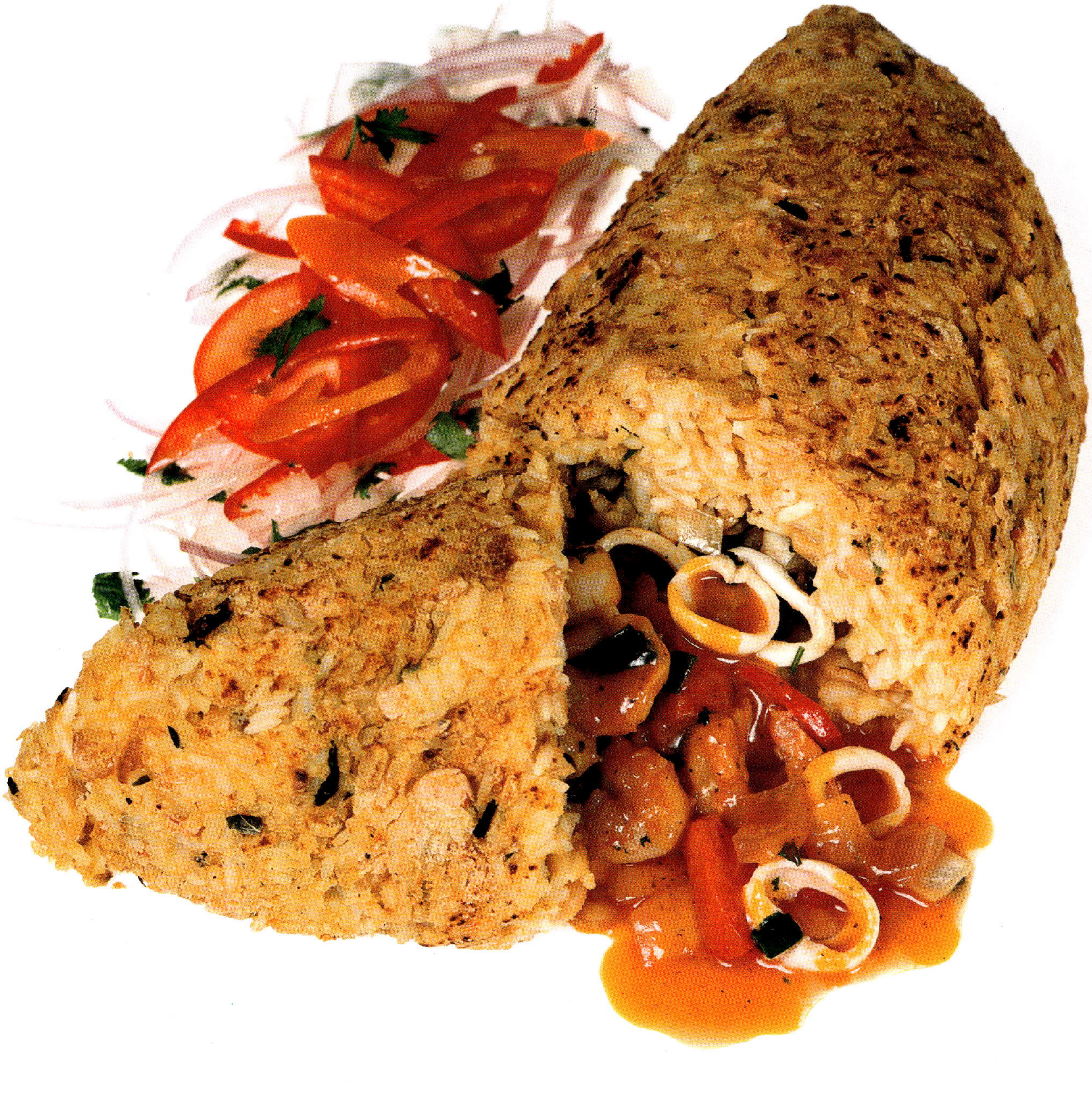

Tacu Tacu en Salsa de Camarones

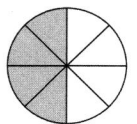

*This dish uses Luis Felipe Arizola's recipe for **Tacu Tacu**, filled with sautéed crayfish tails and swamped in a rich and delicious crayfish coral sauce. We have also integrated Rosita Yimura's precepts on the crayfish filling.*

Ingredients:

- 7 oz (200 g) lima or butter beans, soaked overnight
- 1 cup cooked rice (see **Arroz a la Peruana**, p.225, without the corn kernels)
- ½ cup vegetable oil
- 1 red onion, chopped fine
- 3 cloves garlic, minced
- 4 tbsp **ají amarillo** paste (p.228)
- ¼ cup evaporated milk
- Oil for frying
- Salt and freshly ground pepper

Filling:

- 4 ½ oz (125 g) peeled fresh crayfish tails
- 1 tsp butter
- Salt and freshly ground pepper

- 2 cups **Crayfish Coral Sauce** (p.104)

Preparation

To make the Tacu Tacu:
Drain the soaked beans in a colander and rinse before covering them with plenty of fresh cold water in a large saucepan. Simmer until tender, about 1 hour. When cooked, peel to remove the outer skin.

In a large skillet, heat oil and sauté onion and garlic over medium heat until golden, about 5 minutes. Add **ají amarillo** paste and cook for a further 2 or 3 minutes. Remove from heat.

In a large bowl, combine the beans, rice, cooked onion mixture and evaporated milk. Mix well and season with salt and pepper.

To make the filling:
Sauté crayfish tails in the butter until they turn pink. Season with salt and pepper to taste. Set aside.

Cover the base of a medium skillet with a thin film of oil and heat over high heat until very hot, almost smoking. Place a thick one inch layer of the **Tacu Tacu** mixture in the skillet as if to make a tortilla.

Cook for a few minutes and lift the edges gently to see if it is browned. When it is lightly browned on one side, carefully flip over to cook the other side.

To assemble the Tacu Tacu:
Place some of the crayfish tails in the center of the tortilla. Bring sides together over filling to form a large croquette. Slide onto a warmed serving plate and pour warmed crayfish coral sauce around the outside.

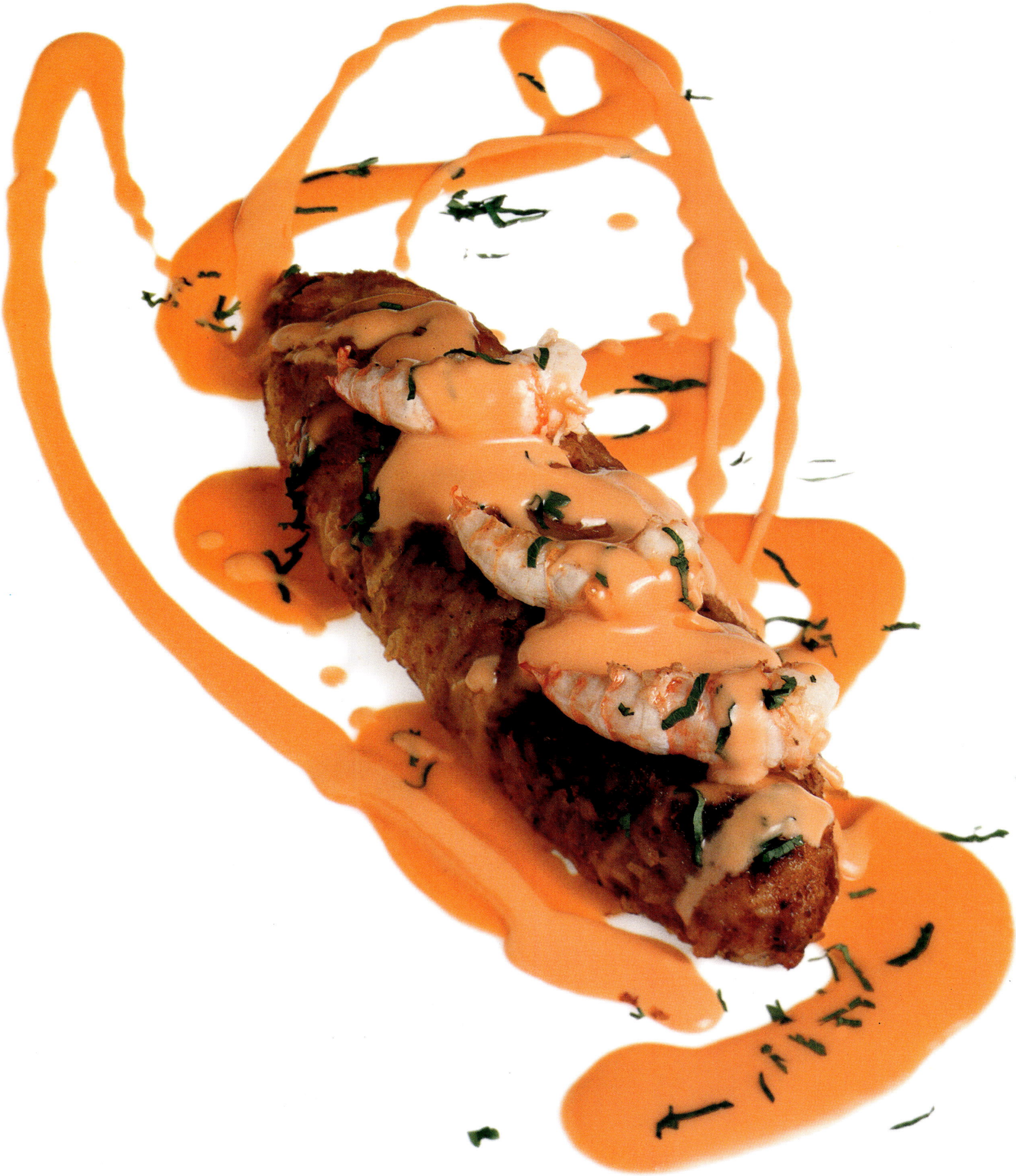

SIDE DISHES

The main side dish found in Peru is rice. Brought to Peru by the Spanish, it quickly became a staple food and is eaten with almost every meal. The preparation is slightly different from European or Asian methods and includes oil and garlic. The recipe here includes sautéed corn kernels but this is optional. Beans have also traditionally always been eaten in Peru and make a very popular side dish, both seasoned and puréed the recipes are included here.

Arroz a la Peruana

The Spanish brought rice to Peru and first cultivated it in the coastal areas. Peruvians love rice and will eat it alongside its Quechua equivalent, the potato. In fact, few meals in Peru are complete without it. Rice and potato served together is the most permanently visible and most essential example of the fusion of Andean and European cuisines and ingredients.

Ingredients:

- 4 cups rice
- ¼ cup vegetable oil
- 1 heaped tbsp minced garlic
- 8 cups water
- 2 tbsp butter
- 3 cups fresh corn kernels, cooked
- Salt to taste

Preparation

In a large pan heat the oil over medium heat and sauté the garlic for 2 or 3 minutes until cooked but not brown. Add rice and combine well. Cook, stirring for a couple more minutes. Season with salt and add the water.

Bring to a boil. Lower the heat and simmer, covered, on very low heat for 15 minutes. Then turn off heat and leave covered for 5 more minutes.

Meanwhile sauté the corn kernels in the butter. Remove lid from the rice pan and add the corn kernels. Mix gently with a fork to separate grains and integrate the corn kernels.

Spoon onto plates or use cup molds to form in individual servings.

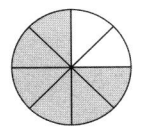

Frijol Guisado & Puré de Pallares

*The most common bean used in Peru is the **frijol canario** or yellow canary bean. Sweetened, Peruvians even make a dessert from them. Here they are seasoned and served as a savory side dish. Any dried white beans or even kidney beans can be substituted as a variation. **Puré de pallares** is a perfect accompaniment to **adobo de chancho** as well as **seco** and other fish and meat dishes. You may like to add more than one cheese. There are some recipes with up to four cheeses, one of which is a blue cheese.*

Ingredients:

- 3 cups yellow canary beans
- ¼ cup vegetable oil
- 1 cup chopped red onion
- 4 cloves garlic, crushed
- ¼ cup **ají panca** paste (p.228)

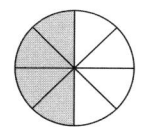

Preparation - Frijol Guisado

Soak beans overnight. Heat oil in a large pan and sauté onion and garlic, over medium heat, until golden, about 5 minutes.

Add **ají panca** paste and cook for a further 2 or 3 minutes.

Drain beans and add to the pot, stirring to cover with seasonings. Cover with plenty of water and bring back to the boil. Lower heat and simmer until beans are soft, about 1 hour.

Ingredients:

- 4 cups large dried white lima or butter beans
- 3 tbsp butter
- ½ cup Parmesan cheese
- ½ cup heavy cream
- Salt and white pepper

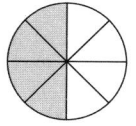

Preparation - Puré de Pallares

Soak beans overnight. Drain and remove outer skins from beans. Place in a large pan of cold salted water and bring to the boil. Cook for 30 to 40 minutes until the beans are tender.

In a blender or food processor fitted with a steel blade, process bean purée until smooth.

Scrape into a bowl and add butter, Parmesan and heavy cream. Mix well, season with salt and pepper, and serve warm.

Condiments & Sauces

*Ajíes or hot peppers in their various forms are what give every Peruvian dish its essential flavor. **Ajíes** feature prominently in pre-hispanic mythology; one of the legendary brothers who were the forefathers of the Inca Empire, Ayar Uchu, is named for **ají** in Quechua. **Ajíes** are used in two basic forms; as an **aderezo** which is a seasoning or dressing included in the preparation of a dish or as accompanying sauces or salsas. They are used dried or fresh and can be blanched to reduce spiciness. The various **ajíes** can also be bought in jars ready made in markets and specialty food stores. **Aderezos** are not, however, lovely to look at, so we sought inspiration for the picture in my favorite book "Le Petit Prince".*

Salsa Madre

Ingredients:

- 1 red onion, diced fine
- 1 tbsp pepper or paprika
- 1 tsp dried oregano
- ¼ cup vegetable oil
- Salt

*This simple mixture of herbs and spices can be used to add flavor to many dishes. It can be kept handy in the refrigerator in a sealed container for 3 to 4 days. Here, Rosita Yimura, a grand dame of Peruvian **nikkei** cooking, brings us her version*

Preparation

Heat a small skillet over medium heat and then add the oil. When the oil is hot, add all the ingredients and sauté until the onion is completely translucent and just starting to turn golden, about 5 minutes. Remove from the heat and let cool before storing.

Pasta de Ají Amarillo

Ingredients:

- 1lb (½ kg) **ají amarillo**
- ½ cup sugar
- ¼ cup vinegar
- 2 tbsp vegetable oil

Preparation

Wash, stem, seed and devein **ají amarillo**. Place in a large pot of cold water and bring to the boil. Reduce heat and simmer for 30-40 minutes until **ajíes** are soft. Strain **ajíes** and place in a blender or the bowl of a food processor fitted with a steel blade. Add the other ingredients. Blend to form a creamy paste. Press through a fine mesh sieve to remove any pieces of skin.

Pasta de Ají Mirasol & Ají Panca

Ingredients:

- 2 tbsp vegetable oil
- 1lb (½ kg) dried **ají mirasol** or **ají panca**
- Water

Preparation

Stem, seed and devein the **ajíes**. (For a very spicy paste you can keep some of the veins.) Toast them in a dry skillet over high heat for a few minutes and then blanche them. Depending on the amount of spiciness you want your paste to have you can blanche just once, or two or three times (in a change of water each time). The spiciness will reduce with each blanching. In a blender or food processor fitted with a steel blade, process the **ajíes** with just enough vegetable oil and water to make a thick paste. Push the mixture through a fine sieve and discard any remaining skin and veins.

Note: The above recipes make 1 cup.

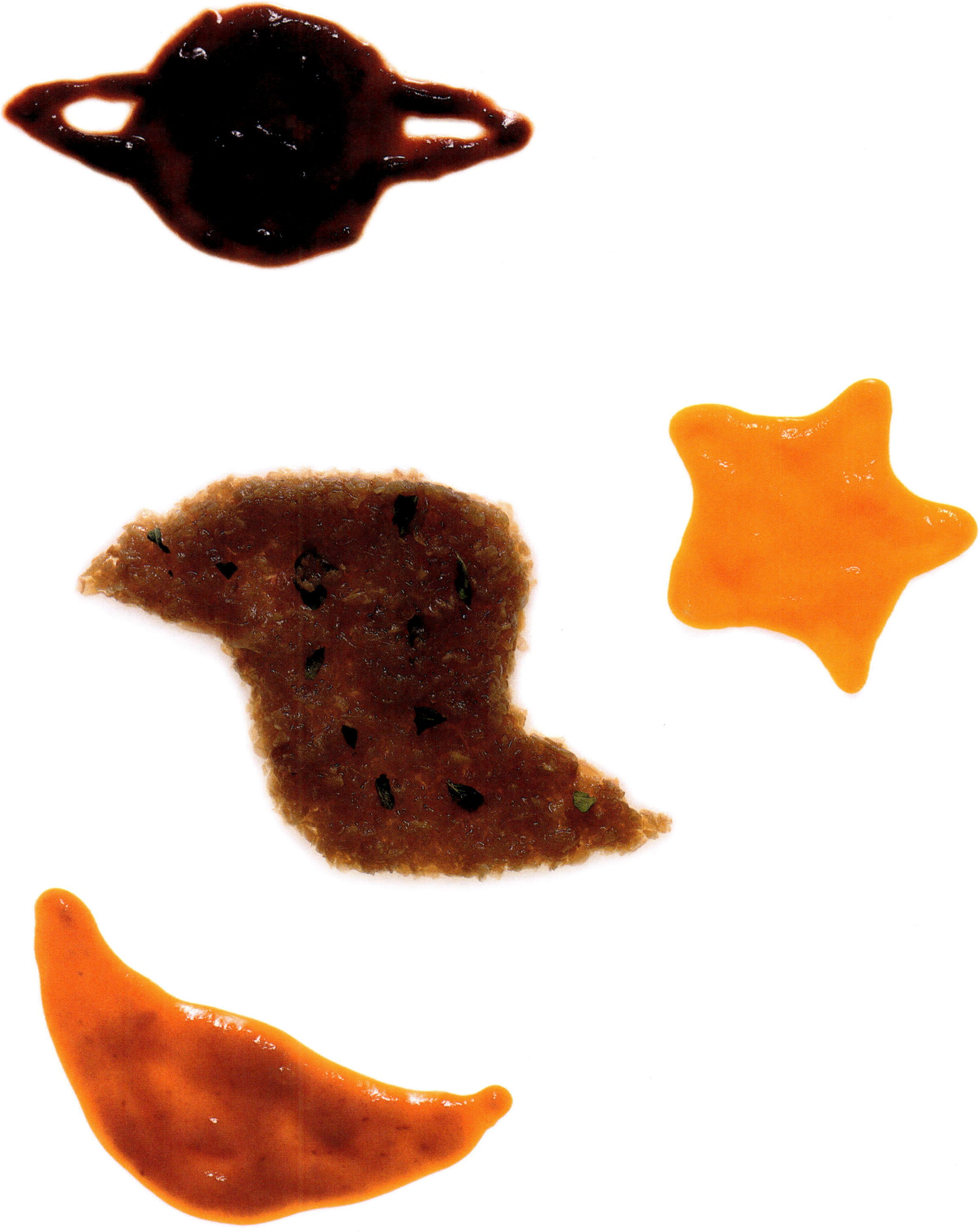

SALSAS

Mayonesa de Rocoto

Make the mayonnaise as for **Mayonesa de Ají** (p.232). Scrape into a bowl and set aside. To make the **rocoto** paste stem, seed and devein the **rocotos**. Blanche in about 4 cups (1 ltr) water, with ½ tbsp sugar and 1 tsp vinegar. Repeat process three times, changing water, sugar and vinegar each time. Drain and place in blender. Process until the **rocoto** forms a creamy paste. Add **rocoto** paste to mayonnaise and mix thoroughly until the sauce is a rosy pink color. Add salt to taste.

For the rocoto paste:
- 2 red rocotos
- 1½ tbsp sugar
- 3 tsp vinegar

Jalpahuaica (hal-puh-whycuh)

Blend first five ingredients in a blender to make a creamy paste. Scrape into a bowl. Mix in chopped scallions and serve as a condiment. Also, as in the picture, you can mix the ingredients without blending them.

- 1 **rocoto**, seeded and deveined
- 2 tomatoes, seeded and chopped
- 2 tbsp vegetable oil
- 2 scallions (white part only) finely chopped
- Juice of one key lime
- Salt

Each recipe makes about 1 cup of salsa

Clockwise from top right: Salsa Cruda de Rocoto, Huacatay, Salsa de Ají & Cebolla China, Salsa Criolla (variation with radishes), Jalpahuaica, Mayonesa de Ají, Mayonesa de Rocoto. **Middle:** Salsa Criolla.

Huacatay

Wash and dry the **huacatay** leaves well. Blend with ají amarillo in a blender or processor while adding oil, vinegar and salt to form a smooth paste.

- 1lb **ají amarillo**, seeded, deveined and chopped
- ½ cup fresh **huacatay** leaves
- Vinegar
- Vegetable oil
- Salt

Salsa de Ají & Cebolla China

Mix all ingredients thoroughly in a small bowl. Serve as a condiment or dipping sauce for **anticuchos**. Cilantro can also be used with, or as a substitute for, the scallions.

- 1 cup **ají amarillo** paste (p.228)
- 1 tbsp olive oil
- 2 scallions, green part only, very finely chopped
- Juice of 1 key lime
- Salt and pepper

Salsa Cruda de Rocoto

Seed, devein and dice rocotos. Place in a large bowl of water with sugar and vinegar. Soak for 5 minutes. Drain and rinse well in 2 changes of water. Add vegetable oil, lime juice, chopped scallions and salt and pepper to taste. Blend well and serve as a condiment.

- 2 large red **rocotos**
- ¼ cup sugar
- ¼ cup vinegar
- 1 tbsp vegetable oil
- 4 scallions, white part only, very finely chopped
- Juice of 1 key lime
- Salt and pepper

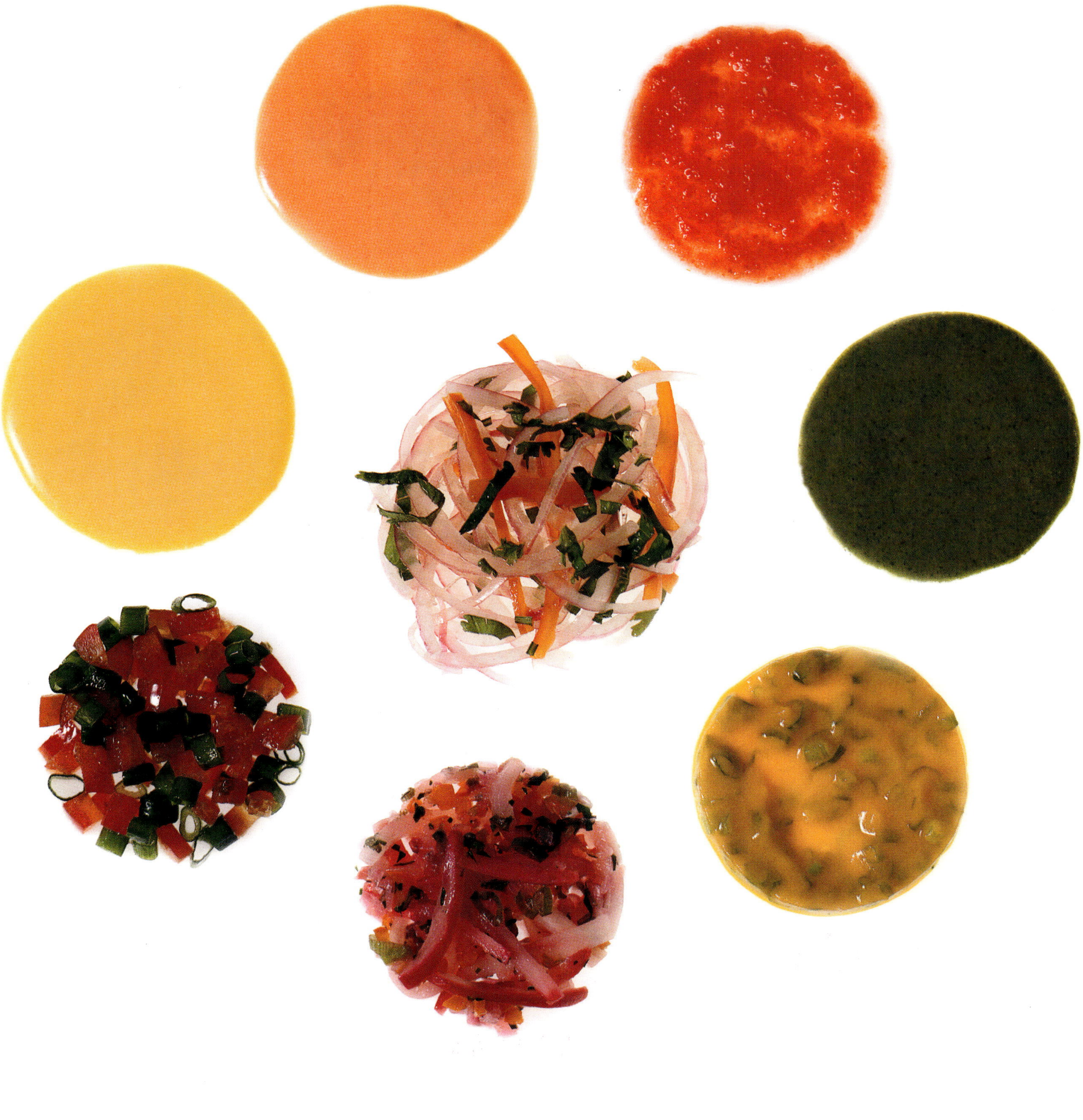

Mayonesa de Ají

Combine egg, mustard, lime juice, salt and pepper in a blender or food processor fitted with a steel blade. Process for 1 minute. With the motor running, add the two oils in a slow steady stream to form a well-emulsified mayonnaise. Taste the mayonnaise and add seasoning if necessary. Scrape mayonnaise into a bowl and add pasta de **ají amarillo**.

- 1 egg
- ¼ tsp freshly ground pepper
- 1 tbsp mustard
- 1 cup vegetable oil
- ½ cup olive oil
- 1 tbsp **ají amarillo** paste (p.228)
- Juice of 1 key lime
- Salt

Makes 1 cup

Salsa Criolla

Season the sliced onion with a little salt. Rinse in plenty of cold water and drain thoroughly. Place the onion in a small bowl and season again with salt, key lime juice and vinegar. Add the **ají amarillo**, vegetable oil and cilantro or parsley. Mix well.

- 2 red onions, sliced as fine as possible
- 1 tbsp vegetable oil
- 1 **ají amarillo**, seeded and finely sliced
- 1 tbsp vinegar
- 3 sprigs of cilantro or parsley, finely chopped
- Juice of 2 key limes
- Salt

Makes 1 ½ cups

Tip: For a variation, add 1 cup of radishes in fine julienne.

Marinade: Beef Heart Anticucho

Prepare marinade by mixing all the ingredients. Alternately, you may use the marinade for the tenderloin **anticucho** with wonderful results.

- ½ cup light vinegar
- 1-2 tbsp **ají panca** paste (p.228)
- ¼ tsp vegetable oil
- Salt

Marinade: Chicken Anticucho

Prepare marinade by mixing all the ingredients.

- 2 cloves of garlic, minced
- 1 tbsp **ají amarillo** paste (p.228)
- 1 tbsp vegetable oil
- 1 tsp dried oregano
- Freshly ground pepper
- Pinch cumin

Marinade: Chicken Liver Anticucho

Prepare marinade by mixing all the ingredients.

- 1 tbsp **ají panca** paste (p.228)
- 1 tsp vinegar
- 2 bay leaves
- ½ tsp dried oregano
- 1 tbsp vegetable oil
- Pinch cumin

Marinade: Tenderloin Anticucho

Peel ginger root with a sharp knife and blend all ingredients in a food processor.

- 1 cup **ají panca** paste (p.228)
- 3 cloves of garlic
- 1 piece of fresh ginger root (approx ¾ in)
- ½ tsp cumin
- 6 tbsp vinegar
- 2 tbsp soy sauce
- 1 tbsp salt

Desserts

All Peruvian desserts spring from Colonial times when a household and its hostess' worth was judged by the quality of the desserts served. They are not complicated but are often time consuming and need to be prepared with love and respect for tradition. Someone who has been bringing those elements to Peruvian cooking for more than thirty years is the greatly loved and respected caterer Marisa Guiulfo. A highly successful self-made business woman, Marisa believes in cooking from the heart with no short cuts. Her culinary expertise and flair for decoration have made her a legend in her own right in Peru. At weddings, baptisms or state occasions, Marisa puts her own mark on some of the happiest and most significant events in our lives. All but two of the following set are from the extensive stock of dessert recipes she shared with us.

ALFAJORES

*There are many variations of traditional **alfajor** pastry. This simple recipe is easy to make and will produce melt-in-the-mouth results every time. The cookies can be filled with either **manjar blanco** or a thick syrup called **miel**.*

Ingredients:

- 2 ¼ cups all purpose flour
- ½ cup (230 g) margarine
- 3 ½ tbsp (100 g) confectioners' sugar

For the miel filling:

- 4 cups firmly packed dark brown sugar
- 1 cinnamon stick
- 2 cloves
- 2 cups water
- ½ tsp white vinegar

Preparation

Preheat oven to 375ºF / 190ºC. Sift the dry ingredients onto a lightly floured board and make a well in the center. Place the softened margarine in the center and, using your fingertips, gradually work in the dry ingredients. Work the dough lightly, pushing it away from you with the palm of your hand and then drawing it back into a ball until it is smooth.

Chill for 30 minutes.

Roll chilled dough out on a floured work surface to 1/6 in (4 mm) and cut into rounds with a 2½ - 3 in-(7 cm-) diameter cookie cutter. Place on a greased and floured cookie sheet and bake for about 12 minutes until barely golden. Be careful not to let them brown at all. Cool on racks and, when completely cool, fill with the **manjar blanco** (p.246) and coat all over with confectioners' sugar.

To make a miel filling:

Place the first four ingredients in a large heavy based pan and bring to a boil. Lower heat and simmer mixture gently until it forms a thick syrup, (238°F/approx. 115°C on a candy thermometer). Mix in the vinegar and remove from the heat. Remove cloves and cinnamon stick and leave to cool before using.

Enough for 30 medium-sized alfajores

Tip: To check if the miel filling is done, put a drop in a bowl of cold water, it should form a soft ball.

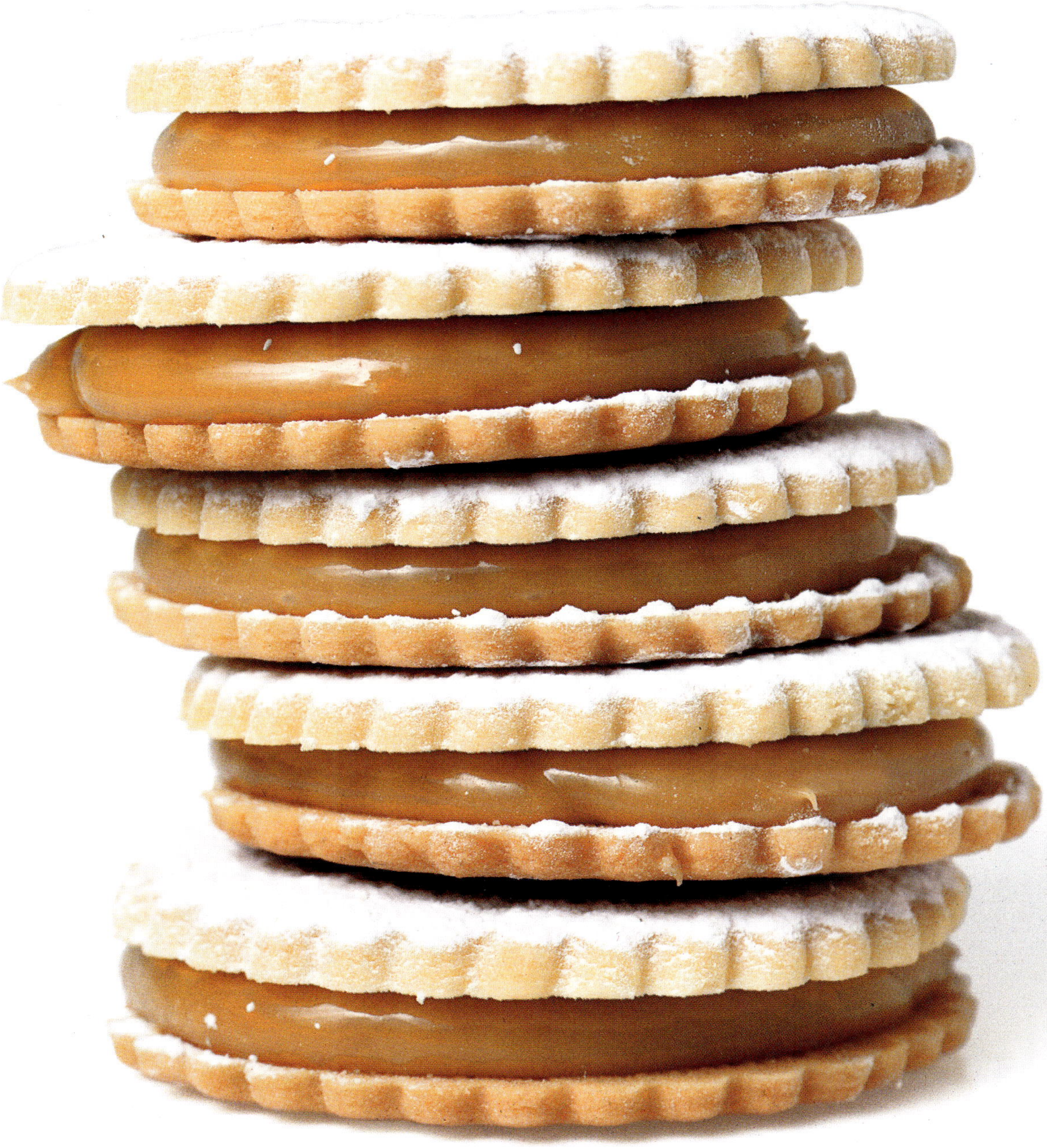

Arroz con Leche

Ingredients:

- 1 cup rice
- 5 cups water
- 1 large stick of cinnamon
- 2 cloves
- 1 can (14 ½ oz) evaporated milk
- 2 cans (28 oz) condensed milk
- 10-12 raisins, soaked overnight in water or liquor
- 1 egg yolk
- ½ cup port
- 1 egg white
- 4 tbsp sugar
- Ground cinnamon to decorate
- Peel of ½ large orange
- Pinch salt

*The Spanish brought rice to Peru and also established the convent where this sweet milk pudding has its roots. The Santa Clara convent, founded in 1606 by Saint Toribio de Mogrovejo, still lists **Arroz con leche** as one of its best sellers.*

Preparation

Blanche the orange peel in three changes of boiling water. Wash the rice very thoroughly in a strainer under running water until it runs clear.

Put the water in a saucepan with the orange peel, cinnamon stick and cloves. Bring to a boil. When the liquid is boiling, add the rice, cover and simmer on low heat until all the liquid has been absorbed, about 30 minutes.

Add the evaporated milk and stir to avoid it sticking, while bringing back to a boil. When the mixture is boiling again, add the condensed milk and the raisins. Cook for a further ten minutes, stirring continuously, until the mixture thickens.

Remove from the heat and stir in the egg yolk, ¼ cup of the port and a pinch of salt.

Heat the remaining port and the sugar together in a small heavy-based pan to form a light syrup.

Beat the egg white until it forms soft peaks, gently fold in the syrup and then fold this frothy meringue into the pudding.

Pour into a serving dish. Decorate with ground cinnamon and, if you wish, with a stick of cinnamon as well.

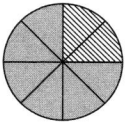

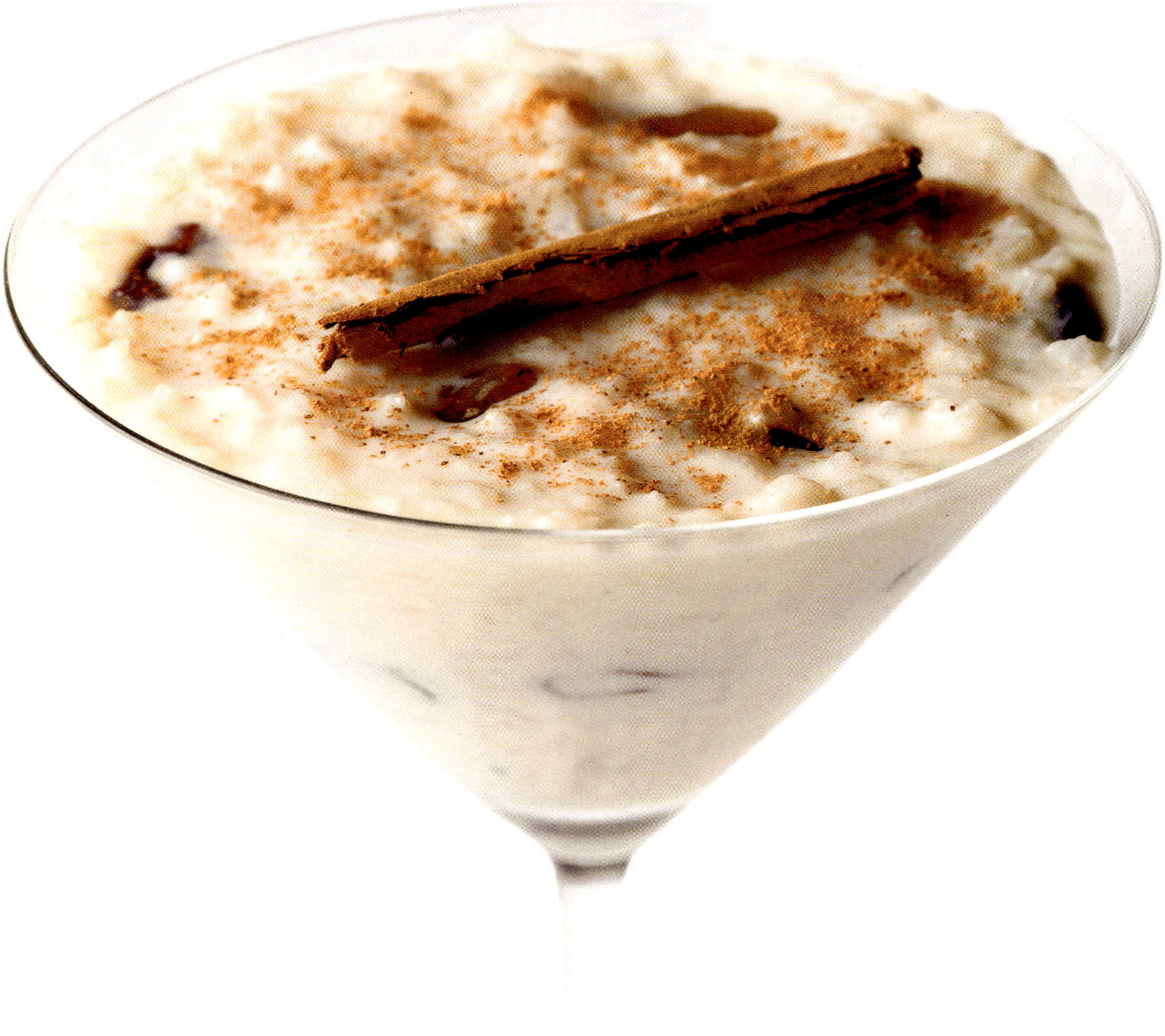

Encanelado

Ingredients:

- 10 eggs
- 10 tbsp sugar
- 7 tbsp self-rising flour
- 3 tbsp cornstarch
- 4 tbsp water
- 2 tsp vanilla extract
- ¼ cup confectioners' sugar
- 5 tbsp ground cinnamon

For the syrup:

- 1 cup sugar
- 1 cup water

- **Manjar blanco** for filling (p.246)

Where would Peruvian desserts be without cinnamon? Here we have the king of cinnamon dishes, called simply a "cinnamoned" dessert. It's wonderful, enjoy.

Preparation

Preheat oven to 350 ºF / 175 ºC. Lightly grease and flour an 8 x 7 x 3 in- (20 x 18 x 7 cm-) cake mold.

With an electric beater, beat the eggs and sugar together until all the sugar has dissolved and the mixture is thick and creamy. With the beater still running add vanilla essence and water little by little.

Sift flour and cornstarch over egg mixture and gently fold in.

Bake for 15 minutes or until cake is light golden and has started to shrink away slightly from the sides of the mold. Test to see if it is done by lightly pressing the top with your fingertip. If it is done it should spring back into shape.

Remove from oven and set aside to cool on a cake rack.

To prepare the syrup:
Boil the sugar and water together, stirring, in a small pan until all the sugar has dissolved, about 10 minutes. Don't let the syrup caramelize. Remove from the heat immediately and set aside to cool.

Unmold and cut cake in half horizontally. Moisten each center face of the two cake halves with the syrup and fill with **manjar blanco**. Replace one on top of the other.

Sift together the cinnamon and confectioners' sugar. Drizzle a little more of the syrup on top of the cake and dust with the cinnamon sugar mixture. Decorate with cinnamon sticks and/or mint leaves.

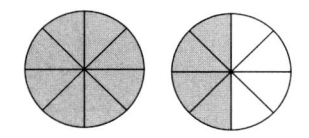

Note: This cake can also be made in a jelly roll pan, baked, cooled, spread with the filling and then rolled into a Swiss roll shape. In this form it is known in Peru as **Pionono**.

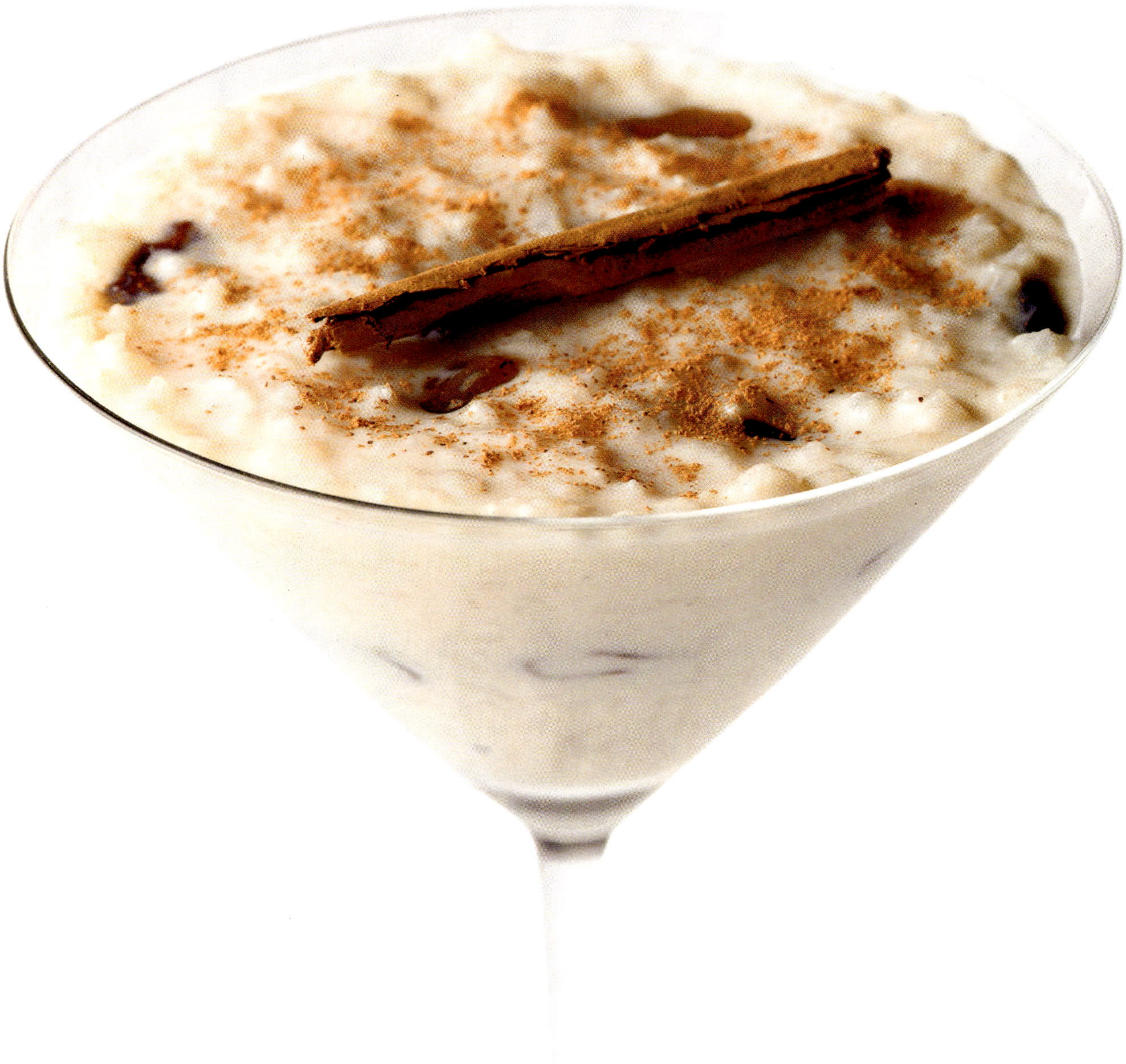

Bien me Sabe

Bien me sabe or 'it tastes good to me' speaks for itself. A luxurious desert made in the convents of Lima during Colonial times with sponge cake, syrup, fruit and nuts, this version takes a slightly different form. These individual sweets make a perfect gift or after dinner treat.

Ingredients:

- 2 cans (29 oz) evaporated milk
- 2 cans (28 oz) condensed milk
- 1 oz (30 g) chopped pecans
- 1 oz (30 g) caramelized orange peel
- 50 pecan halves
- 3 ½ oz (100 g) ground cinnamon
- 3 ½ oz (100 g) confectioners' sugar

Preparation

Combine the two milks in a heavy based saucepan and simmer gently over low heat until they form a firm paste which pulls away from the sides of the pan, about 1 ½ hours.

When the mixture has reached this consistency, stir in the nuts and the candied orange peel and cook for ½ minute more.

Remove from the heat and set mixture aside until cool enough to handle.

Form the mixture into small balls or small oval spheres covering each individual pecan half.

Sift the ground cinnamon and sugar together and dust each sweet all over with the mixture.

With the blade of a butter knife, make small decorative indentations on the top of each sweet.

Makes about 50 sweets

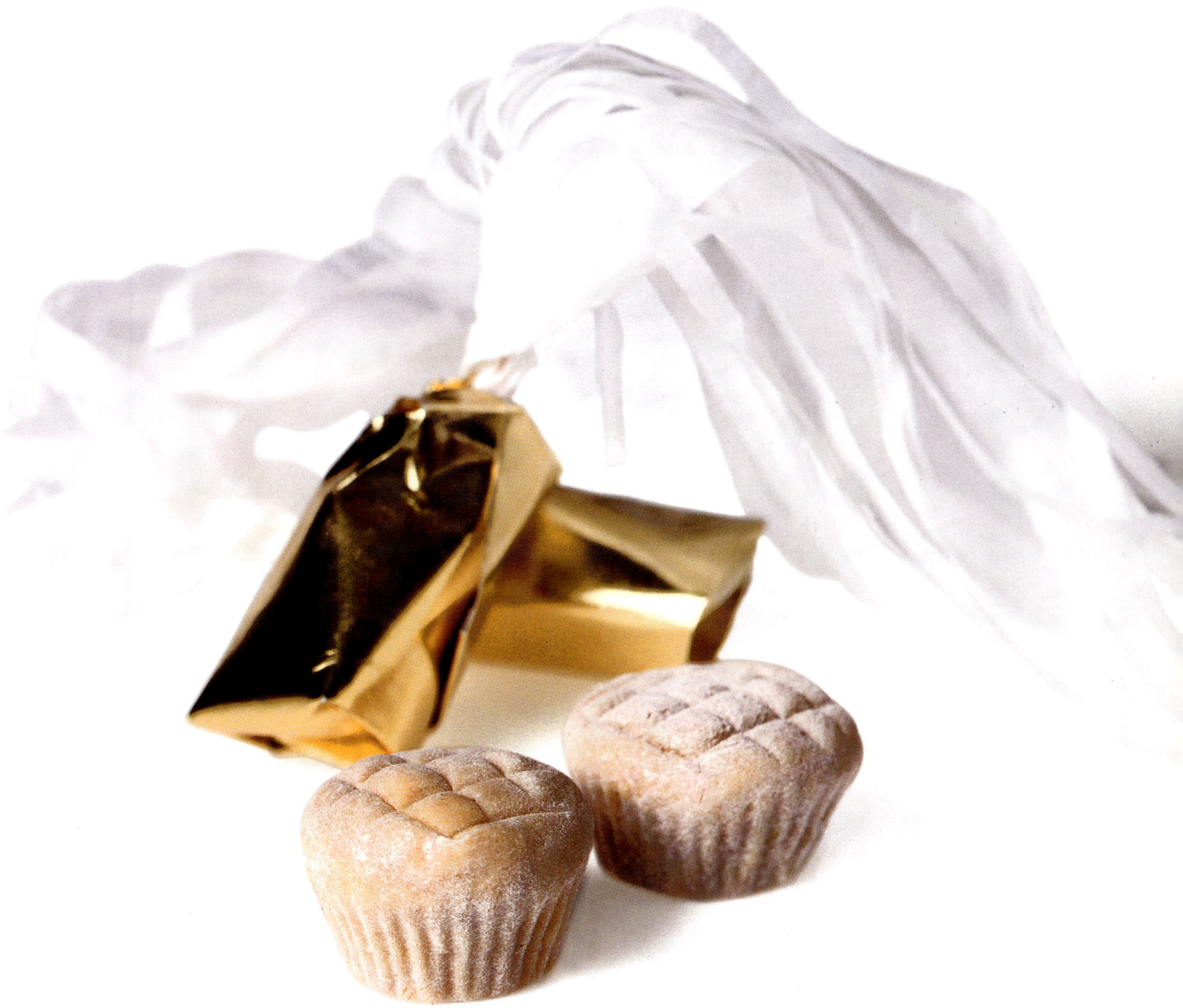

Encanelado

Where would Peruvian desserts be without cinnamon? Here we have the king of cinnamon dishes, called simply a "cinnamoned" dessert. It's wonderful, enjoy.

Ingredients:

- 10 eggs
- 10 tbsp sugar
- 7 tbsp self-rising flour
- 3 tbsp cornstarch
- 4 tbsp water
- 2 tsp vanilla extract
- ¼ cup confectioners' sugar
- 5 tbsp ground cinnamon

For the syrup:

- 1 cup sugar
- 1 cup water

- **Manjar blanco** for filling (p.246)

Preparation

Preheat oven to 350 ºF / 175ºC. Lightly grease and flour an 8 x 7 x 3 in- (20 x 18 x 7 cm-) cake mold.

With an electric beater, beat the eggs and sugar together until all the sugar has dissolved and the mixture is thick and creamy. With the beater still running add vanilla essence and water little by little.

Sift flour and cornstarch over egg mixture and gently fold in.

Bake for 15 minutes or until cake is light golden and has started to shrink away slightly from the sides of the mold. Test to see if it is done by lightly pressing the top with your fingertip. If it is done it should spring back into shape.

Remove from oven and set aside to cool on a cake rack.

To prepare the syrup:

Boil the sugar and water together, stirring, in a small pan until all the sugar has dissolved, about 10 minutes. Don't let the syrup caramelize. Remove from the heat immediately and set aside to cool.

Unmold and cut cake in half horizontally. Moisten each center face of the two cake halves with the syrup and fill with **manjar blanco**. Replace one on top of the other.

Sift together the cinnamon and confectioners' sugar. Drizzle a little more of the syrup on top of the cake and dust with the cinnamon sugar mixture. Decorate with cinnamon sticks and/or mint leaves.

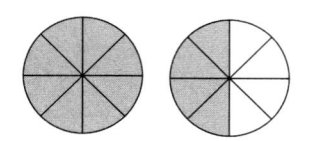

Note: This cake can also be made in a jelly roll pan, baked, cooled, spread with the filling and then rolled into a Swiss roll shape. In this form it is known in Peru as **Pionono**.

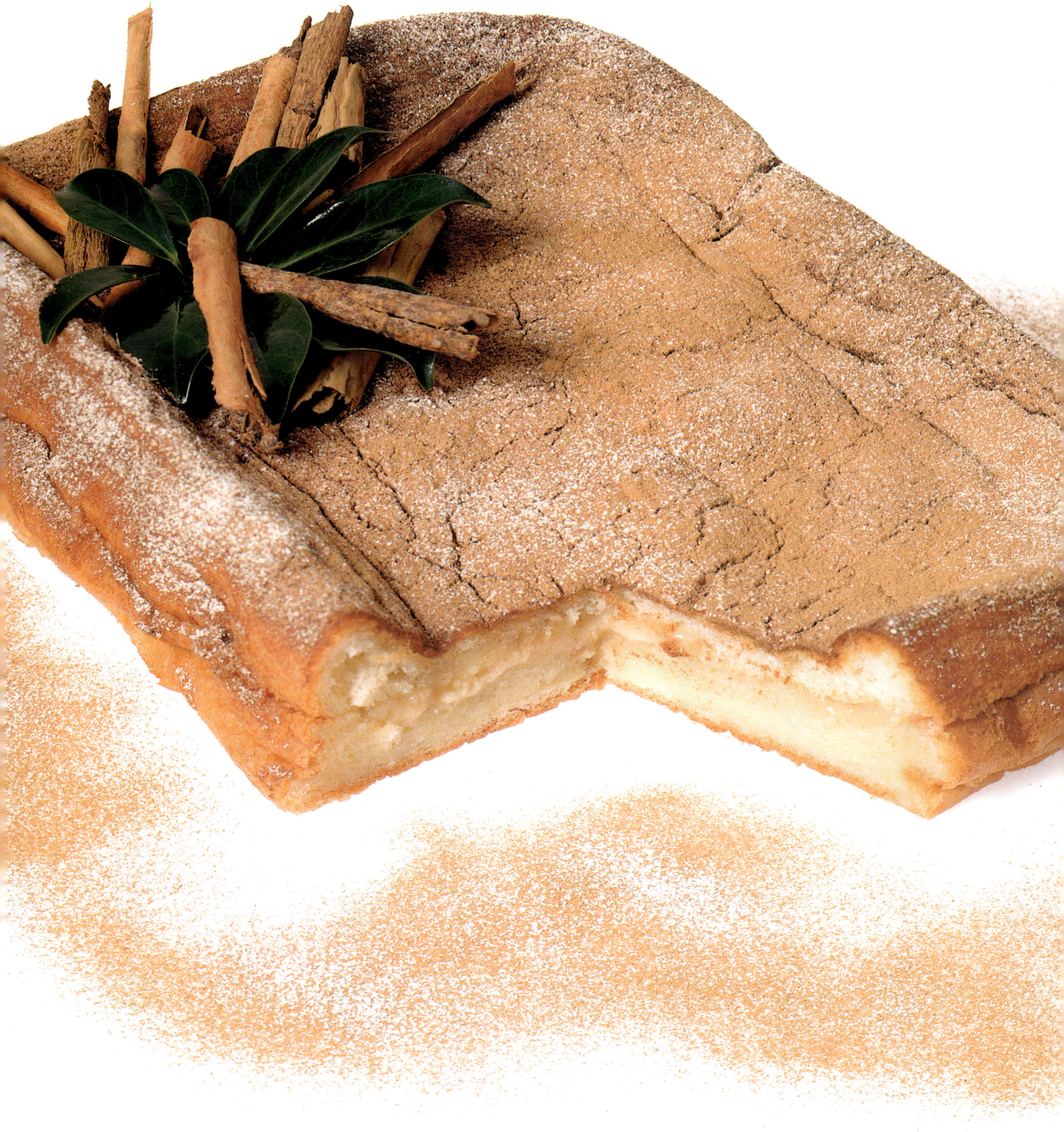

Huevo Chimbo

This is the Peruvian version of the Eastern European Baba au Rhum. In this recipe a rich egg based cake mixed with the Peruvian distilled brandy pisco is then soaked in syrup made with even more pisco before serving. How much more deliciously decadent can you get?

Ingredients:

- 18 egg yolks
- ⅛ cup pisco or brandy
- 2 eggs

For the syrup:

- 1 lb (½ kg) granulated sugar
- 2 cups pisco
- 2 cups water
- 3 ½ oz (100 g) toasted almonds
- ½ cup raisins (you can set them to marinate in Port the night before so that they are 'drunk').

Preparation

Pre-heat oven to 300ºF / 150ºC. Line the base and sides of a 9 x 11 x 2½ in- (22 x 32 x 6 cm-) cake mold with greased wax paper.

With an electric beater, beat the egg yolks, the whole egg and the pisco together until the mixture turns a pale lemon color.

Pour the mixture into the mold and bake in a bain marie in the oven for 40 minutes or until set. It should resemble a sponge cake and be firm to the touch.

Remove from the double boiler and leave to cool for 15 minutes before unmolding.

To prepare the syrup:

Meanwhile, boil the sugar, pisco and water together until the mixture thickens to a light syrup, about 10 minutes. Remove from the heat and leave to cool.

Unmold the huevo chimbo and cut into squares. Soak each individual piece thoroughly in the warm syrup for about 5 minutes and then transfer to a platter.

Serve at room temperature, drizzled with the rest of the sauce, and decorated with raisins and toasted almonds.

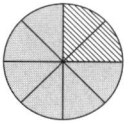

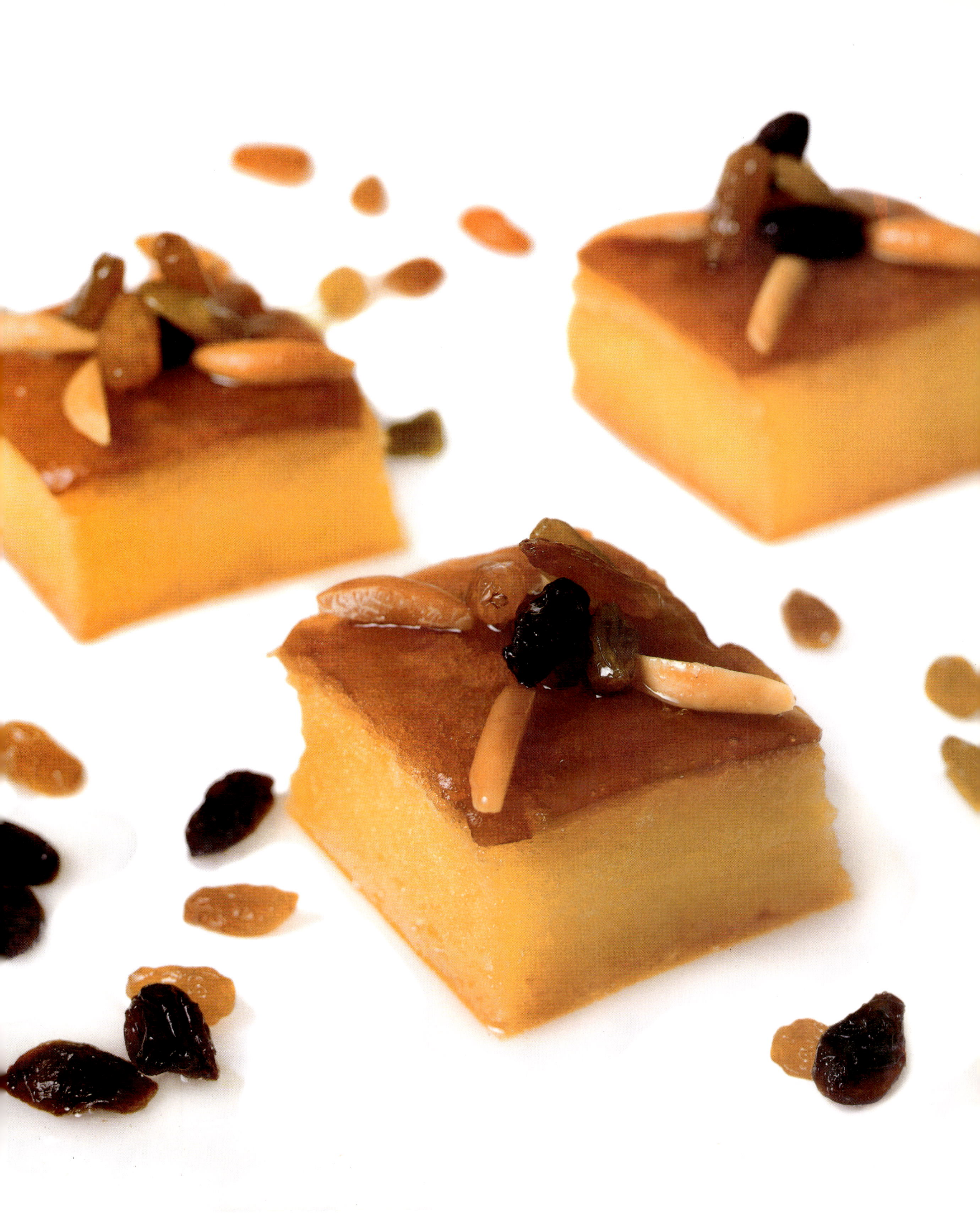

MANÁ EN FRUTITAS & BOLA DE ORO

Ingredients:

For the cake:
- 6 eggs
- 7 oz (200 g) granulated sugar
- 7 oz (200 g) self-rising flour
- 1 tsp vanilla extract

Fillings:
- 1 ½ cups **manjar blanco**
- 1 ½ cups pineapple or apricot jam
- 1 ½ cups **manjar de nueces**

For the manjar de nueces:
- 14 oz (400 g) ground nuts
- 2 cans (29 oz) evaporated milk
- 1 lb (½ kg) granulated sugar

For the maná de yemas covering and frutitas:
- 12 egg yolks, beaten
- 2 cans (29 oz) of evaporated milk
- 2 cups granulated sugar
- 1 lb (½ kg) sifted confectioners' sugar
- Food colorings
- Almond oil
- Royal icing for decoration

Preparation

To make the Bola de Oro:
Preheat oven to 400ºF / 200ºC. Butter a 24 x 18 in-(60 x 45 cm-) jelly roll pan. Line with wax paper and butter and flour paper. With an electric beater, beat the eggs and the sugar together until light and fluffy. Add the vanilla extract. Sift and gently fold in flour, taking care not to deflate the mixture.

Bake for approximately 10 to 12 minutes until the cake is just slightly golden. It should be soft to the touch and just beginning to shrink away from the sides of the pan. Be careful not to overcook. Cool in pan for 10 minutes, then turn onto rack. Meanwhile make the manjar de nueces; simmer all ingredients together in a heavy-based pan over low heat, stirring with a wooden spoon, until mixture thickens and the spoon leaves a track across base of pan. Set aside to cool.

To assemble the Bola de Oro:
Take a six-cup capacity mixing bowl. Cut the sponge cake into 7 or 8 rounds, ranging in size to fit in layers from the base to the rim of the bowl. Line the base of the bowl with the smallest sponge round. Spread with a layer of **manjar blanco** and place another sponge round on top. Spread with a layer of jam and then add another sponge round. Spread with **manjar de nueces** and top with another sponge layer. Repeat the process, adding one more layer of jam and one more of **manjar blanco**. Finally, top with the largest sponge layer and press down firmly. Allow to rest for at least two hours before unmolding.

To unmold invert pudding bowl over serving dish and tap on the base. Cover all over with a fine layer of filling in order for the coating to stick. Decorate with royal icing and miniature fruits shaped from the **maná de yemas**.

To make the maná de yema covering and the miniature fruits:
In a large heavy-based saucepan combine the evaporated milk and the beaten egg yolks with the sugar. Cook the mixture over medium heat, stirring continuously until it thickens to a paste and the spoon makes tracks across the bottom of the pan. The mixture will be granulated and look almost as if the milk has curdled. Remove from the heat and beat vigorously with an electric beater until the mixture becomes thick and shiny. Add the sifted confectioners' sugar, little by little as necessary, enough to bring the mixture together to form a very soft dough.

On a work surface that has been finely dusted with confectioners' sugar, roll out the dough and use to coat the cake. With the excess dough, form miniature fruit shapes; paint or airbrush with different food colorings and 'varnish' with almond oil.

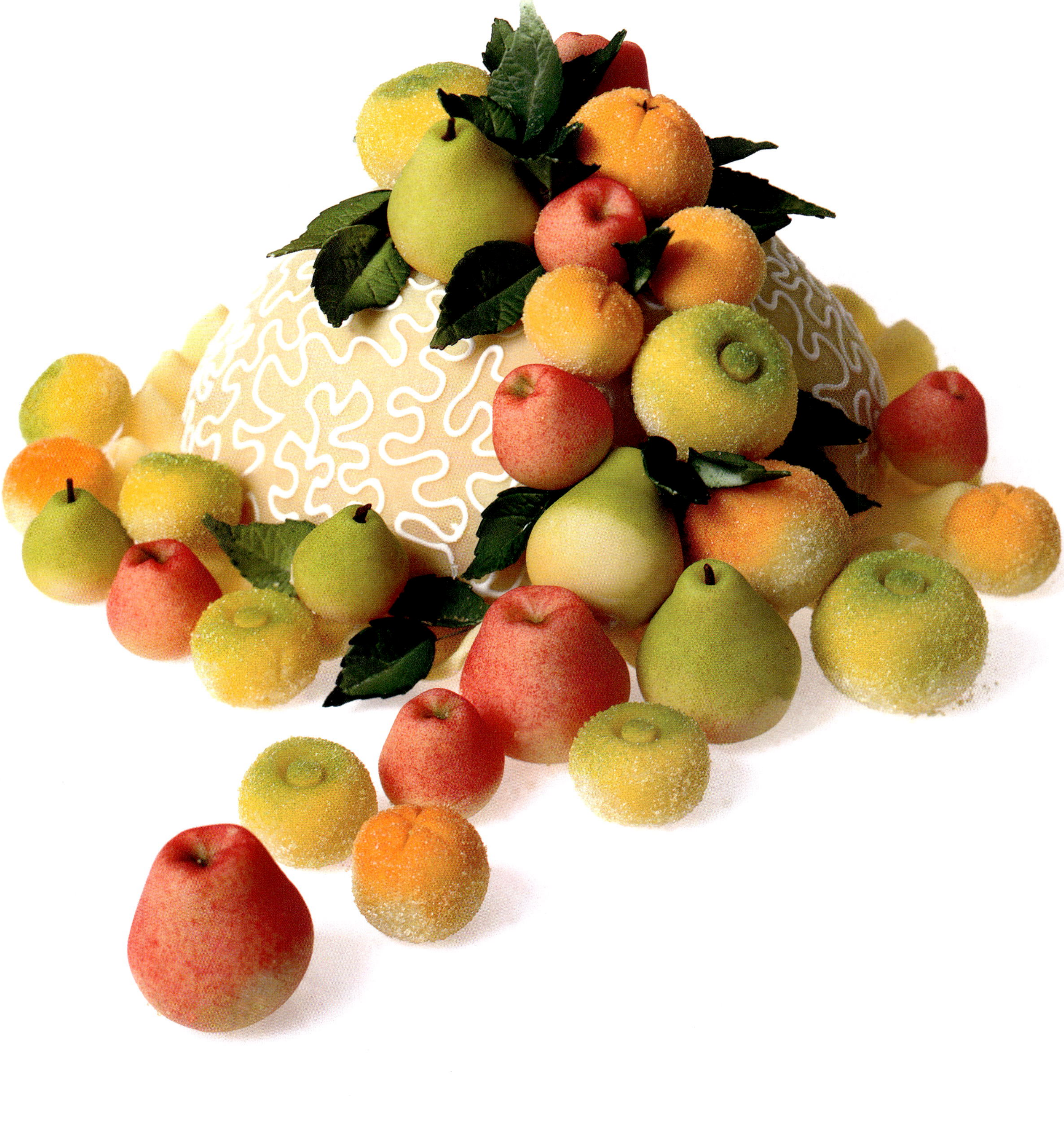

Manjar Blanco
Manjar Blanco de Lúcuma & de Chocolate

*Manjar blanco, or 'white treat', sometimes called **dulce de leche**, is an essential ingredient in many Peruvian desserts. A sweet milk caramel used as a filling or base for puddings, it's a little time consuming to make but well worth the effort. Once made, it will keep for several weeks in the refrigerator, and makes a delicious spread for your favorite breads or crackers. **Manjar Blanco** can also be flavored and eaten as a delicious pudding, which makes it comfort food, fine eating and elegant buffet fare all at once.*

Ingredients:

- 1 can (14 ½ oz) evaporated milk
- 1 can (14 oz) condensed milk

Makes about 2 cups of **manjar blanco**

Ingredients:

- 1 can (14 oz) evaporated milk
- 2 cans (28 oz) condensed milk
- 2 ½ cups (550 g) **lúcuma**, peeled

Ingredients:

- 2 cans (29 oz) evaporated milk
- 2 cups granulated sugar
- ½ cup sifted cocoa powder
- 1 tsp vanilla essence
- 1 tsp butter
- 20 g chopped nuts for decoration

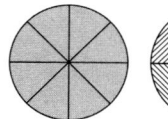

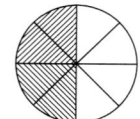

For each recipe

Preparation - Manjar Blanco

Combine the two milks in a heavy-based saucepan and simmer gently over low heat, stirring continually with a wooden spoon, until the mixture thickens to a dropping consistency and you can see the bottom of the saucepan, about 1 hour. Let cool before using.

Preparation - Manjar Blanco de Lúcuma

Blend the evaporated milk and the fruit together and then sieve to remove any tough fibers. Combine the mixture with the condensed milk in a heavy based pan and follow the same procedure as for **manjar blanco de chocolate**.

Preparation - Manjar Blanco de Chocolate

In a heavy-based saucepan, simmer the first four ingredients together over low heat, stirring continuously with a wooden spoon until the mixture thickens to a coating consistency, about ¾ to 1 hour. Mix in the butter and remove from the heat. Pour into a serving dish and allow to set. Decorate with chopped nuts and sifted cocoa.

Note: To make delicious **coconut flavored manjar blanco** simply add ½ cup (or more to taste) of dried grated coconut to the basic recipe. For the richer **manjar blanco de yemas** whisk in 5 beaten egg yolks to the basic mixture when it has cooled.

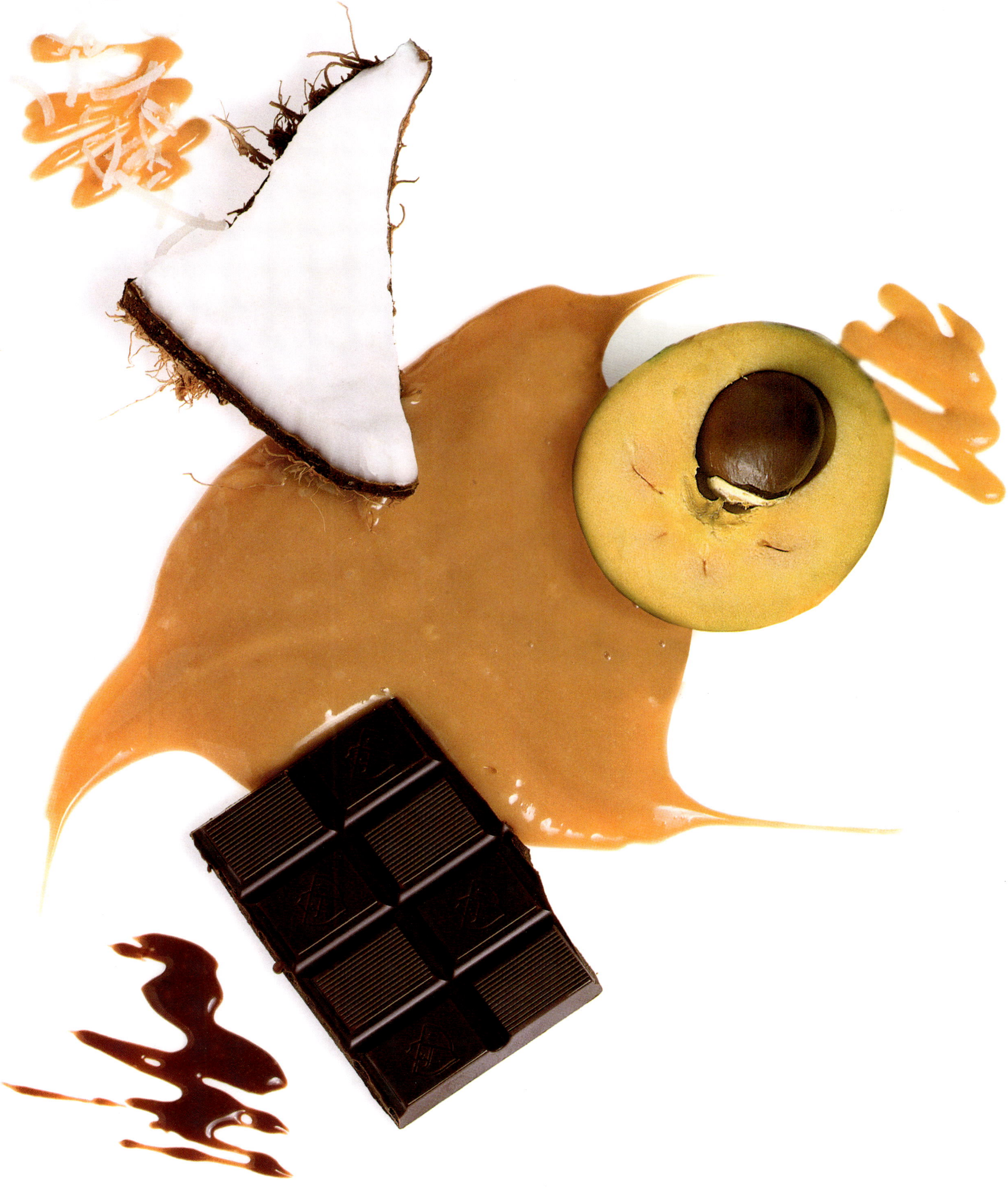

Mazamorra Morada & Limeña

*Pre-Inca cultures made many different varieties of puddings thickened with sweet potato or potato flour. Purple corn gives **Mazamorra Morada** its **criollo** signature and the distinctively purple dessert continues to be a firm Limeño favorite. **Mazamorra Limeña** is a sweeter, richer version based on molasses. Cornstarch gives just as good results as **camote** (sweet potato) flour.*

Ingredients:

- 1 large quince
- 1 small pineapple
- 1 large cooking apple
- 1 stick cinnamon
- 3 cloves
- 2 lbs (1 kg) ears of purple corn
- 1 ¾ oz (50 g) dried apricots
- 1 ¾ oz (50 g) plums or apricots
- 1 ¾ oz (50 g) prunes
- 1 ¾ oz (50 g) sun dried peaches
- 1 cup + 1 tbsp sugar
- 3 ½ oz (100 g) potato flour or cornstarch
- Ground cinnamon
- Juice from 2 key limes

Preparation - Mazamorra Morada

Soak the dried fruit overnight. Peel the quince, pineapple and apple. In a large pan bring to the boil the purple corn and the fruit peels with the cinnamon and cloves in about 3 liters of water.

Boil for about 15 minutes or until the liquid has taken on a deep purple color. Strain liquid and put aside a small amount to cool. Return the corn to the rest of the liquid and boil again for a few more minutes until the corn kernels start to burst open. Remove the corn and strain liquid again through a fine mesh sieve or muslin-lined strainer.

Dice the pineapple, apples and quinces. Add the soaked dry fruit to the purple corn liquid and then add sugar and the diced fresh fruit. Bring the mixture back to the boil. In a small bowl dissolve the cornstarch thoroughly in the previously reserved cold corn liquid, and stir into the fruit mixture. Lower the heat and cook, stirring with a metal spoon, until the mixture thickens, about 15 to 20 minutes. Stir in the key lime juice and remove from the heat. Pour into an 8 x 11 in-(20 x 18 cm-) serving dish or individual cups and let cool. Serve dusted with cinnamon.

Ingredients:

- 2 lbs (1 kg) molasses sugar
- 2 ½ cups water
- 1 ½ cans (22 oz) evaporated milk
- 1 cup all-purpose flour
- 1 cup cold water
- ½ cup port
- 1 tbsp butter
- ½ cup raisins
- ½ cup dried coconut
- ½ cup nuts, peeled and chopped

Preparation - Mazamorra Limeña

In a large saucepan, bring to the boil the molasses, cinnamon, and cloves with the 2 ½ cups of water. When all the molasses sugar has dissolved, skim off the froth and strain the liquid to remove the cinnamon and cloves. Add the evaporated milk. When the liquid returns to the boil, add the flour dissolved in the remaining cup of water.

Lower the heat. Add the coconut, raisins, butter, port and the nuts and simmer gently over low heat until the mixture has thickened to a dropping consistency. Pour into an 8 x 7 in-(20 x 18 cm-) serving dish or individual cups and allow to cool. Serve dusted with ground cinnamon.

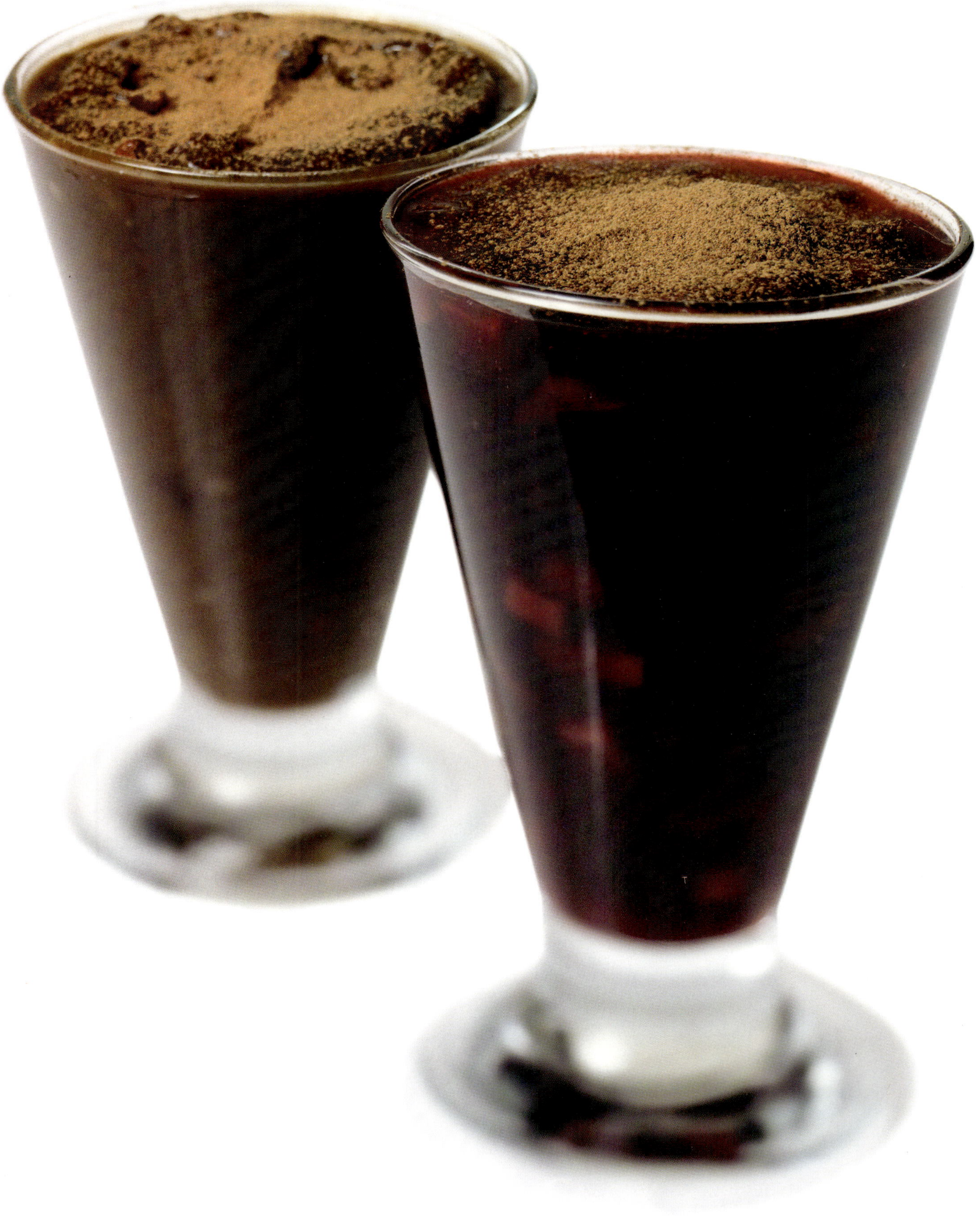

Merengue de Lúcuma

*This, along with nearly all Peruvian desserts, has its roots in Europe. The Quechua people sweetened their foods with natural fruits but did not eat sugar. The Spanish brought sugar cane to the New World and within a short time Peru became the largest single consumer of sugar in the colonies. Peruvians still have an extremely sweet tooth. This delicately crisp meringue cake filled with **lúcuma** and smothered in crème chantilly is a feast for the eyes and the palate.*

Ingredients:

For the meringues:

- 3 egg whites
- ½ cup (200 g) granulated sugar

For the filling:

- 4 **lúcumas** peeled and chopped
- 1 cup granulated sugar
- 1 cup water

For the crème chantilly:

- 2 cups whipping cream
- ¼ cup granulated sugar

Preparation

Preheat oven to 212ºF / 100ºC. Grease and flour a large baking sheet. Mark out 4 rounds on the baking sheet approximately 8 in-(20cm-) in diameter. Beat the egg whites and the sugar together until they form stiff peaks.

With a pastry bag, pipe the meringue mixture to cover the circles in an even layer. Bake in a slow oven for 2 hours, until crisp and dry but not browned.

To prepare filling:

In a small pan simmer the water, sugar and lime juice together on medium heat until all the sugar has dissolved, about 10 minutes. Set aside to cool a little.

When the syrup is cool enough to handle, blend together in blender with the **lúcuma** and then push mixture through a sieve to remove any seeds. When both meringues and filling have cooled, sandwich together the meringue circles and fill with the **lúcuma** fruit mixture.

Fill a pastry bag fitted with a fine tip with the remaining **lúcuma** filling and pipe lattice design on top of the cake. Whip the cream and sugar together to make the crème chantilly and cover sides with an even layer. Pipe more crème chantilly around the rim and the base. The completed cake will keep for up to 24 hours refrigerated.

Serve with chocolate curls and chocolate fudge sauce.

Tip: Once cooked and cooled the meringue rounds will keep in a sealed container for several days.

Note: This recipe will also make about 6 individual meringues, approximately 3in-(7cm-) in diameter.

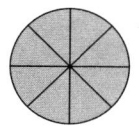

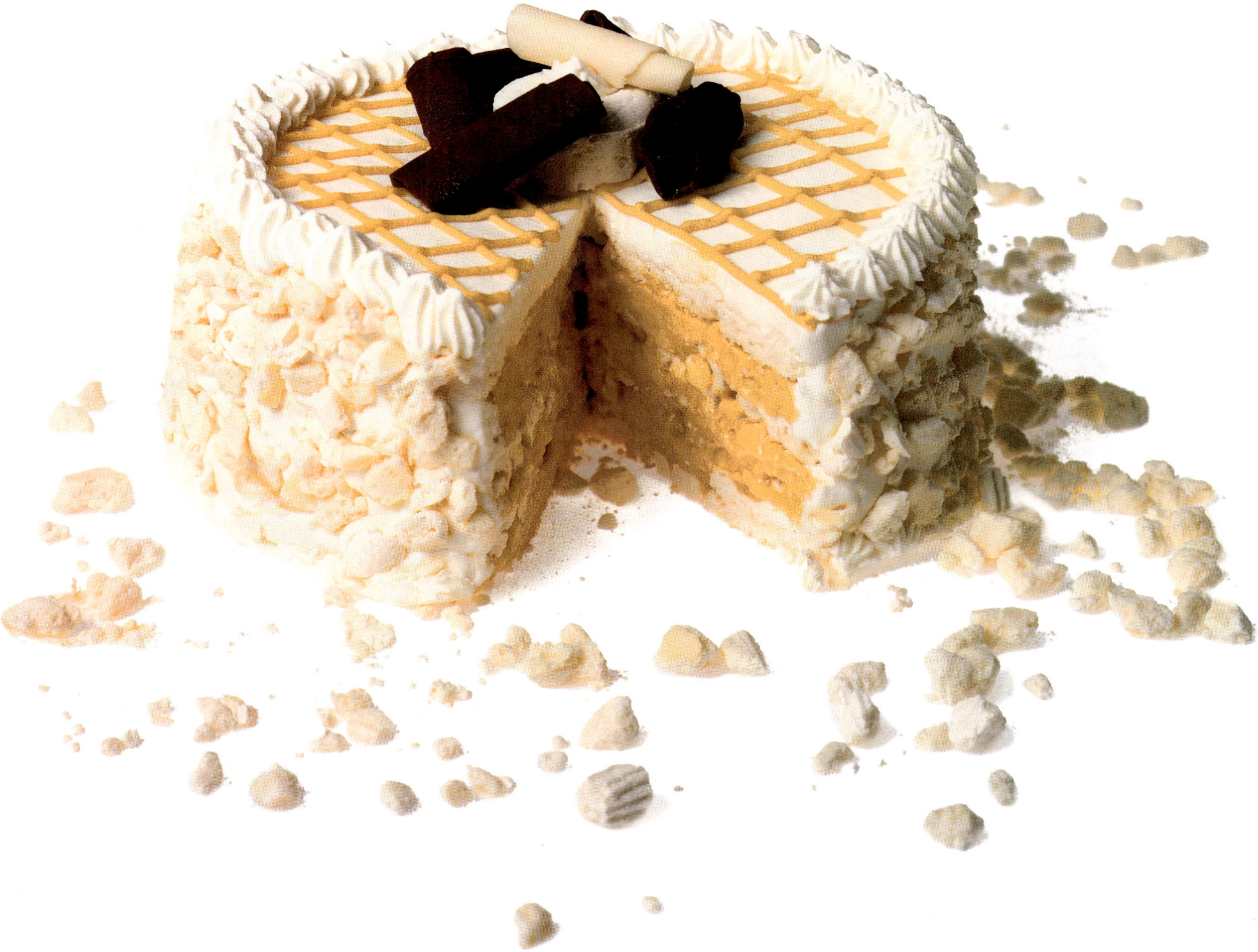

MOUSSE DE CHIRIMOYA

Ingredients:

- 2 lbs (1 kg) **chirimoya**
- 3 leaves gelatin
- 4 tbsp water
- ¾ cups heavy cream, chilled

For the passion fruit coulis:

- 1 cup passion fruit juice
- 3 tbsp sugar

Along with many other revolutionary 'libertadores', Bolivar studied in France. As a result, mousse began to appear on the menu for government parties and receptions from the 1820s onwards. Here this French classic is given a very New World makeover with the inclusion of the Andean native fruit **chirimoya** *or 'custard apple'. The result is a symphony of flavor and an elegant finale to any meal.*

Preparation

Peel the **chirimoya** and remove the black shiny seeds. Mash the flesh coarsely, (you should still be able to see bits of fruit in the finished mousse).

Whip cream to soft peaks and fold gently into the **chirimoya**. Soak gelatin in cold water until dissolved. Stir thoroughly into the **chirmoya** mixture. Lightly oil 6 individual dessert cup molds, and spoon in mousse. Refrigerate for at least 1 hour before serving.

To make the passion fruit coulis:
Bring the passion fruit juice and sugar to a boil in a small pan. Lower the heat and simmer gently for about 15 minutes until the mixture reduces to a syrupy consistency. Set aside to cool.

To unmold, invert mousse onto a dessert plate and tap gently or run a sharp knife around the edges of the mold. Serve with passion fruit coulis.

Note: **Chirimoya Alegre** or "Happy Chirimoya" is a delightful summertime alternative to this mousse. Simply peel and chop chirimoya. Remove seeds and pour fresh orange juice over the fruit. Serve chilled.

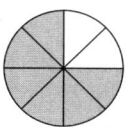

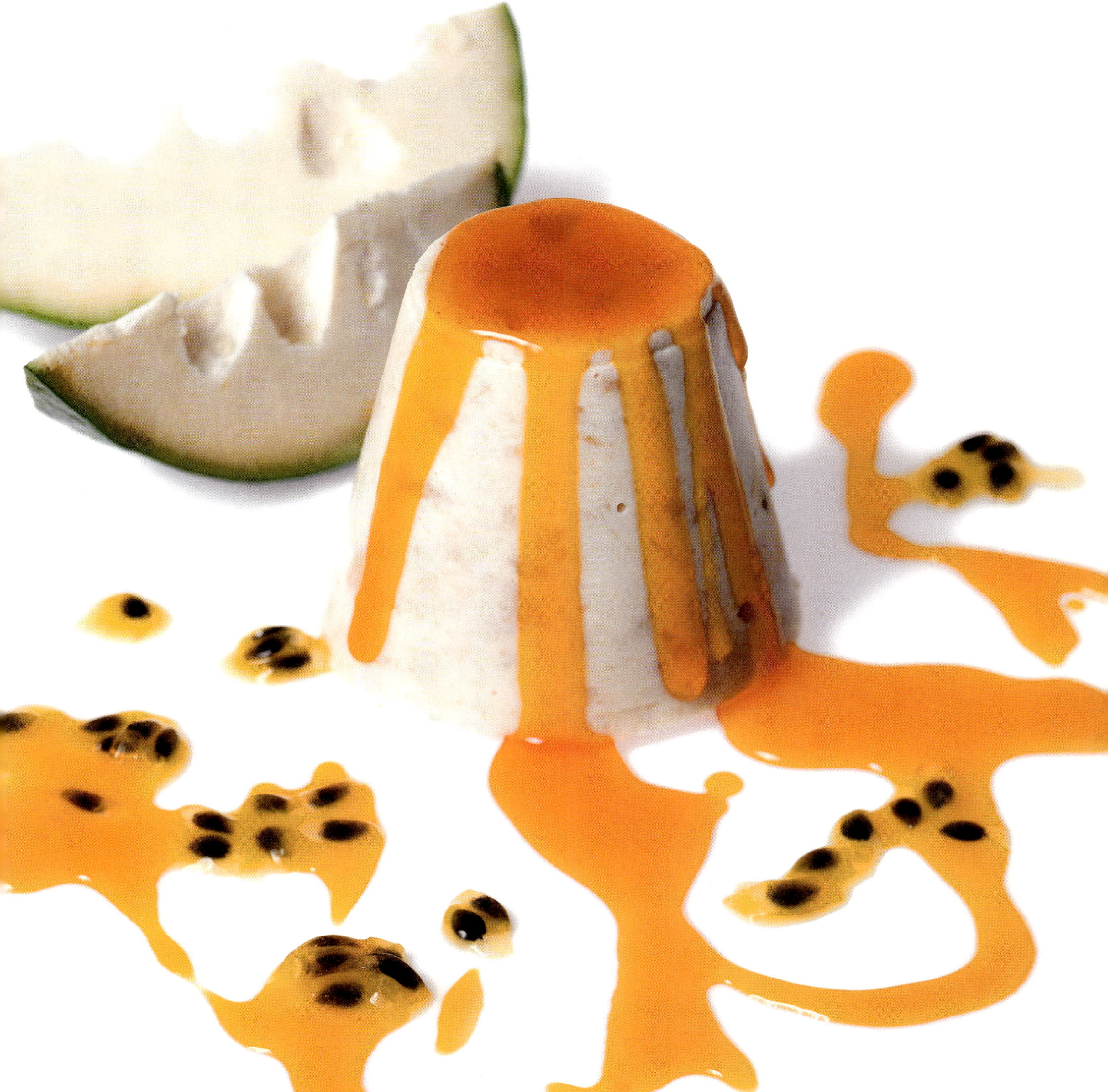

Picarones

*Arabic in origin, **Picarones** were introduced to Peru by the Spanish, where they were again adapted by black African cooks who replaced wheat flour with mashed pumpkin. 'Get your hot **picarones** here!' was a popular cry of the street vendors in 19th century Lima. Present day Limeño families will take a Sunday afternoon trip to the **picaronerías** along the shore to get these fragrant donut-like beignets, always dipped in syrup.*

Ingredients:

For the picarones:

- ½ lb (250 g) peeled and chopped pumpkin
- 1 lb (½ kg) peeled and chopped sweet potato
- 4 tbsp sugar
- 1 egg, lightly beaten
- 3 tbsp fresh yeast
- 2 cups self-rising flour
- 2 ½ tbsp aniseed
- 1 stick cinnamon
- 1 tbsp cloves
- Oil for frying
- Pinch salt

For the syrup:

- 2 cups firmly packed dark brown sugar
- 2 cups white sugar
- 1 fig leaf
- 2 (4-inch) cinnamon sticks
- 1 tbsp cloves
- 2 cups water
- Peel of 1 orange, cut into large strips

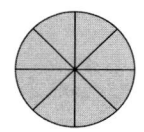

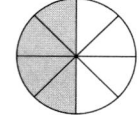

Makes 40 **beignets** or **picarones**,

Preparation

Fill a large pan with 14 cups of water and bring to a boil with the cinnamon sticks, cloves and aniseed. Lower heat to medium and simmer for 10 minutes to make an aromatic infusion. Strain to remove spices and then boil the sweet potato and pumpkin in the infusion until tender, about 10 - 15 minutes. Strain, reserving 2 cups of the cooking liquid. Pass the sweet potato and pumpkin through a fine mesh sieve. Leave the purée and the reserved cooking liquid to cool. In a small bowl, combine the reserved infusion, sugar and yeast and let stand in a draft free place to prove, 10 -15 minutes.

Place the strained sweet potato and pumpkin purée in a large bowl; add the salt, yeast mixture and egg, and blend thoroughly. Fold in the flour and continue to stir vigorously to make a soft, smooth dough which doesn't stick to your hands. Place the mixing bowl in a warm, draft free place, cover with a damp cloth and leave to rise for about 1 hour or until the mixture has doubled in volume.

To prepare the syrup:
Combine the brown sugar, white sugar, cinnamon sticks, cloves, orange peel, fig leaf and water in a medium-sized saucepan. Cook over low heat for 20 -25 minutes, stirring occasionally until the mixture thickens to a syrup. Strain.

To fry the picarones:
In a large pan or deep fryer, heat the oil to 325ºF / 165ºC. Form one tablespoon of the dough into a ring shape and fry until golden. Repeat until all the dough is used, rinsing your hands from time to time in ice water to make dough rings more manageable. Remove **picarones** from hot oil with a slotted spoon and drain on kitchen paper. Serve immediately bathed in syrup.

Tip: You can also process the dough mixture in a food processor or bread maker for 10 minutes on speed level 2. To make good picarones the dough must be elastic. Some people recommend that you put a cork into the hot oil to prevent the picarones from burning.

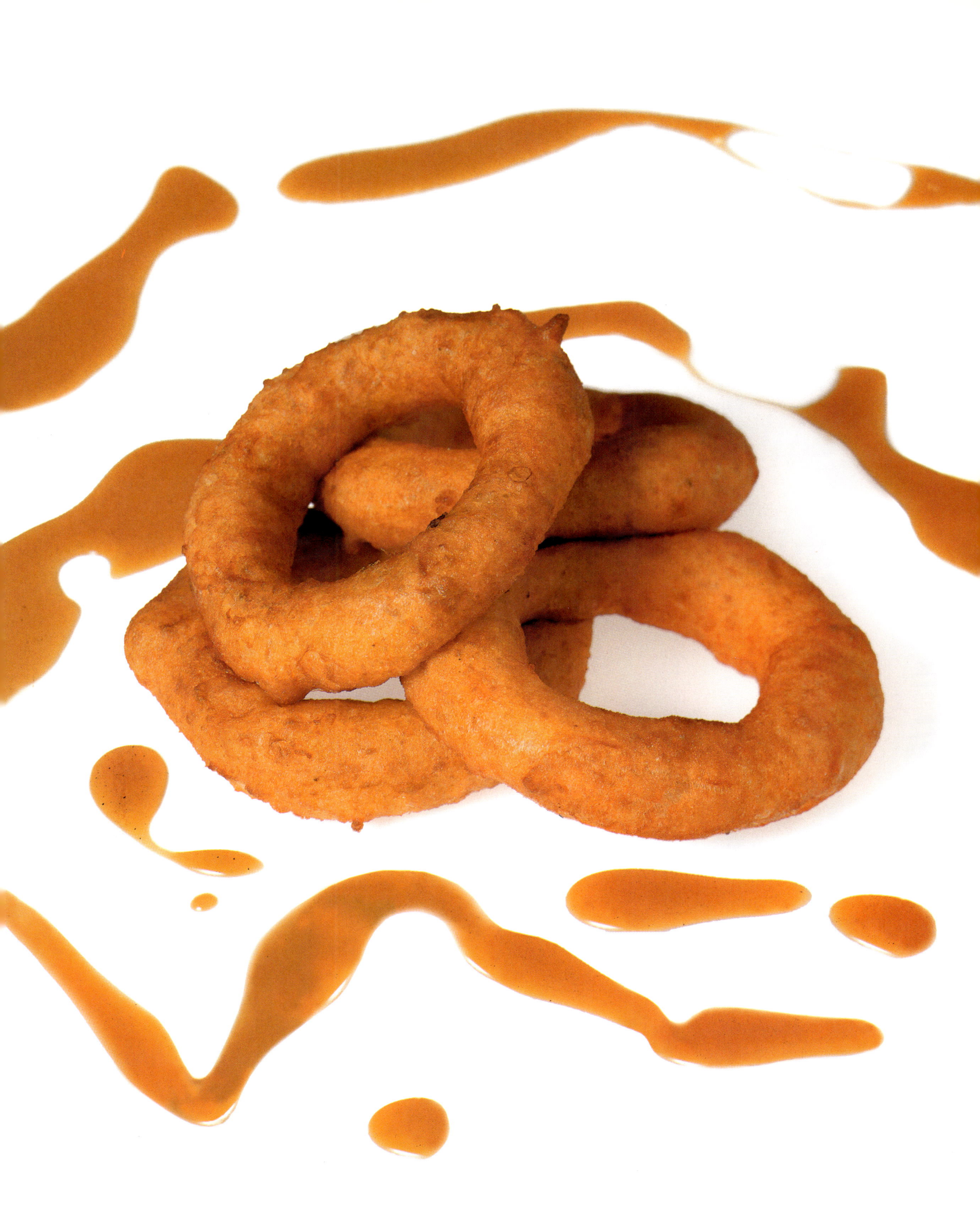

PONDERACIONES

This typical dessert from the viceroyalty takes a little practice to make. The traditional spiral shaped iron batter molds are made especially for the convents and pastry shops in Lima where these lighter than air 'meditations' are produced. Any shape can be used as long as it is heat resistant.

Ingredients:

- 3 eggs
- 1 cup milk
- 1 cup all purpose flour
- Oil for deep frying

For the manjar blanco de yemas:

- 2 cans (28 oz) condensed milk
- 2 cans (29 oz) evaporated milk
- 10 egg yolks lightly beaten

The traditional spiral shaped **ponderación** iron.

Makes about 15 **ponderaciones** and 4 cups **manjar blanco de yemas**

Preparation

Blend the first three ingredients together to make a smooth batter. Heat the oil in a large, deep saucepan. Heat the iron batter mold in the hot oil and then dip into the batter. Cover with a thin film of the batter, leaving a ½ cm rim clear at the top of the mold. This is because during deep frying the batter will bubble up a little.

Dip the covered mold into the hot oil and deep fry until golden, not more than ½ a minute. Remove from the oil and tap the mold gently to remove **ponderación**. Drain on paper towel.

To make the manjar blanco de yemas:
Follow the recipe for **manjar blanco** (p.246) and set aside to cool before stirring in the egg yolks.

Spoon a little of the **manjar blanco de yemas** onto a plate. Place the **ponderación** on top and dust with sifted confectioners' sugar. Serve with fresh fruits, ice cream and strawberry coulis.

Tip: You can also serve them with honey (miel filling - p. 234).

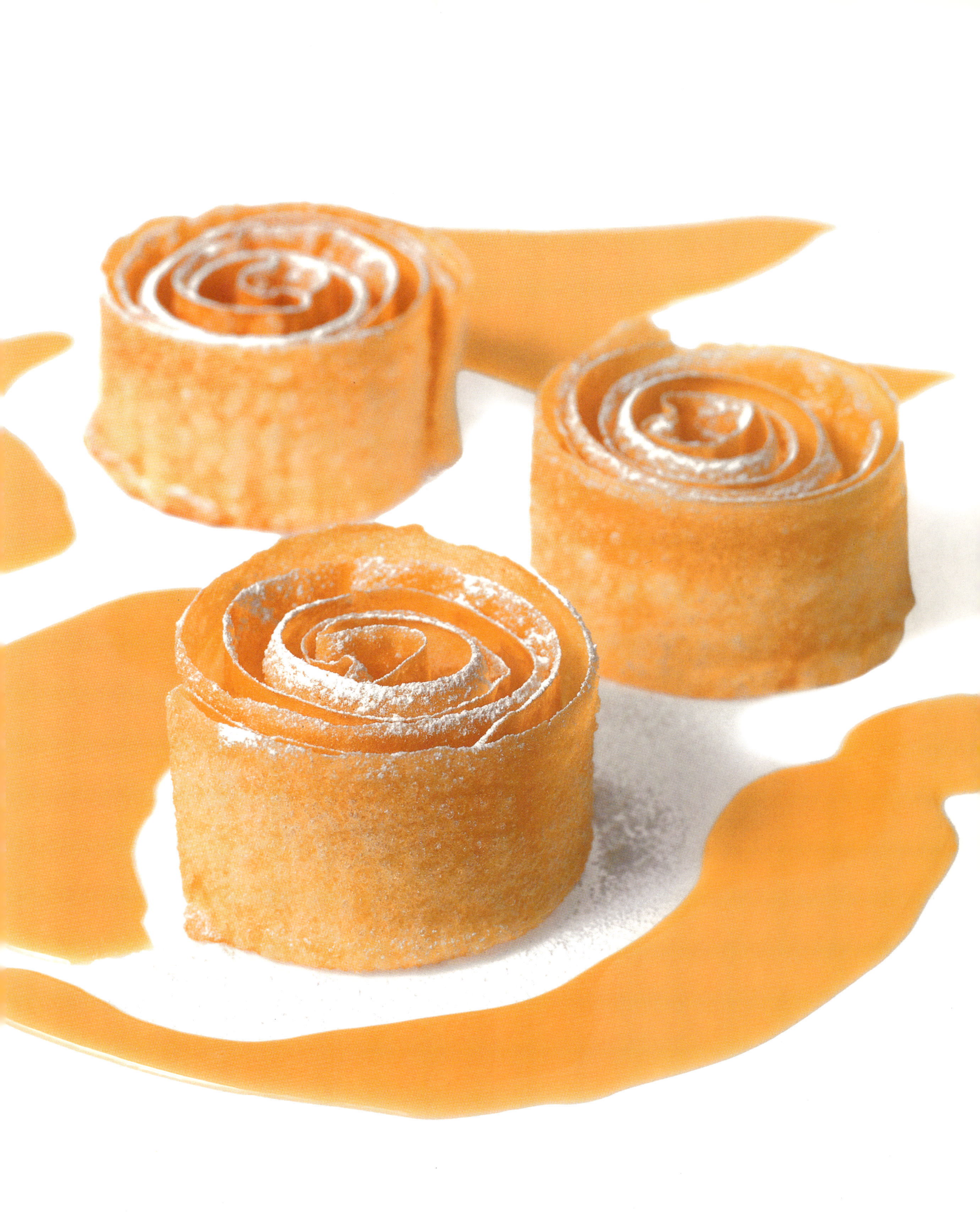

Suspiro de Limeña

Ingredients:

- 1 can (14 ½ oz) evaporated milk
- 1 can (14 oz) condensed milk
- 8 egg yolks

For the syrup:

- 1 cup port
- 1 ½ cups granulated sugar
- 4 egg whites

For serving:

- Ground cinnamon

*This classic **criollo** dessert is said to have been named by the famous Peruvian poet and author José Gálvez whose wife doña Amparo Ayarez was famous for her cooking. When asked what inspired the name, he reportedly replied 'because it is soft and sweet like the sigh of a woman'. In this case, it would be a woman from Lima, a **Limeña**, .*

Preparation

To prepare the caramel:
Combine the two milks in a heavy-based pan and simmer gently over low heat, stirring continually with a wooden spoon until the mixture thickens and the spoon leaves tracks across the bottom of the pan, about 1 hour.

Take off the heat and whisk in beaten egg yolks. Leave to cool and then pour into shallow dessert bowl or individual serving cups.

To prepare the syrup:
Combine sugar and port in a small pan and boil until syrup forms an unbroken thread when dropped from the spoon.

To prepare the meringue:
Beat the egg whites until they form soft peaks. Continue beating, adding hot syrup in a slow steady stream.

In a bowl or individual cups, mound the meringue on top of the caramel mixture and dust lightly with ground cinnamon.

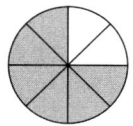

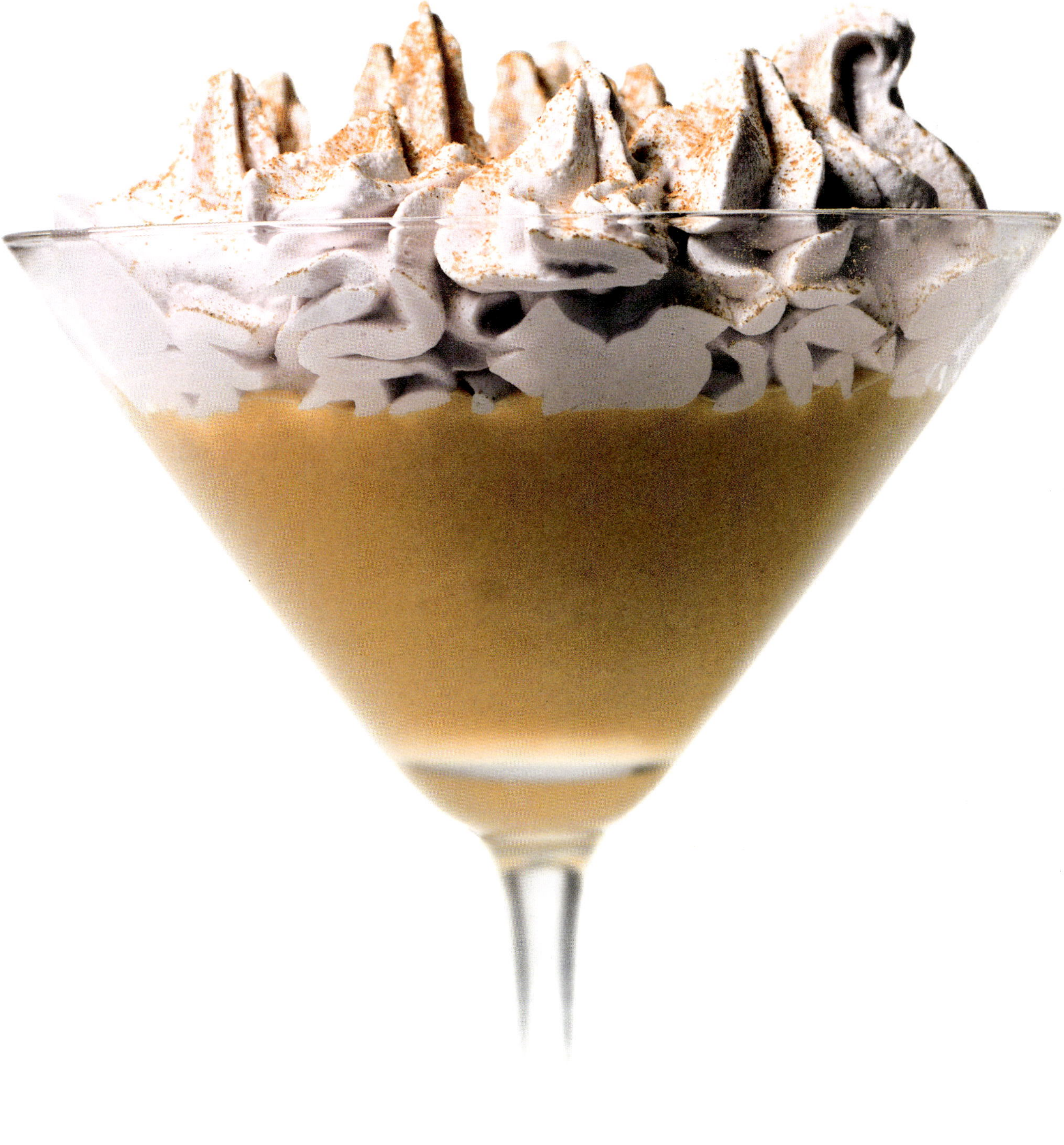

Tejas

Ingredients:

- 5 cups (1 kg) white sugar
- 18 cups (4 ½ ltr) fresh milk or 9 cups (2 ¼ ltr) evaporated milk, mixed with equal parts of water
- 3 ½ tbsp (100 g) butter
- ½ tsp (3 g) bicarbonate of soda
- ½ tsp salt
- ¼ oz (7 g) soy lecithin
- ½ tsp vanilla extract

For coating:

- Fondant (sugar coating)
- Melted chocolate

*These delicious colonial sweets are made by Elena Panizo in her candy factory in the peaceful southern town of Ica. Based on the traditional confection of **manjar blanco** they have become famous all over Peru. Wrapped in pretty paper they make a thoughtful hostess gift or treat for yourself.*

Preparation:

In a copper pan, combine sugar, milk, butter, soy lecithin and salt. Stir until the sugar dissolves and the mixture starts to boil. Wipe the edges repeatedly with a brush or a piece of cloth wrapped around a wooden spoon to avoid the mixture crystallizing.

Continue stirring at intervals until the mixture starts to thicken. Cook for a few more minutes, stirring continuously, until the mixture reaches 210ºF / 99ºC on a candy thermometer.

Just before drawing off the heat, add vanilla to perfume the mixture. Let rest for 24 hours before making the tejas

To form the Tejas:
Form the mixture into a 1 in-(2½ cm-) diameter roll and cut it into 1½ in- (4 cm-) pieces. Top the pieces with the fruit of your choice. Suggested varieties: candied lemons or oranges, preserved fruits, prunes or any type of nut.

For the coating:
Coat with fondant or melted chocolate.

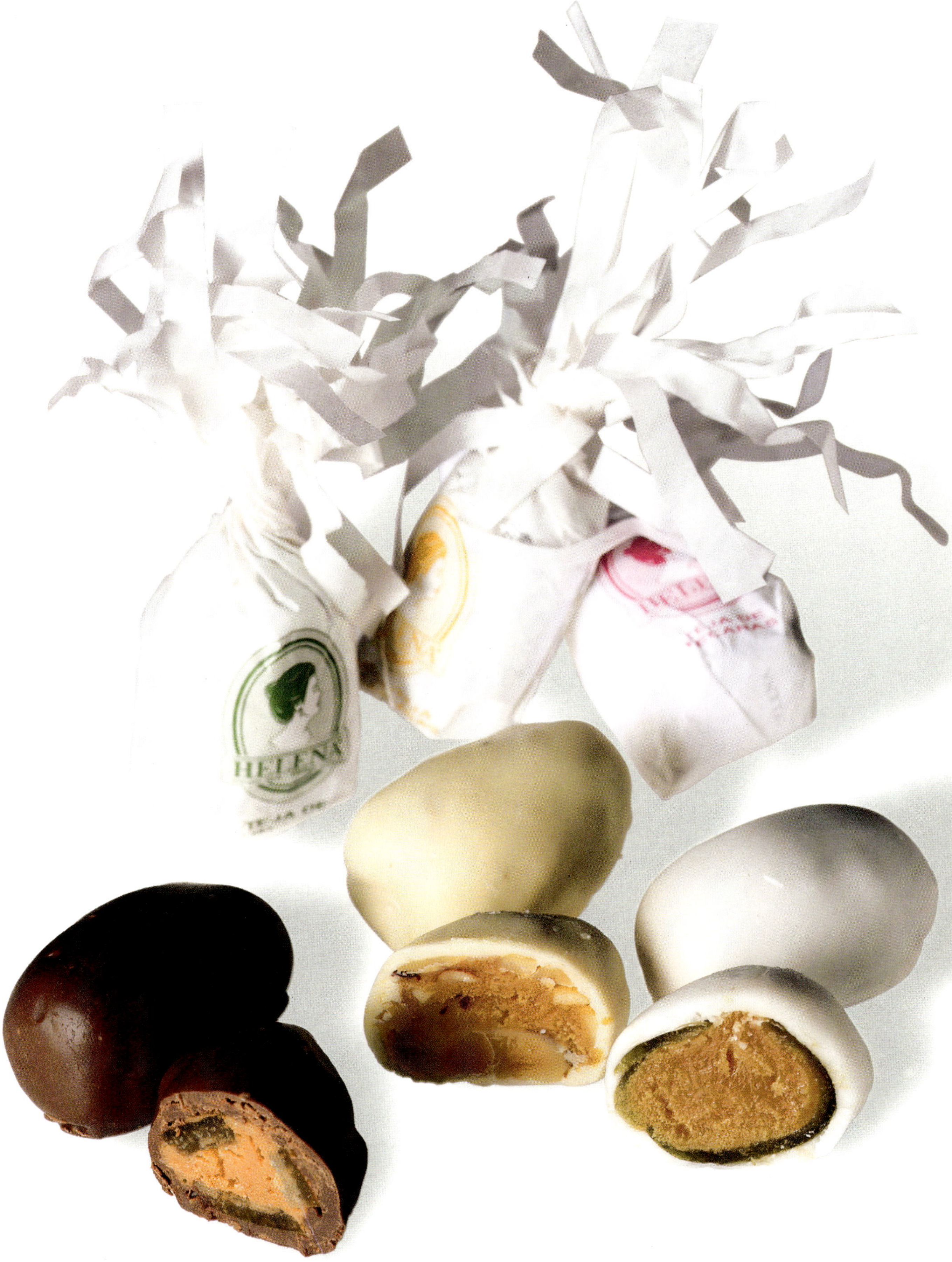
HELENA

Turrón de Chocolate

Ingredients:

- 2 cups vanilla wafers or cookies (broken into small pieces)
- 8 oz (220 g) butter
- 1 cup (200 g) raisins
- 1 cup (200 g) chopped pecans
- ¾ cup sifted cocoa powder
- 1 cup sugar
- 3 eggs

*A friend of mine once told me 'if you ever meet someone who doesn't like chocolate there might be something seriously wrong with him'. The recipe for this delicious chilled chocolate **turrón** is from Lisette Hansa. Serve it with thick chocolate fudge sauce and you have a chocolate lover's double delight.*

Preparation

Melt butter in the top of a double boiler over low heat. Remove from the heat and mix in sifted cocoa powder. In a large bowl, beat sugar and eggs together until the mixture forms soft peaks.

Gently fold butter and cocoa mixture into the beaten eggs with a spatula. Mix in raisins and pecans. (Reserve some chopped pecans for decoration.) Add the broken wafers and mix thoroughly.

Pour mixture into an 8 x 5 in-(20 x 13 cm-) rectangular mold or loaf pan lined with plastic wrap, and refrigerate for at least 3 hours.

To unmold **turrón**, invert onto a serving dish and tap gently on the base. Carefully peel off plastic wrap.

Serve topped with chocolate fudge sauce and decorated with chopped pecans.

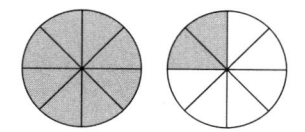

Tip: For an extra special flavor, set the raisins to marinate the night before in Port (so they will be 'drunk').

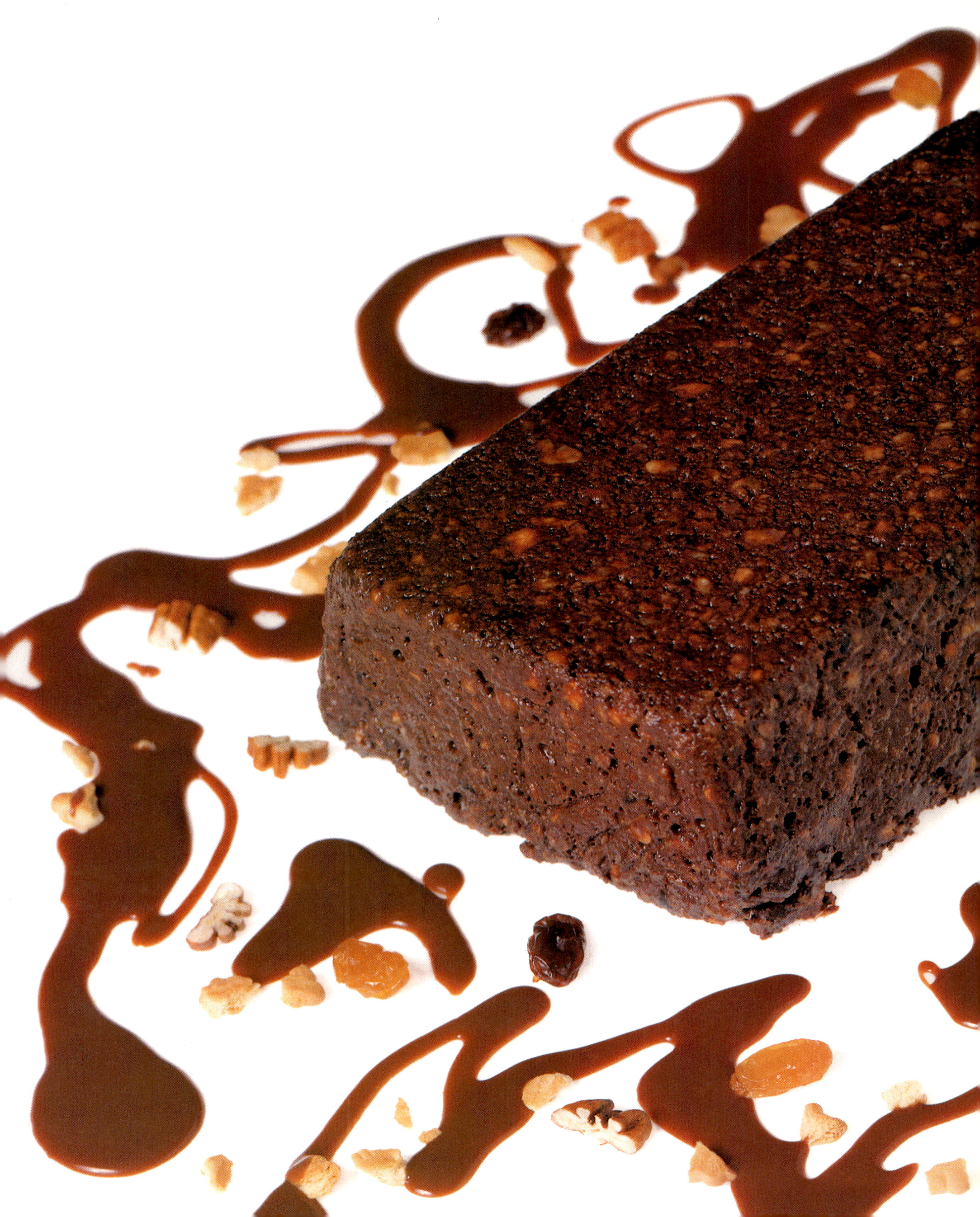

Turrón de doña Pepa

This anise cookie coated with fruit syrup confection has become a national icon. There are varying stories about its origin. One tells that doña Pepa, a black slave named doña Josefa Marmanill, received the recipe directly from the saints in her dreams. It is the traditional holiday pastry eaten throughout the 'purple month' of October when hundreds of Limeños wearing purple robes parade through the streets to celebrate the feast of el Señor de los Milagros. One version is fruit-honey-based and the other is molasses-based.

Ingredients:

- 4 ¼ cups self-rising flour
- 2 cups (500 g) softened vegetable shortening (½ of this can be margarine)
- 1 tbsp salt
- 5 eggs, lightly beaten
- 3 tbsp sugar
- 1 tbsp toasted, ground, sesame seeds
- 2 tbsp toasted, ground, aniseed
- 2 tbsp colored candy sprinkles

For the fruit syrup:

- 1 lb (500 g) fresh peaches or apricots
- ¼ lb (100 g) dried figs
- 1 lb apples
- 1 lb oranges
- 2 quinces
- ½ small pineapple
- 1 banana
- 1 key lime
- 7 cups sugar

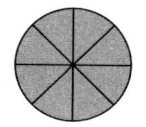

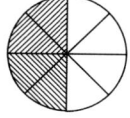

Preparation

Preheat oven to 275°F / 135°C. Grease and flour two large cookie sheets. Sift the flour and salt onto a work surface and make a large well in the center. Into the well, add the eggs, sugar, softened shortening, sesame seeds and aniseed. With your hands bring dry ingredients into the center and incorporate all ingredients, working the mixture into a smooth dough. Break off the dough into small portions and roll each portion into sticks about 12 in (30.5 cm) long and the diameter of a small cigar.

Place the sticks on cookie sheets, leaving about 1cm between each as they will expand a little on cooking. Bake on the middle rack of the oven until barely golden, about 10-15 minutes; be careful because they will burn easily. Remove from the oven and set aside to cool.

To make the fruit syrup:

Wash the fruit well, leave the skins on (except for the banana) and chop coarsely. Place in a large pan with enough water to cover them well, about 8 liters. Bring to a boil, reduce the heat and simmer until the liquid has reduced by half and the fruit has begun to break down, about 20 minutes. Remove from the heat and let cool for a while before straining. You should be left with about 2 liters of fruit juice. Combine the fruit juice with the sugar in a pan and cook over very low heat for about 2 hours or until it starts to bubble halfway up the pan, 240°F / 117°C on candy thermometer. Remove from the heat and let cool for 15 to 20 minutes.

To assemble the turron:

Line the bottom of a shallow 12 x 8 in (30 x 20 cm) dish or platter with wax paper. Place the cookie sticks in even rows touching each other to line the base of the dish, breaking them off to fit the dish if necessary. Any broken pieces can be crumbled, spread on top and lightly pressed down. Spoon some of the syrup over the pastry, making sure it is well coated. Arrange another layer of sticks crosswise over the first layer. Coat well again with syrup and add another layer of sticks again crosswise over the previous layer. Be sure that the sticks are packed tightly together. Spoon the remaining syrup over the entire stack to coat well. Decorate with colored sprinkles and leave for several hours to 'set' before removing from the dish.

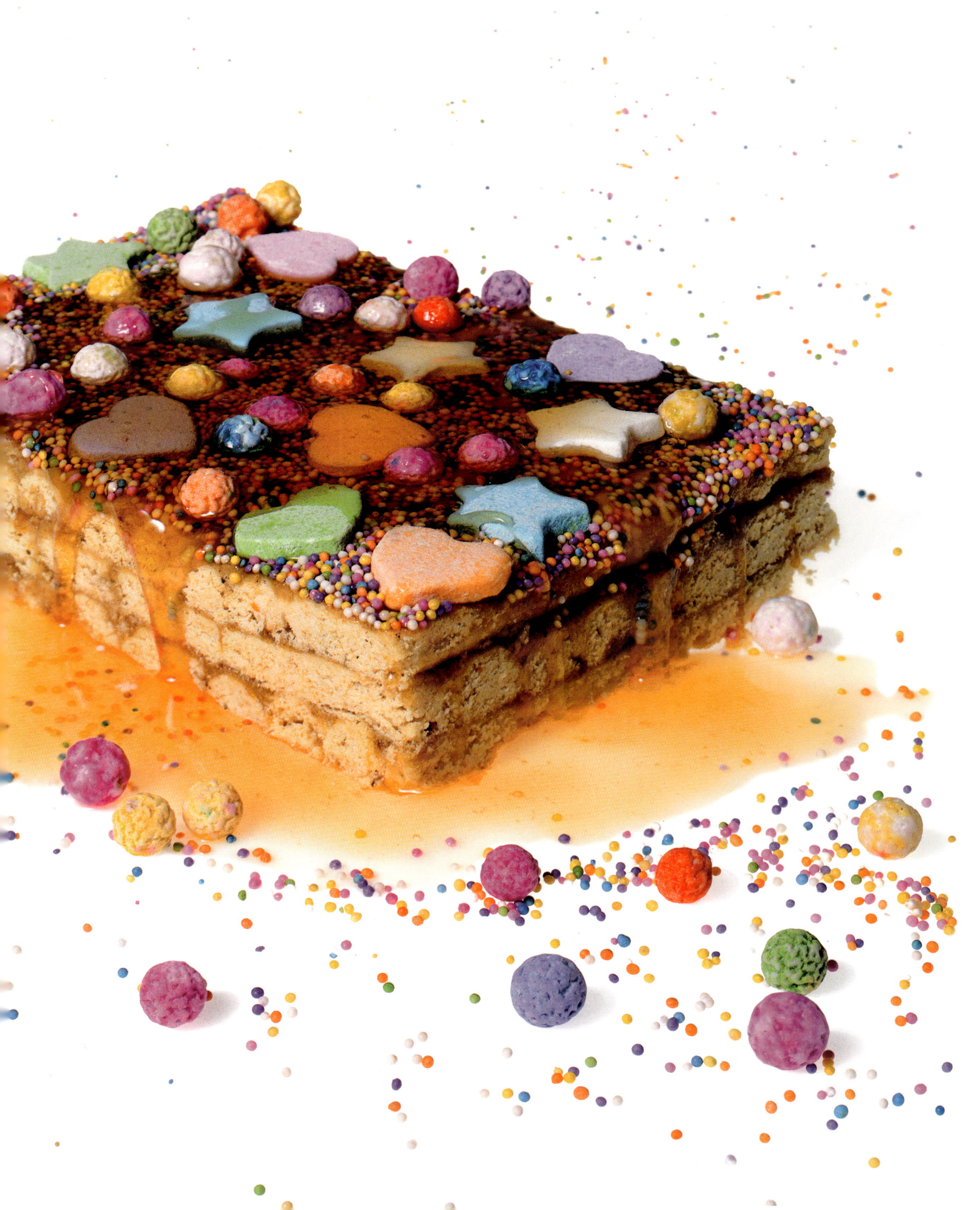

Volador & Guargueros

Ingredients:

- 9 egg yolks, lightly beaten
- 1 cup all purpose flour
- Pinch salt
- Confectioners' sugar

Fillings:

- 1 cup **manjar blanco** (p.246)
- 1 cup pineapple or apricot jam

*Volador is a typical Peruvian pastry which takes its name from the way in which the delicate leaves 'fly up' at the edges. You can also make it in a circular shape. The same pastry is also used for lightly fried crisp little tubes or **guargeros**, the ideal container for sweet and creamy manjar blanco.*

Preparation

Preheat oven to 400°F / 200°C. Sift the flour and salt onto a work surface. Pour the beaten egg yolks into a well made in the center of the dry ingredients. Using one hand gently work the ingredients together to form a ball.

Knead the dough firmly with the palm of your hand until it becomes soft and elastic. Form the dough into a sausage-shaped roll and hit hard against the side of work surface.

Roll out the dough until it is extremely thin (almost transparent) and cut into 18 rectangles measuring 5x4in (12x10cm). Place the pastry leaves on a lightly greased and floured cookie sheet. Bake until the leaves are just cooked and start to rise up off the sheet, not more than 3 or 4 minutes.

Remove from the oven and cool on racks. When cool, sandwich together in threes, making one layer of filling with **manjar blanco** and the other with pineapple jam. Dust with confectioners' sugar.

To make guargueros:

After rolling out the pastry dough, cut into 3 x 4 in-(8 x 10 cm-) rectangles. Bring two diagonally opposite corners of rectangles together to form a small tube. Overlap the points slightly and press firmly with your fingertips to seal well.

Deep fry in very hot oil until lightly golden for about 1 minute, moving gently in the hot oil with a large metal spoon so that it cooks evenly and doesn't burn. Drain on kitchen towel and leave to cool. Fill with **manjar blanco** and dust with confectioners' sugar.

Makes 6 individual voladores or 16 medium sized guargueros

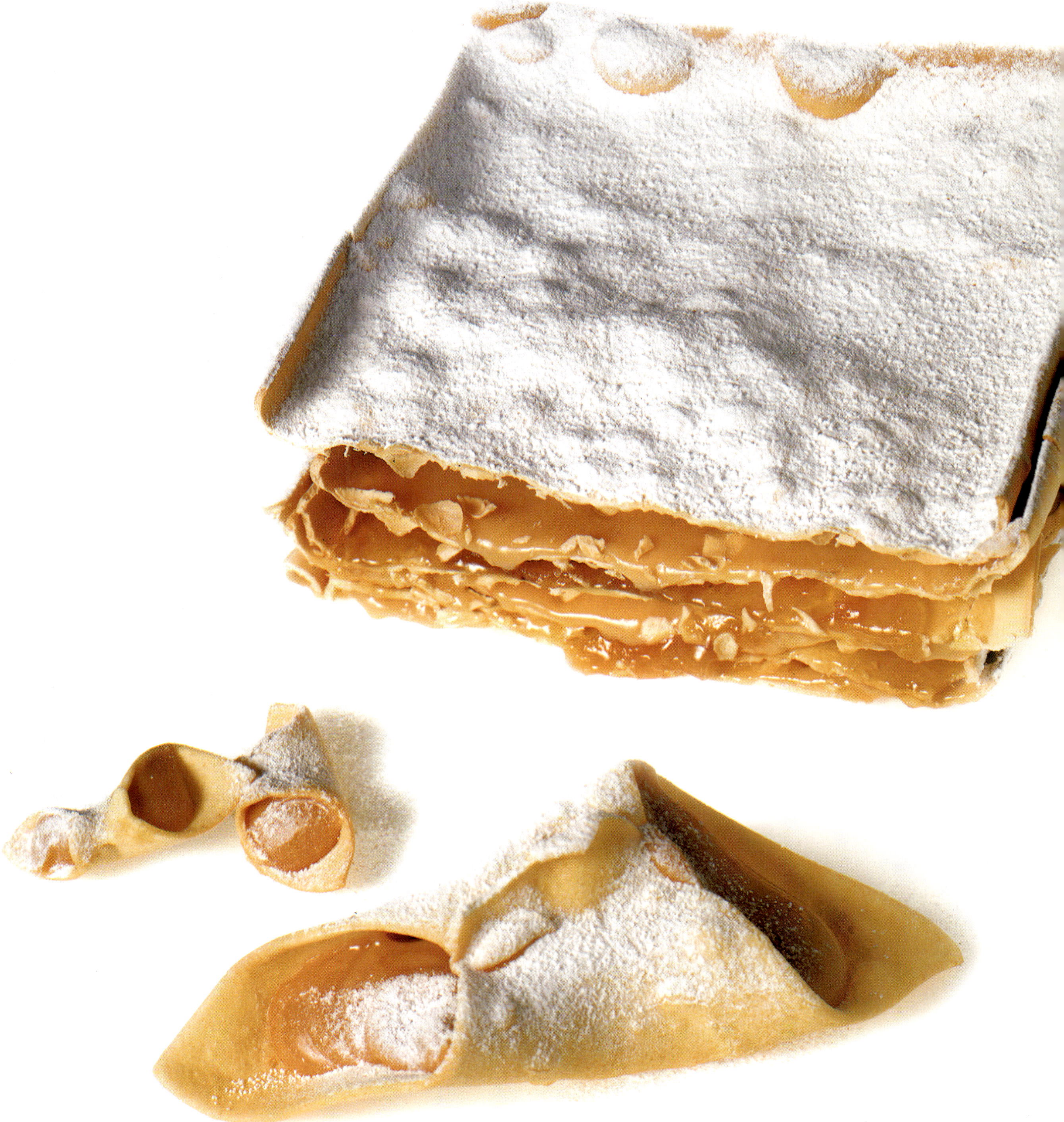

South American Specialty Food Stores or Ingredients Sources

London
Fina Estampa Restaurant
150 Tooley Street, London, SE1
Tel: (44-171) 403-1342

Macchu Picchu Import
PO Box 17348, London, SE9 9WT
Telefax: (44-171) 733-2481

Selfridges food hall
400 Oxford Street, London, W1A 1AB
Tel: (44-171) 629-1234

Sol Andino Services UK
Arch 147, Unit N, Eagle's Yard, Walworth Road, Elephant & Castle, London, SE1 6SP
Tel: (44-171) 740-6147   Fax: (44-181) 906-4757

New York
Dean & DeLuca
560 Broadway at Prince Street
Tel: (212) 431-1691

Macy's
Herald Square, Broadway at 34th Street
Tel: (212) 695-4400

Zabar's
2245 Broadway at 80th Street
Tel: (212) 787-2000

Los Angeles
El Camaguey Meat Market
10925 Venice Blvd., West Los Angeles
Tel: (310) 839-4037

San Francisco
La Palma
2884 24th Street
Tel: (415) 647-1500

Miami
La Tiendita
7971 S.W. 40th Street (Bird Road), Miami 33155
Tel: (305) 266-0212

Washington
Warehouse International Market
3815 A & George Mason Dr., Falls Church.
Tel: (703) 845-260

El Mercadito Hispano
485-B Elden Street, Herndon
Tel: (703) 435-5144

Internet
Tiendas E. Wong - Lima, Peru
www.ewong.com

Some of Lima's Finest Criollo and European Eating

Chef / Owner	Restaurant	Address
Gastón Acurio	*Astrid y Gastón + Bohemia*	Cantuarias 175, Miraflores
Andrea Graña	*"Berango"*	Teniente Romanet 120 - dpto. 201, San Isidro
Luis Felipe Arizola	*A Puerta Cerrada*	Av. Bolognesi 752, Barranco
Alfredo Aramburú	*Alfresco + Alfredo's*	Malecón Balta 790, Miraflores
Arturo Rubio	*Café Ole y Bar Ole*	Pancho Fierro 115, San Isidro
Humberto Sato	*Costanera 700*	Costanera 700, San Miguel
Doris Otani	*El Encuentro de Otani*	Calle San Pedro 182, La Campiña, Chorrillos
Flavio Solorzano	*El Señorío de Sulco*	Malecón Cisneros 1470 Miraflores
Johnny Schuller	*Granja Azul*	Carretera Central Km. 11.5, Santa Clara, Ate Vitarte
Elena Soler de Panizo	*Helena Chocolates*	Nicolás de Ribera 227, Urb. Luren, Ica
Vanessa Graña	*José Antonio*	Bernardo Monteagudo 200, Orrantia del Mar
Luis Enrique Cordero	*Kapallaq*	Av. Petit Thouars 4844, Miraflores
Oscar Velarde	*La Gloria*	Atahualpa 201, Miraflores
Ugo y Sandra Plevisani	*La Trattoría di Mambrino S.A.*	Manuel Bonilla 106, Miraflores
Carlos y Olga Araujo Bado	*Olga y Carlos Mamicé*	Av. Bolivar 291, Pueblo Libre
Cucho La Rosa	*Pantagruel*	Cantuarias 151, Miraflores
Luis Carpio	*Pez Amigo*	La Paz 1640, Miraflores
Adolfo Perret	*Punta Sal*	Conquistadores 948, San Isidro
Raúl Modenesi	*Restaurant Costa Verde*	Circuito de Playas s/n, Barranco
Daniel Manrique	*Segundo Muelle*	Conquistadores 490, San Isidro
Rosita Yimura	*Salón Restaurant Rosita*	Urb. La Taboadita, mz C1- lote 31, Bellavista, Callao
Marisa Guiulfo Felipe Ossio Guiulfo Jorge Ossio Guiulfo	*Ambrosía* *Bar Inca's Grill* *Bar Punto G* *La Bombonnière* *Le Bistrot de Mes Fils* *Marisa Guiulfo Catering*	Av. Malecón de La Reserva 1035, Miraflores Portal de Panes 115, Plaza de Armas, Cuzco Av. Conquistadores 512, San Isidro Av. Sánchez Cerro 2215, Jesús María Av. Conquistadores 510, San Isidro Av. Sánchez Cerro 2215, Jesús María

And Some Great Asian Restaurants

Restaurant	Address
Chifa Real	Manuel Bañón 248, San Isidro
Chifa Titi	Av. Javier Prado Este 1212, Corpac, San Isidro
Fu Sen	Av. Prolongación Javier Prado Oeste 702, Magdalena del Mar
Ichi-ban	Pancho Fierro 194, San Isidro
Makoto Sushi Bar	Las Casas 145 - piso 6, San Isidro
Matsuei Sushi Bar	Manuel Bañón 260, San Isidro
Ming Yin	Amador Merino Reyna 489, San Isidro
O-mei	Av. Javier Prado Este 5902, La Fontana, La Molina
Palacio de Beijing	Av. Benavides 768 - B, Miraflores
Restaurant Oriental Wa Lok	Jr. Paruro 864 - 870, Lima
Restaurant Royal	Av. Prescott 231, San Isidro
Salón Capón	Jr. Paruro 819, Lima

Bibliography - Suggested Further Reading

Balbi, Mariella — ***Sato's Cooking: Nikkei-Style Fish and Seafood***
pub. San Martín de Porres University (1997)

Chifas in Peru
pub. San Martín de Porres University (1999)

Hinostroza, Gloria — ***Cocina Limeña***
pub. San Martín de Porres University (1999)

Ocampo, Teresa — ***Cocina Peruana - Recetas Tradicionales y Prácticas***
pub. SED

Olivas Weston, Rosario — ***La Cocina en el Virreinato del Peru***
pub. San Martín de Porres University (1998)

Rojas-Lombardi, Felipe — ***The Art of South American Cooking***
pub. Harper Collins (1991)

Sison Porras de De la Guerra, Josie — ***El Peru y Sus Manjares***
pub. Mastergraf S.A.

The American Women's Literary Club — ***The American Women's Literary Club Cookbook***
pub. Pacific Press S.A. (1981)

Valderrama, Mariano — ***El Libro de Oro de Las Comidas Peruanas***
pub. Peru Reporting (1996)

Yimura, Rosita — ***The Rosita Yimura Cookbook***
pub. Peru Reporting (1995)